D1562515

"I have often complained that moder███████████████████nt about ethics and worship, often fail to ████ deeply about epistemology, about knowing, about wisdom. They seek to grow in Christ, but they commit their education to secular teachers without any attempt to critique. That leads to spiritual shipwreck. The Bible speaks not only of trusting Christ and serving him in ethics and worship, but also about trusting him as the standard for thought. This is what biblical *wisdom* is about. It is a pattern of thinking that keeps the rest of life in proper order. Robertson's book is the best I know of on this subject. It focuses on what the Bible itself says about wisdom, particularly in the wisdom literature. I have learned much from it, and I hope that many others will as well."

—**John M. Frame**, J. D. Trimble Professor of Systematic Theology and Philosophy, Reformed Theological Seminary, Orlando, Florida

"Once again, O. Palmer Robertson has provided us with a mature fruit of his patient, wise, and meticulous biblical research. From a conservative-evangelical perspective, he explores the wisdom literature of the Old Testament, opening up new vistas of study and understanding of this part of Scripture, which until recently was undervalued and sometimes even neglected in Old Testament research. In his new book, Robertson convincingly argues that the so-called wisdom books do form an integral part of God's Word, with their message and theology deeply embedded in redemptive history. Perhaps surprisingly, Lamentations is also included in this section. To call the books of wisdom 'the how-to [puzzle, lament, love, etc.] books' in the Old Testament canon is an eye-opener, just one of the many that the reader comes across in this rich and insightful work. Robertson's joy in biblical research is contagious, as is his love for God's Word that inspires him. The reading of this book is a joyful experience, and does not disappoint even if the reader disagrees with the author on some minor point."

—**Eric Peels**, Professor of Old Testament Studies, Theological University, Apeldoorn, The Netherlands

"*The Christ of Wisdom* is a major contribution to Christian understanding of wisdom in the Old Testament. As always, Palmer Robertson's work is firmly rooted in the full authority of Scripture and in

REGIS COLLEGE LIBRARY
100 Wellesley Street West
Toronto, Ontario
Canada M5S 2Z5

the supremacy of Christ over all creation. Thus, he helps us explore many portions of Scripture that evangelicals often overlook. He not only addresses academic issues, but also provides enormously helpful insights into the practical application of biblical wisdom to modern life. Every believer will find that this volume expands his or her vision of what it means to follow 'Christ, in whom are hidden all the treasures of wisdom and knowledge' (Col. 2:2–3)."
—**Richard L. Pratt Jr.**, President, Third Millennium Ministries

"The work of wisdom is the purview of the good king. Jesus is a sage greater than Solomon (Matt. 12:42) because he is the true and final son of David, yet many pastors and teachers still find it difficult to preach Christ from the Old Testament wisdom books. This is why Robertson's work is so greatly needed. As with his other writing, he carefully maps out the many ways in which the teaching of the Old Testament speaks to the broader story of redemption and the person of the Redeemer, Jesus Christ. Throughout this book, he reminds us that wisdom literature will not merely make us wise, but also acquaint us with the person and work of our Lord Jesus Christ."
—**John Scott Redd Jr.**, President and Associate Professor of Old Testament, Reformed Theological Seminary, Washington, DC

"How do the Old Testament wisdom books testify to the person and work of Jesus Christ (Luke 24:27, 44)? In what way is Christ the incarnate wisdom of God (1 Cor. 1:24)? Let O. Palmer Robertson answer these questions for you in this book! I can think of no better treatment of this challenging topic from an orthodox, biblical-theological, redemptive-historical, covenantal perspective. As a master teacher, he leads his readers through the ancient world of wisdom literature, demonstrates how this material is vitally relevant for the church today, and magnifies the Christ of wisdom in each successive chapter. Robertson has helped us to heed the call of Scripture to 'get wisdom' (Prov. 4:5; 23:23) and so come to know the One 'in whom are hidden all the treasures of wisdom' (Col. 2:3)."
—**Miles V. Van Pelt**, Alan Belcher Professor of Old Testament and Biblical Languages; Director, Summer Institute for Biblical Languages; Academic Dean, Reformed Theological Seminary, Jackson, Mississippi

THE

Christ

OF

WISDOM

REGIS COLLEGE LIBRARY
100 Wellesley Street West
Toronto, Ontario
Canada M5S 2Z5

THE

Christ

OF

WISDOM

A REDEMPTIVE-HISTORICAL EXPLORATION
OF THE WISDOM BOOKS OF THE OLD TESTAMENT

O. PALMER ROBERTSON

REGIS COLLEGE LIBRARY
100 Wellesley Street West
Toronto, Ontario
Canada M5S 2Z5

PUBLISHING
P.O. BOX 817 • PHILLIPSBURG • NEW JERSEY 08865-0817

BS
1455
R63
2017

© 2017 by O. Palmer Robertson

All rights reserved. No part of this book may be reproduced, stored in a retrieval system, or transmitted in any form or by any means—electronic, mechanical, photocopy, recording, or otherwise—except for brief quotations for the purpose of review or comment, without the prior permission of the publisher, P&R Publishing Company, P.O. Box 817, Phillipsburg, New Jersey 08865–0817.

Unless otherwise indicated, all Scripture quotations are the author's own translation.

Scripture quotations marked (ESV) are from the ESV® Bible (*The Holy Bible, English Standard Version®*), copyright © 2001 by Crossway, a publishing ministry of Good News Publishers. Used by permission. All rights reserved.

Scripture quotations marked (KJV) are from the Holy Bible, King James Version (Authorized Version). First published in 1611.

Scripture quotations marked (NASB) are taken from the New American Standard Bible®, copyright © 1960, 1962, 1963, 1968, 1971, 1972, 1973, 1975, 1977, 1995 by The Lockman Foundation. Used by permission.

Scripture quotations marked (NASU) are taken from the NEW AMERICAN STANDARD UPDATED BIBLE®, copyright © 1995 by The Lockman Foundation. Used by permission.

Scripture quotations marked (NIV) are from the HOLY BIBLE, NEW INTERNATIONAL VERSION®. NIV®. Copyright © 1973, 1978, 1984 by International Bible Society. Used by permission of ZondervanPublishing House. All rights reserved.

Scripture quotations marked (NIV [2011]) are taken from the Holy Bible, New International Version®, NIV®. Copyright © 1973, 1978, 1984, 2011 by Biblica, Inc.™ Used by permission of Zondervan. All rights reserved worldwide. www.zondervan.com The "NIV" and "New International Version" are trademarks registered in the United States Patent and Trademark Office by Biblica, Inc.™

Scripture quotations marked (NKJV) are taken from the New King James Version®. Copyright © 1982 by Thomas Nelson, Inc. Used by permission. All rights reserved.

Scripture quotations marked (RSV) are taken from the Revised Standard Version of the Bible. Copyright © 1952 (2nd edition, 1971) by the Division of Christian Education of the National Council of the Churches of Christ in the United States of America. Used by permission. All rights reserved.

Italics within Scripture quotations indicate emphasis added.

Printed in the United States of America

Library of Congress Cataloging-in-Publication Data

Names: Robertson, O. Palmer, author.
Title: The Christ of wisdom : a redemptive-historical exploration of the Wisdom books of the Old Testament / O. Palmer Robertson.
Description: Phillipsburg : P&R Publishing, 2017. | Includes index.
Identifiers: LCCN 2016052643| ISBN 9781629952918 (pbk.) | ISBN 9781629952925 (epub) | ISBN 9781629952932 (mobi)
Subjects: LCSH: Wisdom literature--Criticism, interpretation, etc.
Classification: LCC BS1455 .R63 2017 | DDC 223/.06--dc23
LC record available at https://lccn.loc.gov/2016052643

This book is dedicated to my *grandchildren* and *great-grandchildren*, with the prayer that they and their coming generations may discover the fullness of Jesus the Christ, in whom are hidden all the treasures of God's wisdom that enlightens the whole of human life.

Grandchildren
Frances, Julia, Laurel, Owen, Sylvia, Nicholas, Jamal

Great-grandchildren
Wade, Willow, Ayla, Adeline

REGIS COLLEGE LIBRARY
100 Wellesley Street West
Toronto, Ontario
Canada M5S 2Z5

CONTENTS

FOREWORD

Few persons will disagree that today's social structures are under enormous attack leading to radical reorganization, especially but not exclusively in Western culture. Concepts of human sexuality, the institution of marriage, the meaning of pain, and reflections on a philosophy of life are just plain "up for grabs" and rootless at the present time. The questions are all too familiar: "How then shall we live?" "How shall we respond to the great questions of life?" Even "How shall we weep in the midst of the tragedies that regularly confront us?" The questioning goes on and on. Society exists in the grip of a huge dilemma to which no one has the answers! Who knows the solution to our quandaries? Where do we go for insight and direction?

Clearly, secular Western society has forgotten its biblical roots. But what now is the excuse that the Christian church might offer for its deficiencies in dealing with today's confused world? Most evangelical believers firmly announce that they believe that "all Scripture is God-breathed" and is profitable and "useful for teaching, rebuking, correcting and training" (2 Tim. 3:15). If that affirmation is truly intended, where then is the evidence that Christians and their pastors are following through on what they acknowledge by their profession? Why have the biblical books that address the practical issues of the day been so greatly neglected in our generation?

Is it not amazing that despite all of society's lack of clear direction, a section of the Old Testament known as the wisdom books speaks with the specific purpose of relieving our confusion and restless searching? In the books of Proverbs, Job, Ecclesiastes, Lamentations, and Song of Songs, God has purposely provided solutions to all the puzzlements over how humans should act and live in times such as these.

As society and even God's own people continue to neglect the directions given in these wisdom books of the Old Testament, a distraught generation stumbles on. What a shame! What a loss because of a famine of the Word of God in the land.

This book by O. Palmer Robertson, *The Christ of Wisdom*, is exactly what should be prescribed for today's Christians, young and old. For people who have lost their way in a confused and upside-down world, for pastors and teachers who have pledged by their ordination vows to teach and preach the whole counsel of God, this stimulating book points to the truth so desperately sought in the convoluted world of today. Pastors have no need for a series of polls to discover where they can find the wisest counsel for congregations trying desperately to cope with life in this topsy-turvy world. The survey is already in. We need the preaching and teaching of the clear Word of God that comes from these books. For they contain enough truth to reshape a whole nation, and even the nations of the world!

Robertson rightly begins with the Bible's teaching on "the fear of the LORD" as the beginning of knowledge (and wisdom) (Prov. 1:7). Simultaneously with that discovery of the fear of the Lord, fathers and mothers must teach their children: "Trust in the LORD with all your heart and lean not on your own understanding; in all your ways acknowledge him, and he will make your paths straight" (3:5–6).

This distinctive treatment of Proverbs not only deals with the message of the book, but also enriches the appreciation of its message by unveiling the book's varied structures. Discovering the larger arrangements of the materials as well as its poetic diversities deepens the reader's appreciation of this practical instruction from the Lord on "how to walk in wisdom's way."

According to Robertson, the wisdom book of Job never fully answers the question, "Why do the righteous suffer?" But it tells how to go about puzzling over the perplexing question of God's dealings with a fallen humanity. Three distinctive aspects of Job emerge: (1) the extensive use of figures of speech as a major contribution to the literary excellence of the book; (2) the progression across the three rounds of Job's dialogue with his friends as their accusations become more and more vitriolic while Job's responses become fuller and more confident; and (3) the process by which the various participants in the dialogue are systematically silenced until only God speaks.

Complementing Proverbs and Job, the book of Ecclesiastes shows how to deal with life's frustrations. This book of wisdom affirms that God "has made everything beautiful in its time. He has also set eternity in the hearts of men; yet they cannot fathom what God has done from beginning to end"—until they find God himself (Eccl. 3:11).

Add to the balanced admonitions of fearing and trusting God the wisdom-based encouragement to saints who sorrow in their suffering: "The LORD is good to those whose hope is in him, to the one who seeks him" (Lam. 3:25 NIV). What perfectly balanced wisdom words for people who simply want to live well despite a seemingly disordered world!

Indeed, a theology of weeping pervades the book of Lamentations, for what will we do when calamity comes? Where and to whom should we go? What shall we do? Are mourning and weeping acceptable to God? Must I accept the inevitability of pain, hurt, and suffering even as a believer? God's wisdom in Lamentations teaches us how to weep in view of these inevitable prospects.

Sex and marriage represent another of our modern neuroses. But should believers be found speaking in church about physical attraction between the sexes, about the intimacies of marital love? Despite all our timid hesitations, Solomon's Song celebrates marital love that is "as strong as death, . . . a mighty flame" from the LORD (Song 8:6 NIV). God in the wisdom of his Word does not avoid the topic of sex. He made it in the first place. He cares about how we handle it. He meant it for our pleasure and joy.

Robertson is not afraid to address the topic of sex from the straightforward perspective of the best Song ever written—the Song of Songs. For too long, parents, pastors, and teachers have danced around the natural meaning of the biblical text and left the waiting church without sober teaching on sex and marital love. The clear teaching of this book of the Bible has been abandoned by the church even while it is affirmed as the Word of God!

When I read Robertson's teaching on this section of the Bible, I shouted for joy! I laughed aloud at the comments of those who have tried their best to avoid affirming what the text was saying. Finally, a teacher, writer, theologian who has found the courage to say what the

Bible says! Yes, many naysayers will gloss over what is plainly taught. But let them show how they arrived at the allegorical, the typological, or the so-called spiritual understanding of the text. In the meantime, our young people are being sadly neglected because of our shyness and false embarrassments. The youth of the church should have heard the real Word of God a long time ago.

Enjoy this feast prepared for you based on the teaching of these wisdom books (sometimes described as the "orphan books") of the Bible. May our Lord use the recovery of these books in our modern era to effect a renewal of our understanding of God's all-embracive truth. Then we may be enabled to get a heart of wisdom and live all of life to the glory of his awesome name.

Walter C. Kaiser Jr.
President Emeritus
Gordon-Conwell Theological Seminary

EDITOR'S PREFACE

In a number of places throughout this work, the divine name *Yahweh*—יהוה—whose distinctly covenantal meaning was revealed to Moses in Exodus 3, is rendered COVENANT LORD or LORD OF THE COVENANT. This representation of *Yahweh* communicates the principal distinctiveness of this name for God.

The term *Yahweh* sounds awkward in English and communicates little to the reader. Substitutions such as the hybrid *Jehovah* and the capitalized *LORD* or LORD do little to communicate the uniqueness of this term. Yahweh is *distinctly* the LORD OF THE COVENANT, the COVENANT LORD.

P&R Publishing

PREFACE

Several decades ago, at the encouragement of colleagues, students, and friends, I laid out a long-term plan for a ministry of writing. The whole endeavor was to focus on the theme "Christ in all the Scriptures." It was to be a programmatic representation of all the various portions of the Bible—God's infallible and inerrant Word—as they variously focused on the anticipation and the realization of the promised Christ.

First on the list came *The Christ of the Covenants* (1980). This work viewed the progress of redemptive history in terms of its movement from creation to consummation. As the successive covenants provide the architectonic structure of Scripture, so these divinely initiated bonds inevitably shape God's working in this world. From Adam to Noah to Abraham to Moses to David to the new covenant in prophecy and fulfillment, the Sovereign LORD OF THE COVENANT determines the course of his grace as it came pouring out across human history.

Next came *The Christ of the Prophets* (2004, with a reorganized edition in 2008). This work asks: What was the focal moment of the entire prophetic movement? What redemptive event was this grand band of spokesmen for God commissioned to interpret? If the exodus was the encapsulating event of the Mosaic period, and the coming of king and kingdom defined the days of David, what event with comparable significance characterized the era of "my servants the prophets"? From Hosea to Malachi the answer is clear. Exile and restoration, death and resurrection, expulsion from God's presence and rejuvenation in his presence describe the days of the prophets. The cataclysmic events of exile and restoration emerge as the key that unlocks the significance of the varied ministries of Israel's prophets. Some prophets anticipate exile, other prophets experience exile, the final prophets return from exile. It's all about the Christ, the Israel of

God, the Suffering Servant of the LORD, who experiences abandonment in sin-bearing and restoration as he sees the travail of his soul and finds satisfaction.

Third in this grand scheme of things was to be "The Christ of the Psalmists and Sages," dealing with the poetical books of the Old Testament. But it was not to be. An initial effort at composing a brief twenty-page introduction to the theology of the Psalms proved to be a rewarding endeavor of personal enlightenment. The three-hundred-page result was *The Flow of the Psalms* (2015), in which the magnificent structure of the Psalter unfolded before my wondering eyes as a life-changing reality leading to God-centered, Christ-focused worship.

So now comes the other half of that originally conceived unity of "Psalmists and Sages." *The Christ of Wisdom* (2017) deals biblically-theologically with five poetic volumes of the Old Testament that plumb the depths of divine wisdom. Internationally respected scholars find no natural resting place for the wisdom books of the Old Testament in a redemptive-historical approach to biblical theology. The books of wisdom resist pressure to take their proper place in the straightaway developmental timeline that stretches from Adam to Noah to Abraham to Moses to David to Christ. In fact, except for Lamentations, you will be hard-pressed to uncover a single reference to the flood, the patriarchs, the exodus, Sinaitic lawgiving, or Davidic king-making in these books of wisdom. So how do you fit these wisdom books into the flow of redemptive history that consummates in the Christ?

By letting them be what they are in their own distinctiveness. They are, it should be remembered, canonical, divinely revealed, and authoritative writings that tell the world how and what to think about the deeper mysteries of human life. Rather than submitting to the moldings and bendings of modernity, these books broaden our understanding of the nature of redemptive history. Divine progress in the complete restoration of reality does not merely move in a purely linear fashion like the flight of an arrow moving across time and space without deviation until it reaches its target. This "third dimension" of redemptive history moves in a cyclical pattern. For certain aspects of God's salvation perform according to a pattern of regulated repetition.

To ignore this dimension of redemptive history is to exclude a major portion of the old covenant canon—and that you do not want to do.

Just as creation has its cycles, so also does redemption. Each year has its seasons, each day its hours. Each life has its birth, its budding, its decline, its death. So the life of faith and repentance in one patriarch somehow repeats itself in each subsequent patriarch. God's people sin; the LORD inflicts judgment; they cry out in repentance; a singular saving hero appears; and the cycle begins again. Six times over, this identical pattern recurs in the age of Israel's judges.

So the wisdom books of the Old Testament conform to this repetitive pattern. A regal father instructs his son how to walk in wisdom's way, and expects him to pass on his enlightened understanding to the next generation (Proverbs). Dialoguing friends young and old come to a climax when they dialogue with the Divine. Joining in the discussion, the Almighty encourages humility whenever a person is forced to puzzle over the deepest challenges of life (Job). Male and female, bride and groom explore the wonders, the beauties of passionate love in vivid detail even as they pass along their perspectives on propriety in sexual relations to maidens of the next generation (Song of Songs). A wealthy king employs his vast resources to learn how to cope with life's frustrations, and shares his insights as the singular Shepherd with other instructors (Ecclesiastes). How to weep rightly in the midst of life's calamities represents an aspect of human wisdom eventually needed by one and all (Lamentations).

How can humanity live life to the fullest without the God-inspired wisdom of the wise? Everyone—young and old, male and female, rich and poor—sooner or later will need every bit of practical advice found in these "how-to" books of the Bible. Indeed, you may bungle along by the impulses of your own brain if you choose. But would it not be far better to "get wisdom," to "get understanding"? With all the powers of your "getting," "get wise!"

If you find yourself tantalized by these wisdom books to seek consummate wisdom, then turn your expectant eyes toward Jesus the Christ. For all the treasures of wisdom and knowledge consummate in him. He is the incarnate Word of wisdom who will willingly teach you his way.

ACKNOWLEDGMENTS

When I first began teaching, I expressed concern to a seasoned colleague about the many things I did not know. "Don't worry," he replied. "Your students will teach you all you need to know."

Having experienced that truth firsthand many times over, I would like to acknowledge my students across the decades for the numerous insights and contributions they have made to my understanding of Scripture:

My students from Reformed Theological Seminary (1967–71)
Jackson, Mississippi

My students from Westminster Theological Seminary (1971–80)
Philadelphia, Pennsylvania

My students from Covenant Theological Seminary (1980–85)
St. Louis, Missouri

My students from African Bible College (1992–2004)
Lilongwe, Malawi

My students from Knox Theological Seminary (1994–2002)
Ft. Lauderdale, Florida

My students from African Bible University (2005–)
Kampala, Uganda

ABBREVIATIONS

AB	The Anchor Bible
ABD	*The Anchor Bible Dictionary*, ed. David Noel Freedman, 6 vols. (New York: Doubleday, 1992)
BCOT	Baker Commentary on the Old Testament
CBQ	*Catholic Biblical Quarterly*
ESV	English Standard Version
JBL	*Journal of Biblical Literature*
JSS	*Journal of Semitic Studies*
KJV	King James Version
LXX	Septuagint (the Greek Old Testament)
NASB	New American Standard Bible
NASU	New American Standard Updated
NCBC	New Century Bible Commentary
NICOT	New International Commentary on the Old Testament
NIV	New International Version
NKJV	New King James Version
RSV	Revised Standard Version
TOTC	Tyndale Old Testament Commentaries
WBC	Word Biblical Commentary

INTRODUCTION TO
WISDOM LITERATURE

CHAPTER OUTLINE

What is *wisdom*? Where is it to be found? Several entire books of the Old Testament summon wisdom to address the critical elements of human existence, such as purpose for life, pain, and romance. But what is wisdom? The patriarch Job wrestled with this question. His poem vivifies the search for wisdom:[1]

---

1. Gerhard von Rad, *Wisdom in Israel* (London: SCM Press, 1972), 146, says that this poem about the search for wisdom in Job "almost luxuriates in words." He notes that the poet underscores the difficulty of discovering wisdom by comparing this search to "the most extreme task ever tackled by the human mind, mining in the heart of a mountain."

Introduction: Job 28

¹ "There is a mine
    for silver
and a place
    where gold is refined.
² Iron is taken
    from the earth,
and copper
    is smelted from ore.
³ Man puts an end
    to the darkness;
he searches the farthest recesses for ore
    in the blackest darkness.
⁴ Far from where people dwell
    he cuts a shaft,
in places forgotten by the foot of man;
    far from men he dangles and sways.
⁵ The earth, from which food comes,
    is transformed below as by fire;
⁶ sapphires come
    from its rocks,
    and its dust contains
nuggets of gold.
⁷ No bird of prey knows
    that hidden path,
no falcon's eye
    has seen it.
⁸ Proud beasts
    do not set foot on it,
and no lion
    prowls there.
⁹ Man's hand assaults
    the flinty rock
and lays bare
    the roots of the mountains.
¹⁰ He tunnels
    through the rock;

his eyes see
    all its treasures.
¹¹ He searches
    the sources of the rivers
and brings hidden things
    to light.
¹² "But where can wisdom
    be found?
Where does understanding
    dwell?
¹³ Man does not comprehend
    its worth;
it cannot be found
    in the land of the living.
¹⁴ The deep says,
    'It is not in me';
the sea says,
    'It is not with me.'
¹⁵ It cannot be bought
    with the finest gold,
nor can its price
    be weighed in silver.
¹⁶ It cannot be bought
    with the gold of Ophir,
    with precious onyx or sapphires.
¹⁷ Neither gold nor crystal
    can compare with it,
nor can it be had
    for jewels of gold.
¹⁸ Coral and jasper
    are not worthy of mention;
the price of wisdom
    is beyond rubies.
¹⁹ The topaz of Cush
    cannot compare with it;
it cannot be bought
    with pure gold.

20 "Where then does wisdom come from?
        Where does understanding dwell?
21 It is hidden
        from the eyes of every living thing,
    concealed
        even from the birds of the air.
22 Destruction and Death say,
        'Only a rumor of it has reached our ears.'
23 God understands
        the way to it
    and he alone
        knows where it dwells,
24 for he views
        the ends of the earth
    and sees everything
        under the heavens.
25 When he established
        the force of the wind
    and measured out
        the waters,
26 when he made a decree
        for the rain
    and a path
        for the thunderstorm,
27 then he looked at wisdom
        and appraised it;
        he confirmed it
    and tested it.
28 And he said to man,
        'The fear of the Lord—
            that is wisdom,
        and to shun evil
            is understanding.'" (Job 28:2–28 NIV)

This introduction to the subject of wisdom will consider several topics:

- The Regal Role of Wisdom
- The Basic Biblical Terminology for *Wisdom*
- The Broader Context of Wisdom in the Ancient Near East
- The Identification of the Books of Wisdom
- The Poetic Form of Wisdom Literature
- The Place of Wisdom in Old Testament Theology
- An Initial Admonition: Get Wisdom!

THE REGAL ROLE OF WISDOM

In Scripture, wisdom manifests itself most fully in connection with kingship, with humanity's capacity to rule. The regal role of wisdom goes back to the time of humanity's creation. God showed his confidence in man's understanding of the essential nature of things by entrusting him with the responsibility of giving appropriate names for all the animals of creation. God brought the subordinate creatures to the man "to see what he would name them" or, as the phrase might be translated, "to see how he would designate them" (Gen. 2:19 NIV). Adam's kingly comprehension of the nature of all creatures enabled him by God's appointment to name the creatures in accord with their essential natures. This naming was not a mindless, random placing of a vocalized label. Instead, it anticipated a zoologist's classification of creatures, displaying a careful analysis of the nature of each and every living being.

From this original beginning, a long line of regal figures connects wisdom with royalty:

All the "wise men" of Egypt fail to interpret Pharaoh's dreams (Gen. 41:8 NIV). But Joseph satisfies the king with his understanding. He then advises him to "look for a discerning and wise man and put him in charge of the land of Egypt" (41:33 NIV). The king can only conclude, "Since God has made all this known to you, there is no one so discerning and wise as you" (41:39 NIV). Because of his extraordinary wisdom, Joseph must be the one to exercise rule over his nation.

Moses as the designated leader of God's people manifests his superiority over the wise men, sorcerers, and magicians of Egypt during the contest of the plagues (Ex. 7:11, 22; 8:7, 18). He later rested his hands on Joshua as a symbolic way of transmitting his ruling authority to his successor. As a consequence, Joshua "was filled with the spirit of wisdom . . . . So the Israelites listened to him and did what the LORD had commanded Moses" (Deut. 34:9 NIV). Only because of this bestowal of wisdom could Joshua succeed in governing the nation.

Samson the judge of Israel appears as a wisdom figure in view of his ability to construct a "riddle," despite all his foibles. He displays his superiority over the Philistines by baffling them with his puzzling sayings (Judg. 14:1–18; 15:15–17).[2]

David the king is declared by the wise woman of Tekoa to possess "wisdom like that of an angel of God." Because of his God-given wisdom, he has no trouble seeing right through the fabricated tale of Joab (2 Sam. 14:19–20).

King Solomon as the paragon of wise sovereigns throughout the world of his day climaxes these manifestations of wisdom among the rulers of God's people. All the fourteen passages in Kings and the ten passages in Chronicles that speak of "wisdom" refer exclusively to King Solomon, with a single exception. Solomon's prayer as he begins his reign underscores this regal role of wisdom as a focal factor in the life of the king:

> Give your servant a discerning heart [lit., "a hearing heart"] to govern your people and to distinguish between right and wrong. For who is able to govern this great people of yours? (1 Kings 3:9 NIV)

---

2. The term used to describe Samson's "riddle," his *chidah* (חִידָה), appears among the various designations for wisdom in the opening verses of Proverbs (Prov. 1:6). It also describes the wise instruction imparted by the psalmist (Pss. 49:4; 78:2). The LXX translates this same word with παραβολή, "parable," which in the New Testament describes the prevailing mode of teaching used by Jesus (Matt. 13:34–35, quoting and applying Ps. 78:2 to the teaching mode of Jesus).

The LORD heard this prayer of the king. As a consequence,

> God gave Solomon wisdom and very great insight, and a breadth of understanding as measureless as the sand on the seashore. Solomon's wisdom was greater than the wisdom of all the people of the East, and greater than all the wisdom of Egypt. He was wiser than anyone else, including Ethan the Ezrahite—wiser than Heman, Kalkol and Darda, the sons of Mahol. And his fame spread to all the surrounding nations. He spoke three thousand proverbs and his songs numbered a thousand and five. He spoke about plant life, from the cedar of Lebanon to the hyssop that grows out of walls. He also spoke about animals and birds, reptiles and fish (1 Kings 4:29–33 NIV [2011]).

Trees, plants, animals, birds, reptiles, and fish embrace essentially every category of living thing on the face of the earth. The breadth of Solomon's wisdom represents a restoration of mankind to his pristine condition as the wise sovereign over all creation.

The regal role of Solomon's wisdom is underscored by the record of international responses to his wisdom: "From all nations people came to listen to Solomon's wisdom, sent by all the kings of the world, who had heard of his wisdom" (1 Kings 4:34 NIV [2011]). The Chronicler is even more explicit: "All the kings of the earth sought audience with Solomon to hear the wisdom God had put in his heart" (2 Chron. 9:23 NIV).

Solomon's role in the production of the Old Testament wisdom books underscores once more the regal role of wisdom. "The proverbs of Solomon son of David, king of Israel" are the words introducing this king as the producer of the bulk of wisdom statements in Proverbs (Prov. 1:1; cf. 10:1; 25:1). The Song of Songs is identified in its opening verse as Solomon's (Song 1:1). The author of Ecclesiastes is described as "son of David," "king in Jerusalem" (Eccl. 1:1). Though not specifically named, Solomon is traditionally regarded as author of this wisdom book as well. The fact that Solomon is associated with these three wisdom books in the Old Testament underscores once more the close association of wisdom with kingship. The king rules effectively over all the various aspects of human life because of his regal wisdom.

In light of this extended treatment of wisdom figures across Israel's history, it is not surprising to find messianic expectation in Israel focusing on a future wisdom figure that would arise at God's appointed time:

> A shoot will come up from the stump of Jesse; from his roots a Branch will bear fruit. The Spirit of the LORD will rest on him—the Spirit of wisdom and of understanding, the Spirit of counsel and of might, the Spirit of the knowledge and fear of the LORD—and he will delight in the fear of the LORD. (Isa. 11:1–3a NIV [2011])

So the first aspect regarding wisdom to be noted in Scripture is its regal role in the life of God's people. As Wisdom personified declares:

> By me kings reign,
> and rulers decree what is just;
> by me princes rule,
> and nobles, all who govern justly. (Prov. 8:15–16 ESV)

From a new covenant perspective, all believers united to the Christ by faith may share in this regal dimension of wisdom. For in him are hidden all the treasures of wisdom and knowledge (Col. 2:2–3).

THE BASIC BIBLICAL TERMINOLOGY FOR *WISDOM*

The Old Testament has no lack of wisdom terminology, as the initial verses of Proverbs indicate. No fewer than seventeen different words or phrases for the concept of wisdom occur in the opening seven verses of the book.[3] This plethora of expressions suggests that wisdom had a significant role to play in the life of God's people under the old covenant. Three of these terms deserve special consideration:

---

3. The terms listed in Proverbs 1 are: (1) "wisdom" (חָכְמָה); (2) "proverb" (מָשָׁל); (3) "instruction, discipline" (מוּסָר); (4) "sayings of understanding" (אִמְרֵי בִינָה); (5) "instruction of the wise" (מוּסַר הַשְׂכֵּל); (6) "righteousness" (צֶדֶק); (7) "justice" (מִשְׁפָּט); (8) "uprightness" (מֵישָׁרִים); (9) "prudence, shrewdness" (עָרְמָה); (10) "knowledge" (דַּעַת); (11) "discretion" (מְזִמָּה); (12) "learning" (לֶקַח); (13) "guidance, counsel" (תַּחְבֻּלוֹת); (14) "enigma, figure" (מְלִיצָה); (15) "riddle" (חִידָה); (16) "fear of Yahweh" (יִרְאַת יְהֹוָה); (17) "torah" (תּוֹרָה).

chokmah ("wisdom"), *mashal* ("proverb"), and *yirat Yahweh* ("fear of Yahweh").

Chokmah, "Wisdom"

This basic term for *wisdom* occurs approximately 150 times in the Old Testament. The related term *chakam,* "wise" (חָכָם), occurs an additional 166 times. The word describes the skill of the artisans who constructed the tabernacle, the expertise of Hiram king of Tyre in working with bronze, and the proficiency of sailors in piloting a ship (Ex. 28:3; 31:3; 35:31; 1 Kings 7:14; Ps. 107:27).[4] The term also describes the capacity of rulers to govern well (Deut. 34:9; 1 Kings 3:28; Prov. 8:15–16). A king who exercises wisdom in his rule creates happy officials and happy people (1 Kings 10:8). But only God can impart true wisdom. It must come as a gift from him (Ps. 90:12; Prov. 2:6; Eccl. 2:26; Dan. 1:17).

Several passages employing this term for *wisdom* underscore the fact that the only way to properly understand this world is to perceive it as a creation arising out of God's wisdom and governed by divine understanding (Job 38:37–38; Ps. 104:24; Prov. 3:19; Jer. 10:12).[5] The inclusion of righteousness, justice, and uprightness as defining factors of wisdom clearly indicates that wisdom is a moral issue, not simply a matter of exercising shrewdness in coping with life (Prov. 1:3).[6]

---

4. In describing the frustration of the sailors in managing their ship in the sea storm, the phrase literally says, "And all their wisdom was swallowed up."

5. Leo G. Perdue, *Wisdom and Creation: The Theology of Wisdom Literature* (Nashville: Abingdon, 1994), regards creation as the major defining factor of wisdom in the Old Testament. Cf. Gerhard von Rad: "Since for the Hebrews the world was a created order, held and governed by God, it could never be regarded as self-existent, nor could it for one moment be understood apart from God" ("Some Aspects of the Old Testament World-View," in *The Problem of the Hexateuch and Other Essays* [Edinburgh: Oliver & Boyd, 1966], 152). The radicalness of the concept of the One God Yahweh, the COVENANT LORD of Israel, as the alone Creator of all things contrasts drastically with the permeating polytheism of all other wisdom literature of the ancient Near East as well as the modern-day mythology of evolution. For a thorough discussion of the significance for wisdom of a single Creator God over all things, see Craig G. Bartholomew, *Old Testament Wisdom Literature: A Theological Introduction* (Downers Grove, IL: InterVarsity Press, 2011), 262–70.

6. James L. Crenshaw, *Urgent Advice and Probing Questions: Collected Writings on Old Testament Wisdom* (Macon, GA: Mercer University Press, 1995), 498, understands "righteous living" according to the wisdom literature to be living in accord with the order of

Mashal, "Proverb"

This term appears in the heading of Proverbs, but identifies principally a particular form of wisdom sayings. *Mashal* generally refers to a brief, pithy, memorable statement that encapsulates truth about God and his created world. It cannot be clearly established that the term *mashal* derives etymologically from the same root that means "to rule" (*mashal*).[7] Yet to formulate a "proverb" is indeed to demonstrate control by capturing the essence of a matter in its relation to God's creation by a succinct, memorable statement. Solomon's proverb about the ant accurately describes the true mode of the creature's way of life in a manner that challenges the human reader to manifest the same wisdom (Prov. 6:6–8). Proverbs that depict a sluggard hinged to his bed and calling for "just a little more sleep" expose the folly of this tragicomical figure (26:14; 6:9–11).

When Jesus as messianic King taught about the kingdom of God, he spoke "many things in parables [παραβολαῖς]" (Matt. 13:3 NIV). By adopting this form of teaching, he was bringing to fullest realization the words of the Old Testament poet:

---

the universe. This "righteous" living will bring blessing because by it a person places himself in harmony with creation. Says Crenshaw: "Life's ambiguities make it highly desirable, if not absolutely essential, to secure God's presence. By living in accord with the rules of the universe established at creation, one obtains God's presence" (498). Crenshaw takes little or no notice of sin, of wrongdoing, and of the necessity of reconciliation with God because of violating his moral law, not merely creation's rules. Yet folly in contrast with wisdom is inseparably connected with wickedness in the book of Proverbs. Job begins by offering sacrifice for each of his children, since they may have sinned (Job 1:5). God ultimately requires Job's friends to offer sacrifice, since they have wrongly accused him (42:7–8). Job humbles himself and repents in dust and ashes (42:6). Ecclesiastes repeatedly acknowledges humanity's sinfulness, a sinfulness firmly rooted in humans' basic nature despite their being created upright (Eccl. 7:29); and every chapter in Lamentations includes explicit confession of sin. This permeating testimony of the wisdom books regarding human sinfulness establishes the fact that righteousness is not simply living in harmony with the rules of creation. True righteousness involves conformity with God's moral law as revealed to Israel.

7. "The sense of *mashal* is difficult to precisely define, although the concept of 'similitude' and 'ruling word' appear to cover the broad spectrum of usage. Both meanings are possible. The former focuses on the sense of likeness, while the latter takes its departure from the root meaning 'to rule, have dominion, reign,' thus a 'word spoken by a ruler or a word bearing special power' (Crenshaw, *Urgent Advice*, 57). Tremper Longman III, *Proverbs* (Grand Rapids: Baker Academic, 2006), 30, notes that it is "possible but not likely" that *mashal* draws on both meanings. "If so, it would point to the fact that the proverb intends to draw comparisons so the recipient can stay in control of a situation."

I will open my mouth in parables [παραβολαῖς], I will utter hidden things, things from of old. (Ps. 78:2 NIV; Matt. 13:34–35; cf. Ps. 49:3–4)

The Gospel writer indicates by this quotation that Jesus' kingdom parables correspond to the regal "proverbs" of the Old Testament. The Greek Old Testament (the LXX) lays the foundation for this connection by translating the Hebrew term *proverb* (מָשָׁל) by the Greek term *parable* (παραβολή), so that the New Testament "parable" corresponds to the Old Testament "proverb." The king's "proverbs" find their counterpart in the kingdom parables of Jesus. In a deceptively simple, succinct, and memorable form, Jesus uncovers the true nature of the kingdom of God and defines the relation of various peoples to that kingdom. The parables of the mustard seed, the good Samaritan, and the wicked vinedressers display his genius as a wisdom figure propounding kingdom truth in parabolic form (Matt. 13:31–32; Luke 10:25–37; Matt. 21:33–45). Any individual attempting to duplicate Jesus' method of parabolic teaching will soon discover the superior nature and the profundity of his parables.

Yirat Yahweh, "Fear of Yahweh"

This descriptive phrase occurs eighteen times in Proverbs, with representations of the phrase in all major sections of the book.[8] A classic passage defines the basic nature of wisdom:

> The fear of Yahweh
>> is the beginning of knowledge,
>> but wisdom and discipline
> fools despise. (Prov. 1:7)

Several passages underscore the single most significant effect of this "fear of Yahweh." It is, simply and profoundly, "life"!

> The fear of Yahweh will prolong life. (Prov. 10:27)

> The fear of Yahweh is a fountain of life, turning a person from the snares of death. (Prov. 14:27)

---

8. The references are as follows: Prov. 1:7, 29; 2:5; 3:7; 8:13; 9:10; 10:27; 14:2, 26–27; 15:16, 33; 16:6; 19:23; 22:4; 23:17; 24:21; 31:30.

The fear of Yahweh leads to life; any person following this principle will live in contentment, without being plagued by trouble. (Prov. 19:23)

The consequences of humility and the fear of Yahweh are riches, honor, and life. (Prov. 22:4)

But exactly what is this "fear of Yahweh"? If it has such far-reaching consequences concerning the essence of life itself, every person should greatly desire this wisdom that fears Yahweh.

Though regularly overlooked, this fear first focuses on none other than the one true God who has revealed himself as "Yahweh." It is not a fear of God in general, not an indefinable terror of an "unknown god" that has no capacity to bring life and blessing. Superstitious fear of a false god invariably brings curse rather than blessing. Only as a person knows, fears, and trusts the one true living Yahweh, LORD OF THE COVENANT, can he expect the blessings described in these verses.

Second, this "fear" should not be reduced to a simple "reverence" of Yahweh, though this aspect of the fear of Yahweh must be recognized. The fear of Yahweh must include an acknowledgment that he is the Judge, that he will execute his just judgments both in this life and in the world to come. "Fear of Yahweh" means fully appreciating the fact that he will call to account every person who has ever lived on this earth. He will punish or reward all people on the basis of their deeds, whether good or bad.

Third, this fear should never be set over against a continuing trust in Yahweh, his goodness, and his grace. The "fear of Yahweh" serves as one of the root definitions for *torah*, the law of the LORD; and the essence of *torah* is to love the LORD your God with all your heart, soul, mind, and strength (Ps. 19:9; cf. Deut. 6:5; Matt. 22:36–38; Luke 10:25–28). Fear of Yahweh means loving him with all that you are and trusting him with all that you possess.

So these three major terms capture the essence of wisdom. Wisdom is the ability to understand the basic principles inherent in God's created order, and to live by those principles. Wisdom enables a person to summarize these basic principles in a succinct and memorable

fashion. Wisdom is living out the whole of life with a constant awareness of accountability before a loving, gracious, and just Creator and
Redeemer.

THE BROADER CONTEXT OF WISDOM IN THE
ANCIENT NEAR EAST

The letters of the apostle Paul took on the form of the common
epistolary pattern of the first century, beginning with an identification of the author, followed by a salutation and then the body of the
correspondence. The book of Deuteronomy gives strong evidence of
following the pattern of the ancient Hittite suzerainty treaties, including
an opening statement concerning the glories of the conquering lord,
a review of the past favors that he has shown his vassal, a summary
of the stipulations required by the suzerain, a rehearsal of potential
curses and blessings for the vassal, and a formula for the renewal of
the treaty.

So it should not be surprising that the wisdom materials of the
old covenant Scriptures parallel similar materials discovered by archae-
ologists in countries neighboring Israel. Even the contents of some
of Scripture's proverbial statements, as well as the themes found in
other wisdom books of the Bible, find their parallels in the wisdom
traditions of other lands.

Scripture itself recognizes the existence of wisdom materials
among the traditions of surrounding nations. Disturbed over his dream
concerning cows emerging from the Nile, the pharaoh calls for the
diviners of Egypt "and all her wise ones" (וְאֶת־כָּל־חֲכָמֶיהָ) (Gen. 41:8).
The narrative of Exodus further confirms the presence of "wise men"
in Egypt during the time of Moses by its reference to the "wise ones"
(לַחֲכָמִים) that Pharaoh summons (Ex. 7:11). According to the testimony of the new covenant Scriptures, Moses was educated "in all the
wisdom of the Egyptians" (πάσῃ σοφίᾳ Αἰγυπτίων) (Acts 7:22). Later
in Israelite history the prophet Isaiah explicitly refers to the ancient
wisdom tradition of Egypt that had been transmitted in his own day:

The officials of Zoan are nothing but fools; the wise counselors of Pharaoh give senseless advice. How can you say to Pharaoh, "I am one of the wise men, a disciple of the ancient kings"? Where are your wise men now? Let them show you and make known what the LORD Almighty has planned against Egypt. (Isa. 19:11–12 NIV)

When setting the cultural context for the special wisdom granted to Solomon, Scripture makes a specific comparison with other lands where wisdom played a major role in the culture of the people. The wisdom of the king of Israel is said to surpass "the wisdom of all the people of the East, and greater than all the wisdom of Egypt" (1 Kings 4:30 NIV [2011]). These two locales represent major sources of wisdom tradition in ancient times that were immediately in contact with the people of Israel.[9]

So it is quite evident from these several references that the producers of the old covenant Scriptures were fully aware of the presence of wisdom traditions in lands neighboring Israel. Still further, it seems clear that Israel had significant interaction with these other wisdom traditions.

In addition to the Bible's own testimony to the presence of wisdom traditions among other nations, a great deal of evidence outside Scripture itself confirms the existence of a body of material that could properly be classified as wisdom literature. Proverbial sayings have a very ancient history. The teaching of Imhotep of Egypt dates to the period between 2700 and 2400 B.C.[10] Some manuscripts of this material date as early as 2000 B.C., a thousand years before the time of Solomon. Sumerian proverbs from Mesopotamia exist in copies dating to 1800 B.C. Canaanite princes of the fourteenth century B.C. quote old proverbs from the Amarna letters addressed to the pharaohs of Egypt.

---

9. R. B. Y. Scott, *Proverbs, Ecclesiastes: Introduction, Translation, and Notes*, AB 18 (Garden City, NY: Doubleday, 1965), xli, and others identify the "people of the East" not with the people of Mesopotamia but with people along the desert fringes of Israel, tribes east or northeast of Canaan. For biblical references that may support this perspective, cf. Gen. 29:1; Judg. 6:3, 33; 7:12; 8:10; Job 1:3; Isa. 11:14; Jer. 49:28; Ezek. 25:4, 10. But the "East" could just as well refer to the civilizations of the Tigris-Euphrates valley. Cf. Ps. 107:3; Isa. 41:2; 43:5; 46:11; Zech. 8:7; Matt. 2:1.

10. See Kenneth A. Kitchen, "Proverbs," in *The Biblical Expositor*, ed. Carl F. H. Henry (Philadelphia: A. J. Holman, 1960), 2:72, for the dating of this material.

Ugaritic materials of the fourteenth century B.C. contain proverbs comparable to the literature in Israel. So it may be said that Israelite culture of the tenth century B.C. was literally surrounded with the wisdom of the ancients. In addition to materials that compare closely with the form and content of the biblical proverb, a number of parallels have been found to the narrative concerning Job and other biblical wisdom materials.[11] In Mesopotamia a document dating a thousand years before Solomon discusses the perplexity that arises over a righteous sufferer. Babylonian documents dating between 1300 and 1000 B.C. have been designated the "Babylonian Job" and the "Babylonian Ecclesiastes."[12] From Nippur near Babylon have been found two large collections of aphorisms dating into the second millennium B.C. A sample reads as follows:

> "Build like a [Lord],
>   go about like a slave."
> "Build like a [sla]ve,
>   go about like a lord."[13]

So what is the precise relation of these various bodies of wisdom literature to the biblical material? Is a direct relationship of these extrabiblical documents to the wisdom books of Scripture possible?

In view of the verified awareness by Israel of various wisdom traditions, it may be appropriately proposed that the parallels of expression could be explained by access to a common tradition of wisdom known in Israel, Egypt, Canaan, and the East. Their interrelationship may be best explained through presuming studied interaction among the schooling experiences of the wisdom scribes of the various nations,

---

11. The principal ancient Near Eastern texts related to the wisdom literature of the Old Testament may be found in James B. Pritchard, ed., *Ancient Near Eastern Texts Relating to the Old Testament*, 3rd ed. (Princeton, NJ: Princeton University Press, 1969), with a listing of the various texts on pages xiii–iv. For a brief overview of the available documents, see Roland E. Murphy, *Wisdom Literature: Job, Proverbs, Ruth, Canticles, Ecclesiastes, and Esther*, Forms of the Old Testament Literature 13 (Grand Rapids: Eerdmans, 1981), 9–12. William McKane, *Proverbs: A New Approach* (Philadelphia: Westminster, 1977), 51–208, offers an extensive discussion of the documents.

12. Derek Kidner, *The Proverbs: An Introduction and Commentary* (Downers Grove, IL: InterVarsity Press, 1969), 18.

13. Ibid.

which "undoubtedly provided opportunity for the study of a wide range of Wisdom writings."[14] It is quite possible to imagine Solomon and the "wise men" of his kingdom as scrutinizing the wisdom materials of Egypt, and transforming them so that they would conform to the larger truths arising from their unique knowledge of Yahweh, the one and only God of creation and covenant who revealed himself to Abraham, the patriarchs, Moses, the people of Israel, and David the organizer of Israel's worship practices.

At the same time, foundational theological differences inevitably exclude direct dependence, whether speaking of pithy aphorisms or extended discourses.[15] If in any way Israel derived some of its expressions from the wisdom of other cultures, the comments of one biblical scholar are well worth noting:

> Egyptian jewels, as at the Exodus, have been re-set to their advantage by Israelite workmen and put to finer use.[16]

> Revelation transfigures what it touches.[17]

> To purge heathen thought-forms and fill them with truth is what Scripture regularly does in the realm of human words and expressions. In this sphere, as in others, former enemies can make good apostles.[18]

The Identification of the Books of Wisdom

Various sayings and narratives focusing on wisdom appear throughout the Old Testament historical and prophetic books. Particular psalms also underscore the role of wisdom in the life of God's

---

14. Scott, *Proverbs*, 20–21.

15. Kitchen, "Proverbs," 73. Michael V. Fox, *Proverbs 1–9: A New Translation with Introduction and Commentary*, AB 18A (New York: Doubleday, 2000), 18, observes that "even in the case of Amenemope, the contact was probably mediated."

16. Kidner, *Proverbs*, 24.

17. Derek Kidner, "Wisdom Literature of the Old Testament," in *New Perspectives on the Old Testament*, ed. J. Barton Payne (London: Word Books, 1970), 122.

18. Ibid., 121.

people, though the idea of so-called wisdom psalms has been brought under serious scrutiny.[19]

But the most distinctive manifestation of wisdom material in the Old Testament finds its focus in several entire works properly characterized as "wisdom books." All these books are found in the "Writings," the third category of the Jewish canon alongside the "Law" and the "Prophets."

The materials included in the Writings of the Jewish canon fall into three types: the historical books (Ruth, Chronicles, Ezra, Nehemiah, Esther); a prophetical work (Daniel, though not strictly speaking a "prophetic book"); and the poetical books (Psalms, Job, Proverbs, Ecclesiastes, Song of Songs, Lamentations). Some question may be raised regarding the poetic nature of Ecclesiastes. As has been observed, however, Ecclesiastes "uses strongly cadenced, evocative prose, perhaps qualifying as prose-poetry," which "in two extended passages moves into formal verse."[20]

The preponderance of usage of *chokmah* as the most basic term for *wisdom* in the Old Testament is divided among three of these books of poetry: Proverbs (38 uses), Ecclesiastes (28 uses), and Job (18 uses). These three literary works have been traditionally identified as belonging to the category of *wisdom books*.[21]

---

19. Cf. the discussion in R. N. Whybray, "The Wisdom Psalms," in *Wisdom in Ancient Israel: Essays in Honour of J. A. Emerton*, ed. John Day, Robert P. Gordon, and H. G. M. Williamson (Cambridge: Cambridge University Press, 1995), 152–60. Whybray concludes that it would be justifiable to designate a particular psalm as a "wisdom" psalm "only if its resemblance to some part of the Old Testament wisdom books . . . were so close as to be undeniable" (158). Despite the virtual impossibility of meeting this criterion, he concludes that Psalms 34, 37, and 73 qualify as wisdom psalms (158).

20. Robert Alter, *The Wisdom Books: Job, Proverbs, and Ecclesiastes: A Translation with Commentary* (New York: W. W. Norton, 2010), xvi. An informal count indicates that over half the verses of Ecclesiastes are poetic in form (136 out of 222).

21. The phrase *wisdom literature*, as has been observed, "is not a form-critical term; it is merely a term of convenience, derived apparently from ecclesiastical usage, to designate the books of Proverbs, Job, and Ecclesiastes, and among the Apocrypha, Ben Sira and the Wisdom of Solomon" (Murphy, *Wisdom Literature*, 3). Neither the Jewish nor the Protestant canon of inspired Scripture includes the apocryphal books of Ben Sira (Ecclesiasticus—second century B.C.) and the Wisdom of Solomon (c. 50 B.C.), though they are often included in studies of wisdom literature.

Several aspects of these three works underscore their commonality: (1) as just indicated, they are all located in the third section of the Hebrew canon; (2) as also noted, they are poetic in form; and (3) they all seek to provide answers to the way in which people can make the best of human life in a manner acceptable to God, to oneself, to one's neighbor, and to a world created by God but fallen as a consequence of man's sin.

As a further point of their identity as *wisdom books*, Job, Proverbs, and Ecclesiastes stand outside the categories that define other types of literature in the canon of Scripture. None of these three books contains narrations of God's redemptive work in the world as recorded in the historical books of the Old Testament. Patriarchs, exodus, covenant, Sinai, wilderness, conquest, and kingship find no place in these three books. Neither do they contain apodictic or casuistic law, characterized elsewhere in Scripture by the traditional introductory phrases "Thou shalt not . . ." and "If a person [does such and such] . . ." These three books do not take the form of prophetic declarations introduced by an authoritative "Thus says the LORD . . ." They do not take a shape appropriate for liturgy in worship as found in the book of Psalms. In contrast with all these other categories of literature in the Old Testament canon, Job, Proverbs, and Ecclesiastes focus on practical issues faced by all humans through the medium of a variety of poetic forms. Thus, they may be appropriately designated as *wisdom books* of the Old Testament.

Although not traditionally regarded as works of wisdom, two additional books will be treated among Old Testament wisdom literature in this material because of their substance in providing wise counsel regarding critical issues in people's lives: Song of Songs and Lamentations. Indeed, the basic words for *wisdom* and *the wise* do not appear in these two books. Wisdom is never urged on the reader, as in the case of Job, Proverbs, and Ecclesiastes. Yet several factors make it appropriate to treat Song of Songs and Lamentations in the context of wisdom literature.

As in Job, Proverbs, and Ecclesiastes, both these books are a part of the third section of the Hebrew canon. According to one scholar, Song of Songs and Lamentations are grouped together with Job, Proverbs, and Ecclesiastes in the Talmudic arrangement of this third section of the canon.[22] These circumstances do not in themselves establish Song of Songs and Lamentations as "wisdom books." But their placement in the Hebrew canon does put them in the same canonical grouping with Job, Proverbs, and Ecclesiastes, which has some significance.

This canonical placement has particular significance with respect to the Song of Songs, identified specifically with Solomon, who has been described as "the source of Israel's wisdom literature."[23] According to one author:

> The ascription of the Song of Songs to Solomon by the Hebrew canon sets these writings within the context of wisdom literature. Indeed this song is the "pearl" of the collection. . . . The Song is to be understood as wisdom literature.[24]

Beyond their locale in the third category of the Hebrew canon, both the Song of Songs and Lamentations are poetic in form. The Song of Songs is structured as an extended poem of interactive dialogue, similar to the book of Job. Lamentations is distinctive in its poetic form as the most extensive example of acrostic poetry in Scripture. Obviously, poetic form does not in itself qualify these two books as belonging to the category of wisdom literature. But it does indicate one further link with Job, Proverbs, and Ecclesiastes.

Still further, as in the case of Job, Proverbs, and Ecclesiastes, these two books do not conform to any of the other categories of canonical literature as previously discussed. They do not take the shape of history, law, prophecy, or liturgy.

---

22. Cf. S. R. Driver, *An Introduction to the Literature of the Old Testament*, 9th ed. (Edinburgh: T. & T. Clark, 1913), ii (in Introduction proper). The collection of books in the Writings has taken on various arrangements in terms of their order, which makes it difficult to affirm a specific order for the wisdom books. Driver's representation of differing orders indicates that the Talmudic arrangement groups together the books of Job, Proverbs, Ecclesiastes, Song of Songs, and Lamentations. Cf. Tremper Longman III, *Job* (Grand Rapids: Baker Academic, 2012), 23.

23. Brevard S. Childs, *Introduction to the Old Testament as Scripture* (London: SCM Press, 1979), 574.

24. Ibid. Murphy, *Wisdom Literature*, xiii, states: "As a whole, the Song emphasizes values which are primary in wisdom thought." Murphy notes that recent scholarship has been open to "ascribing the preservation and transmission" of the Song of Songs "to the sages of Israel" (xiii).

A question may be raised in conjunction with the historical setting of Lamentations in the context of the fall of Jerusalem. In one sense, this circumstance sets Lamentations outside the pale of wisdom books because of its clear connection with the destruction of Jerusalem by the Babylonians as a specific moment in redemptive history. But it may be noted that other works generally regarded as wisdom books also include references to the history of redemption. The first verse of Proverbs identifies the book as "the proverbs of Solomon son of David, king of Israel" (Prov. 1:1).[25] Similarly, the opening verse of Ecclesiastes deliberately sets this book in the redemptive-historical context of the "son of David, king in Jerusalem" (Eccl. 1:1). In addition, the two apocryphal works generally regarded as wisdom books (Ben Sira and the Wisdom of Solomon) both contain extensive records of redemptive history, stretching from Adam to Nehemiah—far more extensive in recording history than the setting of Lamentations in the time of Jerusalem's collapse before the Babylonians.[26]

Lamentations may not formally fit into the category of a wisdom book as traditionally viewed. But most significantly, in terms of its substance, the book addresses a very practical dimension of human life. Lamentations, though specifically recording the grief of Israel associated with the historical moment of the fall of Jerusalem, at the same time presents a godly pattern for the LORD's covenant people to express their grief in all the various tragedies of life. As has been observed:

> One of the results of incorporating the events of the city's destruction into Israel's traditional terminology of worship was to estab-

25. Cf. the comment of Bruce K. Waltke, *The Book of Proverbs: Chapters 1–15*, NICOT (Grand Rapids: Eerdmans, 2004), 52, in noting Proverbs as a product of Solomon as king in Israel: "Solomon as king of Israel looked at humanity and his world through the lens of Israel's covenants and drew the conclusion that one could enter the world of wisdom only through the fear of the LORD." At least to this degree, Proverbs is set in the context of the progress of redemptive history. This relationship would not be far off from the connection of Lamentations to Israel's exile.

26. Ben Sira chapters 44–47 trace the biblical history from Enoch through Nehemiah. The Wisdom of Solomon includes specific references to individuals from Adam through the conquest (chaps. 10–19). Note the qualification regarding Ben Sira and Wisdom of Solomon by R. B. Y. Scott, *The Way of Wisdom in the Old Testament* (New York: Macmillan, 1971), 4n6, that in these two books "the streams of wisdom and prophecy have mingled." The stream of redemptive history might also be included.

lish a semantic bridge between the historical situation of the early sixth century and the language of faith which struggles with divine judgment. For this reason the book of Lamentations serves every successive generation of the suffering faithful for whom history has become unbearable.[27]

More than any other consideration, the treatment of two very practical issues of human life by these two books encourages considering their message in the context of the wisdom books of the Old Testament. Song of Songs deals with the very human issue of "how to love" in a marital situation.[28] "How to weep" in response to tragic events, both corporately and individually, is the element of wisdom provided by the book of Lamentations. At the most basic level, Song of Songs and Lamentations offer wisdom's rich insights into these practical dimensions of human life.

In view of these observations, and despite the traditional restriction of wisdom books to Job, Proverbs, and Ecclesiastes, the current work will include a treatment of the Song of Songs and Lamentations. It is hoped that the generous reader will manifest a tolerance that will allow him to derive some benefit from the practical wisdom provided by these two books, even though he may not find himself prepared to embrace the Song of Songs and Lamentations as, strictly speaking, wisdom books.

So the poetical books of the Old Testament, with the exception of the book of Psalms, may be treated in the context of Old Testament wisdom literature. This observation naturally leads to these questions: Why does the wisdom literature take on the form of poetry? What various poetic forms are found in these Old Testament wisdom books?

The Poetic Form of Wisdom Literature

The poetry of Old Testament wisdom literature takes on a vast variety of forms. This extensive poetic material displays the basic ele-

---

27. Childs, *Introduction*, 596.

28. The framework for interpretation of the Song of Songs will be dealt with in chapter 5 of this book.

ment of Hebrew parallelism throughout, including representations of all its diversity. The book of Proverbs contains two-line couplets, four-line quatrains, the measured *middah* (the "measurement" of typically "three or four" things), and the extended poem, parable, or discourse. Job represents an epic poem sandwiched between two narrative sections. Its larger poetic middle appears in the form of an interactive dialogue, with each subsequent speaker identified by name. In similar form but with distinctive differences, the Song of Songs represents a poetic interchange between a man and a woman designed to provide instructions regarding love and marriage. In contrast with the form of Job, no explicit identification of speakers is provided, which quite possibly indicates that the book was designed for dramatic reading or chanting by featured individuals, though without dramatic enactment. The book of Ecclesiastes opens and closes with narrative observations regarding wisdom, while the central poetic bulk of material is cast mostly in the first person. The book of Lamentations in its total substance is the longest acrostic poem in the Old Testament, even longer than the familiar acrostic of Psalm 119 with its 176 verses. Despite a basic uniformity of the five chapters of Lamentations with their verses arranged in acrostic form, significant diversity appears throughout. The fifth poem may be called a *quasi-acrostic*, containing the standard twenty-two verses, but without any semblance of alphabetic order.

So a wide range of distinctive poetic material characterizes the various wisdom literature of the Old Testament. In each of these instances, it is not simply a matter of poetic materials that have been integrated into the various books. The entirety of each of these books, perhaps with the exception of Ecclesiastes, is deliberately structured in poetic form. In two cases a prose section at the beginning and end is set in contrast with the poetic body of the book. No other portion of Scripture except the Psalms and some portions of the Prophets presents poetic material comparable to these masterpieces of literary composition.

But why? What in the subject of wisdom inspires such extensive poetic expression? As one commentator queries, "is there something about the poetic form that makes it particularly useful for evoking wisdom?"[29] The author answers his own question with an example: "To say that God is 'transcendent' or 'omniscient' . . . is qualitatively different than declaring that God 'rules the raging sea.'"[30]

Beyond the larger impact made by poetic literature, the practical purpose of these discourses may be a primary factor that brought about this all-embracive poetic mode of expression. These inspired works do not focus on history or theology. Scattered admonitions address the people, but these poems contain nothing resembling the "Thus says the Lord" of the Prophets.

These books of wisdom may be called the *how-to books* of the Old Testament. God's people desperately need to know the how-tos that make life possible in the midst of a world that challenges every aspect of human life. Furthermore, they need this practical advice to be preserved in memorable fashion, which partly explains the books' poetic rather than prosaic form.[31] God's people need to carry these God-inspired words of wisdom along with them as they walk along the road, barter in the market, and return each evening to the privacy of home and family.[32]

From this perspective, these five books of the Old Testament may be characterized as follows:

29. Bartholomew, *Old Testament Wisdom Literature*, 68.

30. Ibid., 69.

31. Cf. the comments on memorization as a critical factor in the use of poetry in ancient oral societies in Nicholas Carr, *The Shallows: What the Internet Is Doing to Our Brains* (London: W. W. Norton, 2011), 55–56.

32. Some significant recognition has been given to the role of the family as a formative element in communicating Israel's wisdom tradition, in accord with the manifold times that Solomon addresses his "son" or "sons" in Proverbs. R. E. Clements, "Wisdom and Old Testament Theology," in *Wisdom in Ancient Israel: Essays in Honour of J. A. Emerton*, ed. John Day, Robert P. Gordon, and H. G. M. Williamson (Cambridge: Cambridge University Press, 1995), notes that wisdom in the Old Testament underscored the importance of a right attitude to life in general based on a religious commitment. Regarding the critical role of the family, he notes regarding wisdom in a biblical theology: "The most obvious is that, in the post-exilic period, wisdom appears to have flourished as a part of a programme of education carried out with the approval of, and probably within the location of, the individual household" (281). Again, he states: "The very roots of religion and virtue are seen to rest within the relatively small household context of family life" (281). Though uncertain about the sociological setting of Old Testament wisdom, Crenshaw notes: "In all probability, the central place of instruction was the family" (*Urgent Advice*, 595).

- Proverbs: How to Walk in Wisdom's Way
- Job: How to Puzzle
- Ecclesiastes: How to Cope with Life's Frustrations
- Lamentations: How to Weep
- The Song of Songs: How to Love

Following the conclusion of this brief introduction to Old Testament wisdom literature, the present work will explore each of these books individually. The goal will be to capture the essence of wisdom in each book from a biblical-theological perspective, so that it speaks with practical effectiveness into the current context of the lives of God's people. Special attention will be paid to the varied poetic dimensions of the various books.[33]

THE PLACE OF WISDOM IN OLD TESTAMENT THEOLOGY

For decades, the biblical-theology movement has focused altogether on the history of redemption. The record of the "mighty acts of God" across Israel's historical experience has dominated the study of Old Testament theology. Though producing numerous insights into the biblical message, a sad side effect has been the neglect of the wisdom literature of the Old Testament.[34] In the wisdom literature almost no mention is made of the promise to the patriarchs, the exodus from Egypt, the lawgiving at Sinai, the wilderness wandering, the conquest, Davidic kingship, exile, and restoration.[35] As a consequence, the wisdom materials have been essentially treated as an appendix to the drama of redemption. Some have even gone so far as to dub

---

33. One Old Testament scholar who has given his life to research in the wisdom literature notes that the top of the list for future studies in the field must be "literary artistry." Underscoring this observation, he continues: "There is no more appropriate endeavor, since such analysis takes its cue from ancient sages who labored to master the art of speaking and writing" (Crenshaw, *Urgent Advice*, 32).

34. Says Clements: "It is a significant feature of the influential work of Gerhard von Rad that his attention to the role of wisdom in the growth of the biblical tradition emerges after the completion of his *magnum opus* on Old Testament theology" ("Wisdom and Old Testament Theology," 269).

35. As an exception, as previously noted, Lamentations represents a faith reaction to Israel's redemptive-historical experience of exile.

the wisdom literature of the Old Testament an "alien corpus."[36] This significant aspect of Israel's life of faith has had no opportunity to make its positive contribution to the understanding of God's revelation to Israel. God's people as a consequence have been significantly impoverished.

This neglect of wisdom's contribution to the faith and life of God's people has occurred in part as a consequence of viewing redemptive history from a purely linear perspective. Abraham's faith points to Moses' exodus followed by David's kingdom consummating in Messiah's coming. A straight line across history has provided the pattern for understanding the life and faith of God's people.

A critical modification of the manner in which redemption progresses across history may bring into fuller focus the true nature of God's ongoing work among a fallen humanity. Not only is there the straight line of continuum from the age of the old covenant to the new, but a spiral of repetition must be taken into account—repetition with increased intensity. The cycle of sun and moon that orders the seasons has its vital role to play in redemptive history. The spiral of the Sabbath must be noted—the weekly Sabbaths anticipating sabbatical years accumulating up to the fifty-year Jubilee, which defines the progress of redemptive history (Lev. 25:1–12; 2 Chron. 36:21; Dan. 9:25). Beyond these basic cycles of creation is the significant cycle of birth, life, and death defining the life span of particular men and women who "served God's purpose in [their] own generation" (Acts 13:36). The cycle of the generations functions as an aspect of God's redemptive work in the world that must never be overlooked. Beyond the cycle of generations is the cycle of epochs, of elongated periods of time. Integral to the cycle of epochs is the cycle of national experiences, as dramatized in the days of Israel's judges. Six times over, national sin provokes divine chastening; divine chastening leads to a cry for deliverance; a cry for deliverance receives divine answer by God's sending a judge as savior. But the salvation brought by the

36. Cf. the allusion to this perspective in Crenshaw, *Urgent Advice*, 1. Note also the references in Waltke (*Proverbs 1–15*, 64) to the acknowledgments of several Old Testament theologians regarding the failure to integrate wisdom literature into Old Testament biblical theology.

judge is soon forgotten, and the nation enters the descending spiral into sin once more (Judg. 2:10–19).

Without this larger picture of the repetitive cycles inherent in humanity's experience as ordered by the Creator, Sustainer, and Redeemer of the world, the understanding of basic reality by God's people will remain deficient. This larger picture of God's working in the world provides the framework for a wise understanding of marriage in youth, labor throughout life, tragedy in crisis, weeping in death, and worship in hope. From this perspective, the Old Testament books of wisdom contribute significantly in every age to the understanding of redemption's progress toward its ultimate goal, which finds its personified climax in Jesus Christ, the incarnate Word, the wisdom of God.

An Initial Admonition: Get Wisdom!

The final word in this introduction to biblical wisdom must speak as wisdom speaks: Get wisdom! "The beginning of wisdom is—Get Wisdom! And with all your getting, get understanding" (Prov. 4:7). The proverb drills this admonition into the head and heart of the reader by multiple repetitions:

> Get wisdom! Get understanding!
> > Do not forget!
> > Do not turn away from the words of my mouth!
> Do not abandon her,
> > and she will protect you.
> Love her,
> > and she will watch over you.
> The principal thing is wisdom.
> Get wisdom!
> > and with all your getting,
> > get understanding. (Prov. 4:5–7)

Five times in three verses the admonition is underlined: Get, get, get, get, get! Make the getting of wisdom your chief goal in life. All these years, all these decades, God's people have suffered from relative neglect of these five books of wisdom. So now the admonition must be heeded. It is imperative. Get wisdom.

But just as was asked at the beginning of this introduction to Old Testament wisdom, the question must be asked again, "Where is wisdom to be found?"

The wisest way to wisdom is to follow the route of the wise men from the East: "We saw his star in the east and have come to worship him" (Matt. 2:2 NIV). They found the young child born of a virgin, conceived of the Holy Spirit, designated the Son of God. As a youth he grew in wisdom and stature and favor with God and man (Luke 2:52). Of himself he said, "[Wisdom] greater than Solomon is here" (Matt. 12:42 NIV). The wisdom of men has been made foolishness by the revelation of God's wisdom in Christ (1 Cor. 1:20–25). As the Creator of all things, he has all the treasures of wisdom and knowledge hidden in himself (Col. 2:3).

So this study of the wisdom of the Old Testament must eventually rest on Jesus the Messiah as the fullness and the fulfillment of all the wisdom of God. While appearing as foolishness in the eyes of men, all the wisdom of the ages focuses on him.

SELECTED BIBLIOGRAPHY FOR INTRODUCTION TO WISDOM LITERATURE

Alter, Robert. *The Wisdom Books: Job, Proverbs, and Ecclesiastes: A Translation with Commentary*. New York: W. W. Norton, 2010.

Bartholomew, Craig G. *Old Testament Wisdom Literature: A Theological Introduction*. Downers Grove, IL: InterVarsity Press, 2011.

Carr, Nicholas. *The Shallows: What the Internet Is Doing to Our Brains*. London: W. W. Norton, 2011.

Childs, Brevard S. *Introduction to the Old Testament as Scripture*. London: SCM Press, 1979.

Clements, R. E. "Wisdom and Old Testament Theology." In *Wisdom in Ancient Israel: Essays in Honour of J. A. Emerton*, edited by John Day, Robert P. Gordon, and H. G. M. Williamson, 269–86. Cambridge: Cambridge University Press, 1995.

———. *Wisdom for a Changing World: Wisdom in Old Testament Theology*. Berkeley, CA: BIBAL Press, 1990.

Crenshaw, James L. *Old Testament Wisdom: An Introduction*. Rev. and enl. ed. Louisville: Westminster John Knox, 1998.

———. *Urgent Advice and Probing Questions: Collected Writings on Old Testament Wisdom*. Macon, GA: Mercer University Press, 1995.

Driver, S. R. *An Introduction to the Literature of the Old Testament*. 9th ed. Edinburgh: T. & T. Clark, 1913.

Fox, Michael V. *Proverbs 1–9: A New Translation with Introduction and Commentary*. AB 18A. New York: Doubleday, 2000.

Kidner, Derek. *The Proverbs: An Introduction and Commentary*. Downers Grove, IL: InterVarsity Press, 1969.

———. "Wisdom Literature of the Old Testament." In *New Perspectives on the Old Testament*, edited by J. Barton Payne, 117–30. London: Word Books, 1970.

Kitchen, Kenneth A. "Proverbs." In *The Biblical Expositor*, edited by Carl F. H. Henry, 2:71–93. Philadelphia: A. J. Holman, 1960.

Longman, Tremper, III. *Job*. Grand Rapids: Baker Academic, 2012.

———. *Proverbs*. Grand Rapids: Baker Academic, 2006.

McKane, William. *Proverbs: A New Approach*. Philadelphia: Westminster, 1977.

Murphy, Roland E. *Wisdom Literature: Job, Proverbs, Ruth, Canticles, Ecclesiastes, and Esther*. Forms of the Old Testament Literature 13. Grand Rapids: Eerdmans, 1981.

Perdue, Leo G. *Proverbs*. Louisville: John Knox, 2000.

———. *Wisdom and Creation: The Theology of Wisdom Literature*. Nashville: Abingdon, 1994.

Pritchard, James B., ed. *Ancient Near Eastern Texts Relating to the Old Testament*. 3rd ed. Princeton, NJ: Princeton University Press, 1969.

Rad, Gerhard von. "Some Aspects of the Old Testament World-View." In *The Problem of the Hexateuch and Other Essays*, 144–65. Edinburgh: Oliver & Boyd, 1966.

———. *Wisdom in Israel*. London: SCM Press, 1972.

Scott, R. B. Y. *Proverbs, Ecclesiastes: Introduction, Translation, and Notes*. AB 18. Garden City, NY: Doubleday, 1965.

———. *The Way of Wisdom in the Old Testament*. New York: Macmillan, 1971.

Waltke, Bruce K. *The Book of Proverbs: Chapters 1–15*. NICOT. Grand Rapids: Eerdmans, 2004.

Whybray, R. N. "The Wisdom Psalms." In *Wisdom in Ancient Israel: Essays in Honour of J. A. Emerton*, edited by John Day, Robert P. Gordon, and H. G. M. Williamson, 152–60. Cambridge: Cambridge University Press, 1995.

PROVERBS
HOW TO WALK IN WISDOM'S WAY

CHAPTER OUTLINE

Introduction
  I. The Origin and Development of the Book of Proverbs
 II. The Relation of Proverbs to Other Ancient Wisdom
     Materials
III. The Form, Substance, and Structure of the Book of Proverbs
     A. Basic Outline
     B. Elements of Form and Substance
     C. Introductory Section: The Worth of Wisdom's Way
        (Proverbs 1–9)
        1. The Commendation of Wisdom (Ten Passages)
           a. Proverbs 1:1–7
           b. Proverbs 1:8–9
           c. Proverbs 1:10–19
           d. Proverbs 2:1–22
           e. Proverbs 3:1–12
           f. Proverbs 3:21–35
           g. Proverbs 4:1–4
           h. Proverbs 4:10–19
           i. Proverbs 4:20–27
           j. Proverbs 6:1–19
        2. The Personification of Wisdom (Five Passages)
           a. Proverbs 1:20–33
           b. Proverbs 3:13–20

      c. Proverbs 4:5–9

      d. Proverbs 8:1–36

      e. Additional Note: The Interpretation of Proverbs 8:22 by Athanasius as the Champion of the Opponents of Arianism

      f. Proverbs 9:1–18

    3. A Special Warning to a Son: Avoid Adultery (Five Passages)

      a. Proverbs 2:16–22

      b. Proverbs 5:1–23

      c. Proverbs 6:20–35

      d. Proverbs 7:1–27

      e. Proverbs 9:13–18

D. The Proverbs of Solomon (Proverbs 10:1–22:16)

  1. Proverbs with a Contrast (Proverbs 10–15)

  2. Proverbs without a Contrast (Proverbs 16:1–22:16)

E. The Words of the Wise Ones (Proverbs 22:17–24:34)

  1. First Collection from the Wise Ones (Proverbs 22:17–24:22)

  2. Second Collection from the Wise Ones (Proverbs 24:23–34)

F. The Hezekian Arrangement of Solomonic Proverbs (Proverbs 25–29)

G. The Words of Certain Wise Men (Proverbs 30:1–31:9)

  1. Agur (Proverbs 30:1–33)

  2. King Lemuel (Proverbs 31:1–9)

H. An Acrostic Poem Celebrating the Godly Woman (Proverbs 31:10–31)

  1. Her Price (Proverbs 31:10–12)

  2. Her Product (Proverbs 31:13–25)

  3. Her Piety (Proverbs 31:26–27)

  4. Her Praise (Proverbs 31:28–31)

  5. Summary

IV. Theological Perspectives on the Book of Proverbs

A. A Secularistic Perspective

30

INTRODUCTION

If any book of the Bible is given over to the practicalities of life, it is the book of Proverbs. "How to walk in wisdom's way" summarizes the message of this book that provides "down-to-earth" advice. But this advice is like no other available in this world. It is advice inspired by God, sent from heaven. This book contains the divinely inspired wisdom by which a father may prepare his son for the many different challenges that he must face in life. How to respond to wealth, to work, to words. What to expect from the constant scheming of wicked people. How to understand calamities. But most of all, how to keep God, the LORD of Creation and Covenant, central throughout your entire life.

This wisdom for the walk of a lifetime does not come in the form of a theological treatise or a collection of lessons from history. It comes instead in the form of poetic proverbs—short, practical summaries of truth that anticipate just about every situation that a person will face. Indeed, longer, more elaborate warnings and counsels also appear in the book. But typically these proverbs may be characterized as "God's existentialism." You may plan out the details of your schedule before you step out into today's world. But how can you anticipate the variety of circumstances that will confront you throughout the day? You bump into an old friend, you receive an unexpected message, you miss your appointment. You stumble on a slippery walkway, you have a serious disagreement with your boss, your child's school principal calls for an appointment to discuss a problem that has arisen.

What can possibly prepare you for all these different situations? They arise unannounced without a moment's notice. Where can you turn for the practical advice that will tell you what to do? You need instant insight so that you can know how to react.

That's what the book of Proverbs is all about. It's the LORD's wisdom condensed into short, pithy, memorable sayings that address the concrete challenges his people face every day.

Every human culture creates its own storage bank of wise words. So it should not be surprising that proverbial sayings had a long history among the people of God under the old covenant. Anonymous sayings embodying wisdom are scattered throughout the Old Testament books of history and prophecy:

> That is why it is said, "Like Nimrod, a mighty hunter before the LORD." (Gen. 10:9 NIV)

> As the proverb of the ancients says, "Out of the wicked comes forth wickedness." (1 Sam. 24:13 NASB)

> Let not the one who puts on his armor boast like the one who takes it off. (1 Kings 20:11)

> Does the ax raise itself
>   above him who swings it,
> or the saw boast
>   against him who uses it? (Isa. 10:15 NIV)

> The fathers have eaten sour grapes and the children's teeth are set on edge. (Jer. 31:29; cf. Ezek. 18:2)

> Everyone who quotes proverbs will quote this proverb about you: "Like mother, like daughter." (Ezek. 16:44 NIV)

Not only in the Old Testament literature of history and prophecy. The psalmist also indicates his intent to preserve the treasures of wisdom with a proverb:

> My mouth
>   will speak words of wisdom;
> The utterance from my heart
>   will give understanding.

> I will turn my ear
>   to a proverb:
> With the harp
>   I will expound my riddle. (Ps. 49:3-4 NIV)

Becoming the object of a proverbial saying could indicate a blessing or a curse. For a wise saying is capable of cutting both ways. The LORD warns King Solomon that if the people of Israel violate his commands, they will become "a byword [proverb—מָשָׁל] and an object of ridicule among all peoples" (1 Kings 9:7 NIV; cf. Deut. 28:37). Having witnessed the devastations of God's judgments on his nation, the psalmist declares: "You have made us a byword [proverb—מָשָׁל] among the nations; the peoples shake their heads at us" (Ps. 44:14 NIV; cf. 69:12). In the words of the prophet Jeremiah, to be a reproach and a proverb, an object of ridicule and cursing, are essentially the same thing (Jer. 24:9).

These biblical aphorisms should not be regarded merely as "timeless truths" that manifest no sensitivity to the progress of redemptive history. Though rooted in concrete circumstances of a specific time and place, these Old Testament proverbs contain an element that anticipates the pattern of a spiral moving across history toward its climax. In ever-increasing intensity, through every age, "the fear of the LORD is the beginning of knowledge" (Prov. 1:7). This central theme of life is manifest across the various periods of redemptive history. So the search for wisdom by the patriarch Job underscores the significance of the "fear of the Lord" (Job 28:28). In facing the prospect of the dark days of the exile, the prophet Isaiah declares that those who live by "fear of the LORD" are set over against those who "light fires" in honor of false gods and who will eventually lie down in torment (Isa. 50:10–11; cf. 59:19). As the era of the old covenant moves toward its conclusion, the prophet Malachi anticipates the climactic day in which God will act in judgment to distinguish the righteous from the wicked. At that critical moment, the prophet promises that those who "fear the LORD" will be his treasured possession and will be spared (Mal. 3:16–17). From 2000 B.C. to 1000 B.C. to 700 B.C. to 500 B.C., the proverbial truth that the "fear of the LORD" is the beginning of wisdom manifests its reality across the ages.

Even in the context of the new covenant, the ever-increasing significance of this proverbial word about the "fear of the LORD" finds its place. When the climactic hour of the Son of God's incarnation draws near, Mary declares that the Lord's mercy extends to all those who "fear him" from generation to generation (Luke 1:50). Subsequently, as the apostle Peter acknowledges God's gift of salvation to the Roman centurion, he affirms that God accepts from every nation those who "fear him," anticipating the worldwide spread of the Christian gospel across nations (Acts 10:35). Other instances of this enlargement of a proverbial principle across redemptive history may be traced in the application of particular proverbs to new situations brought about by the progress of redemption.[1] True in every age, these proverbial sayings increase in their significance as redemptive history progresses toward its climax.

In considering the role of Proverbs throughout the life of God's people, the present study will consider the following topics:

- The Origin and Development of the Book of Proverbs
- The Relation of Proverbs to Other Ancient Wisdom Materials
- The Form, Substance, and Structure of the Book of Proverbs
- Theological Perspectives on the Book of Proverbs

THE ORIGIN AND DEVELOPMENT OF THE BOOK OF PROVERBS

The opening verse of Proverbs traces the book's origin to King Solomon, the quintessence of wisdom in Israel's history:

The proverbs of Solomon son of David, king of Israel.
(Prov. 1:1 NIV)

---

1. Three additional examples of the ongoing significance of a proverbial saying may underscore this expanding role of the biblical proverb throughout the Old Testament and into the New: (1) "My son, do not despise the LORD's discipline and do not resent his rebuke, because the LORD disciplines those he loves, as a father the son he delights in" (Prov. 3:11–12 NIV; cf. Deut. 8:5; Job 7:17; Ps. 94:12; Heb. 12:5; Rev. 3:19). (2) "The LORD resists the proud but gives grace to the humble" (Prov. 3:34 LXX; cf. Ps. 138:6; Isa. 57:15; Matt. 23:12; James 4:6; 1 Peter 5:5). (3) "If your enemy is hungry, give him food to eat; if he is thirsty, give him water to drink" (Prov. 25:21 NIV; cf. Ex. 23:4; Matt. 5:44; Rom. 12:20).

34

The indication that Solomon composed three thousand proverbs (1 Kings 4:32) more than adequately covers the approximately eight hundred verses found in the book of Proverbs. As in the case of the preservation of the words of Jesus, this collection of wise sayings represents a high level of selectivity even if all these proverbs should be attributed to Solomon (cf. John 20:30–31).

Further notations within the book itself indicate that not all the material in Proverbs claims to have originated with Solomon. Certain statements give evidence of a variety of authors and editors. More explicitly, authorship is attributed to:

- Solomon (Prov. 1:1; 10:1; 25:1)
- "Wise men" (Prov. 22:17; 24:23)
- Agur (Prov. 30:1)
- Lemuel the king (Prov. 31:1)

It is not possible to precisely identify the "wise men" responsible for different portions of the book. Traditionally, *Agur* and *King Lemuel* have been regarded as names substituting for *Solomon*, although this conclusion is difficult to confirm.

Critics of an earlier day concluded that despite the claim of Solomonic origin, the biblical proverbs must have originated in approximately the third century B.C. because of their Persian or Greek flavor.[2] More recently, Egyptian and Babylonian parallels have made it clear that the content of the book of Proverbs may be appropriately located in the early days of Israelite kingdom history. In addition, the numerous proverbs referring to kings "presuppose the existence of the Israelite monarchy,"[3] which would not suit a third-century B.C. date for the book's origin. The personification of wisdom in chapters 8 and 9 was once regarded as the latest material in Proverbs. But more recently these chapters have been seen as the closest thing in Proverbs to ancient Canaanite materials.[4]

---

2. W. F. Albright calls Hermann Gunkel's late-date theory a "curious myth." Cf. W. F. Albright, "Some Canaanite-Phoenician Sources of Hebrew Wisdom," in *Wisdom in Israel and in the Ancient Near East*, ed. M. Noth and D. Winton Thomas (Leiden: Brill, 1955), 4.

3. Cf. R. N. Whybray, *The Book of Proverbs: A Survey of Modern Study* (Leiden: Brill, 1995), 152, referring to the opinion of W. O. E. Oesterley.

4. Derek Kidner, *The Proverbs: An Introduction and Commentary* (Downers Grove, IL: InterVarsity Press, 1969), 26.

Despite contrary opinions, both external and internal evidence provides significant support for the Solomonic origin of the bulk of materials in Proverbs.[5] At the same time, as previously noted, Scripture itself attributes portions of the book to authors other than Solomon.

A statement within the book itself provides significant internal testimony to editing after the time of Solomon. The statement indicates a conscious editorial rearrangement of proverbs attributed to Solomon that was carried out by a group of wise men in the days of Hezekiah, working 250 to 300 years after their Solomonic composition.

> These are more proverbs of Solomon, copied by the men of Hezekiah king of Judah. (Prov. 25:1 NIV)

The term translated "copied" (הֶעְתִּיקוּ) comes from a root that means "to move," as in Genesis 12:8: "[Abraham] moved from there to a mountain on the east" (cf. also Gen. 26:22). In the context of the formation of the book of Proverbs, the term suggests a transposing of certain proverbs from one location in a collection of manuscripts to another. As one commentator explains, the word means "'to remove from their place,' and denotes that the men of Hezekiah removed from the place where they found the following proverbs, and placed them together in a separate collection."[6] The arrangement (or rearrangement) of the book by the men of Hezekiah indicates that the final form of the book could not have taken shape any earlier than 250 to 300 years after Solomon.

---

5. Recent biblical scholarship has tended to give more credence to the possibility that Solomon composed at least some of the book of Proverbs. Says R. N. Whybray, *Wisdom in Proverbs: The Concept of Wisdom in Proverbs 1–9*, Studies in Biblical Theology 45 (Naperville, IL: Alec R. Allenson, 1965), 20: "it is difficult to set aside entirely the persistent tradition which connects Solomon with wisdom." He comments further that the ascription of wisdom to Solomon "may have a historical basis." He notes that the ascription of certain collections in Proverbs to Solomon "may not be entirely unfounded," since the cultural circumstances favor it (21). To the contrary, Michael V. Fox, *Proverbs 1–9: A New Translation with Introduction and Commentary*, AB 18A (New York: Doubleday, 2000), 56, says: "Historically, it is improbable that many—if any—of the proverbs were written by Solomon."

6. Franz Delitzsch, *Biblical Commentary on the Proverbs of Solomon* (Grand Rapids: Eerdmans, 1950), 1:5.

THE RELATION OF PROVERBS TO OTHER ANCIENT WISDOM MATERIALS

Already the place of biblical wisdom writings has been considered in the larger context of ancient Near Eastern wisdom material.[7] Exploration of this question as it specifically relates to the book of Proverbs has focused on an Egyptian document, the "Wisdom of Amen-em-Opet."[8] When this document was made public, it was immediately hailed as having a direct relationship to the collection of sayings of the "wise ones" in Proverbs 22:17–24:22. Before its publication, it was assumed that Proverbs was different from other Old Testament books simply in that it elaborated on the ethical teaching of the Law and the Prophets. But once attention turned to a comparison with Egyptian and other ancient Near Eastern wisdom literature, Proverbs suddenly came to be viewed as "what might be called the Hebrew version of an intercultural phenomenon shared with Egypt and Mesopotamia."[9] As a consequence, viewing Proverbs as an authentic expression of Israelite faith was brought into question. Now Proverbs was perceived as providing a secularistic view of life, instructing people how to achieve material success.

The dating of this Egyptian document varies between the twelfth and sixth centuries B.C., which means that its chronological relation to the book of Proverbs cannot be determined with certainty.[10] More recent studies have promoted a twelfth-century B.C. dating.[11] But apart from questions of dating, the "points of contact between the two are too many and too close to be a matter of coincidence."[12]

7. Note the introductory chapter of this book in the section titled "The Broader Context of Wisdom in the Ancient Near East."

8. E. W. Budge presented the document to the British Museum in London, England, in 1888. But it was thirty-five years later, in 1923, that the material was finally published.

9. R. B. Y. Scott, "The Study of Wisdom Literature," *Interpretation* 24, 1 (1970): 24.

10. James B. Pritchard, ed., *Ancient Near Eastern Texts Relating to the Old Testament*, 3rd ed. (Princeton, NJ: Princeton University Press, 1969), 421–25, dates this Egyptian document somewhere between the tenth and the sixth centuries B.C., noting that some weight of evidence favors the seventh to the sixth centuries B.C. Assuming the role of Solomon in the production of the materials found in Proverbs, this dating would place the Egyptian document centuries later than the biblical proverbs.

11. Whybray, *Survey*, 10. Fox, *Proverbs 1–9*, 18, dates the document sometime in the twelfth to the eleventh centuries B.C.

12. Kidner, *Proverbs*, 23.

A comparison of some expressions in these two documents may demonstrate their similarities:[13]

Amen-em-Opet	Proverbs
"To know how to return an answer to him who said it, and to direct a report to one who has sent him." (Introduction)	"To make you know the certainty of words of truth, that you may correctly answer to him who sent you." (Prov. 22:21)
"Give thy ears, hear what is said, give thy heart to understand them. To put them in thy heart is worthwhile." (i, 1–3)	"Incline your ear and hear the words of the wise, and apply your mind to my knowledge. For it will be pleasant if you keep them within you." (Prov. 22:17–18a)
". . . nor encroach upon the boundaries of a widow." (6th chap., viii, 18)	"Do not move the ancient boundary which your fathers have set." (Prov. 22:28)
"Better is a measure that the god gives thee than 5000 [taken] illegally." (6th chap., viii, 18)	"Better is a little with the fear of the LORD than great treasure and turmoil with it." (Prov. 15:16)
"Better is bread, when the heart is happy, than riches with sorrow." (6th chap., ix, 8–9)	"Better is a dish of vegetables where love is, than a fattened ox and hatred with it." (Prov. 15:17)
"Cast not thy heart in pursuit of riches. . . . They have made themselves wings like geese and are flown away to the heavens." (7th chap., ix, 10; x, 4–5)	"Do not weary yourself to gain riches . . . for wealth certainly makes itself wings, like an eagle that flies toward the heavens." (Prov. 23:4–5)
"Do not associate to thyself the heated man, nor visit him for conversation." (9th chap., xi, 13)	"Do not associate with a man given to anger; or go with a hot-tempered man." (Prov. 22:24)
"Do not lean on the scales nor falsify the weights, nor damage the fractions of the measure." (16th chap., xvii, 18)	"Differing weights are an abomination to the LORD, and a false scale is not good." (Prov. 20:23)
"Man knows not what the morrow is like." (18th chap., xix, 13)	"Do not boast about tomorrow, for you do not know what a day may bring forth." (Prov. 27:1 NIV)
"Do not eat bread before a noble. . . . Look at the cup which is before thee, and let it serve thy needs." (23rd chap., xxiii, 13, 16)	"When you sit down to dine with a ruler . . . put a knife to your throat." (Prov. 23:1 NIV)

13. The quotations from Amen-em-Opet are taken from Pritchard, *Ancient Near Eastern Texts*, 421–24. Pritchard omits thirteen of the thirty chapters, describing their content only briefly in a footnote. The omitted chapters are 3, 5, 8, 12, 14, 15, 17, 19, 22, 24, 26, 27, and 29.

So how is the relationship of these two documents to be understood? Basically three approaches have been proposed.

The first approach discovers a specific allusion to the "thirty chapters" mentioned in Amen-em-Opet in Proverbs 22:17–24:22. This section of Proverbs is regarded as containing a direct reference to the "thirty sayings" found in the Egyptian document. A recent translation of the critical verse reads as follows:

> Have I not written thirty sayings for you,
> Sayings of counsel and knowledge[?] (Prov. 22:20 NIV)[14]

Based on this analysis of the relationship between the two documents, this first collection of the proverbs of the "wise ones" (Prov. 22:17–24:22) is then divided into thirty "sayings."[15]

The second approach uncovers various expressions scattered throughout Amen-em-Opet that correspond to a number of the "sayings" of the wise ones as recorded in this same section of Proverbs (Prov. 22:17–24:22). Random aphorisms of Amen-em-Opet are compared with similar statements coming from Proverbs.[16]

---

14. NIV (1984, 2011). The earlier NIV footnotes the following optional readings: (Have I not) "formerly written" (to you)? and (Have I not) "written excellent" (things to you)? The later NIV (2011) does not include these optional readings. Though not in the NIV of 1984, the NIV of 2011 identifies thirty consecutive "sayings" by inserting headings across this section of Proverbs. The *ESV Study Bible* (2008) also renders Proverbs 22:20 as "thirty sayings." The enumerations of the two versions differ in that the NIV (2011) counts the introductory verses of the section (Prov. 22:17–21) as "Saying 1" and then merges Proverbs 24:10–12 into a single "saying" to achieve the number "thirty." The *ESV Study Bible* study note begins its enumeration with Proverbs 22:22–23 and separates Proverbs 24:10–12 into two "sayings," also concluding with the number "thirty."

15. This arrangement is extensively developed in Bruce K. Waltke, *The Book of Proverbs: Chapters 15–31*, NICOT (Grand Rapids: Eerdmans, 2005), 225–88. Cf. also Bruce K. Waltke, *The Book of Proverbs: Chapters 1–15*, NICOT (Grand Rapids, Eerdmans, 2004), 21–24. In support of the "thirty sayings" reading of the text, see also Kidner, *Proverbs*, 23, 249–50; Tremper Longman III, *Proverbs* (Grand Rapids: Baker Academic, 2006), 415; Roland E. Murphy, *Proverbs*, WBC 22 (Nashville: Thomas Nelson, 1998), 291–94.

16. An illustration of this approach may be found in Pritchard, *Ancient Near Eastern Texts*, 424n46, citing D. C. Simpson, "The Hebrew Book of Proverbs and the Teaching of Amenophis," *Journal of Egyptian Archaeology* 12, 3/4 (1926): 232–39. Pritchard cites no parallels with forty-seven of the seventy verses from this section of Proverbs.

The first proposal explaining the connection is based on the assumption that Proverbs 22:20 actually refers to "thirty" (sayings).[17] But the written Masoretic Hebrew text (*Ketib*) reads "[on] the third [day]" (*shilshom*, שִׁלְשׁוֹם), which means "[on] the day before yesterday," and is found elsewhere only as an idiomatic expression meaning "in the past" or "formerly." With this understanding, the verse gives expression to a rhetorical question: "Have I not written formerly to you . . . ?"[18] Following this reading of the written Masoretic text, no mention is found in this section of Proverbs to a supposed "thirty" (sayings).

Indeed, the Masoretic verbalization of the text (the *Qere*) has the meaning "thirty" (*shalishim*, שָׁלִישִׁים). Yet the "widespread agreement that the close resemblance to Amenemope ends at 23:11" with only ten comparable units rather than thirty argues against any preciseness of connection between the Egyptian document and Proverbs on the basis of a reference to "thirty sayings."[19] On the other hand, the fact that this section of Proverbs (Prov. 22:17–24:22) can be convincingly divided into precisely thirty sayings supports its connection with Amen-em-Opet.

With respect to the second approach and its concentration on specific parallels of expression shared between Amen-em-Opet and Proverbs 22:17–24:22, the larger framework of these sayings must be taken into account. A polytheistic perspective on life permeates Amen-em-Opet, which is wholly foreign to the biblical document. Repeated reference is made to its various gods. The introduction speaks of the scribe who "sets up the divine offerings for all the gods." He refers to the one who "installs Horus upon the throne of his father," to "God's Mother," and to the one who "protects Min in his shrine." The body of the text appeals to the moon god to establish justice in the land (second chapter), speaks of satisfying god with the will of the Lord [?] (sixth chapter), refers to Fate and Fortune, which are identified as the god Sahy and the goddess Renaenut (seventh chapter), urges making prayer

---

17. The word *sayings* is not in the biblical text.

18. R. N. Whybray, *Proverbs*, NCBC (Grand Rapids: Eerdmans, 1994), 328.

19. Cf. Murphy, *Proverbs*, 292. Waltke, *Proverbs 15–31*, 228, also acknowledges the limitation of the connection at the outset of his comparison: "Recall that it is precisely at 23:11 that material dependent on *Amenemope* disappears."

to Aton when he rises, for he will give prosperity and health (seventh chapter), speaks of safety in the hand of the god, which should enable a person to be sincere (tenth chapter), describes "the ape" that "sits beside the balance" whose god is Thoth (sixteenth chapter), declares that "God is [always] in his success, whereas man is in his failure" (eighteenth chapter), states that "as for wrongdoing, it belongs to the god; it is sealed with his finger. There is no success in the hand of the god, but there is no failure before him" (eighteenth chapter). In addition, the text identifies the "All-Lord" as the pilot of the tongue (eighteenth chapter) and urges its reader not to discover the will of god for his own self without reference to Fate and Fortune (twentieth chapter). In the conclusion, the scribe of Amen-em-Opet identifies himself as Senu, son of the God's Father Pa-miu (thirtieth chapter).

To an Israelite who regularly recited the *Shema* ("Hear, O Israel: the LORD our God, the LORD is one," Deut. 6:4 NIV), this plethora of gods must have appeared as utter abomination. Not knowing how the various gods would react to the different circumstances of life according to their diverse whims must have appeared as totally confusing—which as a matter of fact it is. Given this wholly different context of the aphorisms of Egypt, it may be appropriately observed that far more words of Amen-em-Opet stand in opposition to the teaching of Proverbs than the scattered words that appear to have some formal agreement. Making comparison of phrases or parts of phrases taken out of their total context cannot be a proper way of understanding either the sayings of Amen-em-Opet or the proverbs of Solomon.

How, then, is the connection and sometimes similarity of phraseology between Amen-em-Opet and Proverbs to be understood? The third analysis of the relationship acknowledges the similarities, but at the same time insists that the two different world-and-life views must always be taken into account.[20] Because of the verified awareness by Israel of the wisdom traditions in Egypt, it may be appropriately proposed that the parallels of expression could be explained by appeal to a common tradition of wisdom known in both Israel and Egypt.

20. Whybray, *Survey*, 16, notes that "the more recent studies of Proverbs show a growing tendency, while not denying Egyptian influence altogether, to understand the book as more closely related to Israelite traditions than to outside influences."

Their interrelationship may be best explained through presuming studied interaction among the schooling experiences of the wisdom scribes of the various nations, which "undoubtedly provided opportunity for the study of a wide range of Wisdom writings."[21] It is quite possible to imagine Solomon and the "wise men" of his kingdom scrutinizing the wisdom materials of Egypt, noting the saneness of some of their proverbial sayings, and adjusting them so that they would conform to the larger truths arising from the uniqueness of Yahweh, the one and only true God of Creation and Covenant who revealed himself with consistency to Abraham, the patriarchs, Moses, the people of Israel, David the organizer of Israel's worship practices, and Solomon.

At the same time, foundational theological differences inevitably exclude direct dependence, whether speaking of pithy aphorisms or extended discourses.[22] If in any way Israel derived some of its expressions from the wisdom of Egypt, they must be understood as being wholly transformed by their context in the Old Testament faith of Israel.

THE FORM, SUBSTANCE, AND STRUCTURE OF THE BOOK OF PROVERBS

Form, *substance*, and *structure* are rather elastic terms that can be stretched or shrunk to cover diverse elements of a literary piece. In this instance, the terms anticipate a basic outline of the structure of the book of Proverbs, along with observations regarding larger and smaller elements of form and substance.

Basic Outline

An outline of the basic contents of Proverbs may be helpful in visualizing the flow of the book across its several sections. Both the

---

21. R. B. Y. Scott, *Proverbs. Ecclesiastes: Introduction, Translation, and Notes*, AB 18 (Garden City, NY: Doubleday, 1965), 20f.

22. Kenneth A. Kitchen, "Proverbs," in *The Biblical Expositor*, ed. Carl F. H. Henry (Philadelphia: A. J. Holman, 1960), 2:73. Fox, *Proverbs 1–9*, 18, observes that "even in the case of Amenemope, the contact was probably mediated."

content and the form of the material, along with specific introductory statements, combine to mark out the various materials of the book. The basic sections may be summarized in the following manner:[23]

- Introductory Section: The Worth of Wisdom's Way (Proverbs 1–9)
- The Proverbs of Solomon (Proverbs 10:1–22:16)
  - Proverbs with a Contrast (Proverbs 10–15)
  - Proverbs without a Contrast (Proverbs 16:1–22:16)
- The Words of the Wise Ones (Proverbs 22:17–24:34)
  - First Collection from the Wise Ones (Proverbs 22:17–24:22)
  - Second Collection from the Wise Ones (Proverbs 24:23–34)
- The Hezekian Arrangement of Solomonic Proverbs (Proverbs 25–29)
- The Words of Certain Wise Men (Proverbs 30:1–31:9)
  - Agur (Proverbs 30:1–33)
  - King Lemuel (Proverbs 31:1–9)
- An Acrostic Poem Celebrating the Godly Woman (Proverbs 31:10–31)

Elements of Form and Substance

According to the introductory statements of the book of Proverbs, these words of wisdom arise in the form of communications from the king to his son. As son of the king, he is heir to the throne. He himself will soon be ruling over God's people. In this way the necessity of transmitting wisdom across the generations receives special recognition in the book of Proverbs.

Proverbs concentrates on the theme "How to walk in wisdom's way." It is first and foremost a practical book from cover to cover. The father explains to his son "the way" in which he must walk throughout life.[24]

---

23. See "Chapter Outline" above for a more detailed outline of the book of Proverbs.
24. This concept of "walking in wisdom's way" as the overarching theme of Proverbs is reflected in the title of the book by R. B. Y. Scott: *The Way of Wisdom in the Old Testament*

Specific references to this theme of walking in wisdom's way occur no fewer than twenty-three times throughout the book, without even attempting to calculate the number of times allusion is made to the practical wisdom required for every aspect of human life. Both from a negative and a positive perspective, the author underscores the necessity and the blessing of walking in wisdom. With his son's life stretching before him, the father urges his offspring never to set his foot in the paths of people who search for stolen wealth (Prov. 1:15, 19). His son must not leave the straight paths to walk in ways of darkness (2:13). He must not walk with a perverse mouth, or as a slanderer maliciously revealing secrets that need never be known (6:12; 11:13; 20:19). He must take great caution that he does not suddenly turn and walk after the trail of the adulteress (7:22). He must take care that he not walk as a bully who causes his neighbor to walk in a path that will lead to nothing good (16:29).

From a positive perspective, many blessings and benefits in life come as a person walks in wisdom's way:

- Yahweh will shield you from evil. (Prov. 2:7)
- You will be kept safe, walking securely. (Prov. 10:9; 28:18, 26)
- Your foot will not stumble; your step will not be hindered. (Prov. 3:23; 4:12)
- Your children will be blessed. (Prov. 20:7)
- Your father's directions will guide you when you walk, watch over you when you sleep, and speak to you when you wake. (Prov. 6:22)
- You will grow wise as you walk with the wise. (Prov. 13:20)

Even wisdom personified walks in the path of righteousness (Prov. 8:20). A vivid imagery compares the walk through life to the progressive enlightening of the day:

The path of the righteous
    is like the first gleam of dawn,

(New York: Macmillan, 1971). But the author does little to develop the theme. A brief but insightful treatment of wisdom as the "way" in Proverbs may be found in Cornelius Vanderwaal, *Job–Song of Songs*, vol. 4 of *Search the Scriptures* (St. Catharines, ON: Paideia Press, 1978), 72.

shining ever brighter
    till the full light of day. (Prov. 4:18 NIV)

A phrase that occurs only once in Proverbs but several times elsewhere in the Old Testament deserves some notice: "the way of Yahweh":

A fortress for the person with integrity
    is the way of Yahweh;
but ruination for those who practice evil. (Prov. 10:29)

This "way of Yahweh" could be understood as the "way" that Yahweh himself directs the universe by his thoughts and actions. Or it could refer to the "way" commended by Yahweh for a person to follow. In either understanding, the thought is essentially the same, and has the effect of distancing the God-blessed way of life from any secular perspective of the "way." This "way" cannot be generalized to describe the way of any "god" that might arise in people's imaginations. It is instead the way of *Yahweh*, the one and only LORD of Creation and Covenant.

This phrase, "the way of *Yahweh*," appears in several significant contexts in the Old Testament outside Proverbs. The LORD indicates that he will not keep secret his plans from Abraham. For he has chosen him "so that he will command both his son and his daughter who succeed him to keep *the way of Yahweh* by continually practicing righteousness and justice, so that Yahweh will make everything come to pass for Abraham exactly as he has promised" (Gen. 18:19; cf. also Judg. 2:22; 2 Kings 21:22). As in the case of Proverbs, the revelation to father Abraham comes to him specifically for the sake of his children.

This whole concept of "the way" and "walking in wisdom's way" naturally anticipates the distinctive designation of the life pattern of early Christian believers as recorded in the book of Acts. The life of the Christian is categorized as "the Way." Six times in Acts this term captures the essence of the Christian's existence in this world. Believers in Jesus as the Christ belong to "the Way" (Acts 9:2). Opponents in Ephesus malign "the Way," and as a consequence a great disturbance develops about "the Way" (Acts 19:9, 23). Paul explains that he first persecuted the followers of this "Way," but then himself became a devoted follower of "the Way" (Acts 22:4; 24:14).

What is this Way of the disciple of Christ? Paul defines it very succinctly before Felix the Roman governor. Walking in the Way is equivalent to worshiping "the God of our fathers" in conformity with "everything that agrees with the Law and that is written in the Prophets" (Acts 24:14 NIV). Rather than developing outside the realm of redemptive history as something unique to the substance of biblical theology, "walking in the wisdom of the Way" defines the lifestyle of the redeemed in every age. From the consummative perspective of the new covenant, nothing less than living in unity with Jesus Christ qualifies as walking in the Way. For he embodies in himself "the Way, the Truth, and the Life," the only way of coming to the Father (John 14:6). In him are stored all the treasures of wisdom and knowledge needed for this life (Col. 2:3).

"Walking in wisdom's way" may provide a proper perspective for considering the form and substance of the book of Proverbs. The first portion of Proverbs (chaps. 1–9) comes primarily in the form of extended discourses that introduce a limited number of major topics. The second portion of the book consists mainly of independent two-line or four-line proverbs (chaps. 10–29). The third portion of the book (chaps. 30–31) presents distinctive advice from two wise men, and concludes with an acrostic poem celebrating the godly woman.

Introductory Section: The Worth of Wisdom's Way (Proverbs 1–9)

This introductory material concentrates on commending wisdom as the way to fullness of life. It is distinctively hortatory in style, repeatedly exhorting the reader to seek wisdom. The preface (Prov. 1:1–6) defines the purpose of the whole book, which is to encourage the covenant people of God to seek his wisdom. The spiritual bedrock of all wisdom is identified as "the fear of the COVENANT LORD" (1:7).

Three topics receive extensive development in these first nine chapters of the book. The author repeatedly returns to these focal themes, which are the commendation of wisdom; the personification of wisdom; and a special warning to a son.

The Commendation of Wisdom (Ten Passages)

As an appropriate beginning of his treatment of the subject of wisdom, the author urges his young readers to set a priority on gaining wisdom. These ten passages do not always appear as completely separate entities, but often flow naturally into one another. The extent of this material in the opening portion of Proverbs underscores the significance of wisdom to the writer. But it also suggests the difficulty of convincing the next generation of the importance of placing wisdom as the great priority of life. These passages are:

(1) Proverbs 1:1–7

These verses present the reason for the book and underscore wisdom's moral quality. Over a dozen different terms introduce the subject of wisdom. Godly wisdom is not merely shrewdness in dealing with the various challenges of life. It involves doing what is right, just, and fair. Wisdom's essence is laid out as the heart of the book: "The fear of the LORD is the beginning of knowledge."

(2) Proverbs 1:8–9

These verses provide an initial exhortation to the "son" to listen to his father's instruction and his mother's teaching. Godly wisdom can be acquired only when a person pays attention to his father and mother, those who have been established by God to instruct him in the school of wisdom.

(3) Proverbs 1:10–19

Now the author directly addresses his son a second time, offering an initial warning. Don't give in to the suggestions of sinners. Peer pressure as an alternative to the instruction of wisdom must be resisted. Wisdom is clearly a moral question, a matter of life and death. Sinners who tempt others to join them in their wicked ways only lay a trap for themselves, lying in wait for their own blood.

(4) Proverbs 2:1–22

The young man who devotes himself to seeking wisdom like hidden treasure will understand the fear of the LORD. God will guard the course of the just, and he will protect the way of his faithful ones. For wisdom has the power to protect from evil. As a consequence, the upright will live in the land, while the wicked will be exiled from its borders.

(5) Proverbs 3:1–12

This section makes use of a distinctive style in which admonition precedes promise:

- *Admonition*: Don't forget my teaching and my commands.
- *Promise*: You will have prosperity and long life. (Prov. 3:1–2)

- *Admonition*: Maintain love and faithfulness.
- *Promise*: You will gain favor in the eyes of God and man. (Prov. 3:3–4)

- *Admonition*: Trust the LORD with all your heart.
- *Promise*: He will make your paths straight. (Prov. 3:5–6)

- *Admonition*: Fear the LORD and shun evil.
- *Promise*: You will have health in your body and nourishment in your bones. (Prov. 3:7–8)

- *Admonition*: Honor the LORD with your wealth.
- *Promise*: Your barns will be full. (Prov. 3:9–10)

- *Admonition*: Do not despise the LORD's discipline.
- *Promise*: You will be assured of God's love. (Prov. 3:11–12)

The many positive consequences of wisdom should encourage a person to seek it with all his heart.

(6) Proverbs 3:21–35

The encouragement to seek wisdom in these verses comes in the form of six *Do nots*, followed by a summary of promises for those who will walk in wisdom's way:

- *Do not* let sound judgment out of your sight. (Prov. 3:21)
- *Do not* withhold good from those who deserve it. (Prov. 3:27)
- *Do not* tell your neighbor to come back tomorrow when you can help today. (Prov. 3:28)
- *Do not* plot harm against your trusting neighbor. (Prov. 3:29)
- *Do not* accuse a man for no good reason. (Prov. 3:30)
- *Do not* envy a violent man. (Prov. 3:31)

The consequences of heeding or not heeding these encouragements to live in wisdom are either curse or blessing. The blessings include life, safety, sweet sleep, and absence of fear. The curses are mockery and shame inflicted by God himself.

(7) Proverbs 4:1–4

Once more Solomon admonishes a young man to listen to the wisdom of his father. Only in this case, his word addresses "sons" in the plural rather than a "son" in the singular (cf. Prov. 1:8, 10, 15; 2:1; 3:1, 11, 21). In this unique cameo, Solomon shares his own personal experience: "When I was a boy in my father's house, still tender and an only child of my mother [presumably Bathsheba], he [presumably King David] taught me" (4:3–4). As Solomon the wise king learned from his father David, so he encourages every young man to learn from the wisdom found in previous generations.

(8) Proverbs 4:10–19

These verses develop a contrast between the pathway of the wise and the wicked. The way, the path, the walk, the steps, the running of the wise will always lead them to life (Prov. 4:10–13). But the path, the walk, the traveling, the way of the wicked must be avoided at all costs (4:14–17). The section closes with a classic contrast between the path of the righteous and the way of the wicked:

> The path of the righteous
>   is like the first gleam of dawn,
> shining ever brighter
>   till the full light of day.

But the way of the wicked
   is like deep darkness;
they do not know
   what makes them stumble. (Prov. 4:18–19 NIV)

(9) Proverbs 4:20–27

This section opens with a general admonition to "pay attention" to the words of a wise father. In this regard, it belongs with the many other direct admonitions regarding the way of wisdom in these opening nine chapters of the book. Then the "son" receives one specific admonition after another: "Listen"; "Do not forsake"; "Do not forget"; "Keep my commands"; "Do not despise"; "Do not resent"; "Pay attention"; "Accept what I say"; "Hold on to instruction"; "Listen closely." It is as though the instructor in wisdom is doing everything within his power to get through the natural resistance of youth to the teaching of wisdom. As a concluding promise, the son who accepts the instruction of wisdom will experience health for his entire body, including the heart (Prov. 4:23), the mouth (4:24), the eyes (4:25), and the feet (4:26).

(10) Proverbs 6:1–19

This last section commending wisdom indicates specific follies that wisdom will enable a person to avoid:

• The folly of being security to a neighbor. (Prov. 6:1–5)
• The folly of living like a sluggard. (Prov. 6:6–11)
• The folly of being morally corrupt. (Prov. 6:12–15)
• The folly of becoming any one of the seven things that God hates. (Prov. 6:16–19)

By these ten passages that commend wisdom in the introductory nine chapters of the book, the author lays a strong foundation for all the various wise sayings found in the remaining twenty-two chapters. This concentration on the commendation of wisdom underscores two things: the need for young people (and older people as well) to set a priority on acquiring wisdom; and the innate resistance to wisdom's instruction on the part of people, especially young people, even God's own people.

The Personification of Wisdom (Five Passages)

A reinforcing of the importance of wisdom for life is strongly supported by no fewer than five passages that personify wisdom in this same introductory section of the book. Encountering wisdom is not dealing merely with an abstract idea. Encountering wisdom means interacting with a person, who is none other than God himself. These five passages are:

(1) Proverbs 1:20–33

Madam Wisdom makes her first appearance as she "calls aloud in the street" and "raises her voice in the public squares." She cries out at the intersection of the busy streets, and makes her speech at the gateways of the city (Prov. 1:20–21). By this imagery, personified wisdom enforces the truth that God's wisdom is not like the secrets of a "mystery religion" available only to the initiated. Instead, God openly declares the treasures of his divine wisdom for all who will hear.

In her first speech, Madam Wisdom laments the stubbornness of the simpleminded. Note well! She would have poured out her spirit on every true learner and made her deepest thoughts fully known to every listener (Prov. 1:23).[25] In an earnest effort to recapture the attention of those who have foolishly rejected her, she declares their imminent fate. Disaster, calamity, distress, trouble, abandonment, death, and destruction await all those who stubbornly refuse to accept her advice and foolishly spurn her rebuke. But whoever listens to wisdom will live in safety and be at ease without fear of harm.

(2) Proverbs 3:13–20

In this second personification, Solomon underscores the blessedness of the person who finds wisdom. For Madam Wisdom is much more profitable than silver, yields better returns than gold, and is more precious than rubies. Nothing that a person might desire can compare

---

25. Proverbs 1:23 in the NIV reads, "I would have poured out my heart to you" (1984) or "I will pour out my thoughts to you" (2011). These renderings eliminate possible reference to the outpouring of "my Spirit" on those who heed the call of Madam Wisdom, which is an altogether appropriate rendering of the word רוּחִי. Note the ESV, which reads, "I will pour out my spirit to you."

with her. She brings the blessings of long life, riches and honor, pleasant and peaceful pathways. She is a tree of life to all who will embrace her, bringing unending blessings.

So how is it that wisdom possesses the capacity to bestow all these blessings? It is because wisdom lies at the foundation of the whole of the Covenant Lord's creation. For by wisdom the Lord of the Covenant laid the earth's foundations and set the heavens in place (Prov. 3:19). The ocean's depths as well as the morning's dewdrops are all dispensed by divine wisdom (3:20). So to personally encounter wisdom is to experience intimacy with the Source and Sustainer of all created reality.

(3) Proverbs 4:5–9

This third section personifying Madam Wisdom concentrates on admonitions to the king's sons to "get wisdom," to "get understanding," to love her, esteem her, embrace her. Her rewards will be great if a young man will only seek her. She will protect you, exalt you, honor you. In addition, Madam Wisdom will

> set a garland of grace
>> on your head
>> and present you
> with a crown of splendor. (Prov. 4:9 NIV)

Youthful passions may lead a young person to seek after personal pleasures. But the steady pursuit of Madam Wisdom will provide much more satisfying benefits. For:

> Wisdom is the principal thing;
>> therefore get wisdom.
> Though it cost all you have,
>> get understanding. (Prov. 4:7)

(4) Proverbs 8:1–36

This chapter contains the most extensive passage dealing with the personal nature of wisdom. Yet throughout the ages it has been the most controverted section of the entire book. The Arians of the fourth century A.D. based their heretical teaching on this passage when they declared: "There was a time when the Son was not." But what exactly does this passage affirm about divine wisdom?

First, this personification of wisdom presents itself as freely available to all mankind (Prov. 8:1–5). In accord with the first of wisdom's appearances, it openly manifests itself in the public square, at the gates of the city (cf. 1:20–23). In this passage, wisdom "cries aloud," "raises her voice," and takes her stand on the heights and at the gates leading into the city (8:1–3). Wisdom calls out to all mankind, even to the simpleminded, the most foolish of humanity (8:4–5).

Next, the worth of wisdom's words is affirmed (Prov. 8:6–9). She speaks only worthy things, things that are upright, true, just, and faultless. Far from the mouth of wisdom are words of wickedness, all perverse and crooked words. This introductory statement regarding the inherent value of wisdom's words prepares the way for all the admonitions about words that will follow throughout the remainder of the book.

Then the value of wisdom itself is once more extolled (Prov. 8:10–11). Better than silver or choice gold, more precious than rubies is wisdom. Nothing that a human being might desire can compare with her.

The fruit of wisdom (Prov. 8:12–21) may be seen in its moral productions, including the fear of the COVENANT LORD, the hatred of pride and arrogance, and the rejection of all evil behavior and perverse speech. On the positive side, wisdom serves as the source of power, sound judgment, and the ability of kings to rule by declaring just laws. Wisdom always walks in the way of righteousness and justice, "bestowing wealth on those who love me and making their treasuries full" (8:21 NIV).

Climactically, wisdom displays her all-embracing significance by affirming her presence and place at the creation of the heavens and the earth (Prov. 8:22–31). "The LORD OF THE COVENANT possessed me at the beginning of his works" best represents the opening phrase of this celebrated hymn to the role of wisdom in creation (8:22). The term *qanah* (קָנָה) describes the presence of wisdom within the essence of the Godhead even *before* his deeds of old, *before* the world began, *before* the mountains, *before* he made the earth or any of the world's dust (8:22–26). Five times wisdom is declared to exist "before" the work of creation had begun. Wisdom appears as the personification of a "craftsman" at God's side, filled with delight day after day, rejoicing in his presence, rejoicing in the whole world, and delighting in mankind (8:30–31).

Not as a separated entity existing apart from the Godhead, but as an integral part of the essence of the Creator, this personified wisdom suitably represents in old covenant form the Word that was face to face with God in the beginning. This wisdom-Word was God, and all things were made by him (John 1:1–3). He has the position of priority over all creation, since by him all things were created, things in heaven and on earth, visible and invisible. All things were created by him and for him (Col. 1:15–16). As one commentator has explained the significance of this figure of personified wisdom, it

> paves the way for the New Testament's proclamation of the personal Word and Wisdom of God. . . . The use of such a word [as Wisdom], rather than an impersonal term, such as "order" or "law," . . . carries the implication that God's active thought sustains the world. The further step of portraying Wisdom personified, though only a poetic device, strengthens this emphasis, and provides the New Testament with part of the language it will need for its Christology.[26]

Ancient and modern efforts to read "the LORD *created* me" instead of "the LORD *possessed* me" as an alternative translation for the Hebrew verb *qanah* (קָנָה) have been persistent despite the questionable nature of this understanding of the word in terms of linguistic and lexical usage.[27] The word appears eighty-four times in the Old

---

26. Derek Kidner, "Wisdom Literature of the Old Testament," in *New Perspectives on the Old Testament*, ed. J. Barton Payne (London: Word Books, 1970), 128.

27. The LXX translated the Hebrew word *qanah* as "created" (ἔκτισέν), which played right into the hands of the Arians. For a discussion of the interpretation of Proverbs 8:22 by Athanasius as the "champion" of the opponents of Arianism, see the "Additional Note" at the end of this section. This ancient tradition of seeing wisdom as "created" has recently taken a new turn. Katharine Dell, *'Get Wisdom, Get Insight': An Introduction to Israel's Wisdom Literature* (London: Darton, Longman, and Ford, 2000), 20, sees wisdom as "a poetic personification of the female aspect of God." She resists the idea of a female consort of God as in neighboring religions, citing "majority scholarly opinion" (20). Instead,

Testament, and only six or seven of these instances might allow the understanding "create."[28] As noted by one commentator, "The meaning 'possess' for *qanah* is entirely suitable and is in keeping with the author's usage in 1:5; 4:5, 7. *Yahweh* 'possessed' wisdom as an attribute or faculty integral to his being from the very first, and 'in [with, or by] his wisdom founded the earth.' (3:19)"[29]

One commentator begins his discussion of the term *qanah* by stating that the word means "to acquire": "The word's *lexical* meaning, the semantic content it brings to context, is 'acquire,' no more than that." But from this affirmation he moves from "acquire" to "create": "But one way something can be acquired is by creation." Having deduced that wisdom was "created," he makes a far-reaching conclusion: Wisdom "did not exist from eternity. Wisdom is therefore an accidental attribute of godhead, not an essential or inherent one."[30]

So according to this logic, God first existed without wisdom. Then he created wisdom. From that point on, wisdom helped God

---

wisdom is "Yahweh's creature and therefore created by God" (20). In response to recent feminist interpretations, Karen H. Jobes concludes that "the feminine personification of *Sophia* was completely governed by the grammatical gender of first the Hebrew and then the Greek noun for *wisdom*. Modern feminists have latched onto the language of *sophia* and then have reconstructed it to address gender concerns when it had no such purpose in late-Jewish/early Christian usage" ("Sophia Christology: The Way of Wisdom?," in *The Way of Wisdom: Essays in Honor of Bruce K. Waltke*, ed. J. I. Packer and Sven K. Soderlund [Grand Rapids: Zondervan, 2000], 243).

28. Kidner, *Proverbs*, 79. The passages where *qanah* might mean "to create" are Genesis 14:19, 22; Exodus 15:16; Deuteronomy 32:6; Psalms 74:2; 139:13; Proverbs 8:22. Yet in virtually all these passages, the word may just as well be translated as "possessed" or "acquired" rather than "created."

29. Scott, *Proverbs*, 72. Bruce Vawter, "Prov 8:22: Wisdom and Creation," *JBL* 99, 2 (1980): 213, affirms that Scott is "entirely correct" in rejecting wisdom as God's creation in Proverbs 8:22. But he then resists Scott's assertion of the meaning "possessed" by affirming that *qanah* "is not a stative but a very transitive verb" (214). Yet the idea of "to possess" can be very "active," depending on the thing possessed. "Possessing" wisdom inherently suggests making good use of wisdom's full potential. To possess wisdom is not to hold it as though it were an inanimate stone. As Vawter himself explains, *qanah* means that "Yahweh took possession of a wisdom that he then proceeded to utilize in his work of creation" (215). In other words, the concept of *transitive* or *intransitive* as applied to the possession of wisdom is not a very useful distinction. One can hardly "be in possession of" wisdom without making good use of it.

30. Fox, *Proverbs 1–9*, 279.

create everything else, which he presumably could not have created without wisdom's help.

But where according to this theory did God get the wisdom to create wisdom? If he began with a lack of wisdom (which is unthinkable), needing wisdom to help him create everything else, where did he get the help he needed to create wisdom? More basically from a linguistic perspective, what in the context of these verses suggests the movement from "acquired" to "created"?[31]

Another commentator affirms that in most instances, the verb *qanah* means to "acquire" or "purchase." In order to then arrive at the meaning "created" for *qanah*, he appeals to the Ugaritic usage of a related root, and four verses in the Old Testament (Gen. 14:19, 22; Deut. 32:6; Ps. 139:13).[32] In at least two of these four passages, however, a better case may be made for translating with "possessed" rather than "created." When Abram meets Melchizedek together with the King of Sodom, the main concern in their interchange has to do with the spoils of war. Abram responds to Melchizedek's blessing by presenting him with the tithe. This blessing is pronounced in the name of "God Most High," who is appropriately acknowledged as "'Possessor' [*qanah*] of heaven and earth" (Gen. 14:19–20). In the same context, the King of Sodom proposes that Abram keep the spoils of war for himself. Abram responds by stressing that he has sworn to the COVENANT LORD, God Most High, "Possessor" (*qanah*) of heaven and earth, that he will accept nothing from him (14:21–23). In each case, the context focuses on "possessions," the spoils of war, making it more appropriate to recognize God as "Possessor" of all these things, though he is obviously also their "Creator."

In addition, it is quite clear that "to create" is not the meaning of the term *qanah* in the other ten passages where the term occurs in Proverbs. The person being instructed by Proverbs certainly is not expected to "create" wisdom, knowledge, or truth (Prov. 4:5, 7; 18:15; 23:23). He may be encouraged to "get," "obtain," or "possess" these

---

31. Vawter, "Prov 8:22: Wisdom and Creation," offers an extensive analysis of all the critical texts in which the term *qanah* appears. In summarizing, he states: "I conclude that, as there is not compelling evidence from other OT texts to indicate a Hebrew *qanah* = "created," neither should the verb in Prov 8:22 be translated in this fashion" (213).

32. Longman, *Proverbs*, 204.

most valuable things. But he clearly is not instructed to "create" them. The term may be used even to refer to a person who is identified as a "buyer" (הַקּוֹנֶה) of goods (20:14). Clearly, this person is not a "creator" of the goods that he is attempting to acquire or possess. In this regard, the term "acquire" stands in the closest possible relationship to "possess." For the "acquiring" of an object has as its end the "being in possession of" the same object. The possession of wisdom and its acquisition represent two aspects of the same concept.

More specifically, some thought must be given to the precise sense in which the self-contained God who created all things would "acquire" something outside himself, particularly something as vital as "wisdom." This "wisdom" is said to have served as the "master craftsman" (אָמוֹן) at his side, delighting day by day, rejoicing before him always (Prov. 8:30). Is it then to be supposed that God at first existed without this wisdom that was so vital to all creation? Was God then to first "acquire" this wisdom from somewhere outside himself before he began his work of creation?[33]

To the contrary, the natural meaning of the word *qanah* in this context is that Yahweh "possessed" this wisdom "at the beginning." *Before* his deeds of old he possessed this wisdom. This wisdom was established "from eternity," "from the beginning," "before the world began" (Prov. 8:23). Repeatedly the existence of wisdom before all of God's creative activities is stressed in these two verses (8:22–23).

"I was there!" (שָׁם אָנִי—Prov. 8:27 NIV) declares personified wisdom, "when he set the heavens in place." The passage clearly reflects the processes of creation as depicted in the first chapter of Genesis. When there were no oceans, no springs of water, no mountains or hills, before the earth or any of the dust of the world existed, wisdom was brought forth to do its great work (8:24–26).[34] When God set the heavens in place,

---

33. Vawter speaks of "pre-existent wisdom" that Yahweh "discovers" ("Prov 8:22: Wisdom and Creation," 206). He further notes: "In sum, we are here presented with the concept of a pre-existent wisdom or at least of a wisdom not of the ordinary created order, . . . a wisdom which is not a native attribute of God but a reality accessible to him alone and acquired by him" (215). Not surprisingly, Vawter agrees that this wisdom is "un-Israelite" (215). For from a biblical perspective, wisdom cannot be an entity in itself separated from Yahweh and needed by him to aid him in the creation of the world.

34. The phrase rendered "was brought forth" (חוֹלָלְתִּי) could be translated "was given birth," which functions as a figure of speech. This "giving birth" of wisdom might be

marked out the horizon, established the clouds, gave the sea its boundary, and marked out the foundations of the earth, she was there (8:27–29). As the days of creation progressed, wisdom was rejoicing in the whole world and delighting in mankind, the crown of creation (8:30–31).

So how is this picture of wisdom to be understood? The imagery may be perceived as an elaborate personification of wisdom. Or the description may be judged to be so specific that it posits an actual being, a "hypostatis," that existed alongside but not separated from God.[35] In either case, this image of wisdom anticipates all that would later be described from a new covenant perspective as the "Word" that "in the beginning" was "face to face with God" and "was God" (John 1:1). It was "through him" that all things were made that have been made (1:3). Nothing and no one else can adequately or completely fulfill all aspects of this imagery of personified wisdom as depicted in the description of "wisdom" found in Proverbs 8. This passage is remarkable in its anticipation of a person alongside but separated from the LORD who serves as the Creator of all things.

---

compared to the phrasing of Psalm 2:7: "You are my Son; today I have 'given birth' to you." This phrase is understood in the New Testament as a figure of speech for the Son's resurrection (cf. Acts 13:33–34). In Acts 13, as in Proverbs 8, the figure of "giving birth" does not mean "come into existence." In the context of Proverbs 8, the "birth" of wisdom represents her "coming forth" to be intimately involved in all of God's creative activity, not her coming into existence.

35. Scott, "Study of Wisdom Literature," 42, asks whether wisdom in Proverbs 8 is simply a "poetic personification," or whether it is something more, a *hypostatis*—that is, "an attribute or activity of Yahweh thought of as having an independent personal identity." He cites a number of scholars who have held that in Proverbs 8 "the description of wisdom passes from that of symbolism and personification to that of an independent being, God's master builder and assistant in creating the world." Gerhard von Rad, *Wisdom in Israel* (London: SCM Press, 1972), 153, sees the passage as having "a stylistic dependence . . . on Egyptian texts" that "cannot be denied." He asserts that "there can be no doubt that Israelite teachers have been dependent on the idea of the Egyptian goddess of order and have even borrowed characteristic, individual expressions." He affirms that we can therefore say that in verses 22–29 the style of a specific Egyptian divine proclamation "has clearly been borrowed." An amassing of categorical statements such as "cannot be denied," "there can be no doubt," and "has clearly been borrowed" without supporting evidence inevitably fosters questions about the convincing character of the argument. Von Rad himself proceeds to state that in the process of this transference of Egyptian ideas to the Hebrew thought world, many of the Egyptian concepts have become "completely different." In fact, he affirms that the "wisdom" of Proverbs 8 can be compared "only with difficulty" to the Egyptian concept (153).

Finally, the admonition by personified wisdom directed to his "sons" underscores the blessing that comes to a person from this wisdom of God (Prov. 8:32–36). Twice the word "blessed" is pronounced over those who keep the ways of wisdom (8:32, 34). To enjoy this blessedness, a young man must "watch daily," "wait expectantly" at wisdom's doors. The consummate blessing of eagerly seeking wisdom's blessing is *life*: "For everyone who finds me finds life and receives favor from the Covenant Lord" (8:35). But whoever sins against this personification of divine wisdom "does violence to himself." For as wisdom itself pronounces, "All who hate me love death" (8:36 niv). Let every person, young or old, take heed.

EXCURSUS: *The Interpretation of Proverbs 8:22 by Athanasius as the Champion of the Opponents of Arianism*

Athanasius (c. a.d. 298–373) served as the key figure in the church's determination of the nature of the Trinity and the person of Christ as formulated by the Council of Nicea in a.d. 325. As a young deacon trained by martyr teachers in Alexandria, Egypt, he accompanied his bishop to the council "as an indispensable companion."[36]

The fullest refutation of the errors of Arianism by Athanasius may be found in his four "Discourses against the Arians," consisting of almost 150 double-columned pages.[37] This material was composed during his third exile as a consequence of his uncompromising stand against the Arians (a.d. 356–62). During these years he hid himself from the imperial troops of Emperor Constantius, primarily in the deserts, caves, monasteries, and tombs of the Upper Nile region of Egypt.

These four discourses were originally intended as a "decisive blow" against Arianism. One author observes that the "serious reader" will appreciate "the richness, fulness, and versatility" of his use of Scripture, "the steady grasp of certain primary truths, especially of

36. Archibald Robertson, ed., *Select Writings and Letters of Athanasius, Bishop of Alexandria*, in *Athanasius: Select Works and Letters*, ed. Philip Schaff and Henry Wace, Nicene and Post-Nicene Fathers 4, 2nd ser. (Peabody, MA: Hendrickson, 1994), xviii.

37. Philip Schaff and Henry Wace, eds., *Athanasius: Select Works and Letters*, Nicene and Post-Nicene Fathers 4, 2nd ser. (Peabody, MA: Hendrickson, 1994), 303–447.

the Divine Unity and of Christ's real or genuine natural and Divine Sonship." Above all, in all these discourses may be seen "his firm hold of the Soteriological aspect of the question at issue, of its vital importance to the reality of Redemption and Grace."[38] In other words, Athanasius thought deeply about these matters—in many regards more deeply than modern exegetical treatments of the same topics and passages of Scripture.

His second "Discourse against the Arians" contains an extensive treatment of Proverbs 8:22, with fifteen double-columned pages of introduction to the passage[39] and twenty-one double-columned pages of exposition.[40]

In understanding his treatment of Proverbs 8:22, several factors should be kept in mind. First, as an introduction to Proverbs 8:22, Athanasius offers extensive treatment of a number of passages dealing with the person of Christ that he regards as essential to properly understanding the wording of Proverbs 8:22. He analyzes in great detail Philippians 2:9–10, Psalm 45:7–8, Hebrews 1:4; 3:2, and Acts 2:36, as well as treating numerous additional passages. By this method, Athanasius is displaying his commitment to the basic principles of the "analogy of faith." In other words, a single passage of Scripture must not be interpreted in isolation from the total teaching of Scripture on a particular subject.

As a sample of the depths of his thoughts, his treatment of one element of teaching from John's Gospel may be considered. The brackets have been added by the current writer, in the hopes of aiding the understanding of the passage.

> But if [God] calls into existence things which existed not by his proper [that is, God's own] Word, then the [creating] Word is not in the number of things non-existing and [subsequently] called [into existence]; or we have to seek another Word, through whom He too [the Word] was called [into existence]; for by the Word the things

---

38. As quoted by Robertson in Schaff and Wace, *Athanasius*, 303–4.

39. Athanasius in ibid., 357–72.

40. Ibid., 372–93. Archibald Robertson as editor of this material supports a dating between 356 and 360 for these four discourses (303), which would be a full generation after the Council of Nicea (325).

which were not have come to be. And if through Him [the Word] He [God] creates and makes, He [the Word] is not Himself of things created and made; but rather He is the Word of the Creator God, and is known from the Father's works which He Himself [the Word] worketh, to be "in the Father and the Father in Him," and "He that hath seen him [the Word] hath seen the Father," because the Son's Essence is proper to the Father, and He [the Word] in all points like Him [the Father].[41]

This form of intense analysis may prove to be rather challenging for the modern mind, conditioned as it is to merely "byte-sized" thinking. But Athanasius regarded this type of analysis of related passages from the Old and New Testaments as essential to a proper framework for interpreting the reference to wisdom in Proverbs 8:22.

Second, Athanasius explicitly notes that "what is said in Proverbs, is not said plainly, but is put forth latently."[42] As a consequence, "it is necessary to unfold the sense of what is said, and to seek it as something hidden, and not nakedly to expound as if the meaning were spoken 'plainly.'"[43] Athanasius clearly understood the significance of literary genre such as a "proverb" or a "parable" in analyzing Scripture, even though he would have been altogether unfamiliar with modern linguistic jargon. In this case, Athanasius concludes that the indication that wisdom was "created" in Proverbs 8:22 must be considered in its figurative sense, as the immediately following point regarding his treatment of Proverbs 8:22 will indicate.

Third, Athanasius works altogether with the LXX translation of this passage, which reads:

κύριος ἔκτισέν με ἀρχὴν ὁδῶν αὐτοῦ εἰς ἔργα αὐτοῦ. (Prov. 8:22 LXX)

A literal translation of the passage may read as follows:

The LORD created me a beginning of his ways, for his works. (Prov. 8:22)

41. Ibid., 360.
42. Ibid., 372.
43. Ibid.

Nowhere in his discussion does Athanasius refer to the Hebrew text of Proverbs 8:22. As has been observed, he was altogether "ignorant of Hebrew."[44] As a consequence, he makes no comment on the various possibilities for translating *qanah* as describing God's "acquiring" or "possessing" rather than "creating" wisdom. All his discussion hinges on wisdom's being "created" (ἔκτισέν), as represented in the LXX. But in view of the weight of evidence that he himself had previously cited regarding the eternality of the Son and his equality with the Father, Athanasius concludes that wisdom was "created" in the sense that Christ's human body was the thing created, not his eternal essence. As he explains: "If the text refers to an Angel, or any other created being, let the passage be understood as saying, He 'created me;' but if it be the Wisdom of God, in whom all things originate have been framed, . . . what ought we to understand but that 'he created' means nothing contrary to 'He begat?'"[45]

So having been misdirected by the translation "he created" in the LXX, Athanasius chose to wrestle with this text as a witness to the person and work of Christ in the larger context of the primary teaching of Scripture on this critical topic. As a consequence, it would be unjust to fault Athanasius for treating "created" as a figurative term because of its form as a literary "proverb." At the same time, it would be improper to make a serious appeal to Athanasius's interpretation of Proverbs 8:22 in referring to wisdom as "created," since he had no other textual options before him, and yet interpreted the term "created" as figurative for "begat."

---

44. Robertson in ibid., xiv.

45. Athanasius in ibid., 372. Waltke observes that "a grammatico-historical exegesis of Proverbs 8 does not support patristic exegesis" in its identity of the preexistent Christ with personified wisdom in Proverbs 8 (*Proverbs 1–15*, 127). Yet with regard to Athanasius, full appreciation must be expressed for the carefulness of his exegetical work. Even at the point of his conclusion, he states with great care that *if* Proverbs 8:22 is applied to an angel, the text can be understood as "created"; but if the text refers to the wisdom of God, it must mean "begat." As a point of interest, Athanasius working from the Greek text and Waltke working from the Hebrew text reach the identical conclusion regarding the force of the verb in Proverbs 8:22. According to Athanasius, "he created" means nothing more than "he begat" if applied to Christ. After exploring various options, Waltke concludes that the verb *qanah* "probably means 'to beget,' 'to bring forth' in Prov. 8:22" (409). While the limitation of Athanasius to the Greek text means that a fuller comprehension of the passage was denied him, his work must be appreciated for its thoroughness and care within the whole of the biblical context.

In the end, the consistency of this ancient saint of Christ as well as his cogency in argumentation for the truth must be fully appreciated. For a period of more than forty years, beginning with his critical role as a youth at Nicea to his final days of exile and return in his septuagenarian years, Athanasius held fast to his scripturally based convictions regarding the nature of the Trinity and the person of Jesus Christ. By no means a "slouch" in his exegetical processes and his comprehensive knowledge of Scripture, this one man stood against the tides of time and set the course of future centuries for Christianity along the right path.[46]

46. The history of Athanasius's life is altogether fascinating in itself. A brief review of certain highlights may disclose something of the cost this man paid for his unwavering stand for the truth about the person of Christ, as well as the intrigues of his Arian rivals. From about age twenty-eight to seventy-five, he stood as the champion of truth against Arianism, never succumbing to weariness in well-doing. Based on the rehearsal of his life as presented by Archibald Robertson in Schaff and Wace, *Athanasius*, the life and career of Athanasius may be traced as follows:

He was born in Alexandria, Egypt, in about A.D. 296–98, and was trained under the tutelage of early Egyptian martyrs. His education in Bible and theology followed the tradition of Origen, including his emphasis on the ascetic life. With respect to his intense participation in the formula of Nicea, Robertson comments: "It was not as a theologian, but as a believing soul in need of a Saviour, that Athanasius approached the mystery of Christ" (Robertson in ibid., xiv). This faith was the one thing that sustained him throughout this controversy, even until his decease at the age of seventy-five.

Athanasius played a focal role in the ultimate decision of the Nicean Council, prevailing even over the renowned and respected Eusebius. The small group set against Arius owed much "to the energy and eloquence of the deacon Athanasius, who had accompanied his bishop to the council as an indispensable companion" (ibid., xviii).

Shortly after the conclusion of the Council of Nicea, he was elected bishop over all Egypt and Libya in A.D. 328. He experienced a period of quiet during the beginning years of his role as bishop (328–35). But Eusebius the champion of Arianism was quickly restored from his banishment after Nicea to full favor with Emperor Constantine. By about 330, Eusebius had even obtained the recall of Arius to Egypt. The emperor demanded that Athanasius receive him, but Athanasius refused. The emperor threatened deposition, but Athanasius refused again. Because of a plot against him by Eusebius, Athanasius was summoned by the emperor. A full year was taken up with answering trumped-up charges. In one case, Athanasius was accused of killing a follower of Arius named Arsenius and cutting off his hand. Arsenius had been whisked off to a secret locale in a monastery in Upper Egypt, while a severed hand was circulated as exhibit A in the case against Athanasius. While Athanasius was on trial at Tyre, the hand was introduced as evidence of his brutality. But Arsenius had been found by Athanasius's men and presented at the site of the trial. Arsenius was brought forward wrapped in a cloak, and identified by the exposure of his face. One hand was brought forward, followed by the second. Then it was asked where the arm was for the third hand that had been cut off (ibid., xxxviii–ix).

Though apparently not properly attributed to Athanasius, the Athanasian Creed summarizes well the biblical truth regarding the Trinity as formulated by Athanasius. The first portion of the creed, dealing with the nature of the Trinity, reads as follows:

> Whoever desires to be saved should above all hold to the catholic faith.

Despite this public embarrassment, the Arian prosecutors persisted, now saying that Athanasius had tried to murder Arsenius, who had been forced into hiding for his life. After further charges, Athanasius was eventually exiled by the emperor during the years A.D. 336–37 because of further false charges (ibid., xxxix–xl).

After a brief reprieve, a second exile was forced on Athanasius during the years A.D. 339–46 as a result of the Arians' plots. The first half of these years was spent in Rome (ibid., xliii).

To support his case against the Arians, Athanasius cites a number of atrocities committed by their adherents. In one instance, Lucius, Bishop of Adrianople, who had spoken boldly against the Arians, was bound with iron chains around his neck and hands and driven into banishment, where he died (Athanasius, "History of the Arians," in Schaff and Wace, *Athanasius*, 276).

His second exile was followed by the longest "quiet period" for Athanasius in Alexandria during the years A.D. 346–56 (Robertson in Schaff and Wace, *Athanasius*, xlvii). He was forty-eight years old at the beginning of this era, called his "golden decade."

But this golden age could not endure. Emperor Constans, ruling in the West, was murdered, which gave the opportunity for his brother, Emperor Constantius, to take charge of the entire empire. Troops were sent to Alexandria by Constantius, who assaulted the church where Athanasius was conducting a service in a crowded sanctuary in preparation for a communion service the next day. Athanasius was sitting in his chair in the recess of the apse. As the emperor's troops were breaking into the church, he ordered the deacon in charge of the service to begin Psalm 136, with the people responding at each verse, "For his mercy endures forever." Athanasius refused to escape until all his people were safe. The soldiers crowded up to the chancel. But at the last minute, a crowd of monks and clergy seized Athanasius and in the confusion managed to convey him out of the church "in a half-fainting state" (ibid., l). For the next six years, Athanasius was hidden away in this his third exile (A.D. 356–62). Ironically, but as happens so often among God's people, this exile "marks the summit of his achievement. Its commencement is the triumph, its conclusion the collapse of Arianism" (ibid., li; cf. Paul's letters from prison, Martin Luther's and William Tyndale's translations of the Bible, and John Bunyan's *The Pilgrim's Progress*). Robertson continues: "This period then of forced abstention from affairs was the most stirring in spiritual and literary activity in the whole life of Athanasius" (ibid.). More than half of Athanasius's extant works were composed during this period. The soldiers of the emperor searched for him in vain. "Towns and villages, deserts and monasteries, the very tombs were scoured by the Imperial inquisitors in the search for Athanasius; but all in vain; not once do we hear of any suspicion of betrayal" (ibid.).

Then with the death of Constantius, Athanasius returned as bishop to Alexandria. He called a church council in 362. At this point, he was as a victor surveying the field. The documents produced at the council obviously were from his hand. This council represents the crown of his career (ibid., lviii).

Anyone who does not keep it whole and unbroken will doubtless
   perish eternally.
Now this is the catholic faith:
   That we worship one God in trinity and the trinity in unity,
   neither blending their persons
   nor dividing their essence.
      For the person of the Father is a distinct person,
      the person of the Son is another,
      and that of the Holy Spirit still another.
      But the divinity of the Father, Son, and Holy Spirit is one,
      their glory equal, their majesty coeternal.
What quality the Father has, the Son has, and the Holy Spirit has.
   The Father is uncreated,
   the Son is uncreated,
   the Holy Spirit is uncreated.
   The Father is immeasurable,
   the Son is immeasurable,
   the Holy Spirit is immeasurable.
   The Father is eternal,
   the Son is eternal,
   the Holy Spirit is eternal.
      And yet there are not three eternal beings;
      there is but one eternal being.

Julian the new emperor had recalled the bishops. But soon thereafter he revealed his heart for paganism. He then ordered Athanasius to leave not only Alexandria but Egypt. The new emperor regarded him as "the enemy of the gods," "a contemptible little fellow" (ibid., lix). Athanasius was secure in the support of the populace. He had the power of the people supporting him. But in peace he started up the Nile for a final exile. As he was sailing up the river, he learned that government officials were trailing him. He reversed his direction, passing right by his pursuers. Suspecting nothing, they asked for news of Athanasius. "He is not far off" was the answer, according to Athanasius (ibid.).

After Julian's death, Jovian (a Christian) replaced him (ibid.). But short-lived Jovian died from inhaling fumes from a charcoal fire in his bedroom (ibid., lxi). Valentinian, a convinced but tolerant Catholic, was then elected emperor by the army. Under his reign, Arianism practically died away in the West (ibid.). So in the end, Athanasius's persistence in the faith prevailed.

Under Valentinian's reign, Athanasius enjoyed a deserved period of peace as bishop in Alexandria, though not without facing many challenges (A.D. 366–73). Active to the last, he died at age seventy-five in A.D. 373. Throughout his lifetime, he had "wandered in deserts and mountains, and in caves and holes in the ground" (Heb. 11:38b). Of him it may be appropriately said that "the world was not worthy" (11:38a).

So too there are not three uncreated or immeasurable beings;
there is but one uncreated and immeasurable being.
Similarly, the Father is almighty,
the Son is almighty,
the Holy Spirit is almighty.
Yet there are not three almighty beings;
there is but one almighty being.
Thus the Father is God,
the Son is God,
the Holy Spirit is God.
Yet there are not three gods;
there is but one God.
Thus the Father is Lord,
the Son is Lord,
the Holy Spirit is Lord.
Yet there are not three lords;
there is but one Lord.
Just as Christian truth compels us
to confess each person individually
as both God and Lord,
so catholic religion forbids us
to say that there are three gods or lords.

The Father was neither made nor created nor begotten from
anyone.
The Son was neither made nor created;
he was begotten from the Father alone.
The Holy Spirit was neither made nor created nor begotten;
he proceeds from the Father and the Son.
Accordingly there is one Father, not three fathers;
there is one Son, not three sons;
there is one Holy Spirit, not three holy spirits.
Nothing in this trinity is before or after,
nothing is greater or smaller;
in their entirety the three persons
are coeternal and coequal with each other.
So in everything, as was said earlier,
we must worship their trinity in their unity
and their unity in their trinity.

66

Anyone then who desires to be saved
should think thus about the trinity.[47]

(5) Proverbs 9:1–18

This final personification of wisdom underscores the open invitation extended by Madam Wisdom to even the simplest, the uninitiates of humanity. The passage also underscores the reward offered by wisdom. This representation of wisdom is set in dramatic contrast over against Madam Folly (Prov. 9:13–18).

First, Madam Wisdom offers her generous invitation to all who will listen to her (Prov. 9:1–6). She dwells in a glorious mansion with seven pillars, representing the perfection of ornamentation joined to firmest stability. Inside this magnificent dwelling she has prepared a luxurious banquet table laden with the finest meats and the sweetest wines. In view of these extravagant preparations, it might be assumed that the people invited to this feast with Madam Wisdom would be necessarily limited in number. But no! Just the opposite is true. Prior qualifications have no place in the issue of invitations to this feast of all feasts. Without exception, all those who are "simple" and "lack judgment" are urged to eat the nourishing food of wisdom and drink her mixed wine.

Sad to say, not everyone responds eagerly to this generous summons (Prov. 9:7–9). Contrariwise, the person making these offers may even expect insult and abuse from wicked mockers.

In all these regards, the wisdom parables of Jesus anticipate these same negative reactions to wisdom's offer of fullness of life. The parable of the banquet with guests who foolishly refuse the gracious invitation to the great banquet and the parable of the wicked vinedressers who eventually slay the son solemnly bring to climax the rejected invitation of personified wisdom, and the consequent death of the foolish and wicked servants (Luke 14:15–24; 20:9–19).

To encourage a proper response to this gracious invitation, Madam Wisdom describes the reward that comes to those who will receive her. A life of many days and extended years will be their reward (Prov.

---

47. This version of the Athanasian Creed was adopted by the Christian Reformed Church Synod in 1988.

9:10–12). The fear of the LORD and knowledge of the Holy One will open the door to a life of ever-increasing wisdom and understanding.

In starkest contrast with this imagery of wisdom is the picture of Madam Folly (Prov. 9:13–18). Rather than maintaining a tasteful decor in the public square, Madam Folly is loud, boisterous, undisciplined. She squats at the door of her house, choosing the most prominent point of the city. As people pass by, she hawks her wares. She makes her appeals to the "simple ones" who pass by. Rather than openly declaring the truth about what she actually offers, Madam Folly proposes "stolen waters," "secret delicacies." But the unsuspecting simpleton, the featherhead who listens to her appeals, has no idea that her guests step down into the depths of the grave, invariably joining the dead.

So the book of Proverbs introduces the reader to this strong contrast between Madam Wisdom and Madam Folly. Each has her own appeal. Accepting the one or the other of their invitations settles the matter of life and death. Young men especially should be duly instructed and warned.

Not only in the Old Testament, but also in the New, wisdom undergoes personification. The Pharisees slander Jesus, trashing him as a glutton and a drunkard because of his association with people who are obviously sinful in their outward behavior. Jesus responds by linking his ministry with John the Baptist's, even as he simultaneously sets up a dramatic contrast between their two modes of ministry. The Baptist came as a strict Stoic, fasting as he denounced sinners, while Jesus came as a friend of tax collectors and harlots, openly welcoming the wicked. "But," says Jesus, "Wisdom is justified by her works" (Matt. 11:19c). By his acceptance of sinners, Jesus embodies personified wisdom as the entity being justified. Though Jesus may not directly link himself with personified wisdom as depicted specifically in Proverbs, the essence of divine wisdom is found in Jesus. For this reason, the lifestyle of Jesus will be ultimately vindicated ("justified"). Wisdom is justified "by its works," and so is Jesus as wisdom personified by his lifestyle despite the carping criticism of his adversaries. "For Jesus, like Sophia, 'Wisdom,' can do no wrong."[48]

---

48. Donald A. Hagner, *Matthew 1–13*, WBC 33A (Dallas: Word Books, 1993), 311.

Still further, Jesus is regularly described in language reminiscent of Proverbs 8. He existed before anything was created, and is supreme over all creation. Through him God created everything (John 1:1–3). He is the "firstborn" of all creation, not as first to come into existence, but firstborn in terms of priority of position. Christ controls all kings, kingdoms, rulers and authorities (Col. 1:15–17), echoing the statement in Proverbs regarding wisdom that "by me kings reign" (Prov. 8:15).

A Special Warning to a Son: Avoid Adultery (Five Passages)

As an extension of the conflicting imagery of Madam Wisdom and Madam Folly, Solomon as a wise father counsels his son quite pointedly concerning the adulterous woman. No fewer than five passages in these introductory chapters reiterate this warning, two of them embracing entire chapters (Prov. 5, 7). Climaxing this series of extended proverbial warnings is a distinctive literary form that may be designated a "fable of exposure."[49] In this literary form, a fictitious narrative exposes the listener's deficiency. Instances of this literary form may be found in both the historical and prophetic books of the Old Testament. Jotham son of Gideon constructs a parable regarding the trees of the forest who decline kingship. Eventually the bramble accepts the post, and institutes a reign of terror (Judg. 9:6–20). By this fable, Jotham exposes the folly of the people's desire for a monarch. Nathan's tale about the man who confiscates his neighbor's pet lamb to serve as a supper dish for a passerby vivifies the king's guilt in absconding with his neighbor's wife (2 Sam. 12:1–7). David's General Joab concocts a tale that surreptitiously compares Absalom's banishment to "water spilled on the ground, which cannot be recovered," dramatized before David by the wise woman of Tekoa (2 Sam. 14:14; cf. 14:1–17). The fictitious parables of Ezekiel depicting the apostasy of the kingdoms of Israel and Judah as two adulterous women fit into the same category (Ezek. 16:1–63; 17:1–24; 23:1–49). In each of these cases, the fictitious narrative results in the exposure of the listener's deficiency.

This literary form represents the closest anticipation of some of Jesus' best-known parables, as in the case of the good Samaritan

49. This literary form deserves further research, in both the Old and the New Testaments.

(Luke 10:25–37), the Pharisee and the tax collector (Luke 18:9–14), the four soils (Matt. 13:1–23), the rejection of invitations to the great banquet (Luke 14:15–24), and the wicked vinedressers (Luke 20:9–19). In each case, the parable exposes some deficiency in the listeners' actions or attitudes.

This particular literary form serves well to paint in vivid colors a foolish youth's encounter with an adulteress (Prov. 7). This wise father portrays to his son the step-by-step entrapment of the unsuspecting youth by the adulteress.

The five passages in Proverbs dealing with this subject are as follows:

(1) Proverbs 2:16–22

The adulteress leaves the partner of her youth and ignores the covenant she has made not merely with her husband, but with her God. Marriage as ordained by the Creator is a solemn three-way bond among the man, the woman, and their Creator God, the God of the covenant. As in all of God's covenants, the marriage bond includes curses as well as blessings. By violating this faithful-unto-death relationship between her God, her husband, and herself, the adulteress denigrates her house so that it becomes a direct pathway to death. None who goes in to her will ever return to normalcy on the pathways of life.

In sharpest contrast, those who heed the warnings of the wise will "walk in the ways of good men" (Prov. 2:20). They will "live in the land," experiencing the blessing of God's people, settled in a land flowing with milk and honey (2:21). This blessing of "inheriting the land" finds reiteration in a psalm hymning a righteous life. The psalmist reiterates this blessing six times (Ps. 37:9, 11, 22, 27, 29, 34). But the foolish son who succumbs to the folly of the adulteress will be disinherited from any possession of the promised land (Prov. 2:22).

(2) Proverbs 5:1–23

This entire chapter develops a contrast between the son who succumbs to the temptations of the adulteress and the son who finds full satisfaction in the wife of his youth. A clear statement of the folly of embracing another man's wife vivifies this contrast (Prov. 5:20–23).

The lips of the adulteress drip honey. Her speech is smoother than oil, which makes it all the more dangerous. For in the end she will make a man's life as bitter as gall. She will cut to the quick as sharply as a double-edged sword. Even though she may not acknowledge it, her steps lead directly to the grave (5:1–14). How much wiser is the son who remains captivated by his love for the wife of his youth, viewing her as a loving doe, a graceful deer who totally satisfies him with her breasts (5:15–19). So why? Why would a young man be captured by an adulteress, another man's wife? The LORD OF THE COVENANT watches every step along this pathway of sin. The erring youth will die for lack of self-discipline, led astray by his own folly (5:20–23).

(3) Proverbs 6:20–35

Both father and mother offer warnings to their son about the snares of an adulteress in this third passage. Walking, sleeping, and waking, their counsel will provide guidance, protection, and warning to their son about this life-threatening issue. The wayward wife may be beautiful, even captivating. But can a man scoop fire into his lap without burning his clothes? Can he walk on hot coals without scorching his feet? So the man who sleeps with another man's wife will not go unpunished. The offended husband will relentlessly pour out his wrathful vengeance on the man who has committed adultery with his wife. A thief who is caught may be required to pay all the wealth of his house as a recompense for his crime. But the man who commits adultery will never have his shame removed. The husband whose jealousy has been aroused will show no mercy as he takes his revenge. No compensation, no bribe will satisfy him, however large it might be.

So the son is urged by his father and his mother to avoid this trap at all costs. He will never escape the consequences of his act of folly.

(4) Proverbs 7:1–27

For the second time a full chapter is devoted to this warning regarding the adulterous woman (cf. Prov. 5). It might seem that the topic is experiencing a literary "overkill." But the very fact of the steady, intensive warning properly recognizes the seriousness of the danger faced by the young man—and by the old man as well. Only the repeated words, the commands, the teachings, the wisdom of the concerned father can keep his son from the adulteress, the wayward woman with her seductive words (7:1–5).

This time the wise father dramatizes the seductive process by which the fool, the simpleton, the featherhead succumbs to the allurements of the adulteress. First, he's in the wrong place at the wrong time. He's near her corner, walking in the direction of her house. It's twilight. Daylight fades, and the dark of night is setting in. This woman—she never stays at home where she belongs. She's loud and defiant, brazenly parading in the public squares, lurking in the corners. She greets him with flattery: "You are the one I came to meet. I've been looking for you, and have finally found you." Then she flaunts her religiosity. She has made fellowship offerings, fulfilling her religious vows this very day. With less-than-subtle suggestiveness, she tells him that she has covered her bed with colored linens from Egypt. She has perfumed her bed with myrrh, and invites him to come and drink deeply of love until the morning. Then she anticipates his cautious objections by informing him that "the man" has gone on a long journey and will not be home for several weeks.[50]

"All at once" he follows her! He's like a dumb ox going to the slaughter. He's like a deer stepping into a noose. Then in an instant a shivering arrow pierces his liver and his life is forever lost.

In a final word, the wise man offers a warning to his sons: Do not let your heart turn toward her ways. Do not stray into her paths. For many are the victims she has brought down. Her slain are a mighty throng. Her house is a highway to the grave leading down to the chambers of death.

This fuller description of the adulterous woman in Proverbs 7 is intentionally placed back to back with the personification of Madam Wisdom as described in the very next chapter (Prov. 8). By this arrangement, the choice between two optional ways of life is effectively dramatized. Either a young man chooses life or he chooses death. Either

---

50. Her reference to "the man" (ha-ish) in distinction from "my husband" (ba'aly) could be understood as a deliberate downgrading of her relationship to her marriage partner, even though ish can mean "husband," particularly since the term baal is specifically used three times for "husband" in Proverbs 31:11, 23, 28.

he embraces the wisdom that comes from God or he succumbs to the allurements of the adulteress. While many other significant choices face the young man, this particular choice determines life or death.

(5) Proverbs 9:13–18

This final warning regarding the adulterous woman completes the first major section of the book of Proverbs. Quite fittingly, the description of the adulterous woman corresponds to the imagery of Madam Folly in this final section. Just as the brazen adulteress sits at the highest point of the city, calling to all who pass by, so Madam Folly parades her wares before the public eye. Their joint invitation is extended to all who are simple and lack good judgment. Both the adulteress and Madam Folly appeal to the special sweetness of stolen waters, of food eaten in secret. But the simpleton who is lured into accepting her invitation doesn't understand that the dead are in her house, that her guests end up in the depths of the grave.

A simple children's poem ("The Spider and the Fly," by Mary Howitt,[51] somewhat modified) might vivify the subtle entrapment of a young man by an adulteress:

> "Will you come into my parlor?" said the Spider to the Fly;
> "It's the prettiest little parlor that ever you will spy.
>
> "The way into my parlor is up a winding stair,
> "I have many things to show you if you'll only come up there."
>
> "O no," said the Fly, "to ask me is in vain;
> "The one who goes up your stair will ne'er come down again."
> . . . .
> "Sweet creature," said the Spider, "you're witty and you're wise,
> "How handsome are your lovely wings, how beautiful your eyes.
>
> "I have a little mirror up on my parlor shelf;
> "Step in for just one moment, sir, and you can see yourself."
>
> "Thank you, gracious ma'm," he said, "for the pleasing things you say.
> "But bidding you good-morning now, I'll come another day."

---

51. Roy J. Cook, ed., *One Hundred and One Famous Poems with a Prose Supplement*, rev. ed. (Chicago: Contemporary Books, 1958), 155–56.

The Spider slowly turned about, and went into her den,
For well she knew the silly Fly would soon be back again.

So she subtly wove her little web, making everything look fine,
And got her table ready for the time when she would dine.

Then out her door she came again, and cheerfully did sing,
"Come in, come in, my pretty Fly, with pearl and silver wing.

"Your robes are green and purple, there's a crest upon your head;
"Your eyes are bright as diamonds, but mine are dull as lead."

So very sad it was! How soon this silly Fly,
Listening to these flattering words, came slowly drifting by.

With buzzing wings he hung aloft, then near and nearer drew,—
Thinking only of his brilliant eyes, his green and purple hue;

Thinking only of his crested head—*poor foolish thing*! At last,
Up jumped the cunning Spider, and fiercely held him fast.

She dragged him up her winding stair, into her dismal den.
He went into her little parlor, but ne'er came out again!

And now to every one of you who may this story read,
To idle, silly, flattering words, be sure you ne'er give heed;

To an evil temptress close your heart, your ear, your eye,
And learn a lesson from this tale of the Spider and the Fly.

The Proverbs of Solomon (Proverbs 10:1–22:16)

This second major section of Proverbs quite possibly preserves the original core of the book. All these proverbs are in couplet form containing two poetic lines, with the single exception of Proverbs 19:7, which contains four lines.[52] By observing that the proverbs of this section are

---

52. William McKane, *Proverbs: A New Approach* (Philadelphia: Westminster, 1977), 2, offers an explanation of the way in which the wisdom literature of proverbial sayings developed. He says that it is "clear" that the "primitive element of form is the one-limbed, single-verse saying," and that the development "proceeds from the unit of one verse to the unit which contains a plurality of verses." In this "natural" process, two or more clauses related in context were next attached for emphasis. Then reasons or consequences were added. Finally, "it was not a great step from this to the larger literary units of the wisdom

grouped primarily on the basis of whether they are *with* or *without* a contrast, this portion of Proverbs may be appropriately divided into two main subsections: chapters 10–15 and chapters 16:1–22:16. Chapters 10 through 15 contain a total of 184 proverbs.[53] Of these, 148 proverbs contain contrasts of various sorts, while only 36 proverbs have no contrast. The most striking aspect of this first grouping is the number of contrasts set up between the righteous and the wicked, the wise and the foolish. Proverbs 16:1–22:16 contains a total of 189 proverbs. In marked distinction from the first grouping, only 34 proverbs in this second collection contain a contrast, while the remaining 155 have no contrast. The comparable reversed proportions of the two groupings are quite remarkable:

Proverbs 10–15	Proverbs 16:1–22:16
184 proverbs total:	189 proverbs total:
148 proverbs with a contrast	155 proverbs without a contrast [54]
36 proverbs without a contrast [55]	34 proverbs with a contrast

Even if the count proves to be slightly inaccurate, the closeness of proportion clearly confirms intentional arrangement as well as a high level of selectivity by the editors of Proverbs on the basis of these groupings. These two subsections of this first collection of Solomonic proverbs (Prov. 10–15; 16:1–22:16) deserve further consideration.

---

literature, the strophes and the didactic poems." Such a neat and reasoned analysis of literary complexities can be achieved only by a rigid avoidance of the recognition of the human capacity for creative genius, not to speak of the vitalizing role of divine inspiration.

53. These tallies may not be exactly accurate because of a number of variables. The counting of John Franklin Genung, "Proverbs, Book of," in *The International Standard Bible Encyclopaedia* (Grand Rapids: Eerdmans, 1936), 4:2473, is slightly different. He counts 184 proverbs in Proverbs 10–15, with only 19 not having some form of contrast. He then counts 191 proverbs in Proverbs 16:1–22:16, with only 18 without a contrast. But in either of these reckonings, the counting should be accurate enough to provide an overall picture of the groupings.

54. This number could be broken down into two groupings: eighty-four "synonymous" proverbs in which the same thought is repeated in the second line, and seventy-one "synthetic" proverbs in which the second line advances the thought of the first line. But in either case, these proverbs contain no contrast.

55. This number could be broken down into two groupings: eleven "synonymous" proverbs in which the same thought is repeated in the second line, and twenty-five "synthetic" proverbs in which the second line advances the thought of the first line.

Proverbs with a Contrast (Proverbs 10–15)

As previously indicated, this section contains 148 proverbs with a contrast out of a total of 184 proverbs. A few examples of this distinctive grouping in this section of the book may be noted as follows:

> A wise son
>   brings joy to his father,
> *but* a foolish son
>   grief to his mother. (Prov. 10:1 NIV)

> Hatred
>   stirs up dissension,
> *but* love
>   covers over all wrongs. (Prov. 10:12 NIV)

> The fear of the COVENANT LORD
>   will prolong life,
> *but* the years of the wicked
>   will be cut short. (Prov. 10:27 NIV)

This distinctive grouping of contrasts underscores the difference between the righteous and the wicked. Proverbs chapters 1 through 9 contain only four references to the "righteous" (צַדִּיק). In contrast, thirteen references to the "righteous" occur in chapter 10 alone, followed by eight in chapter 11, eight in chapter 12, and five in chapter 13, making a total of thirty-four references to the "righteous" in the opening four chapters of this first collection of the proverbs of Solomon.[56]

This extended contrast between the righteous and the wicked explains the rationale behind this first collection with its 148 proverbs *with* a contrast and only 36 *without* a contrast. It appears quite likely that some editor or author intentionally arranged this collection with an opening emphasis on the distinction between the righteous and the wicked. The exercise of wisdom involves serious moral consequences. This initial collection of standardized proverbs strongly accents this

---

56. A similar pattern, though not as marked, occurs in the usage of "upright" (יָשָׁר) in these proverbs attributed to Solomon.

foundational issue of the moral character of the contrast between the wise and the foolish.

The substance of this contrast may be demonstrated from Proverbs 11. A summary of the characteristics and consequences of the righteous and the wicked in this single chapter will underscore the significance of this distinction:

Characteristics of the righteous as illustrated from Proverbs 11. The depiction of the righteous person in Proverbs 11 includes the following characteristics: he uses accurate weights (Prov. 11:1); is humble (11:2); has integrity (11:3); is righteous (11:4–6, 8–10, 21, 23, 28); is blameless (11:5); is upright (11:6, 11); is a man of understanding (11:12); is trustworthy (11:13); is gracious (a wise woman—11:16); is kind (11:17); is a sower of righteousness (11:18); is steadfast in righteousness (11:19); is one whose ways are blameless (11:20); is one who gives freely (11:24); is generous (11:25); is willing to sell (11:26); is a seeker of good (11:27); is one who wins/captures/takes souls (11:30).

Characteristics of the wicked as illustrated from Proverbs 11. In radical contrast, the wicked manifests the following characteristics: he uses dishonest scales (Prov. 11:1); is proud (11:2); is unfaithful in his duplicity (11:3); relies on wealth even in a day of wrath (11:4); destroys his neighbor with his mouth (11:9); evokes shouts of joy at his destruction (11:10); destroys a city with his mouth (11:11); derides his neighbor (11:12); betrays a confidence (11:13); is ruthless (11:16); is cruel (11:17); earns his wages by deception (11:18); lacks discretion (a foolish woman—11:22); withholds unduly (11:24); hoards grain (11:26); searches for evil (11:27); trusts in riches (11:28); brings trouble on his family (11:29); receives his due on earth (11:31).

The contrast between the righteous and the wicked is altogether clear. The lifestyle of the righteous has everything to commend it. But the way of the wicked displeases both God and man.

These two lifestyles have radically different consequences, as this same chapter in Proverbs makes quite clear (Prov. 11):

Consequences of the righteous lifestyle as illustrated from Proverbs 11. The consequences of the righteous life are spelled out quite fully: the righteous one finds favor with the LORD (Prov. 11:1); he comes into wisdom by humility (11:2); he is safely guided through life (11:3);

his righteousness delivers him from death (11:4), makes a straight way for him (11:5), and delivers him (11:6); he is delivered from trouble (11:8); he escapes destruction (11:9); he makes the city rejoice through his prospering (11:10); his blessing exalts the city (11:11); he holds his tongue (11:12); he keeps secrets (11:13); he is safe (11:15); she attains honor (a wise woman—11:16); he does himself good (11:17); he receives a true reward (11:18); he lives (11:19); Yahweh delights in him (11:20); he will be free from punishment (11:21); his desires are only good (11:23); the more he gives, the more he increases (11:24); he will prosper and be refreshed (11:25); he is blessed by the people (11:26); he finds favor (11:27); he will thrive like a green leaf (11:28); he will be like a tree of life (11:30).

Consequences of the wicked lifestyle as illustrated from Proverbs 11. The consequences of living wickedly are not very happy: the wicked one is brought down by his own wickedness (Prov. 11:5); he is trapped by evil desires (11:6); his hope perishes at death (11:7); trouble falls on him rather than on the righteous (11:8); a city shouts for joy when he perishes (11:10); he brings ruin on himself (11:17); he discovers death (11:19); he is detested by the LORD (11:20); he will not go unpunished (11:21); his hope ends in wrath (11:23); he ends up in poverty (11:24); he is cursed by the people (11:26); evil comes to him (11:27); he falls (11:28); he inherits the wind (11:29); he receives his due punishment on earth (11:31).

So this opening section of two-line poems in Proverbs 10–15 amasses 148 proverbs with a contrast out of a total of 184 proverbs. A large number of these proverbs with a contrast clearly and strongly declare the difference between the righteous and the wicked. People prepared to receive the instruction of wisdom will not miss the point of this opening declaration.

In addition to grouping proverbs on the basis of whether they do or do not contain a contrast, arrangement by subject matter in this first section of the Solomonic collection deserves consideration. At times the subject grouping is obviously intentional. Because the original text of Scripture had no chapter divisions, some recognition must be given to groupings that extend beyond currently designated chapter divisions. Significant groupings in this first collection of the proverbs of Solomon include the following:

The critical role of the tongue. In the six chapters of this subsection (Prov. 10–15), twenty-six proverbs refer to the tongue, to speech, to testimony. The concentration on this single member of the human anatomy may be explained in that the tongue sets the human being apart from all other earthly creatures, clearly defining him as being like God. The tongue represents a person's mightiest weapon for either good or evil. With his tongue a person may destroy his neighbor or even an entire city (11:9, 11). Or the tongue may serve as a "fountain of life" "nourish[ing] many" (Prov. 10:11, 21).

The value of the godly woman. Scattered across these six chapters are several references to the godly woman. She is a woman of grace, in contrast with a woman without discretion (Prov. 11:16, 22). She has a noble character (12:4). She builds her house (14:1). Alongside the father, she grieves at her son's folly (10:1; 15:20). So the reader of Proverbs need not wait until the final section of the book to discover words of wisdom regarding the godly woman.

The wise versus the foolish. Alongside the contrast between the righteous and the wicked is the equally significant contrast between the wise and the foolish. In these six chapters, no fewer than thirty-three proverbs refer to the wise or the foolish, with a number of them setting the two over against each other. So the practical proverb reads:

> Walk with the wise
> and be wise,
> for a companion of fools
> suffers harm. (Prov. 13:20)

Proverbs without a Contrast (Proverbs 16:1–22:16)

As previously noted, this section contains 189 proverbs. But now the proportion of proverbs with a contrast compared to proverbs without a contrast is totally reversed. These eight chapters contain 155 proverbs without a contrast over against 34 proverbs with a contrast.

Though expanded in more recent years, the classic distinction among three different types of poetic parallelism in the Old Testament continues to be useful.[57] In *synonymous* parallelism, the second line repeats the thought of the first line, with some moderate variation. In *antithetic* parallelism, the second line states the opposite truth as expressed in the first line. But in *synthetic* parallelism, the second member of a couplet advances the thought of the proverb beyond the level of presentation in the first line.

Already examples of antithetic parallelism have been noted in the treatment of the collection of proverbs with a contrast (Prov. 10–15). Illustrations of synonymous parallelism may be taken from this next section of the book (16:1–22:16). In these proverbs, the second line restates the same observation of the first line, with some modification:

> Better is a patient man
> > than a warrior,
> a man who controls his temper
> > than one who takes a city. (Prov. 16:32)

> Even a fool is thought wise
> > if he keeps silent,
> and discerning
> > if he holds his tongue. (Prov. 17:28 NIV)

> Love and faithfulness
> > keep a king safe;
> through love
> > his throne is made secure. (Prov. 20:28 NIV)

This grouping of large segments of proverbs in these two opening sections on the basis of a comparison or a contrast confirms deliberate arrangement of these materials. Perhaps the "men of Hezekiah" mentioned in Proverbs 25:1 had a hand in this arrangement. But it is highly unlikely that this kind of distribution would have happened without someone's intentional planning.

---

57. This classic categorizing of three basic types of Hebrew poetic parallelism was first proposed by Bishop Robert Lowth in 1753 (*De sacra poesi Hebraeorum*, "Concerning the sacred poetry of the Hebrews"). Lowth distinguished among *synonymous*, *antithetic*, and *synthetic* parallelism.

The synthetic type of parallelism in which the second member of the couplet advances the thought of the initial member may be illustrated by samples taken from chapter 16:

Turn over to the COVENANT LORD
    every one of your plans,
and your projects
    will be firmly established. (Prov. 16:3 NIV)

The LORD detests
    all the proud of heart.
Be sure of this:
    They will not go unpunished. (Prov. 16:5 NIV)

Better to be lowly in spirit
    and among the oppressed
    than to share plunder
with the proud. (Prov. 16:19 NIV)

In each of these cases, the second line of the poem advances the thought introduced in the first line.

An additional significant phenomenon that appears in both the collection of proverbs with a contrast (Prov. 10–15) and the collection of proverbs without a contrast (Prov. 16:1–22:16) is the distinction that can be made between a *statement* and an *admonition*. The statement "simply comments on a situation (e.g., about the world, society, or types of individuals) as it is, without drawing any conclusion or pointing out any moral, while the 'admonition' advises, exhorts, instructs, dissuades or warns about the consequences of specific actions or behavior."[58] At times the distinction between these two kinds of proverbs requires careful consideration, which should not be surprising. For the necessity of close analysis belongs to the very nature of the proverb.

The simple comment of the proverbial statement essentially involves a clear, coherent, and profound analysis of reality. The admonition proverb falls into two subcategories: the *direct admonition* and the *implied admonition*, the latter of which constitutes the far

---

58. Whybray, *Survey*, 43. For further discussion of this distinction, see ibid., 43–48.

greater number in this section of the book. Illustrations of these three categories of proverbs are as follows:

Direct Admonition:

> Stay away from a foolish man,
>> for you will not find knowledge on his lips. (Prov. 14:7 NIV)
> (This proverb gives pointed direction, with an attached reason.)

Implied Admonition:

> Wise men store up knowledge,
>> but the mouth of a fool invites ruin. (Prov. 10:14 NIV)
> (The point is clear, though not explicitly expressed. If you wish to be wise, build up your treasury of truth, and don't talk too much.)

Statement:

> The wealth of the rich is their fortified city,
>> but poverty is the ruin of the poor. (Prov. 10:15 NIV)
> (No value judgment is given about being rich or poor. It's simply a fact that riches protect a person from many problems, while poverty constantly exposes to disaster.)

Direct Admonition:

> Do not love sleep or you will grow poor;
>> stay awake and you will have food to spare. (Prov. 20:13 NIV)
> (A clear direction is given, not merely an observation worth considering.)

Implied Admonition:

> Fools mock at making amends for sin,
>> but goodwill is found among the upright. (Prov. 14:9 NIV)
> (Unless you want to be a fool, admit your sin and do your best to make things right.)

Statement:

> Each heart knows its own bitterness,
>> and no one else can share its joy. (Prov. 14:10 NIV)

(It's simply a fact of life: deep down within, a person experiences his most painful bitterness and his greatest joy, neither of which can be fully appreciated by anyone else.)

Direct Admonition:

> Make plans by seeking advice;
> if you wage war, obtain guidance. (Prov. 20:18 NIV)
> (The father instructs the son to make good use of godly counselors.)

Implied Admonition:

> There is a way that seems right to a man,
> but in the end it leads to death. (Prov. 16:25 NIV)
> (Be very careful about thinking that your way is correct. You can be seriously fooled until you finally realize that your way is "dead wrong.")

Statement:

> The laborer's appetite works for him;
> his hunger drives him on. (Prov. 16:26 NIV)
> (It's simply a fact: God has made humans so that their need for daily provision compels them to work.)

All three types of proverbs communicate insight about human realities in memorable fashion. A proverb in the form of a *direct admonition* exhorts the hearer/reader to take deliberate action. The far more numerous *implied admonition* displays the provocative genius of the proverb, requiring the recipient to "tease out" the point of the proverb in terms of its practical significance. On the other hand, the *statement* doesn't tell the reader anything he ought to do. It simply "tells it as it is." Yet this proverbial information has great value in increasing a person's understanding about life. Riches shelter from certain troubles. Your deepest sorrows and joys will always be your own. A hungry laborer works harder. These are simply "the facts of life," and you're far better off if you understand them.[59]

---

59. The *direct admonitions* are easily identified by their imperative form. The *implied admonitions* require more careful thought. The simple *statements* are sometimes difficult

Distinctive groupings in this section with its 155 proverbs *without* a contrast (Prov. 16:1–22:16) include the following:

(1) Three consecutive proverbs describing three types of wicked men. The parallelism of expression is not clear in English translations, but striking in the original text:

- "A man of worthlessness" (אִישׁ בְּלִיַּעַל—Prov. 16:27)
- "A man of perversities" (אִישׁ תַּהְפֻּכוֹת—Prov. 16:28)
- "A man of violence" (אִישׁ חָמָס—Prov. 16:29)

(2) Five proverbs about the poor, not sequential in arrangement, but alternating between two different words for the "poor" (*rush* and *dal*) (רוּשׁ and דַּל) (Prov. 19:1, 4, 7, 17, 22). The first reference begins with "Better to be poor" (19:1), and the last reference ends with "Better to be poor" (19:22). While these factors could be viewed as incidental, it is quite possible that the text has been deliberately arranged with this alternating employment of two different words for the "poor."

(3) A grouping of ten proverbs on various aspects of commercial life. Six of these proverbs appear in direct sequence (Prov. 20:13–16), while the other four precede or follow the sequential grouping (20:4, 10, 21, 23). These proverbs cover the field of commerce quite extensively, from the folly of the sluggard who does not plow in season (20:4), to the LORD's despising corrupted measurements (20:10, 23), to laziness that brings poverty (20:13), to the buyer's strategy of denigrating the seller's product (20:14), to a lesson about being surety to a stranger (20:16), to fraudulent funds that degenerate to a mouthful of gravel (20:17), to the "easy come, easy go" of an inheritance (20:21). These types of smaller groupings are scattered throughout the book. Detecting these various groupings can enrich the understanding of the passage.

The Words of the Wise Ones (Proverbs 22:17–24:34)

A distinctive introduction that occurs twice in this section marks off this particular material into two different segments (Prov. 22:17–24:22;

---

to distinguish. Additional instances of this third type may be found in Proverbs 13:23; 14:13; 16:1, 4; 19:7; 20:14, 29. This last category deserves further exploration.

and 24:23–34). The first introduction identifies the source of this material as coming from "the wise ones" (דִּבְרֵי חֲכָמִים —22:17). The second introduction notes that "these" (proverbs) are "also from the wise ones" (גַּם־אֵלֶּה לַחֲכָמִים—24:23). Yet both poetic sections identify an "I" who serves as the source of this material. This individual mentions "what I teach" and "what I observed" (22:17b; 24:32). Says one commentator: "The specific teacher appropriates the accumulated wisdom of the tradition as his own in order to pass it on to his disciple."[60] Conceivably Solomon could speak of himself as the "I" who has received this traditional wisdom. But more likely, the "I" represents some other wisdom figure who has drawn from the resources of the past, for Solomon fits more naturally in the role of source of wisdom rather than benefactor of wisdom from others. In both introductions, reference is made to the "sayings" of the wise ones, possibly indicating that at some point these collections had been communicated orally.

First Collection from the Wise Ones (Proverbs 22:17–24:22)[61]

The extended introduction of this first portion of the sayings of the "wise ones" echoes quite closely a number of elements in the first major section of the book (Prov. 1–9). This introduction admonishes the reader to "incline your ear" and "hear" (22:17; cf. 4:1, 10, 20; 5:1). He is to "apply [his] heart" to what is taught (22:17; cf. 2:2). The reference to "trust . . . in the COVENANT LORD" clearly replicates a key phrase in the first section of the book (22:19; cf. 3:5). These parallels in two introductory sections support an intentional structuring of the book of Proverbs.

A number of proverbs in this first collection of the "wise ones" are in the quatrain form, containing four lines to each proverb. Others have more than four lines. Illustrations of the quatrain are as follows:

Do not rob the poor because he is poor
    and do not crush the
disadvantaged in the gate,

60. Longman, *Proverbs*, 415.
61. Already the various possible relationships of this section to the Egyptian wisdom of Amen-em-Opet have been considered. See the section entitled "The Relation of Proverbs to Other Ancient Wisdom Materials," above.

for the LORD himself will plead their case
and will wreck the life of anyone
who damages them. (Prov. 22:22–23 NIV)

Do not join those who drink too much wine
or gorge themselves on meat,
for drunkards and gluttons become poor,
and drowsiness clothes them in rags. (Prov. 23:20–21 NIV)

When you sit to dine with a ruler,
note well what is before you,
and put a knife to your throat if you are given to gluttony.
Do not crave his delicacies,
for that food is deceptive. (Prov. 23:1–3 NIV)

An additional distinctive in this section is the permeation of imperatives in a negative form throughout the three chapters of this section (Prov. 22:17–24:22). As many as twenty-two negative admonitions appear, in significant contrast with their paucity throughout the rest of the book.[62] These admonitions include the following:

"*Do not* exploit the poor because they are poor." (Prov. 22:22 NIV)

"*Do not* make friends with a hot-tempered man." (Prov. 22:24 NIV)

"*Do not* move an ancient boundary stone." (Prov. 22:28 NIV)

"*Do not* wear yourself out to get rich." (Prov. 23:4 NIV)

"*Do not* withhold discipline from a child." (Prov. 23:13 NIV)

"*Do not* join those who drink too much wine." (Prov. 23:20 NIV)

"*Do not* gloat when your enemy falls." (Prov. 24:17 NIV)

"*Do not* fret because of evil men." (Prov. 24:19 NIV)

These negative admonitions do not come in the strong form of apodictic decrees, as found in the categorical commands of the Ten

62. But the collection of six negatives in Proverbs 3:21–35 should be noted.

Words (Ex. 20:3–17). Instead, they come in the milder form of counsel, as a father would address his son.

Second Collection from the Wise Ones (Proverbs 24:23–34)

This brief section continues the words of the "wise ones" (גַּם־אֵלֶּה לַחֲכָמִים), apparently indicating a source for these proverbs other than Solomon. The section includes a call for just judgments (Prov. 24:23b–25), a repudiation of personal vengeance (24:28–29), and a longer poem describing the sad state of the sluggard. Weeds cover the sluggard's neglected ground, and his dilapidated wall is about to crumble. Only a "little sleep," a "little slumber," and his poverty assaults him like an armed man (24:30–34). The sometimes humorous and sometimes pathetic pictures of the sluggard display the capacity of the proverb to make a person with undesirable characteristics into a "proverb."

The Hezekian Arrangement of Solomonic Proverbs (Proverbs 25–29)

The first verse of this section explains the origin and current location of these proverbs within the collection: "These also are the proverbs of Solomon, which the men of Hezekiah collected" (Prov. 25:1 ESV).[63] This statement indicates that Solomon was the author of this material, but that it has experienced rearrangement by the contemporaries of Hezekiah. Three hundred years after Solomon, the book of Proverbs had not yet realized its final form.

Immediately after indicating that King Solomon composed the proverbs in this collection while King Hezekiah's scholars set them in good order, this section immediately begins with four proverbs about the king (Prov. 25:2–7). For appropriate to kingship is the production of the proverb. The first proverb speaks of the glory of God in concealing a matter and the glory of kings in *searching out* a matter (25:2). The next proverb compares the impossibility of *searching out*

---

63. Regarding the reference to Hezekiah, Whybray, *Survey*, 19–20, says: "The historical authenticity of this statement has been generally accepted, and—unless the entire book is held to be post-exilic—there seems to be no reason to doubt it."

the heart of a king to the altogether impossible task of searching out the height of heaven and the depth of the earth (25:3). These two opening proverbs connect God's kingship with man's kingship, and parallel a king's search for wisdom to the search required to comprehend a king.

Worth noting in these proverbs arranged by the men of Hezekiah (Prov. 25–29) is the extensive use of simile and analogy, especially in chapters 25 and 26, as evidenced by the following examples:

> A word aptly spoken
> > *is like* apples of gold in settings of silver.
> *Like* an earring of gold or an ornament of fine gold
> > is a wise man's rebuke to a listening ear.
> *Like* the coolness of snow at harvest time
> > is a trustworthy messenger to those who send him;
> > > he refreshes the spirit of his masters.
> *Like* clouds and wind without rain
> > is a man who boasts of gifts he does not give. (Prov. 25:11–14 NIV)

> *Like* cold water to a weary soul
> > is good news from a distant land.
> *Like* a muddied spring or a polluted well
> > is a righteous man who gives way to the wicked. (Prov. 25:25–26 NIV)

The distinctive use of simile in this subcollection makes it read "like a new species of proverb when we note that in all the earlier Solomonic sections there are only two clearly defined similes (10:26; 11:22)."[64] This type of proverb stresses the harmony of humanity with the rest of creation. It's not merely a matter of finding an apt illustration from the realm of "nature." The connection is much deeper. Because of the symbionic relation of humanity to its environment, realities about different kinds of people find their mirror in realities of creation. Wisdom detects these relationships and comes to a better understanding of both.

So in the context of new covenant fulfillment, it should not be surprising that over ninety occurrences of the word *like* appear in one modern translation of the four Gospels (NIV [1984]). Many of

---

64. Genung, "Proverbs," 4:2473.

these occurrences appear in connection with Jesus' parables of the kingdom. For he is the King, the epitome of the "Wise One" who understands the entire realm of creation in its relation to humanity. On this basis he can pronounce his perceptive proverbs in the form of parables.

In addition to this large collection of *like* proverbs, chapter 26 begins with no fewer than eleven proverbs about the fool (Prov. 26:1, 3–12), followed by four proverbs about the sluggard (26:13–16). Also worth noting in this section is the identical repetition of several proverbs from earlier portions of the book:

- Proverbs 25:24 reproduces Proverbs 21:9
- Proverbs 26:22 reproduces Proverbs 18:8
- Proverbs 27:12 reproduces Proverbs 22:3

Though "context" in Proverbs is difficult to define, one possible explanation for this repetition might be searched out in the specific function of the identical verses in their separate contexts or collections.[65] Whatever the case, the men of Hezekiah must have had some reason for apparently duplicating these proverbs.

The Words of Certain Wise Men (Proverbs 30:1–31:9)

Agur (Proverbs 30:1–33)

The identity of this person named Agur is uncertain. Older tradition has treated the word as a code name for *Solomon*. But this view is generally discounted in modern studies. *Agur*, *Jakeh*, *Ithiel*, and *Ucal* are all names or words of uncertain origin and meaning. Many proposed translations "depend on substantial emendations and/or repointings of the consonantal text."[66] In such cases, it may be wiser to leave the puzzle unsolved rather than to emend the biblical text.

Several *middah* types (from the Hebrew *madad*, "to measure") are found in this section:

---

65. See the various explanations offered by Waltke, *Proverbs 15–31*, 333f., 361, 381.
66. Whybray, *Survey*, 88.

There are three things
  that are never satisfied,
four
  that never say, "Enough":
    the grave,
    the barren womb,
    land, which is never satisfied with water,
    and fire, which never says, "Enough!" (Prov. 30:15b–16 NIV)

There are three things
  that are stately in their stride,
four
  that move with stately bearing:
    a lion, mighty among beasts, who retreats before nothing;
    a strutting rooster,
    a he-goat,
    and a king with his army around him. (Prov. 30:29–31 NIV)

The rationale behind this particular poetic device has been variously explained.[67] In some cases, the illustrations from creation stimulate meditation on the truth regarding humanity's relation to God's world. In the first instance cited above, the point for contemplation is the reality for humanity that the grave never says, "Enough!" All human beings will eventually descend into the grave. To make this reality more vivid, three images depict this fact. Fire forever searches for more tinder; the earth perpetually pleads for more water; the barren womb can never be satisfied; and the grave will absorb its victims until no more humans exist on this earth. In the second case, the stateliness of a king that commands respect finds reinforcement through the combined images of a lion, a strutting rooster, and a he-goat that will not rest until he's top of the hill.

King Lemuel (Proverbs 31:1–9)

King Lemuel has also been identified as Solomon in the past, but the connection is uncertain. In this section, the king passes on to his

---

67. Whybray, *Survey*, 98, suggests that the *middah*-form may be used to encourage reflection, as "an attempt to master the world through attaining to an understanding of it." As an alternative proposal, he suggests that the form "might go back in a sense to a magical view of the world," which has no basis in the text of Scripture.

90

son the oracles of wisdom that his mother taught him. So in this case the mother functions as the source of wisdom. Her son, who is the king, serves only as the conduit of her wisdom. The dowager covers three items: (1) the king must not spend his strength on women, for he would be ruined (Prov. 31:2–3); (2) the king must not crave beer, for he would forget what the law decrees and deprive the oppressed of their rights (31:4–7); (3) the king must speak up, judge rightly, and defend the rights of the poor and needy (31:8–9). All three of these succinctly treated topics have special significance for a ruler.

And who, incidentally, is this mother? If Solomon were the "king" in question, then this wise mother would be none other than Bathsheba.

An Acrostic Poem Celebrating the Godly Woman (Proverbs 31:10–31)

In contrast with the many warnings given regarding the harlotrous woman in the opening section of the book (Prov. 1–9), this concluding alphabetic acrostic poem celebrates the virtues of the godly wife. Conjoined to the immediately preceding section in which the king acknowledges his mother as a major source of his wisdom (31:1–9), the two final sections of Proverbs honor women: the wise mother and the wise wife. The book of Proverbs opens with several "personifications" of wisdom as a woman. These final poems celebrate the "materialization" of wisdom in the lifestyle and the faith of these women. With regard to the godly wife, consider her price, her product, her piety, and her praise.[68]

Her Price (Proverbs 31:10–12)

In this passage, a certain type of female is being sought. Who can find her? Where is she to be found? What is this woman like?

---

68. Whybray, *Survey*, 101f., cites two authors who conclude that the acrostic form has made it impossible for the author of Proverbs to treat the material in a logical manner. He notes the suggestion of some interpreters that the acrostic form "necessarily made a logical sequence of topics impossible, and left the poem a 'mosaic' or jumble." He responds by stating that this conclusion simply overlooks the progression of thought in the poem. Rather than destroying an orderly presentation, the alphabetic acrostic provides a framework for completeness.

Literally, she is a person of "strength" (אֵשֶׁת־חַיִל—Prov. 31:10). The translations of this opening phrase vary:

- "A wife of noble character" (NIV)
- "An excellent wife" (ESV, NASU)
- "A virtuous woman" (KJV)
- "A virtuous wife" (NKJV)

As the different translations indicate, this particular female (אִשָּׁה) could be designated as a "woman" or a "wife." If it is a young man who is "seeking" her (which is altogether appropriate), it may be assumed that he is seeking a "wife." But because the concluding word of praise for this female comes from the entire community gathered at the "gate" (Prov. 31:31), it may be equally appropriate to designate her as a "woman" rather than a "wife." Because of her contribution to the whole community, everyone seeks out this kind of woman.

More specifically, this woman is designated as "excellent," "virtuous," "of noble character." The root meaning of the word (חַיִל) is "strong," "valiant," even "wealthy." The term regularly refers to the strength of an "army."

An informative parallel to this passage is found in the book of Ruth. Boaz addresses Ruth with this identical phrase. Literally Boaz says, "For the whole 'gate of my people' knows that you are a *woman with character*" (אֵשֶׁת־חַיִל—Ruth 3:11), which may be the best option for translating the same phrase in Proverbs. Quite interesting is this reference to the "gate" where the leaders of a community gather. In a way similar to Ruth, this "woman with character" in Proverbs will receive praise in the "gate" (Prov. 31:31). In the biblical context, this "character" of the woman, as in the case of Ruth, involves being morally upright, a responsible citizen, committed to the family, and faithfully devoted to the LORD. She's got strength of character and convictions. The same phrase elsewhere in Proverbs describes a wife who is her husband's crown, contributing to his prominence and lending dignity to his person in the community (12:4a). In contrast, the wife who shames her husband is like rot in his bones (12:4b). His wife tears down his life's superstructure.

"Who can find" this woman of character? A person will have to look hard. If you are seeking a wife with character, don't fall head over heels for the first woman who uses a little flattery. Look diligently! But in your looking, don't trust your own prowess. Only the Lord can enable you to find the right one suited just perfectly for you.

"Far more than the most precious jewels is her worth" (Prov. 31:10b). In a little shop on the peninsula jutting out from Cape Town, South Africa, that divides the Indian and the Atlantic Oceans, you may find hundreds of polished semiprecious gems. For a few coins you can collect a bag of multicolored polished rocks. They look great. But their worth is minuscule.

Is that what you want for a wife? Someone outwardly polished who looks like a fashion model, but has no real worth? The proverbs speak straightforwardly about naked outward beauty:

A ring of gold
    in the snout of a pig
is a beautiful woman
    without discretion. (Prov. 11:22)

Make no mistake. Beauty in a woman is a wonderful thing, a manifestation of God's greatest handiwork. But beauty is neither the only nor the first thing that a person should look for when searching for a wife. What you want is a woman "with character," a godly woman who will stand strong for the principles of the Lord.

When you find this kind of woman, be willing to pay! Whatever it costs, pay it gladly. Her worth is far greater than the most costly precious jewels (Prov. 31:10b).

Why is she worth so much? The next two verses explain:

The heart of her husband trusts in her,
    and he will lack nothing of any worth.
She repays him with good and not evil
    all the days of her life. (Prov. 31:11–12)

You think the dowry is too high? You wonder how you will ever get your hands on four cows! Is this woman really worth it?

Repayment certainly must not be your motivation. But count on it. For the rest of your life you will be repaid a thousandfold. All the days of her life she will repay you for the comparatively little money or effort you spent seeking to find her. Not only in the early days of marriage, but through all the long years ahead she will repay you good and not evil.

The husband can trust altogether in her chastity. She is never flirtatious toward other men, and gives him no reason for jealousy. Her husband lacks nothing of true worth in this life. She is the "helper corresponding to him" (עֵזֶר כְּנֶגְדּוֹ—Gen. 2:18), designed by the Creator to meet all his needs. Though a person of great gifts and accomplishments in herself, the wife with character is careful to know the mind of her husband, that she may accommodate herself to his needs. She is always supportive of him in every good work for the LORD that he undertakes.

So, men, pay the price! Make the investment in a wife with character. You will be repaid a hundred times over.

Her Product (Proverbs 31:13–25)

What does this strong woman, this woman with character, produce? First, she glorifies God by her industriousness (Prov. 31:13–20, 24–25).

> She [carefully] chooses
>> wool and linen,
> and delights
>> to work with her hands. (Prov. 31:13)

Two phrases typically characterize many Western women: "Born to shop" and "Shop till you drop." But these phrases do not describe the woman found in Proverbs 31. These words express the ideal of Western secularism, of modern materialism in which the shopping mall has become the temple and consumerism has become god.

But this woman in Proverbs is a "hands-on" person, working hard night and day. She is up in the morning while it is still dark, preparing food for her family (Prov. 31:15). She works vigorously. She has strength in her arms and determination in her will that enable her to persist at a job until it is done (31:17). She's busily fitting out clothes for her children (31:19). She knows how to manage money and possesses good trading savvy (31:16, 18). She's involved in trading real estate, carefully considering a field, determining whether she can use it well, what the asking price might be, and concluding the deal. She takes the money she has earned and plants a vineyard that will provide more profit in future years. She pays a fair price, but always realizes a good return on her investment (31:18a).

At the same time, she knows how to manage workers around the house. She keeps them happy in their employment and provides for their needs as well (Prov. 31:15c). In other words, she is busy fulfilling the cultural mandate, subduing the earth to the glory of God. She has been remade in the image of God the Creator, and so honors him with the whole of her life.

Yet there is more. Not only does she glorify God by her industriousness, she also glorifies God through her family (Prov. 31:21–23).

Look at her children:

> She has no fear of snow
>> for her household,
>> for all her family
> have a double layer of clothing.[69] (Prov. 31:21)

It's sad to think of children all over the world who will shiver in the cold at night. Sometimes poverty is difficult to escape. But if at all possible, this woman will make adequate provision for her household.

Look at the woman herself:

> She makes coverings
>> for herself;
>> her clothing
> is fine linen and purple. (Prov. 31:22)

In consistency with other portions of Scripture, the personal appearance of this woman would not look extravagant. But she also

---

69. The Masoretic vowel pointing reads "scarlet." But the vowels could just as well read "two" or "double," as in the LXX.

avoids the opposite extreme of not caring for herself and her outward appearance. Neatness, attractiveness, and appropriateness of dress characterize her personal appearance. She does not dress too high, nor does she dress too low for the role she must play according to the orderings of God's providence. As the apostle Paul says: "I also want women to dress modestly, with decency and propriety, not with braided hair or gold or pearls or expensive clothes, but with good deeds, appropriate for women who profess to worship God" (1 Tim. 2:9–10).

Look at her husband:

> Her husband is respected
>   in the gate,
> where he sits
>   among the elders of the land. (Prov. 31:23)

If someone has a disruptive family situation, he will not function well in the public eye. But a godly wife will provide domestic order so that her husband will not be distracted by a malfunctioning household. In the context of the dress she provides for the children and herself, it may be assumed that her husband also appears in appropriate dress. The consequence of a well-ordered family means that her husband quickly gains the respect of the elders of the community. For how can a person govern the church of Christ if he cannot govern his own house well (1 Tim. 3:4–5)?

So the wife's contribution to the family situation gives glory to God. The product of her life starts with the family and spreads from there to the whole community.

Her Piety (Proverbs 31:26–27)

At the heart of her piety is the heart of Proverbs: the wisdom of God and the fear of the LORD. First, consider the wisdom of God as manifest in her words:

> She opens her mouth
>   with wisdom,
>   and the law of covenant faithfulness [תּוֹרַת־חֶסֶד]
> is on her tongue. (Prov. 31:26)

She speaks with wisdom and covenant faithfulness. Wisdom is the great thing in the book of Proverbs. As previously noted, ten different sections declare the worth of wisdom in the opening nine chapters of the book. No fewer than five personifications of wisdom appear in those same opening chapters. This woman is the concretization of Madam Wisdom as introduced in the earlier portion of the book. In the piety of her words she stands as the opposite of Madam Folly.

Proverbs places so much emphasis on words, on the way a person speaks. This woman constantly speaks words of wisdom and covenant faithfulness. Every time she opens her mouth, a gem, a jewel, a pearl of great price blesses the hearer. She never speaks rashly or in anger. Always the graciousness, mercy, and kindness of the LORD come to expression in her words. This is her piety.

Crowning this piety is that focal virtue introduced in the very opening verses of Proverbs: the fear of the LORD:

Charm
    is deceptive,
And beauty
    is hollow.
        A woman who fears the LORD—
        She shall be praised. (Prov. 31:30)

All through the book of Proverbs it has been the "son" who has been instructed in the fear of the LORD. But now, rounding out the book at its conclusion, it is the woman with character who embodies this life-determining truth. The "fear of the LORD" is a many-splendored thing. But in this context it appears as "the law of covenant faithfulness" that is on her lips and in her life (Prov. 31:26). This "torah of hesed" (תּוֹרַת־חֶסֶד) combines law and mercy. In her fear of the LORD she unites righteousness and graciousness. As the psalmist says, "Love and faithfulness meet together; righteousness and peace kiss each other" (Ps. 85:10).

In addition to these essential virtues of wisdom and the fear of the LORD, this godly woman is forever watchful. She "watches over the affairs of her household" (Prov. 31:27). She doesn't have her head in the clouds. She's constantly watching over the comings and goings of her family. She's not naive. She's very conscious of what's going on with her husband and children. If one child begins to stray from the path, she's the first to notice and do something about it.

Even further, her religion has that necessary dimension of practicality. She doesn't eat the bread of idleness (לֶחֶם עַצְלוּת—Prov. 31:27). The root of this word for "idleness" appears repeatedly in Proverbs to depict the life of the "sluggard":

> Go to the ant, you sluggard. (Prov. 6:6 NIV)
> How long will you lie there, you sluggard? (Prov. 6:9 NIV)
> As smoke to the eyes, so is the sluggard to them that send him. (Prov. 10:26)
> The laziness of the sluggard brings deep sleep. (Prov. 19:15)
> I went past the field of the sluggard, . . . the ground was covered with weeds, and the stone wall was in ruins. (Prov. 24:30–31 NIV)

A more modern proverbial poem depicts the same lifestyle:

> Lazy bones, lazy bones, sleepin' in the sun,
> How do you expect to get yo' day's work done!
> Lazy bones, lazy bones, sleepin' in the shade,
> How do you expect to get yo' corn meal made!

Contrary to the foibles of the proverbial sluggard, this woman of "strength" manifests a character that consistently puts faith into action. Not only by her pious words, which are absolutely critical, but by her actions she displays godly wisdom through her fear of the LORD.

Her Praise (Proverbs 31:28–31)

Three people spontaneously praise this godly woman: her children, her husband, and the people at the city gate.

First are her children and her husband:

> Her children rise up
>   and bless her;
> Her husband
>   also praises her. (Prov. 31:28)

The children are not content to just "sit there" in the presence of their mother. They "jump up" and bless her. They pronounce their childhood benedictions on her.

Then it's the husband's turn. He adds his praise to the blessings of the children.

But eventually it all becomes a public thing. In the gate, where the elders, the judges, the kings, and the people assemble, she will be praised. Bless the LORD for the godly woman in your life. Eventually the whole community cannot fail to recognize her.

As though that were not enough, the writer admonishes all his readers to join in the praise of this woman who fears the LORD:

> Give her the fruit of her hands,
> And let her works praise her at the city gate. (Prov. 31:31a)

She deserves this praise. So give it to her.

Summary

So this final section of the book of Proverbs rounds out the picture of a person, whether man or woman, who fears the LORD. All the negative images of the adulterous woman found in the warnings to the son in the early chapters of Proverbs find their counterbalance in this concluding poem celebrating the praises of the godly woman. She embodies the image of Dame Wisdom so vividly depicted in the opening verses and chapters of the book.

THEOLOGICAL PERSPECTIVES ON THE BOOK OF PROVERBS

Obviously, the book of Proverbs has its own distinctive characteristics as a theological work when compared with other books of Scripture. It is not narrative theology as found in the historical books. It is not a collection of "Thus says the LORD" utterances as found in the prophetic materials. It does not partake of the poetic exultations found in the book of Psalms, though it is poetic in form.

In attempting to understand the distinctive theological contribution of the book of Proverbs, two diverging perspectives may be considered:

A Secularistic Perspective

It has been noted that the "wise men" of the book of Proverbs make no appeal to redemptive history. Nothing is said about the specific saving activities of God on behalf of Israel. One author concludes that Proverbs is "clearly a secular work. It makes no pretense to an origin in divine revelation or inspiration."[70] As a consequence, it is proposed regarding proverbs:

> They speak to and about men primarily as individuals. The authority to which they chiefly appeal is the disciplined intelligence and moral experience of good men.[71]

This analysis of Proverbs conforms to the secularistic concept of a proverb as a commonplace statement of local wit characterized by "shortness, sense and salt." These worldly-wise sayings contain "the wisdom of many and the wit of one."[72] They fit quite comfortably into the category of "down-to-earth" verbal gems of practicality found in every culture. "Never try to pass through the legs of an elephant twice," says the African proverb. Or "If you're ugly, learn to sing."

In support of this secularistic perspective on the book of Proverbs, appeal has been made to an impersonal mode of expression found in the book. Instead of noting that God will fill a person's barns, Proverbs states that one's "barns will be filled" (Prov. 3:10). One commentator concludes:

> The author appears to be anxious to avoid attributing even this degree of personal action to God. . . . The idea that the giving of rewards is part of the working of an impersonal order seems to prevail over the concept of a God who has a personal relationship with men and a personal will upon which men depend. The impression is given that this God, even though he is called "Yahweh," is rather a functionary carrying out the requirements of an impersonal order than a God who himself decides man's fate.[73]

70. Fox, *Proverbs 1–9*, 7.
71. Scott, *Proverbs*, xvi.
72. Ibid., 3.
73. Whybray, *Wisdom in Proverbs*, 65.

But when taken in context, this very proverb proves exactly the opposite. The proverb reads in full:

> Honor the COVENANT LORD
>   with your wealth,
>   and with the firstfruits
>   of your harvest;
> Then your barns
>   will be filled to capacity,
> and your wine vats
>   will spill over with new wine. (Prov. 3:9–10)

The author of this proverb calls on his audience to give proper honor to Yahweh the LORD OF THE COVENANT. As a consequence, they may expect material blessings. The implication is clear: Yahweh alone is the source of these blessings. To demand the author of a proverbial statement to explicitly line out the conclusion of his premise would require him to betray the essence of a proverb's literary distinctive, which resides in its provocative nature. Explicitly stating every aspect of a desired conclusion to a proverbial proposition would substitute pedantic prose for poetic creativity and originality. Far from being properly characterized as secularistic in nature, a covenantal perspective permeates the book of Proverbs.

A Covenantal Perspective

A much more accurate view of the theology of Proverbs may be gained from a covenantal perspective. The wise sayings of the book are not presented in a vacuum. They are not purely moralistic aphorisms. Instead, they are steeped in theistic assumptions. These wise observations about how the world works assume that God the Creator is none other than Yahweh, the LORD OF THE COVENANT.

The reality of a covenantal relationship lies at the root of the truths found in this book. In the approximately one hundred proverbs in which God is mentioned, all but a dozen use the covenant name *Yahweh*. Furthermore, this naming of God in one hundred out of the approximately eight hundred verses in Proverbs represents a higher percentage in the use of God's name than any other book in the Bible. The conclusion has been well expressed:

As far as terminology goes, then, the book belongs to the covenant people, and God is the God who revealed His name to Moses.[74]

Quite remarkable is the coordination of admonitions in the book of Proverbs with the legislation of the original covenantal documents as preserved in the books of Exodus through Deuteronomy. A person would be hard-pressed to find a single principle of a moral character in Proverbs that contradicts the legislation of the Pentateuch. From a more positive perspective, the affirmations regarding the various aspects of human life dealt with in Proverbs coordinate appropriately with the legislation of the Pentateuch. Whether speaking of commercial dealings, marital relations, or worship foci, Proverbs and covenant law conform closely to each other. This fact in itself should have the effect of confirming the covenantal context of Proverbs.

This perspective becomes more obvious when other aspects central to the book are examined. These factors include the fear of the COVENANT LORD, trust in the COVENANT LORD, and instruction that comes from the COVENANT LORD.

The Fear of the COVENANT LORD

As previously noted, this summarizing motto opens and closes the book of Proverbs, and is repeated in substance at many other points: "The fear of the COVENANT LORD is the beginning of knowledge" (Prov. 1:7).[75] The concept appears in every major portion of the book except the section that records the words of Agur and Lemuel, which is one of the briefest sections of the book (30:1–31:9). By far the most occurrences of the phrase appear in the first two major sections of the book. It appears six times in the introductory chapters (Prov. 1–9), nine times in the major collection of the proverbs of Solomon (10:1–22:16), and three times in the remainder of the book (22:17–31:31), making a total of eighteen times. The phrase brackets the introductory chapters (1:7; 9:10) as well as the entirety of the book itself (1:7; 31:30).

---

74. Kidner, *Proverbs*, 33.

75. As previously noted, the phrase occurs in Proverbs 1:7, 29; 2:5; 3:7; 8:13; 9:10; 10:27; 14:2, 26–27; 15:16, 33; 16:6; 19:23; 22:4; 23:17; 24:21; 31:30 (18 times).

Proverbs encourages the cultivation of this "fear of the LORD" in its introductory chapters (Prov. 1–9). A person may set himself on a path to increase his fear of the LORD. Three "if" clauses explain what will lead to an increase of the fear of the LORD:

> If you
>> receive my words
>> treasure my commandments
>> make your ear pay close attention to wisdom
>> strain your soul to seek understanding
> If you
>> cry out for comprehension
>> raise your voice for understanding
> If you
>> seek her as gold
>> search for her as hidden treasure
> Then you
>> will come to understand the fear of the LORD
>> will discover the knowledge of God.
> For the LORD
>> gives wisdom
> and from his mouth
>> come knowledge and understanding. (Prov. 2:1–6)

Gladly receiving God's words and treasuring his commandments provides the only way to increase in wisdom and the fear of the LORD (Prov. 2:1, 5). Only by God's gift through the words of his mouth may wisdom become a person's possession (2:6).

This clearly stated principle of the dependence on revelation for the increase of wisdom finds significant repetition at the end of Proverbs (Prov. 30:1–6).[76] The wise sayings of both Agur and Lemuel are described as an "oracle," which places the proverbs in the same category as prophetic revelations coming directly from God (Prov. 30:1; 31:1; cf. Isa. 13:1; Jer. 23:33–38; Nah. 1:1; Hab. 1:1; Zech. 9:1; Mal. 1:1). Nothing in terms of divine authority is lacking in the proverbs of Scripture.

---

76. For a fuller development of the significance of these verses in relating wisdom to revelation, see Waltke, *Proverbs 15–31*, 464–77.

This divine wisdom comes from the "flawless" Word of God. The image is that of metal that has been "refined" or "smelted" so that it has absolutely no admixture of corrupting soil (Prov. 30:5). Because of its origin in the LORD himself, the consequent admonition comes with strongest force: "Do not add to his words, or he will rebuke you and prove you a liar" (30:6 NIV). Based on the "Do not add" command in the lawbook of Deuteronomy (cf. Deut. 4:2; 12:32), this principle consummates in the new covenant with the identical "Do not add" command that concludes the book of Revelation:

> I warn everyone who hears the words of the prophecy of this book: If anyone adds anything to them, God will add to him the plagues described in this book. And if anyone takes words away from this book of prophecy, God will take away from him his share in the tree of life and in the holy city, which are described in this book. (Rev. 22:18–19 NIV)

Often it is suggested that this "fear of the LORD" has been reduced simply to a pious respect for God. But as one commentator observes, there is "no indication that the concept has become so bland in Proverbs or that it has lost the connotation of real fear."[77] In an insightful analysis of the impact of the fear of the LORD, this commentator states:

> The term "fear" allows for a range of pertinent emotions. . . . One person may worry about consequences, another may be uneasy about divine disapproval without thinking about retribution, and yet another may be in trepidation before the otherness of the holy. At the very start, a God-fearing child may simply worry that God will punish him for misdeeds.[78]

A most essential point to note about the "fear of the LORD" in Proverbs is that the one to be feared is "Yahweh," God of the patriarchs, LORD OF THE COVENANT. As one commentator indicates, "in the phrase 'the fear of Yahweh' it is the word 'Yahweh,' implying uniqueness in the divine realm, which is the important and decisive word."[79]

---

77. Fox, *Proverbs 1–9*, 70.
78. Ibid.
79. Whybray, *Survey*, 140, quoting A. Meinhold.

Acknowledging his own ignorance of wisdom (Prov. 30:2–3a), Agur underscores the fact that all true wisdom must focus on the knowledge of the Holy One (30:3b).

In summary, one commentator notes: "The statement that the fear of the Lord was the beginning of wisdom was Israel's most special possession."[80] Quite remarkable is the fact that this broad-ranging statement of principle serves as the motto for a book filled with very individualistic, practical instructions.[81]

In terms of its ongoing significance in the life of God's people, this phrase "fear of the LORD" makes vivid appearances in certain New Testament passages. God gave a period of peace throughout Judea, Galilee, and Samaria, and the Christians were "going on in the fear of the Lord" (πορευομένη τῷ φόβῳ τοῦ κυρίου—Acts 9:31). As a consequence of living in this way, the church experienced edification, the comfort of the Holy Spirit, and multiplication of numbers. These associated experiences suggest that "going on in the fear of the LORD" did not indicate a crippling anxiety. Instead, this "fear of the LORD" inspired vigorous activity that led to great blessings for the church.

One other New Testament passage speaks of fear among the people in connection with the exaltation of the name of the Lord Jesus. When in Ephesus certain Israelite sons of a high priest attempted to imitate Paul in casting out an evil spirit, the man with the evil spirit overpowered them, which caused Judeans and Greeks to fear, and the name of the Lord Jesus was magnified (Acts 19:17). In this case, the fear of the Lord is specifically related to the name of the Lord Jesus. For by his resurrection he has been established as Lord, so that he is the one that should be feared.

Trust in the COVENANT LORD

This principle of "trust in the LORD" may appear to contradict the idea of the "fear of the LORD" as previously developed. Yet the two concepts complement each other perfectly. People may fear an officer of the law because of the power he possesses over their lives,

80. Gerhard von Rad, *Wisdom in Israel* (London: SCM Press, 1972), 68.
81. Ibid., 69.

while at the same time trusting him to protect them from numerous evils. So *fear* and *trust* are not alien concepts.

The unity of these two perspectives of trust and fear in relation to Yahweh is vivified in the account of Israel's exodus from Egypt. What a spectacular scene that must have been! The Red Sea opening, the people passing through the waters on dry land, and the army of Pharaoh destroyed as the waters returned. Scripture records the people's response:

> When the Israelites saw the great power the LORD displayed against the Egyptians, the people feared the LORD and put their trust in him and in Moses his servant. (Ex. 14:31 NIV)

Simultaneously the people "feared the LORD" and "put their trust in him." The awesome events they witnessed would certainly foster fear of the LORD. How could they do otherwise? At the same time, it was the power of Yahweh their Redeemer that was manifest. So they trusted the one in whom they stood in awe.

This key factor of wisdom is summarized in the familiar words of Proverbs:

> Trust in Yahweh
> > with all your heart,
> > and on your [own] understanding
> do not lean.
> In all your ways
> > acknowledge him,
> > and he shall make straight
> your paths. (Prov. 3:5–6)

Several factors may be noted regarding this key verse in Proverbs. First, the word *trust* (בְּטַח) has the primary significance of maintaining confidence, experiencing security. Several other passages in Proverbs use this same term:

> Keep sound wisdom and discretion . . . . Then you will walk on *securely*. (Prov. 3:21, 23)

The one who finds his *security* in Yahweh, he is blessed. (Prov. 16:20)

The fear of man
    will bring a snare,
but the one who *puts his confidence* in Yahweh
    will be kept safe. (Prov. 29:25)

So the wise person is one who puts no confidence in himself or anyone else but only and altogether in Yahweh alone.

Second, this confidence must be placed specifically in Yahweh, the COVENANT LORD of his people. He has shown himself faithful to the words of his covenant across the generations. So people should put their confidence in Yahweh and in no mere figment of human imagination.

Third, the word *all* occurs twice in these two verses. A person's confidence must be altogether in the LORD. Not one bit of confidence may be directed otherwise. In addition, the LORD must be acknowledged in all of a person's ways. No area of life can be lived in separation from him.

In times of outer prosperity and blessing, you should trust in the LORD and the LORD alone as the source of all your blessings. Whenever trials and tribulations arise, the proper response is again to trust in the LORD.

To be effective in providing wise direction for life, this trust in the COVENANT LORD must be embraced with the whole heart and include all of a person's ways. Otherwise, it will do little good. An instructive contrast between the fear of man and trusting in the LORD is found in Proverbs 29:25 NIV:

Fear of man
    will prove to be a snare,
But whoever trusts in the LORD
    is kept safe.

Many frustrations and failures in life will come when a person leans on his own wisdom and resources while simultaneously attempting to manifest trust in the LORD.

Instruction from the COVENANT LORD

Beyond these basic principles of fearing the COVENANT LORD and simultaneously trusting him may be found all the various gems of practical instruction in Proverbs. Directions for life in this book do not come in a sequential narrative. Instead, the book presents small cameos of daily life in ways that communicate God's truth about all the various situations that a person may face.

Yet larger themes also permeate this book of wisdom. Three topics in particular receive special notice as rudimentary factors of life: creation, the family, and work. Each of these themes has massive significance in defining the way of wisdom for the individual and for human society.

Regarding Creation

Creation has been generally recognized as a major theme of the wisdom literature of the Old Testament.[82] "Since for the Hebrews the world was a created order, held and governed by God, it could never be regarded as self-existent, nor could it for one moment be understood apart from God."[83] According to another scholar who has spent a lifetime studying wisdom literature, *wisdom* may be defined as "the quest for self-understanding in terms of relationships with things, people and the Creator."[84] Another study in wisdom theology affirms:

> Wisdom theology is creation theology. That conclusion is something all can and do agree with. Wisdom does work within this sphere, rather than in the area of the covenant tradition.[85]

---

82. Cf. the work of Leo G. Perdue, *Wisdom and Creation: The Theology of Wisdom Literature* (Nashville: Abingdon, 1994), in which the whole book is given over to this subject.

83. Gerhard von Rad, "The Theological Problem of the Old Testament Doctrine of Creation," in *The Problem of the Hexateuch and Other Essays* (Edinburgh: Oliver & Boyd, 1966), 132.

84. James L. Crenshaw, "Method in Determining Wisdom Influence upon 'Historical' Literature," in *Urgent Advice and Probing Questions: Collected Writings on Old Testament Wisdom* (Macon, GA: Mercer University Press, 1995), 315.

85. Roland Murphy, "Wisdom in the Old Testament," in *ABD*, 6:924, col. 2.

It is indeed true that wisdom theology finds its foundation in creation theology. Rather than attempting to explain or to justify Job's sufferings, God's wisdom points to the mysterious source of the snowflake and the depth-churning activity of the leviathan (Job 37:5–6; 41:30–34). "Remember your Creator" is the final reminder from Ecclesiastes to all the peoples of the world struggling with the frustrations of life (Eccl. 12:1). The king as exemplar of humanity in the Song of Songs experiences the renewal of humanity's relationship at creation between man and woman, all placed in the setting of a paradisical garden comparable to the original Eden.

But the idea that "creation theology" somehow excludes the simultaneous presence of "covenant theology" introduces a false dilemma. Yahweh is the God of the Covenant, and Yahweh permeates the book of Proverbs. None other than Yahweh possessed wisdom at the beginning of creation (Prov. 8:22). Rich and poor have this in common: Yahweh is Maker of them all (22:2). Yahweh gives sight to the eyes of both the poor and their oppressor (29:13). Even the basic structure of Proverbs in which a father instructs his son is deeply embedded in covenant theology. Just as the basic covenant document of Deuteronomy directs the father in his responsibility to impress the commandments of the covenant on his children, talking of them when sitting at home or walking in the way, so the book of Proverbs repeatedly charges the father to instruct his son in the ways of wisdom (cf. Deut. 6:6–9).

Sad to say, even as the modern world of academia affirms the foundational role of the theology of creation in biblical wisdom, it immediately embalms Scripture's creation doctrine in pagan mythology. Says one commentator: "Drawing on a rich variety of creation myths and their root metaphors, the sages depicted God as the creator of heaven and earth."[86] In expanding on the pivotal role of these mythological concepts in the biblical world of wisdom, this author asserts that in Proverbs 8 wisdom is portrayed as a "fertility goddess whose lovers include monarchs," while Yahweh is the "father and mother of wisdom."[87] Because in ancient Near Eastern literature myths are "replete with stories of female goddesses who take on

---

86. Perdue, *Wisdom and Creation*, 79.
87. Ibid., 89–90.

human lovers," in Proverbs wisdom "invites humans to become her lovers and to experience the intimacies of her embrace."[88] By reading the testimony to creation in the wisdom books through the twisted lens of mythology, the realities of God's creation are distorted by the degenerative unrealities of myth. Following hard on this scheme of things, the modern myth of evolution mutes all testimony to God's glory as witnessed by the heavens, the earth, the sea, and the God-inspired Scriptures.

People must live out their lives within the context of the cold, hard facts of reality rather than of the unrealistic fantasies of mythology. Thankfully, nothing unrealistic finds a home in the biblical proverbs. To the contrary, everything in Proverbs is "down-to-earth." The knowledgeable control of all creation by Solomon (1 Kings 4:29–34) finds its reflection in the varied forms and substance of the book of Proverbs.

Regarding the Family

A second, larger theme that so obviously permeates Proverbs is the concept of the family. The place of the family in Proverbs has been readily recognized as a major concept in current biblical research. In reconstructing the development of wisdom literature in Israel, one scholar notes the prominence of the family:

> In all probability, the central place of instruction was the family, and the curriculum consisted of folk proverbs, the product of long observation. At what point the shift to formal education occurred remains a mystery.[89]

Another scholar comments that the commitment necessary for the development of wisdom materials "needed to be backed up by a

---

88. Ibid., 89.

89. James L. Crenshaw, "The Perils of Specializing in Wisdom," in *Urgent Advice and Probing Questions: Collected Writings on Old Testament Wisdom* (Macon, GA: Mercer University Press, 1995), 595. Waltke, *Proverbs 1–15*, 58–63, makes a distinction between the "Setting of Composition" and the "Setting of Dissemination." He concludes that the proverbs "originated in a court setting" (61). At the same time, he finds strong support for ongoing education of youth "in a home setting" (62).

willingness to listen to, and heed, the teaching of the individual's parents."[90] Further contemporary confirmation of the priority of the family as the basic school of wisdom in Israel appears in an additional affirmation that the father was responsible for teaching youth their responsibilities "as future heads of families," and that the teaching of the mother was "also authoritative."[91] Repeatedly in Proverbs the father and mother are joined as co-instructors of wisdom for their children as well as sharers in the consequences of the wisdom or the folly of their offspring (Prov. 1:8; 6:20; 10:1; 15:20; 20:20; 23:22, 25; 28:24). Speculation has pointed to subsequent "schools" eventually replacing or supplementing the instruction of the parents, but no evidence of this form of imparting wisdom may be found in Proverbs.

Few other topics receive the all-around treatment in Proverbs as does marriage and family. In numerous extended sections, the godly woman, the mother, and the wife as home-builder stand over against the adulterous woman as the home-breaker. The numberless reminders to parents regarding their duty to instruct their children, not to speak of the very format of the book itself as a father's instruction to his son, underscore the role of the family as the foundation stone and source of transgenerational wisdom. The repeated charge to children to love, respect, and obey their parents completes the picture of the model family in Proverbs.

Implied in this parent-child relationship is the unity of husband and wife. These two people are truly one, standing together in facing all the challenges of life. This unity is not a one-way street in which the husband dictates the wise way of life. Their mutual interaction ensures the discovery of the way of wisdom together. Nabal the fool dies from a sudden stroke of the heart because he was not united to his wife in the wisdom she displayed toward David (1 Sam. 25:14–38).

This unity involves the intimacy of oneness in the sexual relationship. The husband drinks deeply from the well of the woman that he alone possesses. He fully satisfies his sexual urges with the breasts of

90. R. E. Clements, "Wisdom and Old Testament Theology," in *Wisdom in Ancient Israel: Essays in Honour of J. A. Emerton*, ed. John Day, Robert P. Gordon, and H. G. M. Williamson (Cambridge: Cambridge University Press, 1995), 281.
91. Perdue, *Wisdom and Creation*, 70.

the wife of his youth. The significance of this element in the family unit receives repeated underscoring in the stringent warnings against the adulteress, the home-breaker. From the positive perspective, the godly woman appears as the key to solidarity in the family. Her husband, her children, her society rise up and call her blessed.

The Creator originated the order as well as the ardor that has always characterized relationships between male and female humans. As a consequence, all aberrations from this created order must be understood as foolish. Polygamy, homosexuality, promiscuity, adultery, same-sex marriage, transgender explorations all contradict the Creator's purpose in the relationships of men to women. Only when in accord with the wisdom of God's revealed Word may divorce be regarded as a way of wisdom rather than folly (cf. Matt. 5:32; 19:9; 1 Cor. 7:15).

But where is the world today in terms of its hearing and heeding the wisdom of Proverbs regarding family structures and lifestyles? Few indeed are the husbands and wives who live out their entire married lives "forsaking all others" in their exclusive love for one another. Where are the parents that disciple and discipline their children, and where the children that eagerly absorb every drop of wisdom that comes from the lips of their God-given father and mother? If the world will hear and heed, as Proverbs so readily admonishes, wisdom's way will show the way.

Regarding Work

A third theme of permeating significance in Proverbs is the topic of work. A series of proverbs underscores the stark contrast between the lazy and the diligent:

> Lazy hands
>   make a man poor,
> but diligent hands
>   bring wealth. (Prov. 10:4 NIV)

> The hand of the diligent
>   will rule,
> while the slothful
>   will be put to forced labor. (Prov. 12:24 ESV)

Whoever is slothful
   will not roast his game,
but the diligent man
   will get precious wealth. (Prov. 12:27 ESV)

The soul of the sluggard craves
   and gets nothing,
while the soul of the diligent
   is richly supplied. (Prov. 13:4 ESV)

The person who gives himself over to six good days of labor stands in starkest contrast with the tragicomic character, the proverbial sluggard. Hinged to his bed, pleading for just a little more sleep, with his field unplowed and his house falling down around him, the lazybones cannot lift his spoon to his mouth with his food right in front of him.

But making fun isn't intended simply to be funny. Slothfulness, living like a sloth, is serious sin. The sloth is one of those creatures whose main function in this world may be to teach humanity a lesson about laziness. Equipped with firmly set claws, the pear-shaped, overweight sloth spends most of his life hanging upside down from the same tree without moving a muscle. According to some reports, the sloth may sleep fifteen to eighteen hours a day, and it may take a week for his subdormant system to digest a single meal.

But the Lord of the Covenant has brought humanity into a contract that requires work, work, and more work. Six days of labor each week are the Lord's expectations. The wise woman in Proverbs rises before dawn to provide food for her family. The wise man learns from the ant who is never idle, storing up food for the coming winter. He works his land, he plows his field, he scrubs the stall of his ox, however troublesome it may be. All his labor is done in fulfillment of the original mandate for humanity to "subdue the earth" to the glory of God (Gen. 1:28).

Conclusion

In the end, taking the time to understand the proverbs will richly reward every effort. From a positive perspective, the proverbs can lead

113

a person into the enjoyment of the fullness of life with the LORD OF THE COVENANT, both in this life and in that which is to come. At the same time, the proverbs can keep a soul from sin and save him from great grief.

The brevity of statement that characterizes most of the proverbs must not be misunderstood as shallow reflections that fail to deal seriously with the difficult challenges of life. Instead, the proverbs often require serious meditation before a person comprehends the truth stated so memorably.

What is wisdom's ultimate answer to these days full of confusion because of human folly? The answer can be found only in the One "greater than Solomon" who is in our midst (Matt. 12:42; Luke 11:31).[92] He is wisdom personified, namely, "Christ, in whom are hidden all the treasures of wisdom and knowledge" (Col. 2:2c–3 NIV). How hollow, how confusing and confounding are all other answers devised by humanity today. Only a sincere return to the triune God of creation and redemption can save this world from its blindness as it stumbles along in its man-made madness across the ages.

So the book of Proverbs stands as a perpetual reminder of the absolute necessity of divine wisdom for every situation that a person may face as he makes his way through life. The imparting of divine wisdom in its most practical and memorable form provides sufficient guidance for all the different challenges faced in life, whether they be challenges of marriage and family, business and commerce, or personal relationships with God and humanity.

SELECTED BIBLIOGRAPHY FOR PROVERBS

Albright, W. F. "Some Canaanite-Phoenician Sources of Hebrew Wisdom." In *Wisdom in Israel and in the Ancient Near East*, edited by M. Noth and D. Winton Thomas, 1–15. Leiden: Brill, 1955.
Blank, Sheldon H. "Proverbs." In *The Interpreter's Dictionary of the Bible*, 936–40. Vol. K–Q. New York: Abingdon, 1962.
Bridges, Charles. *An Exposition of Proverbs*. Grand Rapids: Zondervan, 1959.

---

92. For a useful summary of the ways in which Jesus Christ manifests himself as "greater than Solomon," see Waltke, *Proverbs 1–15*, 131–33.

Clements, R. E. "Wisdom and Old Testament Theology." In *Wisdom in Ancient Israel: Essays in Honour of J. A. Emerton*, edited by John Day, Robert P. Gordon, and H. G. M. Williamson, 269–86. Cambridge: Cambridge University Press, 1995.

Crenshaw, James L. "Method in Determining Wisdom Influence upon 'Historical' Literature." In *Urgent Advice and Probing Questions: Collected Writings on Old Testament Wisdom*, 312–25. Macon, GA: Mercer University Press, 1995.

———. "The Perils of Specializing in Wisdom." In *Urgent Advice and Probing Questions: Collected Writings on Old Testament Wisdom*, 586–96. Macon, GA: Mercer University Press, 1995.

———. *Urgent Advice and Probing Questions: Collected Writings on Old Testament Wisdom*. Macon, GA: Mercer University Press, 1995.

Day, John, Robert P. Gordon, and H. G. M. Williamson, eds. *Wisdom in Ancient Israel: Essays in Honour of J. A. Emerton*. Cambridge: Cambridge University Press, 1995.

Delitzsch, Franz. *Biblical Commentary on the Proverbs of Solomon*. Vols. 1–2. Grand Rapids: Eerdmans, 1950.

Dell, Katharine. *'Get Wisdom, Get Insight': An Introduction to Israel's Wisdom Literature*. London: Darton, Longman, and Ford, 2000.

Fox, Michael V. *Proverbs 1–9: A New Translation with Introduction and Commentary*. AB 18A. New York: Doubleday, 2000.

———. *Proverbs 10–31: A New Translation with Introduction and Commentary*. AB 18B. New Haven, CT: Yale University Press, 2009.

Genung, John Franklin. "Proverbs, Book of." In *The International Standard Bible Encyclopaedia*, 4:2471–76. Grand Rapids: Eerdmans, 1936.

Hubbard, David A. *Proverbs*. Preacher's Commentary, Old Testament 15. Nashville: Thomas Nelson, 1989.

Jobes, Karen. "Sophia Christology: The Way of Wisdom?" In *The Way of Wisdom: Essays in Honor of Bruce K. Waltke*, edited by J. I. Packer and Sven K. Soderlund, 226–50. Grand Rapids: Zondervan, 2000.

Kidner, Derek. *The Proverbs: An Introduction and Commentary*. Downers Grove, IL: InterVarsity Press, 1969.

———. "Wisdom Literature of the Old Testament." In *New Perspectives on the Old Testament*, edited by J. Barton Payne, 117–30. London: Word Books, 1970.

———. *Wisdom to Live By: An Introduction to the Old Testament's Wisdom Books of Proverbs, Job and Ecclesiastes*. Leicester, UK: Inter-Varsity Press, 1985.

Kitchen, John A. *Proverbs*. Mentor Commentary. Ross-shire, Scotland: Christian Focus, 2006.

Kitchen, Kenneth A. "Proverbs." In *The Biblical Expositor*, edited by Carl F. H. Henry, 2:71–93. Philadelphia: A. J. Holman, 1960.

Longman, Tremper, III. *How to Read Proverbs*. Downers Grove, IL: InterVarsity Press, 2002.

———. *Proverbs*. Grand Rapids: Baker Academic, 2006.

Mayhue, Richard. *Practicing Proverbs*. Ross-shire, Scotland: Christian Focus, 2004.

McKane, William. *Proverbs: A New Approach*. Philadelphia: Westminster, 1977.

Murphy, Roland E. *Proverbs*. WBC 22. Nashville: Thomas Nelson, 1998.

———. "Wisdom in the Old Testament." In *ABD*, 6:920–31.

———. *Wisdom Literature: Job, Proverbs, Ruth, Canticles, Ecclesiastes, and Esther*. Forms of the Old Testament Literature 13. Grand Rapids: Eerdmans, 1981.

Noth, M., and D. Winton Thomas, eds. *Wisdom in Israel and in the Ancient Near East*. Leiden: Brill, 1955.

Oesterley, W. O. E. *The Book of Proverbs with Introduction and Notes*. London: Methuen, 1929.

Perdue, Leo G. *Wisdom and Creation: The Theology of Wisdom Literature*. Nashville: Abingdon, 1994.

Pritchard, James B., ed. *Ancient Near Eastern Texts Relating to the Old Testament*. 3rd ed. Princeton, NJ: Princeton University Press, 1969.

Rad, Gerhard von. "The Theological Problem of the Old Testament Doctrine of Creation." In *The Problem of the Hexateuch and Other Essays*, 131–43. Edinburgh: Oliver & Boyd, 1966.

———. *Wisdom in Israel*. London: SCM Press, 1972.

Robertson, Archibald, ed. *Select Writings and Letters of Athanasius, Bishop of Alexandria*. In *Athanasius: Select Works and Letters*, ed. Philip Schaff and Henry Wace. Nicene and Post-Nicene Fathers 4, 2nd ser. Peabody, MA: Hendrickson, 1994.

Schaff, Philip, and Henry Wace, eds. *Athanasius: Select Works and Letters*. Nicene and Post-Nicene Fathers 4, 2nd ser. Peabody, MA: Hendrickson, 1994.

Scott, R. B. Y. *Proverbs, Ecclesiastes: Introduction, Translation, and Notes*. AB 18. Garden City, NY: Doubleday, 1965.

———. "The Study of Wisdom Literature." *Interpretation* 24, 1 (1970): 20–45.

————. *The Way of Wisdom in the Old Testament*. New York: Macmillan, 1971.

Vanderwaal, Cornelius. *Job-Song of Songs*. Vol. 4 of *Search the Scriptures*. St. Catharines, ON: Paideia Press, 1978.

Vawter, Bruce. "Prov 8:22: Wisdom and Creation." *JBL* 99, 2 (1980): 205–16.

Waltke, Bruce K. *The Book of Proverbs: Chapters 1–15*. NICOT. Grand Rapids: Eerdmans, 2004.

————. *The Book of Proverbs: Chapters 15–31*. NICOT. Grand Rapids: Eerdmans, 2005.

Whybray, R. N. *The Book of Proverbs: A Survey of Modern Study*. Leiden: Brill, 1995.

————. *Proverbs*. NCBC. Grand Rapids: Eerdmans, 1994.

————. *Wisdom in Proverbs: The Concept of Wisdom in Proverbs 1–9*. Studies in Biblical Theology 45. Naperville, IL: Alec R. Allenson, 1965.

Job
How to Puzzle

        c. Bildad's First Speech (Job 8:1–22)

        d. Job's Response to Bildad's First Speech
          (Job 9:1–10:22)

        e. Zophar's First Speech (Job 11:1–20)

        f. Job's Response to Zophar's First Speech
          (Job 12:1–14:22)

    3. Round Two (Job 15–21)

        a. Eliphaz's Second Speech (Job 15:1–35)

        b. Job's Response to Eliphaz's Second Speech
          (Job 16:1–17:16)

        c. Bildad's Second Speech (Job 18:1–22)

        d. Job's Response to Bildad's Second Speech
          (Job 19:1–29)

        e. Zophar's Second Speech (Job 20:1–29)

        f. Job's Response to Zophar's Second Speech
          (Job 21:1–34)

    4. Round Three (Job 22–27)

        a. Eliphaz's Third Speech (Job 22:1–30)

        b. Job's Response to Eliphaz's Third Speech
          (Job 23:1–24:25)

        c. Bildad's Third Speech (Job 25:1–6)

        d. Job's Response to Bildad's Third Speech
          (Job 26:1–14)

        e. Job's Final Statement to His Friends (Job 27:1–23)

    5. Job's Closing Soliloquy (Job 28–31)

        a. Job Searches for Wisdom's Ultimate Source
          (Job 28:1–28)

        b. Job Reminisces about His Former Blessings and
          Puzzles over His Current Distresses
          (Job 29:1–30:31)

        c. Job Pronounces a Self-Maledictory Oath
          (Job 31:1–40)

C. The Speeches of Elihu (Job 32–37)

D. The Speeches of the LORD (Yahweh) (Job 38:1–42:6)

    1. The LORD's First Speech (Job 38:1–40:2)

    2. Job's Modest Response (Job 40:3–5)

INTRODUCTION

Have you really read Job?

> If I did not have Job! . . . I do not read him as one reads another book, with the eyes, but I lay the book, as it were, on my heart and read it with the eyes of the heart, in a clairvoyance interpreting the specifics in the most diverse ways. . . . Every word by him is food and clothing and healing for my wretched soul. Now a word by him arouses me from my lethargy and awakens new restlessness; now it calms the sterile raging within me, stops the dreadfulness in the mute nausea of my passion. Have you really read Job?[1]

Have you really read Job? Many people have read Job. Søren Kierkegaard obviously read Job. Karl Barth the theologian read Job (*Church Dogmatics IV/3.1*, 383–461). John Calvin the Reformer read Job (*Sermons on Job*). Archibald MacLeish the playwright read Job (*J. B.*). C. G. Jung the psychiatrist read Job (*Answer to Job*). G. K. Chesterton the poet and essayist read Job (*Introduction to the Book of Job*).

All these people read Job. But have you read Job? Have you really read Job?

The book of Job is all about wisdom—about how people must respond wisely to the most puzzling circumstances of life. Job does

---

1. Søren Kierkegaard, *Fear and Trembling; Repetition*, ed. and trans. Howard V. Hong and Edna Hong (Princeton, NJ: Princeton University Press, 1983), 204–5, as quoted in Craig G. Bartholomew and Ryan P. O'Dowd, *Old Testament Wisdom Literature: A Theological Introduction* (Downers Grove, IL: IVP Academic, 2011), 156–57.

not give all the answers to life's problems. But to the wise, it teaches "how to puzzle."

Life consists of many challenges. Among the greatest challenges faced eventually by Everyman is the question of how to puzzle over troubles, calamities, and disasters as they inevitably occur.

The book of Job provides insight into the question of how to puzzle. To vivify the process of puzzling, this ancient book of wisdom wrestles with this basic life question by using the literary technique of dialogue in prose and poetry. God dialogues with Satan, Job dialogues with his friends, God dialogues with Job. In the end, profound and appropriate answers are given not to the questions, but to the larger question of how to puzzle.

The present work does not presume to provide all the answers on how to respond to life's deepest puzzlements. But perhaps some greater awareness of God's wisdom on how to puzzle will emerge through a fresh and further consideration of the message of Job.

In exploring the book of Job, this work will consider the following:

- Introductory Matters Essential to a Proper Understanding of the Book
- An Overview of the Development of the Book
- The Ultimate Message of the Book

INTRODUCTORY MATTERS ESSENTIAL TO A PROPER UNDERSTANDING OF THE BOOK

Basic introductory questions regarding the book of Job include date and authorship; literary form; integrity and structure; and outlines of the book's content. This treatment of introductory questions will also explore a distinctive literary device of the book of Job: the use of figures of speech.

Date and Authorship

At the outset, a principal distinction must be made between the time of the events recorded in Job and the date of the book's composition. As in the case of many other pieces of literature, the events presented in the book need not necessarily have occurred in the same time frame as the writing of the material.

Time of the Events

Several factors point to the patriarchal period as the time of the events recorded in Job. The regular offering of sacrifice by Job on behalf of his family suggests a period before the enactment of Mosaic legislation regulating Israel's worship practices (Job 1:5). The calculation of wealth by cattle and servants also suggests a patriarchal setting (1:3; 42:12). The absence of any specified center of worship in Job points in the same direction. In addition, the longevity of Job properly suits the patriarchal period. According to the conclusion of the book, Job lived 140 years after the restoration of all his losses (42:16). The length of his life appropriately fits only the patriarchal era of old covenant history.

The historicity of the events reported in Job has been regularly questioned, partly because of its poetic form. But nothing in the nature of poetry inherently excludes historicity. No good reason exists to deny the historical character of Job. The prophecy of Ezekiel mentions by name Noah, Daniel, and Job as men of righteousness (Ezek. 14:14, 20). The New Testament gives specific witness to Job's historical character. The book of James first refers to the prophets "as an example of patience in the face of suffering," though James names none of the prophets who patiently endured their trials (James 5:10 NIV). But he names Job to further establish his point: "You have heard of Job's perseverance and have seen what the Lord finally brought about" (5:11 NIV). The historicity of Job in his suffering need not be denied any more than the historicity of the unnamed prophets who also suffered.[2]

---

2. Tremper Longman III, *Job* (Grand Rapids: Baker Academic, 2012), 34, states that Job is "not a part of the Bible's redemptive history, which records events in space and time when God accomplishes and applies his grace to his people. . . . The truthfulness of the insights conveyed by the book of Job does not depend on the actual existence of Job." He concludes that in his opinion "Job is not a historical person, or at best there was a well-known ancient sufferer named Job." Yet not considering for the moment the atoning character of Christ's suffering, it makes a great deal of difference to know that our Lord actually suffered. In a similar way, suffering saints will receive much greater encouragement

Date of Composition

Proposed dates for the composition of Job range across a thousand years. As previously indicated, the period of the book's events need not determine the circumstances of the book's composition. The idea that Job represents a translation of a late Aramaic original has virtually no evidence to support it, and is basically untenable, particularly "in light of the greatness of the Hebrew poetry of Job, rich as it is in strong rhythmic effects, virtuosic wordplay and sound-play—qualities that a translation would be very unlikely to exhibit."[3] Hypothetically, the book could have originated "at any time between Moses and Ezra."[4] Arguments for an early or a late dating are not conclusive. As one commentator has noted, the book of Job "is no prisoner of time."[5]

Yet as a brilliant piece of wisdom literature, the book may be appropriately regarded as arising during the days when wisdom flourished in Israel. The time of Solomon would be the most likely era for the composition of a wisdom book of this sort.

Literary Form

The poetry of Job is essentially based on the ordinary form of semantic parallelism. Yet as has been well said, "No other biblical poet . . . exhibits the virtuosity in the command of rich synonymity that is displayed by the Job poet."[6]

The book takes on the form of an epic poem. Two narrative sections (Job 1–2; 42:7–17) provide literary brackets for the larger middle section, which is composed of interactive speeches, all in poetic form (3:1–42:6).[7]

---

to know that Job actually did experience his sufferings, and by God's grace was "more than conqueror." Longman subsequently analyzes the passage in James (280–81), but does not comment on the historicity of Job from the perspective of James.

3. Robert Alter, *The Wisdom Books: Job, Proverbs, and Ecclesiastes: A Translation with Commentary* (New York: W. W. Norton, 2010), 3.

4. Francis I. Andersen, *Job: An Introduction and Commentary*, TOTC (London: Inter-Varsity Press, 1976), 13.

5. Derek Kidner, *Wisdom to Live By: An Introduction to the Old Testament's Wisdom Books of Proverbs, Job and Ecclesiastes* (Leicester, UK: Inter-Varsity Press, 1985), 76.

6. Alter, *Wisdom Books*, 7.

7. James L. Crenshaw, *Old Testament Wisdom: An Introduction*, rev. and enl. ed. (Louisville: Westminster John Knox, 1998), 89, describes this bracketing of poetry with

Integrity and Structure

Questions regarding the integrity of the book of Job arise primarily because of the diversity of literary form and substance. A brief narrative section includes a prose dialogue in heaven between the LORD (Yahweh) and Satan, followed by an extended poetic dialogue on earth between Job and three friends.[8] A fourth friend suddenly appears with no antecedent warning, interjecting his evaluations of both Job and his other friends. The book ends with a dialogue between the LORD and Job, followed by a brief narrative conclusion in which the LORD finalizes the situation of Job and his three friends.

Is all this diversity to be regarded as a unity?

Additional questions regarding the integrity of the book have been raised in view of the abbreviated character of Bildad's final speech and the nonspeech of Zophar in the third round (Job 25:1–6). The legitimate role of the rhapsodic poem depicting the search for wisdom in terms of a mining expedition (Job 28) has raised questions regarding its role in the flow of the book. In addition, the LORD's speech to Job comes in two sections, with two separate responses from Job, which seems quite unusual.

---

prose as a "strange union of incompatible literary strata." Yet he proceeds to cite examples of this literary device among other sages of the ancient Near East. Crenshaw suggests that the epilogue "can be dispensed with altogether," since the poem ends appropriately with the speeches of God. To the contrary, Norman Whybray, *Job* (Sheffield, UK: Sheffield Academic, 1998), 11, observes: "The fact that the book begins in prose but continues in poetical form should occasion no question as regards unity of authorship. Prose is the most appropriate form for narrative: . . . It is equally appropriate that the remainder of the book, apart from the continuation and conclusion of the narrative in the Epilogue, should be in poetical form, for poetry is more suitable than prose for the expression of complex emotional scenes."

8. Cf. Brevard S. Childs, *Introduction to the Old Testament as Scripture* (London: SCM Press, 1979), 529, who notes that "no real consensus" has been reached regarding "the history of composition, authorship, or ultimate purpose" of these two major portions of the book. Childs sees several points of tension in a patient Job commended by God with a happy ending in contrast with a defiant Job rebuked by God in a context that repudiates the doctrine of just retribution and reward (529). But a great deal of this disparity can be explained in terms of Job's differing response to the LORD in contrast to his response to his friends, who accuse rather than comfort him. Job can accept from God's hand the good and the bad (Job 2:10). But he cannot endure having no answer to the accusing queries of his friends, which compels him to seek answers from the Almighty.

So is all this diverse material to be regarded as a unity, as a single literary production of a single individual? Or have many hands contributed to the complex form of the book? Did these diverse elements originate at the same time by the same author? Or are they the combined work of multiple authors and editors across decades or centuries?

Responses to supposed disunities may be found at the various critical points throughout the overview of the book that follows. Suffice it to say at this point that the seams binding the manuscript into one document are extremely strong. Connecting links naturally appear in statements, phrases, and structures deeply embedded in the material. As examples, Job's initial soliloquy with its intense death wish makes no sense apart from the opening narrative. The interacting dialogue with his three friends portrays Job's response in a manner that shows progression and seems quite feasible. The extended poem locating the source of wisdom in the fear of God connects naturally with the opening description of Job as a man who feared God (Job 28:28; cf. 1:1, 8). At the same time, this majestic poem provides a necessary interlude between the dialogue of Job with his three friends and the introduction of a fourth friend.

This fourth friend (Elihu), the youngest of the group, makes numerous allusions to the prior speeches of Job and his friends so that his comments suit well the circumstance created by Job's justifying himself as well as his friends' inability to convince Job of his wrongdoing (Job 32:1–5). In his final comments, Elihu provides a natural bridge to the appearance of the Almighty. He identifies phenomena of lightning and thunder that mark the arrival of God himself (37:1–5). Consequently, when the LORD speaks, he addresses Job "out of the storm" already anticipated by Elihu's speech (38:1). The twofold speeches of God followed by the twofold responses of Job provide a natural progression in the concluding narrative. The rebukes from the LORD to Job as well as to his three friends develop naturally out of the previous narratives.

All these various connecting comments and literary devices display a unity that confirms the integrity of the whole piece. The natural flow of one element into another binds the whole into a unity. The majesty, the beauty of the entire document attests to its wholeness as the work of a single inspired author. A joint authorial committee, though it might work ever so diligently, could never produce a poem of this literary quality.

Outlines of the Book

Outlines of Job may assist the reader in following the flow of the book. A basic outline and a detailed outline are as follows:

Basic Outline
- Narrative Prologue (Job 1–2)
- Job's Dialogue with His Three Friends (Job 3–31)
- The Speeches of Elihu (Job 32–37)
- The Speeches of the LORD (Yahweh) (Job 38:1–42:6)
- Narrative Epilogue (Job 42:7–17)

Detailed Outline
I. Narrative Prologue (Job 1–2)
   [No Further Word from Satan]
II. Job's Dialogue with His Three Friends (Job 3–31)
   A. Job's Opening Soliloquy (Job 3:1–26)
   B. Round One (Job 4–14)
      1. Eliphaz's First Speech (Job 4:1–5:27)
      2. Job's Response to Eliphaz's First Speech (Job 6:1–7:21)
      3. Bildad's First Speech (Job 8:1–22)
      4. Job's Response to Bildad's First Speech (Job 9:1–10:22)
      5. Zophar's First Speech (Job 11:1–20)
      6. Job's Response to Zophar's First Speech (Job 12:1–14:22)
   C. Round Two (Job 15–21)
      1. Eliphaz's Second Speech (Job 15:1–35)
      2. Job's Response to Eliphaz's Second Speech (Job 16:1–17:16)
      3. Bildad's Second Speech (Job 18:1–22)

A Distinctive Literary Device

Job's basic structure of narrative introduction and narrative conclusion encasing an extended poetic middle section is generally recognized (Job 1–2; 42:7–17; 3:1–42:6). But a major literary device that permeates the whole of the poetic section has seldom been properly appreciated for its crucial contribution to establishing the greatness of the book. This distinctive literary device in Job provides insight into the progress of the book's argument. At the same time, it serves to forcefully drive home the book's message.

That distinctive literary device is the use of more than 370 figures of speech, which in itself is an astounding number.[9] Yet despite the permeating character of these images, the reader experiences no sense of excessiveness in use. A number of these images are developed quite extensively, while others are grouped as multiple representations of a single truth. Still others are hardly noticed, since they provide only a passing glimpse into the point being communicated. These images are shaped by their varying contexts, and differ in flavor and intensity, so that the figures used by Job's friends sometimes manifest a harsher nature than those of Job himself. A climax is found in the vividness present in God's own descriptive pictures of the various creatures he has made, which display his indisputable wisdom.

The ability to make appropriate use of figures of speech serves as a sign of the wisdom that belongs only to God and man in their roles as kings, as rulers of creation. This kingly capacity to effectively employ figures of speech closely parallels the role of the parable and the proverb as a manifestation of regal control of creation. King Solomon displayed his wisdom by the composition of three thousand proverbs that described in succinct and memorable fashion the very essence of created realities, including the analysis of plants, mammals, birds, reptiles, and fish (1 Kings 4:32–33). Though a comical figure of tragic proportions, Samson, who served as judge before Solomon became king, displayed a similar capacity as a wisdom figure in his ability to compose riddles or proverbs that baffled his adversaries (Judg. 14:13–14, 18; 15:16). Job specifically calls the teaching of his friends "proverbs" (*meshalim*), even though he characterizes them as "proverbs of ashes" (Job 13:12).

---

9. Appreciation for this significant aspect of Job's poetry has been expressed in the work of Alter, *Wisdom Books*, 8: "The other chief resource deployed in the poetry that Job speaks is its extraordinary metaphoric inventiveness."

This distinctive ability to communicate in memorable form an insightful analysis of realities inherent in creation finds prophetic significance when the psalmist of Israel speaks of teaching by "parables" and "riddles" as a regal function anticipating Messiah (Ps. 78:1–2, 72). In his turn, the Gospel writer employs these very words of the psalmist to explain the parabolic teaching of King Jesus about the kingdom of God (Matt. 13:34–35). In conformity to this well-established tradition of Scripture, the book of Job displays its credentials as a piece of inspired wisdom literature by the extensive use of figures of speech throughout the book.

To properly appreciate the literary genius of the book of Job, we must consider the extent and force of its employment of figures of speech. The connection of these images to the progress of the argument of the book should also be noted. This perspective may be best achieved by following the development of the poetic sections of the book itself, noting first the three "rounds" of interaction between Job and his friends (Job 3–31), then the speeches of Elihu (Job 32–37), climaxing with the speeches of God (38:1–42:6). By following this method, a fuller appreciation of the book's message should be realized even as we recognize the critical role of figures of speech.

An Overview of the Development of the Book

Narrative Prologue (Job 1–2)

The prologue of the book (Job 1–2) sets a cosmic stage that serves as the basis for the book's larger poetic section (3:1–42:6). Without the setting provided by these opening chapters, the book would hang suspended in space and time. At the same time, the narrative form of the prologue underscores the historical reality of the events described. Job is no poetic fictional figure. He is a real person with real struggles and triumphs, as a New Testament writer affirms:

> You have heard of Job's perseverance and have seen what the Lord finally brought about. (James 5:11 NIV)

The opening phrases of the larger poetic section beg for a specific setting, which the prologue clearly provides: "After this, Job opened his

129

mouth and . . . said" (Job 3:1–2 NIV). This introductory "After this" requires an answer to the question, "After what?" To what circumstance is the book referring? It would be incomprehensible for Job to be suddenly introduced as he curses the day of his birth and exclaims, "May the day of my birth perish" (3:3 NIV). This drastic outcry demands a context that answers the question, "Why is this man so possessed by this severe death wish?" The prologue answers this question, and provides a basis for the dialogue contained in the next thirty-eight chapters. In the prologue, Job appears as a righteous man, the wealthiest man of the East. But a series of tragedies come without warning. Job loses all—his wealth, his sons and daughters, his physical health, the loyalty of his wife.

But Job does not lose his trust in God. "Yahweh gave, and Yahweh has taken away. Blessed be the name of Yahweh" (Job 1:21b). His wife cannot persuade him to curse God, in distinction from Eve's success in sharing the forbidden fruit with Adam (Job 2:9; Gen. 3:6).

Three friends arrive to comfort Job in this devastated condition. They sit in silence for seven days, until Job takes the initiative in beginning a dialogue.

Little does Job understand that he is the center of a cosmic contest between God and Satan. By his fidelity, Job displays that Yahweh's work of redemption has succeeded in delivering a fallen humanity from the domination of Satan.

So what factors in the prologue provide a proper framework for understanding the progress of the poem? Several points may be noted.

(1) Behind the rise and fall of human fortune lies this cosmic contest. The ultimate struggle is not between Job and Yahweh. Instead, it is between Yahweh and Satan, whose name means "the Accuser." Satan challenges the effectiveness of Yahweh's redemptive program among a fallen humanity, accusing even God of bribery (Job 1:9; 2:4). Of significance in the opening verses is the fact that Job is not an Israelite (1:1). He is of the land of Uz, outside the land of promise. He is nowhere identified as a member of the covenant people of Yahweh. For this reason, Job stands as representative of the redeemed from the whole of humanity.[10]

---

10. Childs, *Introduction*, 538–39, notes that this setting of Job outside the boundaries of the Israelite people appropriately suits the wisdom tradition of Scripture: "Wisdom is

This ultimate test of the COVENANT LORD's redemptive program may be best appreciated against the backdrop of the first man. Adam in the garden failed the test instigated by Satan. Though perfect in his original creative form, the first representative man sinned against God. The prologue of Job describes a similar but drastically different circumstance. Though an upright man when judged by the standards of fallen humanity, Job is by his own confession a sinner (Job 7:21; 9:28–31; 13:26; 14:16–17). He even acknowledges the classic doctrine of original sin:

> Man born of woman
>   is of few days
>   and full of trouble. . . .
>
> Who can bring what is pure
>   from the impure?
>   No one! (Job 14:1, 4 NIV)

By his own admission, Job is not in a perfected state, as was the original man. In addition, his test involves being stripped of every earthly comfort and convenience. He is not in a garden as was Adam. Stripped of all possessions, taunted by his wife, oppressed by wasting disease, roundly and falsely condemned by his closest comrades, Job in uttering his death wish is fully understandable.

But Job never curses Yahweh his COVENANT LORD, the ultimate source of all his pains. Where Adam in the pristine purity of fresh creation failed, Job with everything against him succeeded. So Satan has been defeated, and Yahweh's redemptive work in behalf of fallen sinners has won the day.

Though leaping across millennia of redemptive history, the lines of another poet underscore the same principle:

> My name from the palms of His hands
>   eternity will not erase;

---

not confined to the chosen people. Nor are the issues being addressed by the book tied to Israel's peculiar national history, as if Job were only a type of the suffering Jew of the exile. The setting assures Job's proper place within Israel's canon, namely as wisdom literature which addresses theological issues basic to all human beings."

Impressed on His heart it remains,
   in marks of indelible grace.
Yes, I to the end shall endure,
   as sure as the earnest is given;
More happy, but not more secure,
   the glorified spirits in Heaven.[11]

The message of Job cannot be properly understood apart from this cosmic perspective of the prologue. To the very end, neither Job nor his friends are informed of this circumstance. Even in his summarizing dialogue, Yahweh never unveils this underlying reality of Job's struggle. But the readers of Job know this background, which provides justification for applying the message of Job to every person redeemed in Christ. Simultaneously it displays the genius of the literary character of the book.

By this introductory structure, the book of Job speaks directly to the circumstances of every generation. The Redeemer of a fallen humanity does not whisper in the ear of every struggling saint the cosmic circumstance behind his struggle. But through the message of Job, you have this truth unveiled to you. As one who trusts in Yahweh the Lord of the Covenant who is ultimately revealed in the person of his Son Jesus Christ, you may understand your struggles in life in terms of this cosmic dimension.

(2) Wisdom and its role in responding to the ways of God with man serve as a focus of the book from beginning to end. Job's initial introduction displays him as a man who "feared God," which points to a poetic climax in the book by defining wisdom as the "fear of the Lord" (Job 1:1; 28:28). Three times in the prologue, Job's fear of God emerges as the principal factor in analyzing his person (1:1; 1:8; 2:3). Without this prologue, the true state of Job's condition in the eyes of the Almighty would remain an uncertainty. But the prologue makes it crystal clear. Job fears the Lord, which is the beginning of wisdom. As a consequence, he is a righteous man, a pious servant of Yahweh the Lord of the Covenant. Throughout the book, Job maintains his innocence—not his sinlessness, but his uprightness as a person devoted

---

11. Augustus Montague Toplady, "A Debtor to Mercy Alone" (1771).

to the LORD.[12] He is a good man. He shuns evil, walking in the ways of the LORD (1:1, 8; 2:3).

The prologue repeatedly displays this essential character of Job. Despite all his disasters, he does not curse God but blesses him instead, contrary to Satan's predictions and his wife's urgings (Job 1:11, 21; 2:4, 9–10). It has been proposed that Job's test was whether he would love God simply for the sake of loving God.[13] But simply loving God for himself is too abstract a concept for a biblical book of wisdom such as Job. Instead, Job's test was whether he would bless God rather than curse him whatever the LORD brought into his life. These alternatives Job himself laid down in clearest terms in his interaction with his wife. In reaction to all his losses, shall he curse Yahweh and die? Or shall he accept trouble and trial from God just as he accepts the good (2:9–10)? By his refusal to curse God and die, Job displays the profundity of his wisdom.

With this perspective in mind, saints of today can learn to expect trials and sufferings in this life that do not always seem to correspond to the extent of their commitment to Jesus Christ. So how should they respond? They should respond as Job did, just as the letter of James advises. This later letter to a suffering Christian community encourages believers to remember the patience of Job, assuring them that "the Lord is full of compassion and mercy" despite all human trials (James 5:11).

(3) Yahweh the LORD OF THE COVENANT is the one true God in the book of Job. The designation *Yahweh* appears thirty-two times in twenty-three different verses. Only once does the name of Yahweh appear in the dialogue between Job and his friends (Job 12:9). The remaining thirty-one appearances occur in the opening prologue (18 times) and in Yahweh's closing dialogue with Job, along with the epilogue of the book (13 times). Fifteen times in Yahweh's interaction

---

12. According to one commentator, the purpose of the prologue is "to make unambiguously clear that Job is completely pure" (J. P. Fokkelman, *Reading Biblical Poetry: An Introductory Guide* [Louisville: Westminster John Knox, 2001], 179). This analysis overlooks Job's multiple acknowledgment of his personal sinfulness (cf. Job 7:21; 9:28–31; 13:26; 14:16–17).

13. Childs, *Introduction*, 536, 539.

with Satan this covenant name for God appears. In marked contrast, various other designations for God appear over a hundred times in Job, the great majority of them occurring in the dialogue between Job and his friends. So while Job's talk about God with his friends centers on a general concept of God, the principal person determining the course of events is clearly Yahweh, the LORD OF THE COVENANT, as seen at the beginning and the end. This deliberate distinction in the composition of Job between sections of listening in on people talking about God and observing Yahweh himself determining the course of events is so marked that it provides a focal aspect of the book. Yahweh the LORD OF THE COVENANT controls the events of human history, encompassing even the negative actions of Satan the Accuser. This truth is dramatically represented in the fact that Satan cannot touch Job or any of his possessions without first receiving Yahweh's consent (1:8–12; 2:3–7).

(4) The narrative prologue as well as the narrative conclusion of Job is quite distinctive from the rest of the book in terms of the paucity of figures of speech. As previously indicated, the book contains over 370 figures of speech. Yet no figures of speech are found in the narrative introduction and narrative conclusion of Job, with the exception of two images employed by Satan. In both these instances, Satan lives up to his name, "the Accuser." In this case, Satan reaches the height of presumption by directing his accusation against God himself. The LORD has "put a hedge" around Job (Job 1:9–10). According to Satan, God is guilty of bribery, which alone explains Job's piety. Then when Satan fails to provoke Job to curse God by removing all his possessions, he accuses God once more. "Skin for skin!" says Satan (2:4). In effect, Satan insinuates, "So long as his flesh remains untouched, he will bless you. But let me at him. Let me afflict his body, and he will curse you."

Only the speeches of the various individuals of the book contain this extensive use of figures of speech. The relative absence of figures of speech in the narrative opening and closing sections provides some support to the conclusion that the book of Job intends to describe real events that occurred in time and history, despite the poetic form of the bulk of the book.

Job's Dialogue with His Three Friends (Job 3–31)

Job's Opening Soliloquy (Job 3:1–26)

Job responds to the seven silent days of his three friends by describing two critical moments in his life: his birth and his death (Job 3:3–10, 11–19). Job wishes that the day of his birth could be turned into darkness, deep shadow, overwhelming blackness, and thick darkness. He declares his desire that the night of his birth be like a barren womb whose morning stars become dark, since it did not shut the doors of the womb to hide him from all of life's troubles (3:3–10). If only no knees had received him at his birth and no breasts had nurtured him, he could have been lying down in peace, asleep in death and at rest. Death could serve him well as the great equalizer, for then he would lie with kings, rulers, stillborn children, and the wicked. He could enjoy the ease of captives who no longer hear the slave driver's shout because he is finally freed from his master. He longs for death more than people who spend their lives searching for hidden treasure. He wishes to join those who are filled with gladness when they finally reach the grave.

By these extended figures depicting birth and death, Job vivifies the despair he feels over the calamities of his life. Merely descriptive words could not convey the emotion he experiences, the agony he endures. More than a clinical analysis of his inner struggles, Job's figures convey the heartache brought about by life's pains. He wishes barrenness of the womb on the night of his birth. He describes death as a welcoming resting place, a hiding place from trouble discovered deep in the ground, a hidden treasure that causes gladness when it is finally found.

Round One (Job 4–14)

Eliphaz's First Speech (Job 4:1–5:27)

From the beginning, Eliphaz and his companions primarily intend to convince Job of his guiltiness before God and the divine justice displayed in all his calamities. The various figures of speech they employ regularly reinforce this intention. Eliphaz notes that people who "plow evil" and "sow trouble" invariably reap what they sow (Job 4:8). His logic inevitably leads him to conclude that Job must have committed a great deal of evil that would be commensurate with his vast troubles. By a merciless use of a figure of speech, Eliphaz compares Job and his wife to a lion and a lioness whose teeth have been knocked out and whose cubs have been scattered. Once-powerful Job is now as unthreatening as a toothless lion who must perish from lack of prey. Having lost her children, his wife is like a lioness without her cubs (4:10–11).

To underscore his analysis of Job's sad situation, Eliphaz claims a divine revelation that has uncovered the reason for Job's sufferings. To make his claim more effective, he depicts this divine revelation as a secret whisper, a disquieting dream, a spirit gliding past his face that made his hair stand on end. He has seen a vague form and heard a hushed voice. This revelatory apparition has compared a frail human being to someone living in a house of clay with a foundation of dust, a creature crushed more easily than a moth, a tent whose cords are pulled up so that it is about to collapse. In view of this divine revelation concerning Job's perilous situation, how could he exalt himself by claiming to be more righteous than God by questioning the justice of his sufferings (Job 4:12–21)?

By using these vivid figures, Eliphaz bypasses formal proof that Job is a greater sinner than Eliphaz himself, since he has not experienced such calamities. He appeals to basic truths that cannot be denied. Whatever a man sows, that shall he also reap. Human life is as fragile as a house of clay, as transient as the brief existence of a moth, as collapsible as a tent whose stabilizing cords have been yanked up. But by his application of these figures as divinely revealed explanations of Job's fragility as a consequence of God's judgment, Eliphaz has twisted the truth to confirm an unproven point.

It should not be surprising that figures of speech seem to tumble so easily from the mouth of Eliphaz and his friends. For "wisdom" is not the exclusive possession of people redeemed and remade. The ungodly also have a "wisdom" of their own, which they may use for their own ungodly purposes. In fact, they may manifest a wisdom about the affairs of this life that exceeds the wisdom of the godly. As Jesus says in summarizing his parable of the shrewd manager: "The sons of this age are wiser in their own generation than the sons of light" (Luke 16:8b). So Paul the apostle applies the words of Eliphaz to the sophistry of the Greek men of wisdom:

> He catches the wise
> in their craftiness. (Job 5:13 NIV; 1 Cor. 3:19)

Paul uses this quotation from an ancient wise man of the East to expose the sophism of his more contemporary West. By this application of the words of Eliphaz, Paul shows that a relative wisdom may be found among the ungodly. But at the same time, he indicates that God may expose human wisdom in all its foolishness. His treatment of the text from Job incidentally shows the way to approach the speeches of Job's very imperfect friends. Their statements may be true enough in themselves—only wrongly applied to the circumstances surrounding Job's situation. They may be used for their instructional value, even as they may be recognized as wrongly applied in Job's case.

For instance, Eliphaz's classic statement is certainly true: "Man is born to trouble as surely as sparks fly upward" (Job 5:7 NIV). No one can dispute his well-phrased figure of speech. How can sparks on a hearth fly downward rather than upward, and who among humanity can deny the inevitability of trouble! The truth of his statement is incontestable.

But in context, Eliphaz implies that Job's sin is the direct cause of his calamity. Resentment over what God brings into life kills a fool [and you, Job, are that fool]. The children of a fool will be crushed in God's court without a defender [just as has happened to your children, Job]. Hardship does not simply spring out of the ground on its own. It comes for a reason [and the reason for your greater suffering is your greater sin]. Because of the folly of your sin, all your troubles have come on you *as surely as the sparks fly upward* (Job 5:2–7).

Eliphaz rounds off his first words to Job with seemingly hopeful figures of speech. If only Job will accept his analysis, if he will cease despising this disciplining of the LORD, then his descendants will be like the grass of the earth, and he will come to the grave in full vigor, like sheaves gathered in season (Job 5:25–26).

137

How helpful does Eliphaz appear to be! If only Job will admit that he is a greater sinner than all his friends, then he can expect the blessing of the Almighty.

But as the Almighty himself declares to Eliphaz in the end, "I am angry with you . . . because you have not spoken of me what is right" (Job 42:7 NIV). Not in the vagueness of a claimed apparition, but with the bluntness and clarity of words spoken directly by the LORD himself, the Almighty judges Eliphaz to be altogether wrong. Despite the vividness and persuasiveness of his figures of speech, his claim to have a revelation from the LORD is nothing more than pretensions that stir up the anger of the Almighty.

Job's Response to Eliphaz's First Speech (Job 6:1–7:21)

In response to Eliphaz's first cutting accusations, Job bares his soul by sharing the depths of his pain. Two figures of speech vivify his agony. His misery is so great that if measured on scales it would outweigh the wet sand of the sea. His pain sinks into the depths of his soul because it arises from absorbing the poison of God's arrows.

But where is the sympathy from his friends that he expected? Should they treat him as though he were as unfeeling as hardened stone or metallic brass? Should they actually expect him to endure his agony without complaint? A wild donkey brays loudly when he hurts. But a good husbandman will not lose his temper at a bellowing ox. He will seek to understand the source of his animal's discomfort. Yet Job has found no help in his friends. Their counsel is as tasteless as the white of an egg without salt (Job 6:5–12). Their support may be compared to an intermittent stream. In the rainy season, they are like an overflowing river made deeply dark by thawing ice and melting snow. But in the dry season when water is sorely needed, the stream evaporates in the heat of the sun. Caravans turn aside to the riverbed, expecting refreshment from their wearying journey, but they are sorely disappointed.

So Job hoped to receive some small refreshment in the counsel of his friends. But he has been sadly disappointed (Job 6:14–20).

Job then depicts the miserable character of his days. They are like the hours of a hardworking slave who longs for the cool shadows of the evening, or the days of a hired servant who eagerly waits for his wages (Job 7:1–4). His days pass by swifter than a weaver's shuttle, coming quickly to their end without hope. The unaltered pattern of a slave laborer makes his days blend into one another so that time passes by swiftly without demarcation of change (7:6). In the end, as a cloud vanishes and is gone, so Job expects to go down to the grave. He will never return to his house again, and his place will know him no more (7:9–10).

Job concludes this first response to Eliphaz by addressing God himself. Figures of speech once more play a critical role in his message to the Almighty. Is Job like the raging sea, or like a monster of the deep, that he must be put under guard by the LORD (Job 7:12)? Why has God made him his special target? Has he become a burden to the Almighty? Is he deserving of these strictures enforced by the LORD? Could not the LORD simply forgive him of his faults (7:20–21)?

In this first interchange between Job and his friend, numerous figures of speech vivify the messages of both Eliphaz and Job. These images include a barren womb, darkened morning stars, a door slammed shut, a peaceful sleep, captives freed from the shout of the slave driver, a search for hidden treasure, plowing, sowing, reaping, a lion and lioness without teeth, a secret whisper, a gliding spirit, a house of clay, a transient moth, a tent with its ropes pulled up, sparks of a fire flying upward, grass of the earth, sheaves fully developed, wet sand on a scale, poisoned arrows, hardened stone and brass, a braying donkey, the tasteless white of an egg, an intermittent stream, disappointed caravans, a hardworking slave, a weaver's shuttle, a vanishing cloud, a raging sea, a monster of the deep, a target of the Almighty, a burden of the LORD. These figures of speech are not disposable incidentals any more than are the intimacies of bodily relationships described in the Song of Songs. The images are of such a character that they communicate the essence of the message of the book. Without the figures of speech, the whole piece of literature would fall flat. But with the images, the book comes to life.

Bildad's First Speech (Job 8:1–22)

Bildad jumps into the dialogue with a blunt accusation directed at Job and his children. Job's words are a "blustering wind" containing nothing of substance. He unfeelingly pronounces sentence over Job's ten dead children. They sinned against God, and so he gave them over to the penalty of their sin (Job 8:2, 4).

Bildad asserts that Job's ignorance of the righteous ways of God's working in the world is due in part to the brevity of human life. For "we were born only yesterday and know nothing, and our days on earth are but a shadow" (Job 8:9 NIV).

Then with three vivid images Bildad explains Job's quick and certain end as the inevitable destiny of all who forget God. Papyrus will never grow tall where there is no marsh. For while it is still growing and uncut, it withers more quickly than grass. The godless relies on a fragile spider's web that cannot possibly hold him up. The ungodly entwines his roots around a pile of rocks as though it were a well-watered plant thriving in the sunshine. But torn from its spot, the place disowns it altogether and other plants grow in its soil (Job 8:11–19). So by obvious implication, Job's sudden loss of fortune may be properly understood. He has forgotten God, and as a consequence all his prosperity has vanished.

Job's Response to Bildad's First Speech (Job 9:1–10:22)

Job's response to Bildad's first speech might be viewed as "over-kill." Job's speech is twice as long as Bildad's, and goes well beyond a necessary answer to Bildad's accusations. In part, the fullness of Job's response may be explained in that at least half his remarks are directed not to his friend but to God. As in the previous speeches, figures of speech play a major role in defining the nature of the response. But in this case, the figures of speech fall into several different categories.

First, Job employs images to show how the power of God orders the course of the universe. The Almighty moves mountains and over-turns them. He shakes the earth and makes its pillars tremble. He speaks to the sun and it fails to shine. He seals off the light of the stars. He stretches out the heavens and treads on the waves of the sea.

So how is it possible for Job to dispute with him? Even if he were innocent, God would crush him with a storm. If he were blame-less, his own mouth would condemn him (Job 9:4–22). Obviously, Job speaks out of his frustration in failing to understand the ways of God toward him. The Almighty is simply too great for him to comprehend.

Second, Job develops images of the brevity of life. His days are swifter than a runner. They fly away. They skim past like boats of papyrus, like eagles swooping down on their prey (Job 9:25–26).

Third, he uses images to describe the impossibility of a person's cleansing himself of guilt. He could wash himself with soap and cleansing soda. But then God would plunge him into a slime pit, so that even his clothes would detest him (Job 9:30–31). God's perception of sin is so much deeper than man's that a person's justification of himself is altogether meaningless.

Fourth, Job employs vivid images of God's creative activity in designing him. God molded him like clay. He poured him out like milk and curdled him like cheese. He clothed him with skin and flesh, and knitted him together with bones and sinews (Job 10:9–11). As in Psalm 139, Job marvels at the amazing work of God and God alone in shaping him in his mother's womb.

Fifth, he uses images to describe God's unexpected assault on him. If Job holds his head high, God stalks him like a lion. The full force of the LORD's increasing anger comes against him "wave on wave," like the incessant crashings of the swellings of the sea (Job 10:16–17).

Sixth, Job makes use of vivid images to depict the awesome reality of death. Death is the place of no return, the land of gloom and deep shadow, the realm of deepest night and utter chaos where even light is as darkness (Job 10:21–22). In view of these sober images of death, Job's constant expression of a death wish is even more striking. In his first speech, he had cursed the day of his birth and lamented the fact that he did not die as he came from the womb (3:1, 11). In his second speech, he gave full expression to his longing to die: "Oh, that I might have my request, . . . that God would be willing . . . to let loose his hand and cut me off!" (6:8–9 NIV). Now in this third speech, he once more expresses his wish that he had died before any eye had seen him. In his despair over life he declares, "If only I had never come into being, or had been carried straight from the womb to the grave!" (10:19 NIV). Despite his depiction of death as the land of gloom, darkest night, and disorder, Job sees it as more desirable than the miseries of his present life. His vivid images of death deepen the pathos of his desire to die.

Zophar's First Speech (Job 11:1–20)

This third friend of Job has heard enough. He feels compelled to humble Job by indicating the folly of Job's presuming to understand anything of the mysteries of God. For his mysteries are higher than the heavens—so what can Job do? They are deeper than the depths of the grave—so what can Job know? Their measure is longer than the earth and wider than the sea (Job 11:8–9). So how can Job expect to understand anything about God's ways with people? A foolish man like Job can no more become wise than a wild donkey's colt can become a man (11:12).

Once more, Job's friend offers no specific evidence that Job has committed sin that could explain God's judgments. But if only Job will put away his sin and allow no evil to dwell in his tent, then his present troubles will be as waters gone by. His life will become brighter than noonday and his darkness like morning (Job 11:14–17). Having prejudicially assumed Job's sin to be fact though without proof, he torments Job with these vivid images of restoration to lost blessing and favor with God.

Job's Response to Zophar's First Speech (Job 12:1–14:22)

Zophar's twenty verses in a single chapter are answered by Job's seventy-five verses in the three subsequent chapters. The shorter the speeches of his adversaries, the longer the responses of Job. But in a form similar to his previous responses, Job begins with an answer to his friends, and then concludes with a soliloquy addressed to God (cf. Job 7:1–21; 10:2–22; 13:20–14:22). Each of these soliloquies consists of a battery of questions addressed to God: seven questions in the first, nine questions in the second, and eight questions in the third. Interestingly, when God finally addresses Job, he responds with over fifty questions, and answers none of Job's. God will be God.

Zophar has scorned Job's ability to understand anything about God's mysterious ways of wisdom. Yet this friend has propounded his own analysis of the source of Job's troubles (his sin) and the way of restoration (his repentance). In response, Job answers with a proverbial statement that stands as a classic in its own right: "Does not the ear test words as the tongue tastes food?" (Job 12:11 NIV). With a touch of sarcasm, Job puts his friends in their place. Without any doubt they are "the people," and wisdom will come to its final end when they die (12:2)! Contrary to Zophar's analysis, Job contends that he has a bit of understanding.

To enforce his point, Job lists eleven categories of leaders, including counselors, judges, kings, priests, advisers, elders, nobles—the most respected people on the earth. All of them God deprives of their reason (Job 12:17–24a). Job then employs three figures of speech to underscore the lostness of the wisest of the world apart from insight that God alone can give. God sends them wandering through a trackless wasteland. They grope in darkness like blind men with no light. He makes them stagger like drunkards (12:24b–25).

Job scorns the supposed wisdom of his friends. Their memorable statements are proverbs that have the consistency of ashes. Their apologetics are no stronger than defensive mounds made of soft clay (Job 13:12).

Having received no satisfaction in his dialogue with his three friends, Job now turns to God himself (Job 13:20–14:22). By multiple images, he lays before God his sense of weakness before the assaults of the Almighty, and his hopelessness in view of the brevity of human life. He is nothing more than a leaf whipped about by the wind, dried chaff chased by the breeze (13:25). God has fastened his feet in shackles so that he cannot escape. He makes Job inherit the sins of his youth for the rest of his life. In a most vivid imagery, he describes God as scrutinizing his every path by putting marks on the soles of his feet so that he cannot get out of God's sight for a single moment (13:26–27). As a consequence, Job wastes away like something rotting, like a garment that is slowly, silently being eaten by moths (13:28).

Following this theme, Job employs six different illustrations depicting the brevity of human life. Man springs up like a flower and quickly withers away. He is like a fleeting shadow that cannot last. He puts in his time like a hired man bored with his tiresome work. There is more hope for a tree than for a man. For if a tree is cut down, it will sprout again. The roots may grow old in the ground and the stump die in the soil. Yet at the scent of water it will bud and put forth shoots like a plant. But man dies and is laid low in the earth. He breathes his last and is no more. As water evaporates from the sea and as a riverbed becomes parched and dry, so man lies down and does not rise. Even until the heavens are no more, men will not awaken or be roused from their sleep. Truly, man born of woman is few of days and full of trouble (Job 14:1–12).

Viewed from the perspective of what man can see with his physical eyes, Job's descriptions of the brevity of human life ring true. Man finishes his brief time on earth, and then is seen no more. Yet with all the prevalence of this seemingly hopeless pessimism, Job gives expression to his anticipation of future expectations. If only God will hide him in the grave, conceal him until his anger passes by. Then he will wait for his renewal to come. God will call, and he will answer. The LORD himself will long for the creature that his own hands have made. In the end, God will keep no record of his sins, but will seal them up in a bag (Job 14:13–17).

What more could be expected in terms of faith in resurrection life beyond the grave in this ancient patriarchal period? Though seeing through a glass darkly, Job sees.

At the same time, he is painfully aware of the gradual erosion of his life as it is lived out under the chastening hand of the LORD. Again he resorts to the vividness of figures of speech to convey his insights. As even a mountain erodes and crumbles, as a boulder can be moved from its place, as water wears away stones, and as torrents wash away the soil, the LORD destroys man's hopes and overpowers him once and for all (Job 14:18–22).

In this further series of interchanges between Job and the second and third of his friends, the extensiveness and intensiveness of the figures of speech are quite noteworthy. In these first interchanges between Bildad, Zophar, and Job, no fewer than sixty figures of speech may be found. The following list illustrates something of the extensiveness of these images: a blustering wind, withering papyrus, a fragile spider's web, a plant with roots wrapped around rocks, moving mountains, a shaking earth, a failing sun, stars sealed off, the stretching of the heavens, treading on waves of the sea, a swift runner, flying days, swiftly sailing boats of papyrus, a swooping eagle, washing soap, cleansing soda, a slimy pit, molding clay, poured milk, curdled cheese, clothing of skin and flesh, knitting with bones and sinews, a stalking lion, pounding waves, crashing seas, a place of no return, a land of gloom and deep shadow, a realm of deepest night, utter chaos, light as darkness, mysteries higher than the heavens, deeper than the grave, longer than the earth, and wider than the sea, a wild donkey's colt, bright noonday, morning light, an ear tasting words, a tongue tasting food, a trackless wasteland, blind men groping in darkness, staggering drunkards, crumbling ashes, mounds of clay, a windblown leaf, dried chaff blown by the breeze, shackled feet, soles of feet with telltale marks, rotting substance, a moth-eaten garment, a withering flower, a fleeting shadow, a hired servant bored with his work, a chopped-down tree sprouting roots that smell water, evaporating seawater, a parched riverbed, the sleep of death, a hiding place in the grave, a sealed bag, an eroding mountain, a transported rock, water wearing away stone, soil washed away by torrents of water.

Hardly can this vast array of images be relegated to merely incidental window-dressing in the book of Job. As vital parts of a piece of epic poetry, these figures of speech belong to the very essence of this literary masterpiece. To use one of the book's own images, the book of Job would be as tasteless as the white of an egg apart from these diversified illustrations. The essence of wisdom may be found in the ability to analyze human realities in terms of the Creator's handiwork as displayed throughout the whole of his creation. From the fragile spider's web to the vast expanse of the heavens, true wisdom can discern the unity of humanity with its created environment, as well as man's distinctiveness as a moral, accountable creature.

Round Two (Job 15–21)

As might be anticipated, this second round of interchanges between Job and his three friends displays an increased intensity of expression on both sides. On the one hand, the friends intensify their accusations against Job. In response, Job intensifies his affirmations. Accusations answered by affirmations. In both cases, the critical role of figures of speech continues.

145

Eliphaz's Second Speech (Job 15:1–35)

Eliphaz opens with a barrage of mockery aimed at Job. Would a wise man fill his belly with the hot east wind? As the desert sirocco consumes everything in its path, so Job by his remarks has undermined piety and hindered devotion to God (Job 15:2–4). Does Job think of himself as the first man ever born, as one brought forth before the ancient hills (15:7)?

Eliphaz then relentlessly assaults Job and pronounces the inevitability of his destruction. Characterizing the previous speeches of himself and his friends as "God's consolations" spoken ever so gently, he describes Job as "vile and corrupt," one who "drinks iniquity like water" (Job 15:11, 16). The gray-haired and the aged are on their side, men even older than Job's father (15:10). No longer does Eliphaz merely hint that Job's sin might be the cause of his calamities. Even the words coming from Job's mouth are prompted by his sin, so that his own mouth condemns him (15:5–6).

In the darkest possible colors, Eliphaz describes the horrors of the life of a sinner like Job. Terrifying sounds, attacking marauders, being marked for the sword, becoming food for vultures—the ancients have made it plain that these are the inevitable experiences of the wicked. He has shaken his fist at God, defiantly charging against him with a thick, strong shield. As a consequence, distress and anguish overwhelm him like a king poised to attack (Job 15:21–26).

To vivify the destruction of the wicked, Eliphaz employs a series of images. The wicked will be paid off in full before his time. His branches (perhaps an image of Job's children) will not flourish. He will be like a vine stripped of its unripe grapes, like an olive tree dropping its blossoms before fruit can form. As a godless person, he will be barren, and fire will consume his tents. All this calamity comes because deceit takes its shape in the womb of the wicked (Job 15:32–35).

A more unfeeling expression could not be found in the mouth of an avowed enemy, much less a trusted friend. Job has been betrayed by his closest allies, and perhaps that is his deepest wound. He must bear his pain all alone.

Job's Response to Eliphaz's Second Speech (Job 16:1–17:16)

But by the grace of God, and as a trophy of God's grace alone, Job answers intensified accusation with intensified affirmation. It is as though the utter disappointment he experiences from his friends drives him more completely into an unbroken trust in his God. Yet his faith never completely numbs his hurt and his confusion.

God gnashes his teeth at him. As a threatening opponent, the Almighty fastens his piercing eyes on him. God has made him his target. His archers surround him. He pierces his kidney and spills his gall on the ground. He rushes against him again and again like a well-armed warrior (Job 16:9–14).

But then, in a dramatic turn of perspective, Job develops extensive imagery of a court proceeding. In a startling, unexpected twist, he approaches God, who appears simultaneously as his Judge and his advocate. He has a witness in heaven who will testify on his behalf. He has an advocate—yes, even an intercessor who is his friend—who will plead with God on his behalf. That advocate can be none other than God himself (Job 16:18–21).

So Job lays his case before God, whom he considers to be both his Judge and his advocate. To this point, Job has been spared the ultimate moment in which he will stand for judgment before the Almighty. So God can rightfully demand a pledge, a security, until the final hour of accountability. But who other than God himself will come forward to take up responsibility for his cause? His children are dead, his wife has encouraged him to curse God and die, and his closest friends have become his accusers. In Job's mind, only God could have closed the minds of his friends to the extent to which they have been blinded in analyzing his case. As a consequence, God cannot let them triumph over him. The Almighty is the only one left to put up the security that he himself demands. As Job argues:

> Give me, O God, the pledge you demand. Who else will put up security for me? You have closed their minds to understanding; therefore you will not let them triumph. (Job 17:3–4 NIV)

Yet with all the manifest declaration of faith in God found in Job, he still must wrestle with the realities that press in on him. His whole frame is but a shadow. His friends treat the night of his despair as though it were daylight. In the face of his darkness, they have such small perception of his distress that they audaciously declare, "Light is near" (Job 17:7, 12).

So what can he say? Job responds with a series of images depicting the hopelessness of death. Is he to spread out his bed in darkness? Is he to call fleshly corruption his father, the consuming worm his mother or his sister? Is all his hope to perish in the dust of the grave (Job 17:13–16)?

So Job struggles to the edge of hopefulness in God as his advocate and Judge. Then he falls back to the brink of despair over death. In both these circumstances he gives expression to his perception of reality. But between these two options there must be a resolution. In the end, only the revelation of God himself can confirm his hope and correct his friends.

Bildad's Second Speech (Job 18:1–22)

Now this supposed friend of Job becomes cruelly vindictive in his second speech. Though condemning Job for his sin in his first speech, he offered much encouragement, as might be expected of a friend. At that earlier moment, he gave great hope. If only Job would plead with the Almighty, his earlier blessings would seem trite in comparison to his future prosperity (Job 8:5, 7). God would yet fill Job's mouth with laughter and his lips with shouts of joy (8:21).

But now in this second speech, Bildad can only drum damnation after damnation on the head of his friend. Job has treated his friends as though they were cattle, as stupid in his sight (Job 18:3). In his vindictive reaction, Bildad employs over twenty-five images to depict the fate of a wicked person like Job:

- His lamp will be snuffed out.
- The flame of his fire will stop burning.
- The light of his tent will become dark.
- The lamp beside him will go out.
- The vigor of his step will be weakened.
- His feet will thrust him into a net.

- A trap will seize him by the heel.
- A snare will hold him fast.
- A noose will be hidden for him on the ground.
- A trap lies in his path.
- Calamity is hungry for him.
- Disaster eats away parts of his skin.
- Death's firstborn devours his limbs.
- He is torn from the security of his tent.
- He is marched off to the king of terrors.
- Fire resides in his tent.
- Burning sulfur is scattered over his dwelling.
- His roots dry up below.
- His branches wither above.
- His memory perishes from the earth.
- He has no name in the land.
- He is driven from light into darkness.
- He is banished from the world.
- He has no offspring or descendants.
- He has no survivor where he once lived.
- Men of the west are appalled at his fate.
- Men of the east are seized with horror.

That's it. That's the only word Bildad can speak to Job. Two of his images anticipating Job's prospects are particularly startling, both of them depicting death in its most horrid colors. The "first-born of Death" will devour his parts (Job 18:13). As only the "son" of Death, it cannot kill. But it can do worse by consuming his flesh. As one translation puts it, "Death's eldest son swallows his organs."[14] Beyond that horrid experience, he will be "marched off to the king of terrors" (18:14). The ultimate terrorizer is Death, who will bring to Job horrors far worse than anything he has undergone up to this point. Because Job is an "evil man" who "knows not God," all these horrors most certainly will be his fate (18:21).

14. Andersen, *Job*, 189.

149

Job's Response to Bildad's Second Speech (Job 19:1–29)

So what can Job say in response? He must admit that God has treated him brutally. All his wealth and possessions are gone. His ten children, sons and daughters, are all dead. Bodily sicknesses torment him. His closest friends can only accuse him. So how can he respond to these accusations?

In acknowledging his calamities, Job once more employs a number of figures of speech to describe his treatment by the Almighty. God has drawn his net around him, trapping him like a wild animal. He has blockaded his way so that he cannot pass by to move on with the simple activities necessary to sustain life. He has shrouded his pathway in darkness so that he has no clear understanding of how to proceed from day to day. He has stripped him of any respect he might have had from the community, and has snatched from his head the crown of royalty that rightly belongs to every man made in God's image. He has torn him down on every side so that he is like a defenseless city without walls, exposed to every adversarial assault. He has uprooted every remnant of hope he might have had for the future. God's anger constantly burns against him. His supernatural troops advance in force against him, building siege ramps in anticipation of a prolonged assault. He sets up his military camps so that they encircle Job's fragile tent. Job has escaped total destruction with only the membranelike skin of his teeth (Job 19:8–12, 20). It seems that Job resorts to more extensive use of figures of speech when the intensity of his responses increases.

Yet square in the midst of seeming despair, Job gives expression to his strongest hopes. It could not be him, but the grace of God at work in him. Repeatedly Job had indicated his determination to speak out and his desire to have an audience before God:

> I will not keep silent; I will speak out in the anguish of my spirit. (Job 7:11 NIV)

> If only there were someone to arbitrate between us, to lay his hand upon us both . . . then I would speak up without fear of him, but as it now stands with me, I cannot. (Job 9:33, 35 NIV)

> Keep silent and let me speak;
> Then let come what may. (Job 13:13 NIV)

Withdraw your hand far from me, and stop frightening me with
your terrors. Then summon me and I will answer, or let me speak,
and you reply. (Job 13:21–22 NIV)
If only you would hide me in the grave, and conceal me till your
> anger has passed!

....

If a man dies, will he live again?
All the days of my hard service I will wait for my renewal to come.[15]
You will call and I will answer you;
you will long for the creature your hands have made. (Job 14:13–15 NIV)

O earth, do not cover my blood; may my cry never be laid to rest!
(Job 16:18 NIV)

But now Job asks for more—more than an opportunity to speak.
He desires a more permanent record of his puzzlings, his complaints.
He wants his words written, preserved in a scroll. No, he wants even
more. He wants a recording that will be more lasting than scribblings
on papyrus. Let his words be inscribed with an iron tool on lead. Even
better, let them be engraved on a rock so that they last forever (Job
19:23–24). (In the end, Job has a far more permanent record than he
could have ever imagined. His words are inscribed on the permanent
pages of Holy Scripture.)

So Job has a hope that God will eventually hear his case. His
friends will not listen to him properly or sympathetically. But he has
good hope that God will listen to him.

In that context, he expresses his confidence. "I know," he says. "I
have a certainty. Nothing can shake me of this confidence. I know that
my *Goel*—my Redeemer, the divinely appointed One who must take
up my cause—I know that he lives!" (cf. Job 19:25). God himself, in
the tradition of the patriarchs, has set up the system of the kinsman-
redeemer. The Almighty has determined that the orphan, the widow, the
disenfranchised will have some recourse in the final appeal before the

---

15. Comments John E. Hartley, *The Book of Job*, NICOT (Grand Rapids: Eerdmans,
1988), 236: "If God hides him in Sheol, there would have to be some way for him to be
restored to earthly life. . . . *Renewal* means a new vigorous life in a restored body. The Hebrew
root is the same one translated *will sprout again* in reference to a tree in verse 7b. Returned
to life, Job would have left his old diseased body and be given a body full of vitality."

courts of justice (Lev. 25:25, 48; Ruth 2:20). So Job claims for himself a permanent hope arising from this same principle of ultimate justice.

But Job has no earthly relatives to take on this role of the kinsman-redeemer. All his relatives have forsaken him. His sons and daughters are dead. His wife urges him to curse God and die. His closest friends roundly condemn him and show not a whit of compassion. So God himself must be his *Goel*, his kinsman-redeemer. Job is confident that he has a Mediator who will argue his case before the Almighty, and that Mediator is the Almighty himself.

Except for the larger image of the kinsman-redeemer, these critical verses in the book of Job are distinctive for their absence of figures of speech. At the point of climax in the book, the author abandons his profuse use of imagery to communicate with unadorned prose the most profound of insights into eternal realities of the cosmos. Note carefully the various elements of his affirmation (Job 19:25–27):

"I know." He has an unshaken certainty despite all his calamities.

"That my kinsman-redeemer lives." He affirms that this defender, this vindicator of his cause, lives forever. He will always exist to stand at his side and speak out in his behalf. Since all other options are eliminated, this kinsman-redeemer must be none other than God himself. So taking the text for what the text says, a peculiar situation arises. God his Judge is at the same time God his Redeemer.

But is it legitimate to "leap the gap" and declare that Christ Jesus is Job's Redeemer, as Handel's *Messiah* so gloriously proclaims? Obviously, Job himself could not make that precise identification. But if it is legitimate to say that Moses' Passover lamb anticipates Christ the sacrificed Redeemer, then Job's resurrection hope, which is the focal point of this passage, must ultimately anticipate Christ the risen Redeemer.

"At the last." At that final great Day when all righteous causes are confirmed as true.

"On the dust [of my grave] he shall stand." Not merely in some esoteric realm of the spirit world, but in that real world of material as well as spiritual substance in which humankind first came into existence when God formed man of the dust of the earth and breathed into his nostrils the breath of life.

"And after this skin of mine is destroyed." The inevitability of the corruption of human flesh in the grave must be fully acknowledged, and Job does not shy away from recognizing that fact.

"Yet from the vantage point of my flesh I shall see God."[16] Not apart from my flesh, but in my flesh I will see God. My contact with the ultimate reality of God himself will be realized with the whole of my being, body and soul.

"Whom I, indeed I, shall see for myself, not some stranger!" No other person can stand in Job's place on that final vindication day. He himself must be present to receive God's judgment on his own behalf.

"My whole being cries out for complete closure within my soul." Nothing less than a finalizing resolution in the presence of the Almighty in which God his *Goel* pleads his case can satisfy Job. His friends have decided that Job must be the greater sinner because of his greater suffering. But the just God must provide an indisputable refutation of these unjust charges.

So nothing less than anticipation of bodily resurrection can satisfy Job, and nothing less than bodily resurrection can satisfy these words of Job. Despite difficulties of wording and rationalizations of unbelief, the conclusion cannot be avoided. Expectation of confrontation

---

16. The choice between "from the vantage point of my flesh" and "apart from my flesh" in interpreting מִבְּשָׂרִי (Job 19:26) has been regularly discussed. Either rendering is grammatically possible, as noted in H. H. Rowley, *Job*, NCBC (Grand Rapids: Eerdmans, 1976), 139. In support of "from my flesh," Norman C. Habel, *The Book of Job*, Old Testament Library (Philadelphia: Westminster, 1985), 294, says: "Job hopes to see with his 'eyes,' which also suggests a physical seeing." Habel quotes Terrien, who demonstrates that "when used with a verb expressing vision or perception, the preposition *min* refers to the point of vantage, the locale from which or through which the function of the sight operates (Ps. 33:13–14; S. of Sol. 2:9)" (294). The phrasing of the next verse supports this understanding: "whom I, even I myself shall behold; and my eyes shall see and not a stranger" (Job 19:27). In support of understanding this critical phrase as meaning "from my flesh" rather than "apart from my flesh," see Kidner, *Wisdom to Live By*, 69n1; Gleason L. Archer Jr., *A Survey of Old Testament Introduction* (Chicago: Moody Press, 1964), 449.

with the living God in the wholeness of human existence comes forth strongly in these classic words of Job.

After his climactic declaration of faith, Job returns to speak with his constantly accusing friends. He answers figure of speech with figure of speech. They are saying that the root of the trouble lies in him. But they themselves should fear the sword of divine judgment that is sure to come. For God's wrath will bring punishment by the sword (Job 19:28–29). For the first time, Job warns his friends about the prospect of divine judgment that they themselves could experience. Earlier he had disputed with them, rejecting the judgments they pronounced. But now he sees that they are not simply wrong. They have put themselves in great danger because of the abusive way in which they are treating him. Perhaps his vivid imaginings of his own appearance before the throne of God for judgment alerted him to the prospect of divine judgment that would confront his friends.

Zophar's Second Speech (Job 20:1–29)

Zophar has absorbed nothing of Job's ringing affirmation of faith. Only Job's concluding warning that they, his friends, might be exposed to the sharp edge of God's judgmental sword has registered in his consciousness. So he responds with a vilifying list of more than twenty pronouncements of doom on Job-the-Wicked. With two contrasting figures of speech he describes how Job has lifted himself up, and how he is sure to be brought down. The pride of the wicked makes his head touch the clouds, but he will perish forever like his own dung (Job 20:6–7). With that vivid starting point, Zophar employs image after image to describe the doom that awaits Job. Like a dream he flies away. He disappears like a vision of the night. Evil is sweet in his mouth so that he hides it under his tongue where he can continually enjoy its flavor. But his food will turn sour in his stomach, and will become the venom of serpents. He will spit out the riches he has swallowed, for God will make his stomach vomit them up. He will suck the poison of serpents. The fangs of an adder will kill him. He will get no enjoyment from rivers flowing with honey and cream. God will rain down blows on him. He may flee to escape an iron weapon, but a bronze-tipped arrow will pierce him. He will pull the gleaming point out of his liver. Total darkness engulfs his treasures. A vigorous fire that burns on its own with no need of being fanned will consume him. The heavens will expose his guilt, and the earth will rise up to accuse him. A flood of rushing waters will carry off his house on the day of God's wrath. Such is the heritage appointed by God for the wicked (20:8–29).

Job's Response to Zophar's Second Speech (Job 21:1–34)

So Zophar has made his case. The wicked suffer from constant divine judgments. They get no enjoyment out of anything in life.

But Job questions this simplified analysis of the ways of God with man. For very often it is the wicked who live on, growing old and increasing in power. Job develops an extensive figure of the happy, prosperous life of the wicked. They see their children established around them. They live in safe homes free from fear. They enjoy music and dance. They go down to the grave in peace, despite their total rejection of their obligation to serve God (Job 21:7–16). So how often does calamity come on the wicked? How often is the lamp of the wicked snuffed out? How often are they like straw before the wind, like chaff swept away in a gale? Not very often. If you question travelers who move about from place to place, they will tell you that the evil man is spared the day of calamity (21:17–18, 29–30). In the end, an honor guard is set at his tomb, the soil of the valley is sweet to him, and a countless throng attends his funeral (21:32–33). Elsewhere Job will agree that God brings many calamities on the wicked (24:18–25; 27:13–23). But a balance must be struck. His images of the prosperity of the wicked must balance out the sweeping claims of his friend Zophar that the wicked invariably experience calamities all the days of their lives.

So this second round of interchanges between Job and his friends presents an intensified dialogue. The saturation of this material with figures of speech also intensifies. Over ninety illustrations may be identified in this section. These images include a belly filled with the hot east wind, a man born before the creation of the ancient hills, drinking iniquity like water, attacking marauders, a man marked for the sword, food for the vultures, a fist shaking defiantly, a shield used

155

for charging, a worker dismissed before his time, branches that do not flourish, a vine stripped of grapes before they are ripened, an olive tree dropping its blossoms before its fruit is formed, a barren life, tents consumed by fire, gnashing teeth, piercing eyes, a target of the Almighty, surrounding archers, a pierced kidney, gall spilled on the ground, a well-armed warrior, a judge and an advocate, a court witness, a legal security, the human frame as a shadow, death as a bed of darkness, fleshly corruption as a father, a consuming worm as a mother or sister, friends treated as cattle, a snuffed-out lamp, a burned-out flame, a darkened tent, an extinguished lamp, a weakened step, feet thrust into a net, a trap that seizes the heel, a snare that holds fast, a noose hidden on the ground, a trap lying in the path, a hungering calamity, disaster that eats parts of the skin, death's firstborn that devours limbs, the lost security of a tent, death as the king of terrors, fire residing in a tent, burning sulfur, dried-up roots, withered branches, memory perishing from the earth, being driven from light into darkness, banishment from the world, no offspring or descendants, no survivors, appalled men of the west, men of the east seized with horror, a trap for a wild animal, a blockaded way, a pathway shrouded in darkness, a crown of royalty, a defenseless city, hope uprooted, siege ramps, a military camp, an encircled tent, the skin of the teeth, an arbitrator, blood crying from the earth, a papyrus scroll, an iron tool for writing on lead, an engraved rock, a kinsman-redeemer, a root of trouble, a judgmental sword, a head touching the clouds, perishing dung, a dream that flies away, a vision in the night, a sweet taste in the mouth hidden under the tongue, food soured in the stomach, the venom of serpents, vomiting, sucking the poison of serpents, the deadly fangs of an adder, rivers flowing with honey and cream, blows repeated like rain, an iron weapon, a bronze-tipped arrow, a gleaming arrow-tip in the liver, a vigorous fire, an accusing earth, a flood of rushing waters, a heritage, a happy home, a peaceful grave, a snuffed-out lamp, windblown chaff, travelers moving about, an honor guard at a tomb, sweet soil for the dead, a countless throng.

In the first twenty-one out of forty-eight chapters of the book of Job, over 150 figures of speech have been noted. These images must be regarded as integral to the entire message of the book. By their very bulk, they claim a critical role in communicating the message of Job. They take on a defining role in the poetic shaping of the book. But still more, they function as substance that constitutes the essence of the message. Rather than merely serving as intensifying devices, they contribute vitally to the essence of the word from God being communicated.

Round Three (Job 22–27)

This third round of interactive speeches between Job and his three friends is distinctive because it underscores the role of the "silencing motif" that runs through the book. Once a person is "silenced," he is "out of the game." In the continual challenge to resolve the questions surrounding Job's suffering and the mysterious puzzle of the Almighty's ways, an inability to provide appropriate response to the previous speaker indicates defeat.

So the friends of Job repeatedly express their sense of compulsion to speak. The very first of these friends makes this point quite strongly. In responding to Job's opening soliloquy, the oldest (and presumably the wisest) of his friends gives expression to his compulsion to speak:

> Then Eliphaz the Temanite replied: "If someone ventures a word with you, will you be impatient? But who can keep from speaking?" (Job 4:1–2 NIV)

The first response of Job's second friend also arises because of his agitation over what he regards to be the impropriety of Job's words, which cannot be left unanswered:

> Then Bildad the Shuhite replied: "How long will you say such things? Your words are a blustering wind." (Job 8:1–2 NIV)

When his turn comes, Job's third friend expresses the necessity he feels to offer a response, for if he remains silent Job will be vindicated:

> Then Zophar the Naamathite replied: "Are all these words to go unanswered? Is this talker to be vindicated? Will your idle talk reduce men to silence? Will no one rebuke you when you mock?" (Job 11:1–3 NIV)

157

When a fourth friend emerges, the implication that Job will be proved correct if his friends are silenced stirs him to speak:

> So these three men stopped answering Job, because he was righteous in his own eyes. But Elihu . . . the Buzite . . . was . . . angry with the three friends, because they had found no way to refute Job . . . . Now Elihu had waited before speaking to Job because they were older than he. But when he saw that the three men had nothing more to say, his anger was aroused. So Elihu . . . said: . . . "They are dismayed and have no more to say; words have failed them. Must I wait, now that they are silent, now that they stand there with no reply?" (Job 32:1–6, 15–16 NIV)

A series of silencings traces the progress of the book. First, Satan is silenced by the faith response of Job despite the devil's dire predictions. Satan is then heard no more throughout the remainder of the book.

Then in this third round of speeches, Zophar the third friend has nothing to say, while Bildad the second friend offers the briefest of speeches (6 verses—Job 25:1–6).[17] This shortness of speech may be contrasted with the greater length of his earlier speeches (22 verses—8:1–22; 21 verses—18:1–21). Eliphaz finds himself incapable of opening a fourth round of speeches, and is silenced. This silencing of the three friends arouses Elihu's ire. At the same time, Job's final speech to his three friends is his longest, encompassing six chapters (26:1–31:40). But he in his turn is silenced by Elihu, seen by the fact that Job offers no response to this fourth friend. In the end, Job experiences his final put-down by the speeches of God himself—not once but twice. He speaks only to declare that he must remain speechless:

> Then Job answered the LORD: "I am unworthy—how can I reply to you? I put my hand over my mouth. I spoke once, but I have no answer—twice, but I will say no more." (Job 40:3–5 NIV)

17. Cf. Meredith G. Kline, "Job," in *The Wycliffe Bible Commentary*, ed. Charles F. Pfeiffer and Everett F. Harrison (Chicago: Moody Press, 1962), 479, in commenting on the extreme brevity of Bildad's third speech and the absence altogether of a third speech from Zophar: "Bildad's brief, feeble effort represents their expiring breath. Zophar's subsequent failure to speak is the silence of the vanquished (cf. 29:22)."

Then Job replied to the LORD: ". . . Surely I spoke of things I did not understand, things too wonderful for me to know." (Job 42:1, 3b NIV)

So in this third and final round of speech interactions between Job and his three friends, a termination of their dialogue takes shape. First Eliphaz will speak and Job will respond. Then Bildad will make his briefest and weakest effort, followed by Job's longest and strongest. Zophar will have not a word to add to this third round of speeches. As a consequence, Job emerges as the champion of the competition.

As an alternative interpretation of this closing down of the comments of the three friends, many commentators have posited a corruption of the text at this point. Bildad's shortened speech and Zophar's "missing" speech, it is proposed, indicate a dislocation of portions of the original text.[18] But the absence of any textual evidence supporting this hypothesis and the warp-and-woof role of the silencing motif throughout the book from beginning to end argue strongly against this hypothesis of a corrupted text.[19]

---

18. Alter, *Wisdom Books*, 6, suggests that the third round of the debate "was somehow damaged in scribal transmission." Roland E. Murphy, *Wisdom Literature: Job, Proverbs, Ruth, Canticles, Ecclesiastes, and Esther*, Forms of the Old Testament Literature 13 (Grand Rapids: Eerdmans, 1981), 16, says: "It is generally recognized that the text has been scrambled in chs. 24–27, where no speech is attributed to Zophar." In a similar tone, cf. Tremper Longman III and Raymond B. Dillard, *An Introduction to the Old Testament*, 2nd ed. (Nottingham, UK: Inter-Varsity Press, 2007), 228: "The third cycle probably suffers from an error in textual transmission . . . in that Job's words in 27:13–23 are either a part of the Bildad speech or the missing Zophar speech."

This oft-repeated perspective regularly overlooks this silencing motif that provides a critical contribution to the book's progress. Satan is silenced, then the three friends beginning with the youngest, then Job. In the end, only God speaks, with Job responding in abject humility. So the whole narrative combines to make the point: wisdom ultimately resides only in God. All others should remain silent and accepting of his will in the face of life's most puzzling problems.

19. Though noting that most commentators agree on the "high probability of serious dislocation" in the third round of speeches, Childs recognizes Job's triumph in the contest of the dialogue, as indicated by the abbreviated character of his friends' closing remarks: "The dialogue between Job and the three friends ended with their defeat. They failed to come forward, thus admitting failure to sustain their case against Job" (*Introduction*, 530, 539).

Eliphaz's Third Speech (Job 22:1–30)

Finding himself incapable of making any concrete point against Job, Eliphaz now becomes downright nasty. By a collection of figures of speech, he plays on Job's calamities. Snares are all around him, trapping him in whatever direction he turns. Sudden peril terrifies him, and the darkness that envelops him is so dense that he cannot see. Floodwaters reach so high that they cover his head (Job 22:10–11). All these distressful circumstances must have come on Job because of his great sin. Previously Job's friends had made specific accusations only indirectly, using the third person to identify the wicked: "*his* pride reaches to the heavens . . . for *he* has oppressed the poor; *he* has seized houses he did not build" (20:6, 19). But now Eliphaz charges Job directly, to his face: "*you* stripped men of their clothing . . . . *You* gave no water to the weary and *you* withheld food from the hungry" (22:6b–7 NIV). Without a stick of evidence, Eliphaz denounces Job for sending away widows and the fatherless empty-handed (22:9). So is Job going to continue on the path of evil men, who assume that God is veiled in such thick clouds that he cannot see what is happening on earth, and whose foundations are invariably washed away by a flood (22:14–16)?

Moving beyond his unfounded charges, Eliphaz once more offers Job the possibility of restoration to God's favor. But he must first disregard the value of his most precious things, so that he counts his nuggets of gold as nothing more than rocks and dust. Then the Almighty will become his glittering gold and his choicest silver (Job 22:24–25). Then light will shine on all his ways, and he will be God's instrument for lifting up the downcast and delivering the guilty through the cleanness of his hands (22:28–30). Eliphaz has painted a beautiful picture of the blessing of God on the repentant, but it is all wrongly directed, since it is based on false accusations. Ironically, it is the prayer of Job for Eliphaz that finally delivers his friend from the judgment of God (42:8).

Job's Response to Eliphaz's Third Speech (Job 23:1–24:25)

Job will provide a full answer to Eliphaz's unfounded charges in his response. He will even call down curses on himself if he has ever neglected the widow, the orphan, the hungry, or the naked as Eliphaz has charged (Job 29:12–17; 31:16–28). But his immediate response is to struggle over his inability to achieve an audience with God. He can travel east, west, north, and south without ever finding God so that he can come to understand what the Almighty is doing with him. Yet Job is confident that when God has completed his severest process of testing, he will come forth as purified gold (23:8–10).

Still, Job cannot comprehend the ways of the Almighty. With vivid imagery, he rehearses the desperate circumstances that characterize the life of the needy. The poor are like wild donkeys in the desert, foraging for food in the wasteland for their children. Lacking clothes, they hug the rocks for shelter and are drenched by the cold mountain rains. They carry sheaves but go hungry. They crush olives and tread winepresses even while they suffer thirst. When night falls, the murderer rises up and kills the poor and needy. Men break into houses and the adulterer keeps his face covered, claiming deep darkness as their light of morning (Job 24:5–17). It appears that God charges no one with wrongdoing (24:12c).

Yet Job affirms that the LORD ultimately brings his judgment on the wicked.[20] With a series of images he vivifies their end. The wicked are nothing more than foam on the surface of the water. The grave snatches them away even as heat evaporates the melting snow. The womb that has brought them into the world forgets them, and the

---

20. Job 24:18–25 along with 27:7–23 is often taken as Job's contradicting his earlier opinion as expressed throughout the dialogue. Cf. Childs, *Introduction*, 542; Longman, *Job*, 38. In these later passages, Job appears to be agreeing with his three friends that the wicked will indeed experience judgmental disaster at the hand of God. This perspective appears to directly contradict Job's observation that the wicked "spend their years in prosperity and go down to the grave in peace" (Job 21:13; cf. his vivid description of the charmed life of the wicked and their children in 21:7–13). Yet is not this setting of one principle over against another the very essence of wisdom? Cf. the classic illustration of back-to-back proverbs: "Do not answer a fool . . ."/"Answer a fool . . ." (Prov. 26:4–5). Must not wisdom recognize on the one hand that the wicked often prosper, while also affirming that God judges the wicked? Must not these two perspectives be held in tension, with wisdom applying the one or the other to a particular concrete situation? Job's friends wrongly applied the concept of God's judgment on the wicked to righteous Job. Job rightly resisted that application. Yet now he affirms the principle in general, but without making specific application. These two perspectives on God's response to the wicked do not represent contradiction in Job. Instead, they manifest true wisdom in Job as he sets one principle over against another with proper discernment.

worm in their grave feasts on them. They are broken like a tree. For God drags away even the mighty among them. They are cut off like heads of grain (Job 24:18–24). In the end, Job recognizes that God is not so far away. He may let the wicked rest with a feeling of security for a while. But his eyes continually watch their ways, and they are finally brought low (24:23–24).

Bildad's Third Speech (Job 25:1–6)

In his shortest speech, Bildad can only appeal to the innate sinfulness of all humankind. Perhaps Job's picture of the vileness of humanity has touched him. Bildad asks the classic question: "How can one born of woman be pure?" (Job 25:4b NIV). He speaks not so much of the wickedness of the woman, but of the universality of humanity's sinful nature, a reality that is difficult to deny. He expands on the theme of mankind's universal sinfulness with more telling images. If the moon is not bright and the stars are not pure in God's eyes, how much less man, who is but a maggot, or a son of man, who is only a worm (25:5–6). Bildad's final speech would be more convincing if it were clear that he did not intend to point his accusing finger at Job.

Job's Response to Bildad's Third Speech (Job 26:1–14)

Bildad's shortest speech of 6 verses is answered by Job in the first 14 verses of his longest speech (161 verses, spanning Job 26–31). Clearly, Job has not been silenced by the speeches of his friends. They are the ones who have been silenced, never to be heard again. Zophar cannot rouse himself to make further comment, and Eliphaz does not initiate a fourth round of interchanges.

Only chapter 26 is addressed specifically to Bildad, as seen by the singular use of the *you* throughout the chapter. With six stinging sarcasms, Job disparages the wisdom of this supposed friend. What a help to the powerless is he! What salvation he provides for the feeble! What sterling advice for someone who supposedly has no wisdom! What great insight! Who gave you these wonderful words?! With the help of whose spirit have these gems flowed from your mouth (Job 26:1–4)?!

Then with a series of images Job depicts the unfathomable wisdom of God that embraces both death and life. The dead lying beneath the waters are in deep anguish. But before God, death and destruction with all their mysteries are openly exposed, lying naked (Job 26:5–6).

To create and sustain life, God in his wisdom spread out the skies over empty space and hung the earth over nothing. He wraps the rainwaters in his clouds, but somehow the clouds do not burst under their weight. He covers the full moon with the clouds, and draws a line on the horizon as a boundary between light and darkness. He makes pillars that uphold the heavens and churns up the depths of the sea. In his wisdom he has brought fair skies from chaos simply by the breath of his mouth (Job 26:7–13).

So if mankind can hardly grasp the significance of his "faint whisper" or the "outer fringe" of his works, how can he expect to understand the full force of his power (Job 26:14)?

[No Third Speech of Zophar]
Zophar has been silenced.

Job's Final Statement to His Friends (Job 27:1–23)
By a shift from the singular to the plural *you*, Job indicates that he has completed his response to Bildad, and now offers his final word to all three of his friends. First he asserts that he cannot in good conscience admit that they are right. For he must not deny his personal integrity (Job 27:5). Worth noting is the fact that God himself as well as Job's wife had earlier confirmed his integrity despite the assaults of Satan (2:3, 9). Job has a unity of purpose in his soul that he cannot contradict without denying his very essence.

But then he proceeds to describe with a number of vigorous figures of speech what he conceives to be the fate that God allots to the wicked. The plague will bury his descendants. The wicked may heap up silver like dust, and clothes like piles of clay. But the righteous will eventually wear the wardrobe of the wicked, and the innocent will divide his silver. The house of the wicked is like a moth's cocoon, like a flimsy watchman's hut. Like a flood his terrors overtake him. A tempest snatches him away in the night. The east wind hurls itself

163

against him as he flees headlong from its power. The mighty wind claps its hand in derision and hisses its victim out of his place (Job 27:15–23). So God will deal with the wicked in the end.

[No Round Four Started by Eliphaz]
Eliphaz has been silenced.

Job's Closing Soliloquy (Job 28–31)
Having made his final response to his three friends, Job now addresses an extended soliloquy to someone, to anyone who will hear him. This closing soliloquy includes a magnificent poem describing humanity's search for wisdom (Job 28:1–28); a reminiscence over former blessings joined to a puzzling over current distresses (29:1–30:31); and the solemn pronouncement of a self-maledictory oath (31:1–40).

Job Searches for Wisdom's Ultimate Source (Job 28:1–28)[21]
This exquisite poem has been called "a reorienting respite from the strife of tongues."[22] Job begins his soliloquy with an extended

---

21. Questions have been repeatedly raised about the authenticity of this chapter. See the extensive discussion in Whybray, *Job*, 18–22. Gerhard von Rad, *Wisdom in Israel* (London: SCM Press, 1972), 148, observes that there is "unanimity about the fact that the poem has been inserted secondarily into the dialogue section of the book of Job." But he offers no proof of its secondary nature. In a similar vein, Alter, *Wisdom Books*, 114, says that the "strong scholarly consensus" is that it is an editorial interpolation. Alter states that "this looks like the work of another poet with a very different worldview." But he offers no specifics in support of this conclusion. He cites Robert Gordis as supporting the authenticity of the poem by identifying it as an interlude before Job's final confession of innocence. Alter regards this proposal as "fanciful," though "beguiling." Whybray, *Job*, 19, rejects the claim that the nature of wisdom in Job 28 is irrelevant to the preceding debate in the book. He observes that this analysis "betrays a misunderstanding of the nature of that debate. . . . In a real sense the question of wisdom is the main issue of the dialogue." Claus Westermann, *The Structure of the Book of Job: A Form-Critical Analysis* (Philadelphia: Fortress Press, 1981), 137, correctly treats Job 28 as "an intermezzo in the pause between the first and second acts of the drama, a concluding response to the speeches of the friends." But his analysis that the chapter teaches that wisdom is simply not at human disposal but belongs only to God overlooks the concluding statement of the chapter that the fear of the LORD is wisdom (Job 28:28), an identical analysis as found in the opening chapter of Proverbs (Prov. 1:7). The point of both Job and Proverbs is that wisdom is attainable for humans through the fear of the LORD.

22. Kidner, *Wisdom to Live By*, 80.

metaphor in which he compares the search for wisdom to a mining operation. Man searches for ore in the farthest recesses of the earth, in the blackest darkness underground. He cuts a shaft, he dangles and sways, he discovers sapphires, nuggets of gold that transform the earth below as by fire. No bird of prey, no falcon's eye, no proud beast, no prowling lion has ever seen the depths of this shaft. Man alone assaults the flinty rock, lays bare the roots of the mountains, tunnels through solid rock. He alone eyes these hidden treasures (Job 28:1–11).

But where can wisdom be found? Where does understanding dwell? The deep says, "It is not in me." The sea responds, "It is not with me." Destruction and Death say, "Only a rumor of it has reached our ears." It cannot be found in the land of the living, and its worth cannot be comprehended. Wisdom cannot be bought with gold, sapphires, crystal, jewels, coral, jasper, or topaz (Job 28:12–22).

God alone knows where wisdom dwells. When he created the powerful variables of this world, such as the force of wind and water, rain and the thunderstorm, then he appraised, confirmed, and tested true wisdom. Because God alone determines the disbursement of these powerful elements, he alone understands the way of wisdom. So then Job rightly concludes, "*The fear of the Lord—that is wisdom, and to shun evil is understanding*" (Job 28:12–28 NIV).

Job has experienced for himself the forces of wind and water, rain and thunderstorm. So he can speak from experience. In view of these variables that exist totally out of man's control, the fear of the LORD is wisdom, to shun evil is understanding. Whatever life may bring, the LORD must be feared. This is wisdom.

Job Reminisces about His Former Blessings and Puzzles over His Current Distresses (Job 29:1–30:31)

Thinking of these powerful variables that define life's experiences, Job expresses his longing for his former days. Again, figures of speech communicate his feelings far more effectively than a mere prosaic description might have done. Once God's lamp shone on his head, his path was drenched with cream, and the rock poured out streams of olive oil for him. Out of respect, young men stepped aside and old men rose to their feet. The tongues of nobles stuck to the roofs of their

165

mouths when he was present, for he rescued the poor, the fatherless, and the dying. He made the widow's heart sing. Righteousness was his clothing, justice his robe and turban. Job was eyes to the blind, feet to the lame, and a father to the needy. He broke the fangs of the wicked and snatched victims from their teeth (Job 29:3–17). Because of their great respect, men waited for his comments as though they were anticipating refreshing showers. They drank in his words as the spring rain. The lightened face of his smile was precious to them. He sat as their chief, dwelt as a king among his troops, and was like one who comforts mourners (29:21–25). He assumed that he would die in his own comfortable house, his days as numerous as the grains of sand. He expected that his roots would reach deeply to the refreshing waters and that the dew would lie on his branches all night long. He thought his glory would remain fresh and his bow ever new in his hand (29:18–20).

"But now"! Three times he repeats this phrase, dramatizing his change of fortune (Job 30:1, 9, 16). But now! But now! The respect he once had has turned to disgust and disdain. Sons of the shiftless mock him in song. Their fathers were a base and nameless brood banished by their fellow men. They brayed like senseless donkeys among the bushes and could not be trusted to keep his sheepdogs. But now their sons do not hesitate to spit in his face. Now that God has unstrung his bow, he has no arm for defense. His opponents throw off all restraint. They attack as an armed tribe, they lay snares for his feet, they build siege ramps against him, they break up his road, they advance through a gaping breach in his defenses. Every ounce of his dignity is driven away as by the wind, and his safety vanishes like a cloud (30:1–15).

So now! His life is poured out like water, night pierces his bones, God binds him like the collar of a garment that is too tight. He throws him into the mud and reduces him to dust and ashes. He drives him before the wind and tosses him about in the storm. The churning inside him never stops. He has become a brother of jackals, a companion of owls. His harp is tuned to mourning and his flute to the sound of wailing (Job 30:16–31).

Extensive use of figures of speech vivifies the contrast between Job's previous experience and his present circumstance. He has lost all material blessings and all respect from his fellow men.

Job Pronounces a Self-Maledictory Oath (Job 31:1–40)

As a final support for his cause before God and men, Job pronounces the horrors of a self-maledictory oath upon himself. Nineteen times he uses the conditional *if* to specify the circumstances in which he calls down curses on himself. Though a patriarchal figure living before the specific revelation of the law to Moses, Job anticipates at least six of the Ten Commandments. If he has given false witness against his neighbor, if he has been guilty of covetousness, if he has committed adultery by look or by action, if he has stolen by unjust dealings, if he has murdered by mistreating the orphan, widow, or needy, if he has worshiped the sun, the moon, or his gold as an act of idolatry, then he specifies the curses that he calls down on himself. Both the transgressions and the consequences are made vivid by the use of concrete figures of speech. The ruin of the wicked is his heritage from the Almighty. God weighs him in scales. The worship of sun or moon is likened to a kiss of homage, which would be sin that must be judged. An open door to his home displays his care for the traveler. A land crying out against him and furrows wet with tears would describe the pain of unpaid workers if he should abuse them. The fourfold curse he speaks over himself is most striking, whether it be taken literally or figuratively:

> May others eat what I have sown, and may my crops be uprooted. (Job 31:8 NIV)

> May my wife grind another man's grain, and may other men bow over her. (Job 31:10)

> Let my arm fall from the shoulder, let it be broken off at the joint. (Job 31:22 NIV)

> Let briers come up instead of wheat and weeds instead of barley. (Job 31:40 NIV)

In his desperation for a hearing before God, Job pleads for an indictment written out against him. He would proudly wear this formal accusation as an epaulet on his shoulder. He would put it on his

167

head as a crown. With this decoration he would approach God like a prince (Job 31:35–37).

This last imagery shows the extent to which Job will go to reinforce his point. A formal criminal indictment by God has been turned into a decorative insignia and crown for the head. No stilted prose could convey the emotive impact inherent in this striking imagery. By this figure of speech, the author has brought Job's expression of frustration to a literary climax.

Once more the number of images employed in this third round of interchanges between Job and his three friends is somewhat overwhelming. More than 110 figures of speech are found in these chapters (Job 22–31). These figures include a blustering wind, surrounding snares, enveloping darkness, floodwaters rising up to the head, thick clouds, foundations washed away, glittering gold, choicest silver, light shining on a path, traveling in every direction of the compass, purified gold, wild donkeys in the desert, hungry poor carrying sheaves that they cannot eat, thirsty poor treading grapes that they cannot drink, foam on the surface of water, melted snow, a worm feasting in a grave, a broken tree, heads of grain cut off, a dull moon, impure stars, man as a maggot, man as a worm, dead lying beneath the waters, exposed mysteries lying naked, earth hung over a void, a full moon covered with clouds, a line drawn across the horizon, pillars upholding the heavens, a churning sea, the breath of God's mouth, a faint whisper, an outer fringe, silver heaped up like dust, clothes heaped up like piles of clay, a moth's cocoon, a flimsy watchman's hut, a flood and a tempest, a hurling east wind, hissing wind clapping hands, a dangling miner, the fiery appearance of precious stones, a bird of prey, a falcon's eye, a proud beast, a prowling lion, the roots of mountains, tunnels in the rocks, hidden treasure, the unknowing deep, the lonely sea, personified Destruction and Death, the force of wind and water, a lamp shining on the head, a path drenched with cream, a rock pouring out streams of olive oil, a tongue stuck to the roof of the mouth, a singing widow's heart, righteousness as clothing, justice as a robe and a turban, eyes for the blind, feet for the lame, a father to the needy, broken fangs of the wicked, victims snatched from the teeth, refreshing showers, spring rain, a face lightened by a smile, a sitting chief, a king among his troops, days as numerous as grains of sand, roots reaching to refreshing waters, dew lying on branches throughout the night, an invigorated bow, sons of the shiftless, a mocking song, braying donkeys, watchers of sheepdogs, spit in the face, an unstrung bow, an armed tribe, snares for the feet, siege ramps, a road broken up, a gaping breach, a driving wind, a vanishing cloud, life poured out like water, night piercing the bones, a neck bound by its clothing, being cast into the mud, reduced to dust and ashes, driven before the wind, tossed about in a storm, a churning within, a brother of jackals, a companion of owls, a harp tuned to mourning, a flute tuned to wailing, a heritage from God, being weighed in the scales, a kiss of homage, an open door to travelers, the cry of an oppressed land, furrows wet with tears, a written indictment serving as a decorative insignia, and a crown proudly worn.

A number of these figures of speech might be judged as commonplace. But many others are quite distinctive if not altogether original, communicating far more than mere words could convey. Noteworthy among these are hungry poor carrying sheaves that they cannot eat, thirsty poor treading grapes that they cannot drink, earth hung over a void, a moth's cocoon, hissing wind clapping hands, a mining venture depicting the search for wisdom, a path drenched with cream, a singing widow's heart, broken fangs of the wicked, sons of the shiftless, furrows wet with tears, a written indictment serving as a decorative insignia, and a crown proudly worn.

The Speeches of Elihu (Job 32–37)[23]

Job has silenced his three friends. They have nothing more to say (Job 32:1, 3, 5). This very fact arouses a fourth friend who has

---

23. The authenticity of the speeches of Elihu has been regularly questioned. Says Alter, *Wisdom Books*, 133: "Though some scholars have tried to save the Elihu speeches as an integral part of the book, the plausible consensus is that it is an interpolation, the work of another poet." Childs, *Introduction*, 530, cites a wide consensus that the Elihu speeches are "secondary and disruptive." Westermann, *Structure*, 139, agrees with this assessment: we may "say with certainty that the speeches of Elihu are a subsequent addition" to Job. But the comment of Whybray, *Job*, 23, is appropriate: "The arguments for and against the Elihu speeches as an integral part of the book have each their own plausibility; but inasmuch as the onus of proof lies upon the proponents of a negative judgment, it may be concluded that their case is not proven." Among other arguments against the authenticity of the Elihu

been present all along. As the youngest of the group, he has deferred to the wisdom of the aged. But they have failed to refute Job, and yet have condemned him (32:3c). In addition, Job has seriously erred by justifying himself rather than God (32:2). These reasons compel Elihu to speak. The three friends are rationalizing their failure to effectively answer Job by saying, We have found the wisest way to deal with this problem. We will let God refute him, rather than man (Job 32:13). So they stand before Job without a thing to say. Words have failed them. They have gone silent in defeat.

The speeches of Elihu may be divided into six segments. A formal introductory statement by the author of Job precedes four of these segments, such as "So Elihu said"; "Then Elihu said" (Job 32:6; 34:1; 35:1; 36:1). The basic thrust of these six speeches is as follows:

- Elihu introduces himself into the dialogue. (Job 32:6–22)
- Elihu makes an initial address to Job. (Job 33:1–33)
- Elihu addresses Job's three friends. (Job 34:1–37)
- Elihu makes a second address to Job. (Job 35:1–16)
- Elihu continues his address to Job. (Job 36:1–33)
- Elihu announces the imminent appearance of the LORD in the storm. (Job 37:1–24)

More than once Elihu invites Job and his three friends to respond to his speeches (Job 33:5, 32; 34:34). The fact that neither Job nor his

---

speech, Westermann, *Structure*, 140, notes that Elihu alone quotes earlier speeches of Job in his critique, and that "such a thing never happens in a real disputational discourse." Yet is that not exactly what Job does when he quotes God's earlier statement: "Who is this that obscures my plans without knowledge?" (Job 42:3; cf. the identical words spoken by God as recorded in Job 38:2: "Who is this that obscures my plans with words without knowledge?")?

A number of considerations support the authenticity of the Elihu speeches: (1) his opening comments accurately reflect the narrative up to the point of his entry into the dialogue; (2) Elihu's analysis of Job's deficiency is identical with the LORD's, which comes subsequently (Job 32:2; 40:8); (3) Elihu advances the discussion by introducing two ways that God has indeed spoken despite Job's protestations of his silence (Job 33:12–30); (4) Elihu's ninefold admonition to "Listen" prepares the way for Job to pay attention to the multiple queries that will come from the Almighty; (5) Elihu's repetitious reference to the thunderous voice of God directly anticipates the twofold description of the LORD's answering "out of the storm" (Job 37:2–5; 38:1; 40:6). These numerous and coherent allusions to the material both before and after Elihu's speeches support the authenticity of the Elihu material.

three friends offer any response indicates that Elihu is the victor in the ongoing silencing game. By his speeches he has silenced them all.

Clearly, Elihu is correct in his critique of the three friends. They have not proved Job wrong. They have swung haymakers at him by accusing him of gross sins that have caused his calamities. But they have offered no clear proof that Job is a greater sinner than other people, thereby deserving greater suffering. The three friends have not proved their case against Job. In the end, this fourth friend will be confirmed in his judgment about the three friends by God himself (Job 42:7).

But is Elihu also correct in his analysis of Job's self-defense? Has Job, all this time, been busy justifying himself rather than justifying God? Has his main concern been to prove himself an upright person rather than attempting to prove that God has been altogether just in his treatment of him?

Yes, Elihu is correct in his critique of Job as well. This conclusion is confirmed by a comparison of Elihu's evaluation of Job when compared with God's. Elihu was angry with Job "for justifying himself rather than God" (Job 32:2b NIV). With virtually the identical thought, God queries Job: "Would you condemn me to justify yourself?" (40:8 NIV).

Although Job has spoken of God what is right in comparison to what the three friends have said, he has concentrated more on justifying himself than on justifying God's ways with him. Admittedly, it would have been far more difficult for Job to interact with his friends in ways that would justify God rather than himself. But that is precisely what he should have done. Elihu in his speeches establishes the rightness of God's ways with man. In providing this insight, he serves as a transitional figure, clearing the way for Job's ultimate face-off with God himself. In the end, Job will get the audience with God that he so earnestly desires. But the outcome will not be exactly what Job has expected.

Elihu employs two figures of speech to describe his compulsion to speak. He is like bottled-up wine. He is like new wineskins ready to burst. So he must find relief by opening his lips and answering Job and his three friends. He is full of words, and the spirit within him compels him to speak (Job 32:18–20).

Elihu makes a positive contribution to the entire process of interchange by noting that God continues to speak despite Job's sense of frustration over the LORD's seeming silence.[24] Why has Job complained that God answers none of his words? For the LORD speaks in two distinct ways, though man may not perceive it. First, in accord with the revelational experiences of the patriarchal period, God speaks "in a dream, in a vision of the night, when deep sleep falls on men as they slumber in their beds." He speaks in order "to turn man from wrongdoing and keep him from pride, to preserve his soul from the pit, his life from perishing by the sword" (Job 33:14–18 NIV). Subsequently God will honor Job by a theophany, and will speak to him in a form even clearer than a dream or a vision in the night.

But God also speaks in another way. According to Elihu, a man may be "chastened on a bed of pain with constant distress in his bones . . . . His flesh wastes away to nothing, and his bones, once hidden, now stick out. His soul draws near to the pit, and his life to the messengers of death" (Job 33:19–22 NIV). God does these things more than once to a man "to turn back his soul from the pit, that the light of life may shine on him" (33:30 NIV). He "speaks to them in their affliction" (36:15b NIV).

This is undoubtedly Job's experience. All this time, through all these trials, God has been speaking to him, not in judgment but in grace. By this speaking, God has been humbling Job, keeping him from wrongdoing, preserving his soul. In analyzing Elihu's distinctive perspective, one commentator notes:

> Affliction, he tells [Job], is not a token of God's displeasure, but one of the measures of his grace. It is not sent in wrath, but with a kind of merciful design. It is one of the ways in which God speaks to men to draw them away from sin and to promote their highest welfare.[25]

So now what can Job expect? Elihu describes the way God works in showing his grace through the trials and sufferings of life. If there is a

---

24. Crenshaw, *Old Testament Wisdom*, 91, regards Elihu's speeches as hardly contributing to a resolution of the conflict between Job and God. Yet Elihu's distinctive insights clearly move the argument of the book along.

25. William Henry Green, *Conflict and Triumph: The Argument of the Book of Job Unfolded* (Edinburgh: Banner of Truth, 1999), 267.

messenger on the side of the afflicted, a mediator to plead his cause and to provide a ransom for him, "then his flesh is renewed like a child's; it is restored as in the days of his youth. He prays to God and finds favor with him, he sees God's face and shouts for joy; he is restored by God to his righteous state. Then he comes to men and says, 'I sinned, and perverted what was right, but I did not get what I deserved. He redeemed my soul from going down to the pit, and I will live to enjoy the light'" (Job 33:23–28 NIV).

Figures of speech appear throughout Elihu's message, though perhaps not as extensively as in other portions of the book. He speaks of the flesh of the afflicted as being renewed like a child's (Job 33:25). He makes use of Job's earlier imagery: "the ear tests words as the tongue tastes food" (34:3; cf. 12:11). He characterizes Job as a man who "drinks scorn like water" (34:7), which is a milder description than Eliphaz's judgment that man "drinks iniquity like water" (15:16). He encourages Job with the declaration that God is wooing him "from the jaws of distress" and bringing him to a "table laden with choice food" (36:16). He depicts the breath of God as producing ice and causing the broad waters to freeze (37:10). God spreads out the skies "hard as a mirror of cast bronze" (37:18). Generally Elihu's speech is not permeated by images as extensively as in the case of the other dialogue portions of the book. But he has made a major contribution to the advancement of the book's argument by interpreting the chastenings of the LORD from a positive perspective. As has been noted, *"Elihu saw chastening in its redemptive context, as informed and governed by the principle of sovereign grace. Since grace is by its very nature sovereignly free, it may bestow the blessing of chastening most abundantly on the saint who has relatively least need!"*[26]

Elihu's attitude toward Job is more that of true friendship than of the vindictiveness of the other three friends. His desire is that Job be cleared even as he acknowledges his sin. As he explains:

> If you have anything to say,
>   answer me;
>   speak up,
> for I want you to be cleared. (Job 33:32 NIV)

26. Kline, "Job," 484 (emphasis added).

The speech of Elihu silences Job, and prepares him for his final confrontation, his interchange with the Almighty himself. It is quite likely that the thunder announcing the coming storm to which Elihu refers anticipates the actual approach of God himself. For he declares with some sense of alarm, "At this my heart pounds and leaps from its place. Listen! Listen to the roar of his voice, to the rumbling that comes from his mouth" (Job 36:33–37:2 NIV). With that foreboding of an approaching thunderous voice, the stage is set for Yahweh the COVENANT LORD to answer Job "out of the storm" (38:1). This dramatic entry of God himself introduces the climax of the book.

In the face of Elihu's argumentation, Job now in his turn has been silenced. As was the case with Satan before Yahweh, as was the case of each of Job's three friends in their turn, so now Job has nothing to say. He attempts no response. By the speech of Elihu Job has been prepared to *listen* rather than to speak.

Elihu's determination to bring Job to the point of listening rather than speaking has been one of his major goals from the beginning of his address to Job. His opening words to Job directly speak to this matter:

> But now, Job,
>   listen
>   to my words;
>   pay attention
>   to everything I say. (Job 33:1 NIV)

Nine times Elihu directly admonishes Job and his friends, "Listen!" (Job 32:10; 33:1, 31, 33; 34:2, 10, 16; 37:2, 14). These admonitions serve to bind over the Elihu speeches to the speeches of God, which immediately follow.

The Speeches of the LORD (Yahweh) (Job 38:1–42:6)

The LORD's First Speech (Job 38:1–40:2)

Instantly the narrative announces that it is the LORD, Yahweh, God of the Covenant, who finally speaks to Job. All through the interchanges with his four friends, over a hundred times it has been "God" (*Elohim, Eloah, El, Shaddai*), and only once "Yahweh" (Job 12:9) as the common point of reference. But now, as in the prologue to the book (1:1–2:13), Yahweh is the one who speaks and acts.

Distinctly in the books of wisdom in the canon, God's wisdom is for all the peoples of the world. But this wisdom is no less for God's covenant people. The Creator, Sustainer, Redeemer, and Judge of all humanity is no other than Yahweh, the LORD OF THE COVENANT. By this name, Yahweh uniquely reveals his nature as the great, the unchanging "I Am."

From the perspective of the new covenant, God's name has changed, even as the fuller understanding of his nature has become known. His new revelatory name is "the Father, the Son, and the Holy Spirit." This name is singular, underscoring the unity and singularity of the deity. Yet *the* Father, *the* Son, and *the* Holy Spirit attest to the authenticity of the three distinct persons that constitute the essence of this single, unified God. In this name is hidden all the treasures of wisdom and knowledge. Every aspect of unity and diversity in this world finds its ultimate explanation in the reality of this triune God. "All nations" may claim for themselves the treasures of wisdom and knowledge found in the self-revelation of the God of this name (Matt. 28:19–20).

The LORD's speech to Job comes "out of the storm," as anticipated by Elihu. This speech does not articulate what might have been expected. Rather than defending his servant Job in face of his opponents' unfounded accusations, Yahweh the LORD OF THE COVENANT puts Job on the defensive. Who is this person that darkens his plan, his purpose for the world, with words without wisdom? Job is finally getting his audience with the Almighty. But instead of God's answering him, he must answer God. In rapid-fire succession, the LORD poses over fifty questions for Job to answer.[27] The LORD builds on Elihu's preparation of Job to *listen*. For how can a person answer any question without first listening? The initial sign of increase in wisdom is the capacity to listen before presuming to speak.

This final phase of the book's dialogue climaxes with a virtual flood of images that permeate the speeches of God. The LORD's first

---

27. Quite interestingly, asking questions served as a principal method of Jesus' interaction with his audience as a teacher. The Gospel of Mark records Jesus as asking no fewer than sixty questions of his hearers. The Son reflects the wisdom of the Father.

words to Job contain over twenty images drawn from his activities at creation and the resulting weather phenomena (Job 38:1–38). One noteworthy author, being a gifted word-crafter in his own right, has underscored the climactic nature of the poetry coming at this point from the mouth of God himself:

> The poet, having given Job such vividly powerful language for the articulation of his outrage and his anguish, now fashions still greater poetry for God. The wide-ranging panorama of creation in the Voice from the Whirlwind shows a sublimity of expression, a plasticity of description, an ability to evoke the complex and dynamic interplay of beauty and violence in the natural world, and even an originality of metaphoric inventiveness, that surpasses all the poetry, great as it is, that Job has spoken.[28]

The humbling of Job before the majestic workings of the Creator and Sustainer of the universe becomes immediately apparent by Job's being struck dumb before these queries. God wants Job to tell him who has darkened his counsel with words void of knowledge. Job had longed for the opportunity to question God, but now he must brace himself like a man and prepare to answer the questionings of the Almighty (Job 38:2–3).

The Covenant Lord laid the foundation of the earth at its creation. Where was Job at that time? Someone marked off the dimensions of the world's foundations and stretched a measuring line across them. Surely Job must have been there! Yes? So he should have no trouble explaining who made these markings. On what were the earth's footings set? Who laid its cornerstone even while the morning stars were singing and the angels were shouting for joy?

The Lord of the Covenant continues with his plethora of images. He shut the sea behind doors when it burst forth from the womb. He shaped the clouds as a garment for the sea and wrapped it in thick darkness. He fixed a limit for the sea, setting doors and bars in place and halting its proud waves at a predetermined point.

Then God turns to his providential orderings that maintain the creation. He gives orders to the morning, telling it when to appear.

---

28. Alter, *Wisdom Books*, 10.

He shows the dawn where and when it must come forth. He treats the surface of the earth as though it were a cloth that the dawn takes by its edges to shake out the wicked, just as someone might grasp the corners of a tablecloth to shake out its dried and dirty crumbs. In the same way, the emerging light of every dawn shakes the wicked who do their evil deeds under cover of darkness out of their hiding places.

Then the COVENANT LORD depicts the effect of dawn's light on the shapeless mass of the earth. As the gradually increasing daylight strikes the earth's surface, images take on a more refined shape, just like clay molded under the form of a seal. The earth's features stand out like a tailored piece of cloth rather than like a shapeless mass of draped material. So God denies the wicked their enjoyment of his light and exposes their upraised arm for all to see (Job 38:14–15).

Next God queries Job concerning his journeys to the springs of the sea and the recesses of the ocean's depths. Has Job ever seen the gates of death or comprehended the vast expanses of the earth (Job 38:16–18)? Does he know the way to the place where light and darkness reside? Can he lead them both to their proper places? With a cutting sarcasm, the Almighty presses Job: "Surely you know, for . . . you have lived so many years!" (38:19–21 NIV).[29]

Then he asks about the storehouses of snow and hail, the place where lightning and the east wind are dispersed, about cutting a channel for rain, being a father to the dew, locating the womb of ice and frost, and commanding the surface of the deep to freeze (Job 38:22–30).

Can Job control the constellations and their movements according to the seasons? Can he shout to the clouds to activate a flood of water? Does he commission the lightning bolts so that they feel obligated to report back to him? Does he count the clouds and tip over the water jars of the heavens when the dust of the earth becomes hardened? Is he the one that gives wisdom to the human heart and understanding to a man's mind (Job 38:31–38)? By all these questions, God humbles Job before his great glory as Creator and Sustainer of the universe.

---

29. Kidner, *Wisdom to Live By*, 71, analyzes these probings of the Almighty as putting Job in his place "more as a father might do it to a dogmatic adolescent than as a judge to an offender."

Next the Almighty describes the uniqueness of a number of animals and birds as members of his earthly kingdom. Is Job actually capable of providing for them, supervising them, determining the uniqueness of their nature? Does he hunt prey for the lioness and satisfy the hunger of the lions? Who provides food for the raven when its young cry to God? Is Job watching over the mountain goats when they give birth, far away from any human civilization? Did he untie the ropes of the wild donkey, who laughs at the commotion of town? Can he tame the wild ox so that he will plow his furrows? Did he design the ostrich with his short wings and powerful legs? Did he make such a senseless bird who lays her eggs on the sand, but who laughs at horse and rider when she runs? Does Job inspire the horse who catches the scent of battle and eats up the ground in frenzied excitement as he charges into the fray? Can he provide wisdom for the hawk to hunt and the eagle to soar at his command (Job 38:39–39:30)?

As in the case of proverbs and parables, the ability to analyze and describe in short, memorable statements the major characteristics of various members of the animal kingdom demonstrates royal wisdom, the ability of a king to rightly govern his domain (1 Kings 4:32–33). In the present situation, God is the King and the whole world his realm for rule. By establishing that he possesses the wisdom essential for governing this vast world, the LORD shuts off the complaint of Job against the way in which he orders the circumstances of his personal life.

Following the display of God's glory, Job finds himself in a most uncomfortable position. Is he to contend with God, correct the Almighty, accuse him (Job 40:1–2)? God has made no reference to the sin of Job or his own mighty acts in redemption. Yahweh the LORD OF THE COVENANT has concentrated on his glory as Creator and Sustainer. "Just as Jesus invited us to 'consider the lilies of the field,'" so the LORD invites Job as a friend to "join him in a walk around his garden."[30] Too often this basic perception of the reality of God is forgotten. Man's first level of accountability is to God as his Maker and Benefactor.

---

30. Andersen, *Job*, 270–71.

Job's Modest Response (Job 40:3–5)

God humbles Job by this first speech. Job declares himself to be "insignificant." He can speak no more. He in his turn has been silenced. Though properly humbled by the questions that he cannot answer as posed by God, Job is also honored that the Almighty stoops to converse with him so freely and extensively (Job 40:3–5).

The LORD's Second Speech (Job 40:6–41:34)

The integrity of the book of Job has been questioned in view of a second speech of God, followed by a second response of Job. What is the point of a second speech of God? Why a second response of Job? Should not this bifurcation be viewed as uncovering disunity in the literary piece?[31]

A closer reading of the two speeches of God will reveal the inherent progression. Beyond God's control of the created world as displayed in his first speech is God's power to maintain justice and humble the proud, just as he has done with Job. This very factor provides a larger challenge for Job:

> Do you have an arm
> like God's,

---

31. Cf. Childs, *Introduction*, 529. Childs acknowledges the "general agreement" that this section "forms an integral part of the original poetic composition." Yet he finds it a "puzzlement" that there are two divine speeches that "vary considerably in literary quality." Childs states that "the question has not been satisfactorily resolved" as to why the book concludes with two speeches from God rather than a single speech (539).

The clearest answer to this question resides in the progression realized across the two speeches. In the first instance, God challenges Job by asking him to display his control of creation and the weather—the earth, the stars, clouds and sea, the morning, light and darkness, snow, hail, winds and rain, the constellations (Job 38:2–38). Then God points to some of the lesser members of the animal world, asking Job to display equal wisdom to that which designed and sustains the raven, mountain goat, doe with fawn, wild donkey and ox, ostrich and battle-horse, hawk and eagle (38:41–39:30). Job is appropriately humbled. But in his second speech, God offers what clearly is a more ominous challenge, one that suits perfectly the circumstance of the book. If Job is going to discredit God's justice, then let him be the one to establish justice in the earth. Let Job humble every proud man and crush the wicked where they stand (40:11–14). This second challenge by God draws out from Job a much more heartfelt repentance (42:1–6), arising from Job's inability to respond to the much greater challenge of humbling the proud and establishing righteousness in all the earth. But if he cannot do this job, how can he dare to criticize the Almighty?

and can your voice thunder
   like his?
Then adorn yourself
   with glory and splendor,
and clothe yourself
   in honor and majesty.
Unleash the fury
   of your wrath,
look at every proud man
   and bring him low,
look at every proud man
   and humble him,
crush the wicked
   where they stand.
Bury them all
   in the dust together;
shroud their faces
   in the grave.
Then I myself will admit to you
that your own right hand can save you. (Job 40:9–14 NIV)

Can Job do this difficult work that God continually does in maintaining justice and humbling the proud? Well beyond the challenge of ordering the weather phenomena is sustaining righteousness, humility, and justice among all humanity.

To drive home his point, the LORD resorts once more to a number of figures of speech. Does Job have an arm of strength like God's? Can his voice thunder like the Almighty's? If so, then Job has the challenge set before him to do this work of God. He must put on clothing of honor and majesty. He must bury every proud and wicked person in the dust, and shroud their faces in the grave. Every proud man he must bring low, and every wicked man he must crush even as he stands defiantly in his own strength. If Job presumes to criticize God and contend with him, then he must show that he can do a better job than God. A major aspect of God's work is humbling the proud and crushing the wicked, so Job must display his ability in this critical area (Job 40:6–14).

With the assumption that this task will be too difficult for Job, God offers him a lesser challenge. He presents before him two of his creatures that can present a worthy challenge to Job, one from the land and one from the sea. If humbling all human beings appears as too great a task, then perhaps Job can prove his prowess by taking on one of these lesser creatures.

The first of these creatures is the behemoth, most likely identified with the hippopotamus, among the largest and most challenging of land animals (Job 40:15–24). The description fits the hippo: he feeds on grass and is powerful in muscle and bone. Yet the reference to his tail as being like a cedar tree is puzzling. One possible explanation might be to understand the verb (*chafatz*) in its more common significance: he "delights" in his tail as though it were a cedar. Small though it may be, its waving back and forth shows the delight of the creature.[32]

So can Job trap the hippo? Can anyone tame him by piercing his nose (Job 40:24)? Would Job like to give it a try? Though he is too much for man to subdue, his Maker can approach him and humble him with his sword (40:19).

Then there is the leviathan, the most challenging of sea creatures, quite possibly the crocodile. In this case, the description is filled with multiple images. Numerous figures display the futility of attempts to tame him. Is he to be caught with a fishhook, his tongue tied with a rope, a cord slipped through his nose, a hook planted in his jaw? Will he beg for mercy, agreeing to be a slave, made a pet like a bird, put on a leash for little girls, purchased by traders? The ridiculousness of it all underscores Job's incapacity to subdue this creature. As this imagery is summarized:

> If you lay a hand on him, you will remember the struggle and never do it again! Any hope of subduing him is false; the mere sight of him is overpowering. (Job 41:8–9 NIV)

The multiple use of figures of speech continues. This creature's outer coat cannot be stripped off. No one can bridle him. Who would dare open the doors of his mouth? Rows of shields are on his back,

---

32. The idea of a mythological figure is contradicted by the statement that God made him along with humanity (Job 40:15). The proposal that this beast represents a dinosaur stumbles over the fact that no such creature walked the earth as recently as the days of the biblical patriarchs.

his snorting throws out flashes of light, his eyes are like the rays of dawn, firebrands stream from his mouth, smoke emerges from his nostrils as from a boiling pot over a fire of reeds, his breath sets coals ablaze, flames dart from his mouth, his chest is hard as a rock, hard as a lower millstone, he treats iron like straw, bronze like rotten wood. Slingstones are like chaff to him, a club as a piece of straw. He laughs at the rattling of the lance. His underside is like jagged potsherds, leaving a trail in the mud like a threshing sledge. He makes the depths churn like a boiling caldron, he stirs the sea like a pot of ointment, the deep seems to have white hair (Job 41:12–33).

What kind of lasting impression would be made on the reader if this amazing creature were simply designated by his name? But the manifold use of figures of speech heightens the reader's awareness of the awesomeness of this creature.

So what is the point of it all? God's challenge for Job to humble the proud still stands at the center. This single creature "looks down on all that are haughty" and is "king over all that are proud" (Job 41:34). This creature of God—he is able to humble the proud. But can Job humble this creature? As the LORD declares:

> No one is fierce enough to rouse him. Who then is able to stand against me? Who has a claim against me that I must pay? Everything under heaven belongs to me. (Job 41:10–11 NIV)

The Almighty is debtor to no one. Particularly sinful man has no claim on him. God has never given to anyone more troubles than he deserves. If Job cannot humble even the lower creatures of this world, how can he presume to declare what is right and wrong about the LORD's dealings with humanity?

So God has completed his second speech to Job. He has not answered Job's questions as to why he is suffering. He has not tried to establish Job's sinfulness. He has not stooped to defend his own actions. He has simply shown himself to be the incomparable Creator and Sustainer of his world. If Job cannot handle even one of the lesser of God's creations, not to speak of humanity, how can he presume to contend with God the Maker of it all? One commentator provides insightful comments on the significance of Job's inability to control even a sample or two of God's creatures:

> But there is no mistaking the thrust of it . . . . It cuts us down to size, treating us not as philosophers but as children . . . whose first and fundamental grasp of truth must be to know the difference between our place and God's, and to accept it. We may reflect that if, instead of this, we were offered a defence of our Creator's ways for our approval, it would imply that he was accountable to us, not we to him.[33]

In reviewing the speeches of Elihu and God, we find that the number of figures of speech continues to be rather overwhelming. These two speakers employ a combined total of over eighty images. Adding this total to previous numbers, the book of Job contains over 370 figures of speech. The number is astounding in itself, not even considering the impact of these images on the communication of the book's message.

The images used in the speeches of Elihu and God include the following: bottled-up wine, new wineskins ready to burst, chastening on a bed of pain, distress in the bones, flesh renewed like a child's, the ear testing words as the tongue tastes food, drinking scorn like water, jaws of distress, a table laden with choice food, the breath of God producing ice, skies hard as a mirror of cast bronze, thunder as the roar of God's voice and the rumbling of his mouth, earth's foundations, a measuring line for the earth, earth's footings and cornerstone, singing morning stars, angels shouting for joy, sea shut behind doors, sea bursting forth from its womb, clouds a garment for the sea, commands given for the morning, the earth as a shaken cloth, the earth as clay molded under a seal, a tailored cloth, a journey to the springs of the sea, the gates of death, the residence of light and darkness, storehouses of snow and hail, a place of dispersal for lightning and wind, a channel for the rain, a father to the dew, the womb of ice and frost, a shout to the clouds, commissioning of lightning, tipping the water jugs of heaven, hunting prey for the lioness, providing food for the ravens, watching over mountain goats as they give birth, taming

---

33. Kidner, *Wisdom to Live By*, 72.

the wild ox, a senseless, laughing ostrich, a frenzied battle-horse, an arm like God's, a thunderous voice, clothing of honor and majesty, burying the proud in the dust, shrouding the faces of the wicked in the grave, bones as tubes of bronze, limbs like rods of iron, caught with a fishhook, a tongue tied with a rope, a cord through the nose, a hook in the jaw, a pet like a bird, a pet on a leash for girls, doors of the mouth, shields on the back, snorting flashes of lightning, eyes like rays of the dawn, firebrands streaming from the mouth, smoke from the nostrils, a boiling pot, breath that sets coals ablaze, a chest as hard as a rock or a lower millstone, iron as straw, bronze like rotten wood, slingstones like chaff, a club like a piece of straw, the rattling of a lance, jagged potsherds, a trail in the mud, a threshing sledge, a boiling caldron, a pot of ointment, the deep like white hair, a king over the proud.

Job's Repentant Response (Job 42:1–6)

In the end, Job responds with appropriate humility and repentance before his Maker. God has a plan, as is clearly shown by the fact of his creation. God will carry out every plan he has made. He will bring his own counsel to a satisfactory conclusion (Job 42:1–2). Twice Job quotes earlier statements of God (42:3a, 4). He acknowledges that he is the one who spoke of things he did not understand. As a consequence, he despises himself and repents in dust and ashes (42:3–6).

It might be argued that Job now does exactly what his friends had urged him to do all along. Is he not finally repenting, just as Bildad, Zophar, and Eliphaz had directed him to do (Job 8:5–7; 11:14–15; 22:23–27)? Is it now at this late date in the book that Job finally does what his friends had said he should do? That would appear to be exactly the case.

Yet the repentance urged by Job's three friends and the repentance actually expressed by Job are two different things. His friends had informed Job that he must repent of all the evil he had done that was the cause of all his tragedies. But Job never falls into line with their directives. Instead, in both his responses to God, Job acknowledges wrongdoing with respect to what he said about God in responding to

his friends. He does not repent for the wrongdoings that they identified as the cause of his disasters:[34]

I spoke once,
　　but I have no answer—
twice,
　　but I will say no more. (Job 40:5 NIV)

Surely I spoke of things
　　I did not understand,
things
　　too wonderful for me to know. (Job 42:3 NIV)

Job's repentance should be understood as genuine and necessary. But
it must also be perceived as something other than an ultimate submis-
sion to the skewed judgment of his friends.

Narrative Epilogue (Job 42:7–17)

Having concluded his interaction with Job, God turns to his
three friends. He specifically addresses Eliphaz, the oldest of the
three. These friends have not spoken what is right, particularly with
respect to God. Their wrong evaluations of God's ways stand in
contrast with God's evaluation of his servant Job. Four times Job
receives from God the honorary designation "my servant" (Job 42:7,
8 [3 times]). The book's narrative begins with Job's designation as
"my servant Job" (1:8) and ends with this fourfold identification of
"my servant Job."

Most challenging in terms of understanding is this final contrast
in which the LORD declares that he is angry with Elihu and his two
friends because they have not spoken about him "what is right, as my
servant Job has" (Job 42:7c). For four chapters the LORD has peppered
Job with over fifty questions, identifying him as the one who "darkens
my counsel with words without knowledge" (38:2). He has brought
Job to the point of repenting in dust and ashes (42:6). Job is now in
his turn silenced, committed to speak no more (40:5). How is it that

---

34. This distinction in the repentance of Job is helpfully brought out in Longman, *Job*,
65–66.

now Job is twice described as the one who has spoken of the LORD *"what is right"* (42:7–8)? In what sense may it be said that Job has spoken of the LORD what is right?

As might be expected when a few words incisively define the solution to a long-standing puzzle, numerous explanations of these words have been offered. Some have concluded that Job's "right" words must be his repentant words just spoken.[35] But the repentance of Job seems too recent and the reference to his speaking what was right seems too broad to refer only or primarily to his recent humbled condition.

A more all-embracive understanding of the LORD's approval of Job's words fits the flow of the narrative much better. As this perspective has been summarized:

> In the prologue the narrator announced that Job did not sin with his lips or express contempt for Yahweh (1:22; 2:10). Now Yahweh's answer announces that Job's bold assertions in the dialogue speeches were likewise free from blame in spite of some rather vitriolic moments (e.g., 16:9ff.). The blunt and forthright accusations of Job from the depths of his agony are closer to the truth than the conventional unquestioning pronouncements of the friends.[36]

A further connection to the narrative prologue in this final pronouncement of the LORD helps to identify what was "correct" or "true" in Job's sayings. As just noticed, twice in the prologue and four times in the epilogue, Yahweh bestows the honorary title "my servant" on Job (Job 1:8; 2:3; 42:7, 8 [3 times]). The epilogue echoes the prologue. Job never lost this position as the LORD's servant in the LORD's eyes, and Job never relinquished this position by anything he

---

35. Says Kline, "Job," 489: "it seems necessary to think primarily of Job's confession and the friends' lack of such repentance . . . . For in terms of the theology expressed in their debate, the difference between them was merely one of degree. The words of all of them were in part censurable." Cf. Whybray, *Job*, 172–73: "Yahweh is here referring to what Job has *just said* . . . . There he has not only confessed that God and his works are incomprehensible, but has shown humility in admitting his own insignificance and ignorance. Such humility was wholly lacking in the friends, who had confidently claimed that they understood God's nature." Cf. also Longman, *Job*, 459: "In the final analysis, it appears that God is including Job's repentance in his declaration that Job did what was right. He repented, and now the three friends need to repent."

36. Habel, *The Book of Job*, 583.

said. Despite the questioning nature of many of Job's remarks, he speaks always as "my servant." Quite striking is the consistency of Job's astounding affirmations of faith throughout the entire course of the dialogue with his three friends, displaying the unbroken assurance of his personal relationship with the Almighty. At first he longs for someone to arbitrate between himself and God (9:33). Then he reminds the Almighty that it was God's own hands that shaped him, molded him like clay, indicating that the LORD had taken a personal interest in his original formation (10:8–9). Then he cries out through his agonizings, "Though he slay me, yet will I trust him" (13:15). Next he describes his future expectation in terms of God's longing for him—a most amazing expression of hope in the midst of deepest sufferings:

> All the days of my hard service
> I will wait for my renewal to come.
> You will call and I will answer you;
> *You will long for the creature your hands have made.* (Job 14:14–15 NIV)

Truly astounding are these words coming directly from Job's heart of his confident trust in the undying love and commitment of God. Here he scales the pinnacle of divine mystery as expressed later by the Son of God: "The Father seeks such to worship him" (John 4:23). Yet there is more. Job speaks properly of the LORD when by a persistent faith he affirms that "even now my witness is in heaven; my advocate is on high. My intercessor is my friend as my eyes pour out tears to God" (Job 16:19–20). Job boldly implores God to give the pledge that God himself demands, since no one else would dare put up security for him (17:3). Climactically he declares from the fullness of his faith: "I know that my Redeemer lives . . . . I myself will see him with my own eyes . . . . How my heart yearns within me!" (19:25–27 NIV).

Does not the consistency of these faith responses to the carping criticisms of Job's friends attest to the propriety of the LORD's assessment that Job has spoken "what is correct" about him? The LORD must have been greatly pleased with these noble words of undying hope. Yet not an inkling of this kind of wording is found among the multiple speeches of Job's three friends. In this unique way, Job remains as God's beloved "servant" through it all. By these expressions of unmoved trust in God, Job speaks "correctly," on the "solidly established" basis of his faith throughout all his challenging days.[37]

Even Job's humblings take on unique characteristics. No threat of consuming wrath is employed to bring Job to his senses. Instead, God humbles Job by displaying his ongoing wonders as Creator, Sustainer, and Redeemer of a fallen world.

But these three friends! Puffed up in their self-centered piety, they experience a different humbling. They stand before a God of justified wrath who threatens to consume them in a moment. In addition, they must humble themselves before men as well as before God, which Job was not required to do. These three friends must go to Job and offer sacrifice as they acknowledge their sin. Job will then pray for them even though he is "still unsightly and unhealed."[38] Then and only then will they be graciously delivered from divine wrath.

Never had Job's friends even considered the possibility that they, rather than Job, could be the targets of God's wrath. As has been well stated:

> In the course of their speeches, not one of them even hinted that they, not Job, might be the object of God's wrath (Job 42:7) and in need of his grace. Now they discover (it is a delightful irony) that unless they can secure the patronage of Job (the very one they had treated as in such need of their spiritual resources), they might not escape the divine displeasure.[39]

Job perceives that his accusing friends have a need that he alone can supply, and so he prays for them. Even before he experiences personal restoration, he manifests a genuine concern for his friends by interceding on their behalf. Then the LORD "made him prosperous again and gave him twice as much as he had before" (Job 42:10; cf. Job 1:3; 42:12). In addition, his brothers, his sisters, and all his

---

37. The word normally translated as indicating that Job spoke "what is right" does not refer primarily to moral rightness. The root idea of the term (נְכוֹנָה) describes a thing "established," and may refer to "truth." Says Habel, *The Book of Job*, 583: "The term rendered 'truth' (*nekona*) refers to what is correct and consistent with the facts (Deut. 17:4; 1 Sam. 23:23). Job's answers correspond with reality."

38. Kidner, *Wisdom to Live By*, 73.

39. Andersen, *Job*, 293.

acquaintances who had previously known him came and comforted him over all his troubles.[40] Even though everything had been restored to Job, he still had need for comfort over his earlier losses. Each one gave him a piece of silver and a gold ring (42:11).

From a new covenant perspective, the good news from Jesus is that he will send "another Comforter," the Holy Spirit, who will minister to Christ's people in their times of affliction (John 14:16). He will not leave his people as abandoned orphans. By the sending of the Spirit, he will come to them (14:18). In this world they will have tribulation. But they can take heart, for the one who is with them has "overcome the world" despite all its challenges and distresses (16:33).

THE ULTIMATE MESSAGE OF THE BOOK

So what is the ultimate message of the book of Job? People have sought an answer to this question across the centuries. But no consensus has been reached. One author rhapsodizes about the genius of the book of Job: "Nothing that has survived from the ancient world achieves such sublimity of thought and expression."[41] Yet this same author proceeds to describe God as he appears in Job as "this guilty Lord."[42] He speaks of the "sublime irrelevance" of God's challenges to Job in asserting that he exercises authority over the animal world.[43] He concludes that Job acquiesced to God's might only when he "finally realized the futility of arguing with one who rose above the law."[44] This God is described as someone "taking leave of one's senses" like Job's wife.[45] Such blasphemous depictions of the God of

---

40. Kenneth Laing Harris, "Job," in *ESV Study Bible* (Wheaton, IL: Crossway, 2008), 872, says that the word *comfort* is "the most important key word in the book." A number of verses using the word *comfort* are cited (Job 2:11; 6:10; 7:13; 15:11; 16:2; 21:34). These references to "comfort" in Job offer a significant insight into the book, though not sufficient to establish its place as the "key word" of the book. The effort to substitute "comforted" in place of "repented" in dust and ashes in Job 42:6 is not convincing.

41. Crenshaw, *Old Testament Wisdom*, 106.

42. Ibid., 94.

43. Ibid., 99.

44. Ibid., 103.

45. Ibid., 105.

Job clearly contradict one clear message of this book: humans should never presume to call God to account.

So what is the ultimate message of Job? What is the unique word of wisdom communicated with such majesty of literary style? Because of the persistence of certain views regarding the message of the book, it may be useful to begin by discussing what the book of Job does not say. Then the actual message of Job may be considered.

What the Book of Job Does Not Say

First, the book of Job does not directly answer the question, "Why do the righteous suffer?" Job suffers terribly and is relatively innocent. But the "Why" question remains unanswered. The LORD studiously avoids any hint of an answer to the question of Job's sufferings. Indeed, the prologue to the book places the sufferings of God's servants in the context of a cosmic struggle between the LORD's redemptive program and the destructive schemes of Satan. But this behind-the-scenes interchange between God and Satan remains forever unknown to Job, meaning that the LORD's servant who suffers can only vaguely deduce this unseen cosmic scene as the solution to the puzzle of his sufferings. People living since Job have not had any more opportunity than Job to actually witness firsthand the cosmic interchange between God and Satan.

Second, the book of Job is not a theodicy. It does not seek to justify God in relation to the existence of evil in this world. Nowhere in the concluding speeches of Elihu and of God himself is the effort made to vindicate God in view of what he has brought into the life of Job. As has been well stated: "So the book is not a theodicy—for man cannot arrogate to himself the right to justify God without deifying himself."[46] In the end, Job ceases his demands that God explain why he suffers so extensively.

What the Book of Job Does Say

So what is the message of the book? From a positive perspective, what truth about God and his creation does Job communicate?

---

46. Kidner, *Wisdom to Live By*, 86.

First, the book of Job clearly affirms that God ultimately rewards the righteous and punishes the wicked. From an opposing viewpoint, Job has been described as a "radical challenge to the doctrine of reward for the righteous and punishment for the wicked."[47] On the surface, this evaluation of Job's message may seem correct. But reading to the end of the book firmly contradicts this negative analysis. How does Job end up? He is totally vindicated before the face of the world, his relatives, and his friends. He is fully restored in health and family, with twice the wealth he previously possessed.

In a similar vein, what is the final picture of the so-called friends of Job who persistently pummeled him? Certainly the effort to justify them is wrongly conceived.[48] Job's stinging sarcasm goes a long way to putting them in their place, making them into a "proverb," so that the derogatory cliché "Job's comforters" continues to this day to communicate disdain. Openly exposed in their error for all to see, they must offer sacrifices in Job's presence and before the watching world to gain the intercession of the very one they so cruelly tormented.

But there is more. The LORD is "angry" with Eliphaz and his two friends. This wrath of the Almighty will be meted out with precise justice. Eliphaz, presumably the eldest, bears the greatest responsibility and the severest accountability. But all three friends experience public shame for their irresponsible accusations. Before Job, still in his disheveled state, they must appear and plead. He has been appointed their judge. Only in the context of their humbling sacrifice before him, their humiliating plea to him, does he pray for them. Their personal access to God has been denied. Only through Job's intercedings will they be spared the outpouring of a righteous God's wrath. They have not spoken the truth about "my servant" Job. So their public

---

47. Alter, *Wisdom Books*, 3.

48. Though finally affirming that Job's friends "exceed proper bounds when praising God at the expense of human beings," Crenshaw, *Old Testament Wisdom*, 109, nonetheless comes to their defense: "While their conviction that a just God ruled the universe brought extreme spiritual consternation to Job, we must not forget that they suffered considerable abuse from their friend. In addition, who can say that adherence to religious conviction in the face of contradictory evidence is wholly wrong? . . . In a way, Job's friends are partly victimized by the literary genre in which they appear."

wrongdoing of slandering Job's character is dealt with publicly. No one in the community could miss this moment. The tormentors stand meekly before the tormented. They depend altogether on the good graces of Job's forgiving spirit as he receives their confession of wrongdoing and intercedes on their behalf.

So the book of Job makes it quite clear. The faithful servants of the LORD will be duly rewarded, while the wicked stand under the condemning shadow of God's wrath. If they fail to repent, confess, and seek reconciliation with the one they have pained, they will experience the fullness of the Almighty's anger.

The New Testament pointedly confirms this very principle as it relates to Job. "You have seen the consummation of the Lord [τὸ τέλος κυρίου] with respect to Job," says James (Jas. 5:11). The account, written plainly, reads as follows:

> The LORD blessed the latter part of Job's life more than the first. He had fourteen thousand sheep, six thousand camels, a thousand yoke of oxen and a thousand donkeys. And he also had seven sons and three daughters. . . . After this, Job lived a hundred and forty years; he saw his children and their children to the fourth generation. And so he died, old and full of years. (Job 42:12–13, 16–17 NIV)

Faithful to his covenantal promises, the LORD rewards his faithful servant.[49] In the end, Job possesses twice the number of sheep, camels, oxen, and donkeys than he previously owned (cf. Job 1:3). Yes, he must have grieved deeply over his first family of lost children. But God has his way of compensating.

So despite current protestations, the message of Job comes through clearly. The LORD rewards the righteous and humbles the wicked, though in his own time rather than in accord with people's expectations. Even Job himself acknowledged that the suffering righteous might have to wait patiently until after the resurrection to witness his

---

49. R. B. Y. Scott, *The Way of Wisdom in the Old Testament* (New York: Macmillan, 1971), 148, says that this conclusion of the narrative involving a material compensation of the hero "suggests that the epilogue was contributed by a dull mind on which the whole great argument had been lost." Yet Job's hope of bodily resurrection discussed earlier clearly anticipates material compensation, and suggests anything but a dull mind.

own vindication. But that vindication would eventually come, as the next point discussed immediately below indicates.

Second, the latter part of Job's life may be regarded as one grand "image" or "figure of speech." Certainly it is not a figure of speech in the sense that it represents an unhistorical record. The New Testament's reference to the "final end" of Job confirms the reality of these events (James 5:11). Yet at the same time, Job's final condition serves as an image of restoration to all the blessings that God will ultimately bring to his people. Job's restoration experience depicts the fullness of life that will come through bodily resurrection, even as Job himself anticipated (Job 14:14–17; 19:25–27). Job ends up with twice as many material possessions as he had at first, along with the restoration of a full family of seven sons and three daughters (42:12–15).

This "latter end" of Job may be appropriately connected with the "many mansions" that Jesus has gone to prepare for his disciples. The reward for any suffering by God's people in this life will be far more than simple compensation. For the sufferings of this present life are not worthy to be compared with the glories of the world to come (Rom. 8:18). Through God's restoration of Job, the propriety of Job's anticipation of bodily resurrection is confirmed. This same perspective may be claimed for all who suffer in this life as servants of their Creator, Sustainer, and Redeemer.

Third, the message of Job provides answers to the important question of how to puzzle. Life inevitably brings its puzzles, unanswerable from a human perspective. Yet a human being will invariably puzzle over the difficult issues of life, which is altogether appropriate. The larger question is: "What is the proper way to puzzle over such questions?" Several factors in the book of Job contribute toward answering this question of how to puzzle:

(1) You should not puzzle over sufferings and trials in life by seeking answers in terms of degrees of sinfulness. Job was the most righteous man of his time, and yet he suffered the most. The measure of grace in the mercy and severity of God's treatment of his people is impossible for the human mind to discern. Greater severity may indicate greater grace, and extended mercy may graciously cover a multitude of sins.

(2) As you puzzle, you should never presume to accuse God of any wrongdoing or injustice in his treatment of sinners. Because every sin deserves ultimate separation from God, no one in this life receives what he deserves in terms of divine judgment. At the same time, you should not assume that there is never a correlation between sin and calamity. The failure of Moses to enter the land, the unending strife within the household of David, and the sickness and death of many in Corinth clearly indicate that some correlation between sin and calamity may exist in accord with the wisdom of God (Deut. 3:23–25; 32:50–52; 2 Sam. 12:9–10; 1 Cor. 11:30).

(3) As you puzzle, you should understand that a cosmic drama of redemption ultimately lies behind every experience in the life of every human being. The purposes of God toward a fallen creation focus on consummate redemption of the entire cosmos, and that focus is never lost. It never becomes secondary to any other consideration. Even the smallest of human events moves the world toward its cosmic conclusion. Everything that happens in your life, as well as in the course of nations, contributes to the realization of God's ultimate goal.

(4) As you puzzle, you should humble yourself under the mighty hand of God, resting content that whatever occurs in life is for your own good and his glory (Rom. 8:28). Job gave proper expression to that outlook in his first responses to his tragedies: "The LORD gave, and the LORD has taken away; blessed be the name of the LORD" (Job 1:21). Maintaining this perspective throughout all human tragedies may prove to be extremely difficult. Yet it is the only way to remain at peace with God and your circumstances.

(5) As you puzzle, you should recognize the temporal character of all your sufferings. Despite the mockery of an unbelieving world regarding a hope rooted in the world to come, that hope remains an ultimate reality. Job's repeated expressions of hope in the future resurrection of his body along with his longing for vindication before God must not be minimized. All puzzlings about the purposes of God in your life should be placed in the framework of this faith in the future that constantly anticipates the climax and completion of God's work of redemption.

194

CONCLUSION

So the book of Job proves itself to be a masterpiece of literary composition. Not only through the structure of the epic, the substance of the narrative, and the perfections of the poetry, but also through the literary employment of figures of speech, it establishes itself as a book that communicates with greatest effectiveness the realities of God and his sovereign purposes in the world he has made, providentially sustains, and will graciously bring to its proper consummation.

SELECTED BIBLIOGRAPHY FOR JOB

Alter, Robert. *The Wisdom Books: Job, Proverbs, and Ecclesiastes: A Translation with Commentary.* New York: W. W. Norton, 2010.

Andersen, Francis I. *Job: An Introduction and Commentary.* TOTC. London: Inter-Varsity Press, 1976.

Archer, Gleason L. *A Survey of Old Testament Introduction.* Chicago: Moody Press, 1964.

Bartholomew, Craig G., and Ryan P. O'Dowd. *Old Testament Wisdom Literature: A Theological Introduction.* Downers Grove, IL: IVP Academic, 2011.

Childs, Brevard S. *Introduction to the Old Testament as Scripture.* London: SCM Press, 1979.

Clines, David J. A. *Job 1–20.* WBC 17. Dallas: Word Books, 1989.

———. *Job 21–37.* WBC 18A. Nashville: Thomas Nelson, 2006.

———. *Job 38–42.* WBC 18B. Nashville: Thomas Nelson, 2011.

Crenshaw, James L. *Old Testament Wisdom: An Introduction.* Rev. and enl. ed. Louisville: Westminster John Knox, 1998.

Dhorme, E. *A Commentary on the Book of Job.* Nashville: Thomas Nelson, 1984.

Ellison, H. L. *From Tragedy to Triumph.* Sydney: Paternoster Press, 1967.

Fokkelman, J. P. *Reading Biblical Poetry: An Introductory Guide.* Louisville: Westminster John Knox, 2001.

Green, William Henry. *Conflict and Triumph: The Argument of the Book of Job Unfolded.* Edinburgh: Banner of Truth, 1999.

Habel, Norman C. *The Book of Job.* Cambridge Bible Commentary. New York: Cambridge University Press, 1975.

————. *The Book of Job*. Old Testament Library. Philadelphia: Westminster, 1985.

Harris, Kenneth Laing. "Job." In *ESV Study Bible*, 869–73. Wheaton, IL: Crossway, 2008.

Hartley, John E. *The Book of Job*. NICOT. Grand Rapids: Eerdmans, 1988.

Janzen, J. Gerald. *Job*. Interpretation: A Bible Commentary for Teaching and Preaching. Atlanta: John Knox, 1985.

Kidner, Derek. *Wisdom to Live By: An Introduction to the Old Testament's Wisdom Books of Proverbs, Job and Ecclesiastes*. Leicester, UK: Inter-Varsity Press, 1985.

Kline, Meredith G. "Job." In *The Wycliffe Bible Commentary*, edited by Charles F. Pfeiffer and Everett F. Harrison, 459–90. Chicago: Moody Press, 1962.

Longman, Tremper, III. *Job*. Grand Rapids: Baker Academic, 2012.

Longman, Tremper, III, and Raymond B. Dillard. *An Introduction to the Old Testament*. 2nd ed. Nottingham, UK: Inter-Varsity Press, 2007.

Murphy, Roland E. *Wisdom Literature: Job, Proverbs, Ruth, Canticles, Ecclesiastes, and Esther*. Forms of the Old Testament Literature 13. Grand Rapids: Eerdmans, 1981.

Pope, Marvin H. *Job*. AB 15. Garden City, NY: Doubleday, 1965.

Rowley, H. H. *Job*. NCBC. Grand Rapids: Eerdmans, 1976.

Scott, R. B. Y. *The Way of Wisdom in the Old Testament*. New York: Macmillan, 1971.

Westermann, Claus. *The Structure of the Book of Job: A Form-Critical Analysis*. Philadelphia: Fortress Press, 1981.

Whybray, Norman. *Job*. Sheffield, UK: Sheffield Academic, 1998.

3

ECCLESIASTES
HOW TO COPE WITH LIFE'S
FRUSTRATIONS

CHAPTER OUTLINE

Introduction
5

1. Prologue (Eccl. 1:1–11)
2. Body (Eccl. 1:12–12:7)
3. Epilogue (Eccl. 12:8–14)
III. The Message of the Book
  A. The Question of a Unified Message
    1. Two Authors?
    2. One Author in Conflict with Another?
    3. A Unified Perspective
  B. Various Frameworks for Interpreting the Message
    1. A False View of Life
    2. An Allegory of the Gospel
    3. The Best of Human Wisdom
    4. A Realistic Picture of Life
  C. The Message Contained in the Repeated Statements of the Book
    1. Frustration of Frustrations (הֲבֵל הֲבָלִים)
    2. "What Is the Profit?" (מַה־יִּתְרוֹן)
    3. "Under the Sun" (תַּחַת הַשָּׁמֶשׁ)
  D. God in the Gospel of Ecclesiastes
    1. God Is the Maker of All Things
    2. God Has a Prevailing Purpose in Providence That Should Be Searched Out
    3. God Is the Great Benefactor of Humanity
    4. God Expects Men to Revere Him in Worship, and as a Consequence to Take All of Life Seriously
    5. God Is Judge and Distinguishes between the Righteous and the Wicked
    6. God Tests Humanity in a Variety of Ways
    7. God Will Finally Call All People to Account
  E. The Final Message and the Final Messenger
Conclusion
Selected Bibliography for Ecclesiastes

198

INTRODUCTION

Anyone who takes a serious dose of the book of Ecclesiastes will strongly react either with fond appreciation or with frustrated incomprehension. Reputable scholars line up on either side, calling it the "strangest book in the Bible"[1] that has "a false view of life"[2] or agreeing with Martin Luther, who referred to Ecclesiastes as "this noble little book" that should be "read of all men with great carefulness every day."[3]

The reason for these contrary reactions rises primarily out of the strong dose of reality that Ecclesiastes continually serves up. Hard labor, frustrating relationships, dissatisfaction with life, the folly and madness of humanity, the discomforts of aging, the inevitability of a cold and lonesome grave—these are not topics that normally grace table conversation. Yet these experiences constitute the substance of stark reality.

Can God be in it all? Do all these things also come from his hand? Must we face these harsh facts about life?

Indeed we must. One way or another, these realities will come upon us all.

So God has graciously given us Ecclesiastes to ease us into a healthy, wholesome outlook on life as it really is. This book is canon—that is, it comes with the full authority of God's Word to a fallen humanity in desperate need of restoration and redemption. It speaks incisively to the eschatological *already* to help a person grasp with firm assurance that "there is a time, an appointed hour, for everything," and that God has made "everything beautiful in its time" (Eccl. 3:1, 11, 17). In this broader context, Ecclesiastes offers God's wisdom on "how to cope with life's frustrations." Or, from a slightly different perspective, coping with life's transitoriness.

In approaching Ecclesiastes from a biblical-theological perspective, we must give some attention to its original place in the history of redemptive revelation. In this regard, it will be most helpful to

---

1. R. B. Y. Scott, *Proverbs. Ecclesiastes: Introduction, Translation, and Notes*, AB 18 (Garden City, NY: Doubleday, 1965), 191.

2. S. R. Driver, *An Introduction to the Literature of the Old Testament*, 9th ed. (Edinburgh: T. & T. Clark, 1913), 472.

3. Quoted in E. W. Hengstenberg, *Commentary on Ecclesiastes* (Edinburgh: T. & T. Clark, 1869), 32.

remember once more that the wisdom literature of the old covenant Scriptures offers a unique perspective on the basic nature of redemptive history. God's working of salvation among his people does not develop purely and simply along a linear-timeline projection. The movement across history is not to be envisioned as a simple straight line from creation to consummation. Instead, the imagery of an advancing spiral captures more correctly the character of redemption's movement across the ages. In this advancing spiral of God's redemptive working, the age of Ecclesiastes' contribution to redeeming truth arises at a specific period of time, but also addresses the stark realities of every age. It could not have come in an earlier period, and would not come during a later era. At the same time, the imagery of the spiral communicates the idea of repetition, of re-experience of the same essential realities in each successive age. It is not so much a matter of "timeless truths"; instead, it is experiencing the realities of God's timing that recur with ever-heightening intensity across each new era.

The opening scenes depicted by Ecclesiastes vivify this cyclical perspective in a context of stability ensured by the ongoing purposes of God:

> Generations come and generations go,
>   but the earth remains forever.
> The sun rises and the sun sets,
>   and hurries back to where it rises.
> The wind blows to the south and turns to the north;
>   round and round it goes, ever returning on its course.
> All streams flow into the sea, yet the sea is never full.
>   To the place the streams come from, there they return again.
> . . . .
> What has been will be again, what has been done will be done again;
>   there is nothing new under the sun. (Eccl. 1:4–9 NIV)

Keeping this perspective in mind, we note that the current treatment of Ecclesiastes will focus on the following topics:

- Audience, Authorship, and Date of Composition
- Literary Form, Structure, and Synopsis
- The Message of the Book

It should be remembered that this treatment of Ecclesiastes is not a commentary on the book. As a consequence, some challenging exegetical points of significance may not be broached by this treatment. The reader is encouraged to pursue these matters before God for his own edification and for the maturing of Christ's church. For with every increase of wisdom and understanding comes ever-greater blessing in all the changing scenes of life.[4]

Audience, Authorship, and Date of Composition

Target Audience

The question of the authorship of Ecclesiastes has involved long and detailed discussions. But a related question of some significance for understanding the book has been generally neglected. This neglected question is the identity of the "target audience" of Ecclesiastes.[5] Throughout the book, imperatives are addressed to some particular person who can be identified as the target audience, the recipient of the book. This unidentified person is consistently addressed with a singular *you*. No imperatives appear in the first four chapters, which contain the first-person autobiography of the person speaking throughout the book. Then suddenly eight imperatives, found in chapter 5, give instructions about worship. All these imperatives are addressed to a singular (understood) *you*, including directions such as these: Guard your steps when you go to the house of God (Eccl. 5:1); do not be rash when you speak to God (5:2); fulfill your vow to him (5:4).

The bulk of imperatives in Ecclesiastes are found in the second half of the book (chaps. 7–12), with each of these chapters containing at least one exhortation.[6] But who is this singular *you* addressed by these imperatives?

4. A helpful treatment of the substance of Ecclesiastes, including careful analysis of some of the more challenging exegetical points, may be found in Walter C. Kaiser, Jr., *Coping with Change: Ecclesiastes* (Ross-shire, Scotland: Christian Focus Publications, 2013).

5. Michael V. Fox, "Frame-Narrative and Composition in the Book of Ecclesiastes," *Hebrew Union College Annual* 48 (1977): 83, raises questions concerning the literary characteristics of Qohelet as narrative, including who is speaking, how the voices speak, and how they relate to each other. But he says nothing about Qohelet's target audience.

6. The division conventionally made between the first half (Eccl. 1–6) and the second half (Eccl. 7–12) of Ecclesiastes may be more precisely located by including the final three

The only target audiences eventually mentioned at the conclusion of the book are "young man" (Eccl. 11:9), "the people" (12:9), and "my son" (12:12). The "young man" could be any young man, most likely referring to the same person subsequently designated as "my son." In the context of wisdom literature, the "son" should be perceived more generically as every young person willing to hear rather than pointing specifically to an actual son and successor of the king of Israel.

The "people" (הָעָם) that the speaker in Ecclesiastes addresses could be Israel. But the term is rather broad, and does not in itself specifically indicate Israel. It could well refer to "people" in a more general sense.

If the people of Israel actually were the target audience of Ecclesiastes, some explanation must be given for a number of critical aspects of the book. Nowhere does the covenant name of *Yahweh* appear in Ecclesiastes. Always the deity is referred to as *Elohim*, the general name for God (forty times in the twelve chapters of Ecclesiastes). The word used to designate "man" is *adam* (אָדָם), not *ish* (אִישׁ), at a ratio of 49 to 7. One author notes that "there can be no doubt that the text intends *adam* to refer generically to any human being, whether male or female."[7] Never is any particular event of Israel's redemptive history mentioned. Not one word refers to the calling of the patriarchs, the exodus, or Israel's wilderness wanderings. Nothing is said of Sinai and its law-covenant, nothing about the conquest under Joshua, no mention of the period of the judges. How are these omissions to be explained if Israel is the target audience of the book?

An additional factor of significance is the extensive use of the early chapters of Genesis in Ecclesiastes. Man's creation in a morally

---

verses of chapter 6 (6:10–12) in the second half of the book. For further discussion of this precise location of the halfway point in the book, see footnote 48 below.

7. C. L. Seow, *Ecclesiastes: A New Translation with Introduction and Commentary*, AB 18C (New York: Doubleday, 1997), x. Cf. Robert Gordis, "Was Koheleth a Phoenician?," *JBL* 71, 2 (1952): 112, who notes that the reason for designating "man" as *adam* is almost certainly due to "the nature of Qoheleth's discussion of man generically as 'mankind.'"

N.B.: The term *Koheleth* or *Qohelet* represents a transliteration of the first-person speaker throughout the book. The term is traditionally rendered in English as "the Preacher" or "Ecclesiastes," which also serves as the most common title for the book. Its basic meaning is "one who calls (the people) to assemble," "the Convener of the assembly," or "one who addresses the assembly."

upright condition, his fall into sin, the corruption of his whole being, the burdensome character of labor that came as a consequence of God's curse on the ground, the inevitability of death with its return to dust—all these items find their place in the book of Ecclesiastes.[8] These various elements from the early chapters of Genesis have broad application to the whole of humanity.

Beyond these specific references to the early chapters of Genesis is the development of the "creational ordinances" of worship, marriage, and labor that play a vital role in the very infrastructure of Ecclesiastes. These original ordinances established at creation continue to have direct application to the whole of humanity, and quite clearly have a major role to play in the thought world of Qohelet.[9] God sanctified to himself one day in seven (Gen. 2:1–3), and Qohelet expects his recipients to come for worship in the house of God (Eccl. 5:1–7). The Creator commanded the original man and woman to multiply and replenish the earth (Gen. 1:28), and Qohelet encourages the man to enjoy life with his wife whom he loves (Eccl. 9:9). At his creation, the man is told that he may eat of "every tree in the garden" (Gen. 1:29; 2:16), and repeatedly Qohelet underscores the centrality of mankind's enjoyment of food and drink (Eccl. 2:24; 3:13; 5:18; 8:15). Even more expansively, God directed Adam to "subdue the earth" (Gen. 1:28), and Qohelet repeatedly emphasizes the role of labor in the life of humanity (Eccl. 2:24; 3:13, 22; 5:18; 8:15).

How does all this data relate to the question of the recipients, the target audience of Ecclesiastes?

All these factors point to the conclusion that Qohelet does not address Israel specifically. To the contrary, he speaks to humanity, to all mankind, to Adam's descendants and not merely to Abraham's.

This perspective on the intended recipients of Ecclesiastes helps make sense of otherwise perplexing data. It explains the absence of the

---

8. A helpful narrative overview of the use of Genesis in Ecclesiastes may be found in Charles C. Forman, "Koheleth's Use of Genesis," *JSS* 5, 3 (1960): 256–63.

9. For further discussion of these three "creational ordinances" of the Sabbath [worship], marriage, and labor, see John Murray, *Principles of Conduct: Aspects of Biblical Ethics* (Grand Rapids: Eerdmans, 1957), 27–106; O. Palmer Robertson, *The Christ of the Covenants* (Phillipsburg, NJ: Presbyterian and Reformed, 1980), 68–81.

name *Yahweh* and the omission of any reference to redemptive history in Israel. It explains the multiple references to the early pre-Abrahamic history of Genesis. It particularly makes sense of what otherwise appears as an overemphasis on eating, drinking, and enjoying work and wife. For if the targeted audience is the whole of humanity, the message of Ecclesiastes can be clearly seen not as a secularistic call to a hedonistic lifestyle, but as a hopeful recall to the basics of human life as originally designed by the Creator. If the target audience is humanity in general rather than Israel in particular, this perspective may even provide a possible explanation for why the first-person speaker in Ecclesiastes is designated as "Qohelet" rather than "Solomon." Qohelet as king in Jerusalem represents the apex of God's work of redeeming a fallen humanity in the old covenant era. As the divinely designated "Convener" of the whole of humanity, as the apex of wisdom's source, Qohelet rises above the confines of his local kingdom and speaks from a higher position. In this role, he is not to be known primarily as Solomon the localized king; he is Qohelet the Convener of humanity.[10] Indeed, he has not relinquished his role as king of God's elect nation of Israel, residing on his throne in Jerusalem. But in this context, his personhood stretches beyond Solomon, son of David and Bathsheba, to Qohelet, the wisdom figure par excellence. In this capacity, he speaks to all mankind about the cold realities of life and how to cope with the harshest issues of these realities. Frustration, hard work, oppression, seeming injustices will always be a part of humanity's existence in this fallen world. But there is a way to deal with these frustrations: "Fear God and keep his commandments. For this is the whole of humanity" (כִּי־זֶה כָּל־הָאָדָם) (Eccl. 12:13, literal translation).

So it appears that the book of Ecclesiastes addresses an audience that is not specifically identified, but apparently includes humanity as a whole. The overarching intent of the book is to provide some wisdom on how to cope with the inevitable frustrations of the present life. The person addressing these perplexing reality questions is the wisdom figure par excellence, the king of Israel who is placed in the

---

10. As previously indicated, *Qohelet* literally means "one who calls together the assembly," the "Convener."

distinctive role of being the Convener who assembles humanity, that they might benefit from his wisdom.

Authorship

Having considered the targeted audience of Ecclesiastes, we now find it appropriate to look at the question of the book's authorship. For well over two thousand years, virtually all Jewish and Christian scholars agreed that King Solomon, who reigned over the united kingdom of Israel from about 960 to 920 B.C., was the author of Ecclesiastes. In more recent years, particularly since the mid-nineteenth century, the balance shifted so that few people continued to affirm Solomonic authorship. In still more recent days, some of the primary arguments against Solomon's authorship of Ecclesiastes have been seriously questioned. So what have been the main factors in this vacillation among biblical scholars?

In Favor of Solomonic Authorship

Supporting the Solomonic authorship of Ecclesiastes are the following considerations.

(1) The words of the book are specifically attributed to the "son of David, king in Jerusalem" (Eccl. 1:1). In addition, the first-person narrator of the book identifies himself as "king over Israel in Jerusalem" (1:12). Yet only one immediate son of David ever ruled in Jerusalem, and that was Solomon. Indeed, as many as twenty descendants of David sat on the throne in Jerusalem over the next four hundred years. But Solomon uniquely conforms to the glorious status achieved by this son of David as depicted in Ecclesiastes.

(2) All the circumstances of this king as delineated in Ecclesiastes match perfectly the splendors of Solomon in his unsurpassed glory. The wisdom, the pleasures, the projects, the amassing of riches, the multiplication of wives and concubines, the feasting—all these experiences fit Solomon to a *T*. In all these areas he excelled everyone who was before him and who followed him (Eccl. 1:13–2:9; cf. 1 Kings 4:20–34; 10:14–11:3). No other king after Solomon achieved these levels of regal splendor. Solomon clearly excelled all

other monarchs in Israel, and fits nicely into Qohelet's mold as depicted in Ecclesiastes.

(3) The language used to describe the experience of God's people under Qohelet's rule parallels very closely the descriptions of Solomon's kingship. The people of Judah and Israel were "eating and drinking and rejoicing" (1 Kings 4:20). These very words Ecclesiastes uses repeatedly "to express those activities that compose Qoheleth's enjoyment refrain for his listeners."[11] They ate, they drank, and they were happy.[12] The experiences described in Ecclesiastes are depicted in precisely the same language as the experiences of God's people in Solomon's day.

(4) The similarities in the literary composition of Ecclesiastes and the book of Proverbs support the identity of Solomon as author of Ecclesiastes. Solomon's role in the production of Proverbs can, of course, be questioned. This matter has already been considered in an earlier section of this volume. But given the authorship of at least a bulk of the book of Proverbs by Solomon, the similarity of composition and style with Ecclesiastes lends significant support to the idea of Solomonic authorship of Ecclesiastes. One of the "maddening" elements of Ecclesiastes is the difficulty of discovering any coherent development of thought across the pages of the book. Interspersed among extended discourses on specialized topics are proverbial sayings shaped with the classical forms of poetic parallelism. Endless efforts have been made to "outline" Ecclesiastes, to uncover an inherent structure of organized thought-patterns—but to no avail.[13] Yet the whole literary pattern of the book closely parallels the arrangement

11. Daniel C. Fredericks and Daniel J. Estes, *Ecclesiastes & the Song of Songs* (Downers Grove, IL: InterVarsity Press, 2010), 33f.

12. Cf. Eccl. 2:24–25; 3:12–13, 22; 5:18–20; 8:15; 9:7. The comments in the book of Kings about "eating, drinking and rejoicing" immediately precede the narrative of Kings that describes the accomplishments of Solomon (1 Kings 4:21–28). These accomplishments provide the backdrop for Qohelet's frustration over these same experiences (Eccl. 2:4–8). Still further, the superiority of Solomon's wisdom over all other kings in Israel is anticipated in 1 Kings 3:12 as reflected in Ecclesiastes 1:16. Worth comparing also is the description of Solomon's wealth that exceeded the resources of all other kings, which finds its parallel in the description of Qohelet's wealth that exceeded the treasures of all those who were before him in Jerusalem (1 Kings 10:23; cf. Eccl. 2:4, 8–9).

13. Further discussion of attempts to discern the structure of Ecclesiastes may be found later in this chapter under the topic of "Structure." See particularly note 48 below.

of Proverbs. In both documents, proverbial sayings are interspersed among extended discourses on selected topics. The overall arrangement of the two books is unique among all other books of the Bible, with perhaps the exception of the book of James in the New Testament. In both cases, longer sections with a unified topic may be detected. But then verse upon verse of disconnected proverbs abound in both Ecclesiastes and Proverbs.

Furthermore, these proverbs, these parables, these aphorisms—do they not set apart these two books as unique and united? Indeed, some commentators have attempted to demonstrate the differences between the wisdom embodied in the sayings of Ecclesiastes in contrast with similar statements in Proverbs.[14] In some instances there may be a genuine contrast. But even in Proverbs itself, back-to-back sayings may counter each other, such as: "Do not answer a fool according to his folly" and "Answer a fool according to his folly" (Prov. 26:4–5 NIV). Apparent dichotomies only demonstrate the need for discerning wisdom to survive in this disjointed world order.

But the wise sayings, the proverbs themselves. Who can duplicate them? Who is gifted with adequate insight into the essence of God's ordering of his complex creation to summarize within the strictures of succinct, memorable, poetic form a few truth realities that offer no insult to the divine order of things while providing a way through life's dilemmas? Indeed, some parallels may be found in extrabiblical literature, as indicated in the previous treatment of Proverbs in this volume.[15] Virtually every culture has its collection of "wise sayings." Some limited number of proverbial sayings may be found in the writings of Israel's prophets. But hardly anything compares with the quality and extent of proverbial wisdom found in the biblical books of Proverbs and Ecclesiastes.

Since Jesus' day, no other human being has been able to approximate the parabolic form that Jesus used constantly to embody "true truth" in memorable form. A similar thing may be said about the

14. Cf. Tremper Longman III, *The Book of Ecclesiastes* (Grand Rapids: Eerdmans, 1998), 282, who offers his evaluation that the book of Proverbs "has received implicit criticism throughout Qohelet's writings."
15. See the previous discussion of extrabiblical parallels to Proverbs in the section entitled "The Relation of Proverbs to Other Ancient Wisdom Materials" in chapter 1.

failure of efforts to duplicate the proverbs of Solomon as recorded in the book of Proverbs. Yet the book of Ecclesiastes has done it. Indeed, alongside the statement honoring the greatness of Solomon's wisdom, recognition is given of other individuals alongside Solomon who were acknowledged as sources of wisdom (1 Kings 4:31). Notation of the wisdom of Egypt and the men of the East is set alongside the praise of Solomon's wisdom (4:30). Yet the point of these references is to establish the fact that Solomon in his wisdom was greater than all these. None could compare with him, and none of these individuals is also described as "son of David," "king in Jerusalem," greater than all kings who were before them. Who but Solomon fits all these criteria—the great king, son of David, pinnacle of wisdom figures, noteworthy composer of proverbs?

In Opposition to Solomonic Authorship

The following considerations may be noted that stand against recognizing Solomon as the composer of Ecclesiastes.

(1) Solomon is never explicitly named as the author of Ecclesiastes. In Proverbs as well as the Song of Songs, Solomon's name appears at the head of the book. For some reason Solomon's name is not specified as author in Ecclesiastes. The most logical explanation could be that Solomon actually is not the book's author.[16]

(2) The language of Ecclesiastes differs from the form of Hebrew found in earlier books of the Old Testament. The analysis of Franz Delitzsch regarding the impact of linguistic considerations on the dating of Ecclesiastes has been repeatedly affirmed over previous decades: "If the Book of Koheleth were of old Solomonic origin, then there is no history of the Hebrew language."[17] By this criterion, Ecclesiastes

---

16. Hengstenberg, *Ecclesiastes*, 43f., argues that it is "of no little significance" that Solomon does not appear under his own name. He concludes: "The book of Ecclesiastes was not only not actually composed by Solomon, but does not even pretend to have been."

17. Franz Delitzsch, *Commentary on the Song of Songs and Ecclesiastes* (Edinburgh: T. & T. Clark, 1891), 190. A. Lukyn Williams, *Ecclesiastes*, Cambridge Bible for Schools and Colleges (Cambridge: University Press, 1922), xiv, says that the statement of Delitzsch "is irrefutable." Other references to Delitzsch's words are found in Robert Gordis, *Koheleth—The Man and His World* (New York: Bloch, 1955), 59; Seow, *Ecclesiastes*, 11; Longman, *Ecclesiastes*, 4.

is generally dated in the third century B.C.[18] So Solomon could not possibly serve as its author.

(3) Some explicit statements in Ecclesiastes simply could not have been spoken by Solomon. As the book opens, the speaker/author identifies himself as king over Israel at some point in the past: "I *was* king in Israel" (Eccl. 1:12). In order to maintain Solomonic authorship, this statement has led to groundless speculations that after his departure from the faith because of his foreign wives' influence (1 Kings 11:4–6), Solomon was deposed and later returned to compose this document that records the folly of his previous life during his earlier days when he *was* king. But since nothing in the narrative of Kings indicates that Solomon was ever dethroned and restored, this statement that he "was" king must mean something else. A possible explanation is that this statement introduces an "impersonator" of Solomon—not as a way of deceiving the people, and not as a pseudepigraphic document in which the author falsified his identity in an attempt to lead the people into thinking that this book was actually written by Solomon. Instead, with the full and assenting knowledge of the people of Israel, a subsequent "wise" person impersonated Solomon as a literary device for dramatizing his message. As a consequence, Ecclesiastes must be viewed as written not by Solomon, but by this "impersonator" who composed his message long after Solomon's day. The past tense of the verb in the phrase "I *was* king in Israel" may therefore be understood as communicating the fact that Solomon was not the author of Ecclesiastes, and that a later individual impersonated him.

A second phrase in Ecclesiastes makes little sense if Solomon himself was the author of the book. The author speaks of himself as being greater than "everyone who ruled before me in Jerusalem" (Eccl. 1:16). Yet only one person ruled over Israel in Jerusalem before Solomon. So it would make little sense for Solomon to have spoken of "*everyone* who ruled before me in Jerusalem." So someone later than Solomon must be speaking.

---

18. Cf. Thomas Kruger, *Qoheleth: A Commentary* (Minneapolis: Fortress Press, 2004), 19, who affirms that in "recent research" the date for Ecclesiastes is generally set in the second half of the third century B.C. Seow, *Ecclesiastes*, 21, proposes an earlier date in the postexilic period, "specifically between the second half of the fifth and the first half of the fourth centuries B.C.E."

Additional passages in Ecclesiastes are difficult to imagine as coming out of the mouth of Solomon. For instance, would the reigning king have sympathized so deeply with the oppressed of his people while at the same time tolerating the fact that power remained on the side of the oppressors (cf. Eccl. 4:1–3; 5:8–9)? Instead of standing idly by while bemoaning the oppression of the oppressed, would not a reigning king have taken action to relieve his people of this abuse? How could these words, so critical of oppression, have been spoken by the king himself?[19] Solomon clearly would not have spoken so publicly in self-criticism. So Ecclesiastes must not have been written by Solomon.

(4) A final argument against Solomonic authorship of Ecclesiastes appeals to proposed parallels in Akkadian texts that date from the twenty-first to the fourth centuries B.C.[20] These ancient texts contain fictional autobiographies written long after the death of the persons under consideration. Yet these documents are composed in the first person. These documents appear to represent exactly the format adopted

19. Says Kruger, *Qoheleth*, 4: "For a writing that is supposed to go back to a king, Qoheleth develops an astonishingly critical view of power and dominion."

20. Seow, *Ecclesiastes*, 48, accepts the view that the form of the book takes on the literary genre of the "fictional royal autobiography." The author of Ecclesiastes chose to "evoke the memory of Solomon, a consummate wise king who had seen it all, knew it all, and had it all" (47). He assumes that the genre "must have been familiar to Qohelet's audience" (48). Cf. the extensive discussion of this material in Tremper Longman III, *Fictional Akkadian Autobiography: A Generic and Comparative Study* (Winona Lake, IN: Eisenbrauns, 1991), 103–23. Longman compares the form of Qohelet with the Akkadian genre of autobiography, "particularly fictional autobiography with a didactic ending." He notes that similarities can be seen by comparing Qohelet with the Cuthaean Legend of Naram-Sin, found in five exemplars of a Neo-Assyrian version as well as in an Old Babylonian version. The Cuthaean Legend is identified as a distinctive type of fictional Akkadian autobiography in that it has a didactic ending. As a consequence, the three sections of the Cuthaean Legend may be compared with the body of the book of Ecclesiastes: first-person introduction (Eccl. 1:12–18); first-person narrative (2:1–6:9); and first-person instruction (presumably 6:10–12:8). Even though the first-person narrative in Qohelet is "intellectual-religious" and the Cuthaean Legend is "political-religious," Longman still regards them as comparable, since in both cases a first-person narrator rehearses from a later temporal perspective events and thoughts he had previously experienced. Longman concludes that the same threefold structure in the Cuthaean Legend is duplicated in Ecclesiastes (121). These similarities between the first-person fictional Akkadian autobiography and the body of the book of Ecclesiastes lead Longman to conclude in his commentary on Ecclesiastes that the biblical book should be regarded as using the same literary genre (Longman, *Ecclesiastes*, 19–20). As a consequence, Ecclesiastes should be regarded as first-person fictional autobiography composed long after Solomon's lifetime.

by the author of Ecclesiastes. As a standard mode of composition across an extended time in the ancient Near East, this form is viewed as explaining the literary nature of Ecclesiastes. It is a fictional autobiography of a regal figure long dead. This format has been adopted by the author of Ecclesiastes for the purpose of communicating truths about life in a way of speaking that would be familiar to his audience. The conclusion, then, must be that Ecclesiastes could not have been written by King Solomon in the tenth century B.C.

These negative arguments appear quite strong in opposition to the Solomonic authorship of Ecclesiastes. One or more of these considerations has prevailed in the thinking of most scholars in recent days. Yet some balancing responses also merit consideration.

Some Balancing Responses

(1) In his exalted position of kingship, Solomon incorporated within himself many roles and functions. The opening reference to the "words of Qohelet" rather than the "words of Solomon" clearly intends to lay emphasis on the function of the speaker rather than his personal identity. Among these functions was the "assembling" of God's people to hear the word of the LORD, which is the root idea of the "Qohelet."[21] He is the Convener.[22] Being in a situation of multiple roles, the king in this case might understandably choose the title *Qohelet* rather than refer to himself by his personal name, since *Qohelet* would serve as the most suitable term to describe the role he would fulfill by delivering this book of Ecclesiastes to the people. Particularly if the target audience is perceived as being

---

21. The root meaning of *qahal* is "to assemble." The feminine ending refers to a person who fulfills the function of calling an assembly. Other uses of the feminine ending as indicating function or office include *yoshevet* ("one who resides; an inhabitant"; Mic. 1:11); *mevaseret* ("one who brings glad tidings"; Isa. 40:9); and possibly *soferet* ("one who counts or recounts"; Ezra 2:55: "sons of *ha sophereth*").

22. Certain ecclesiastical organizations choose a "Moderator" or "Convener" at the beginning of each annual session. The Moderator of the previous year gives the "Retiring Moderator's Sermon," which compares to the address to the "assembly" by Qohelet the "Assembler" or "Convener." This custom closely resembles the role described for the author of Ecclesiastes. He is the "Moderator," the "Convener," who in his old age offers his "Retiring Moderator's Sermon."

211

humanity as a whole, it would be appropriate for Solomon to drop his localizing name and speak from a broader perspective as Qohelet the Convener.

In a distinctive passage in the New Testament, a similar substitution of a title for a personal name occurs in Jesus' words: "The *Wisdom of God* said . . ." (Luke 11:49). In this passage, the wisdom of God functions in a way similar to Qohelet in Ecclesiastes. The wisdom of God speaks for God, just as Qohelet speaks for God on behalf of Solomon. In both cases, the title substitutes for the name of the person.

As the wisdom figure par excellence of the old covenant, Solomon has as his task the imparting of God's wisdom as it relates to every aspect of life. In this role, he is *Qohelet*, the one who convenes and addresses the assembly. Indeed, he has not shed his regal robes, for he identifies himself as "king of Israel." But now, even more than in the book of Proverbs, he speaks in the first person in this very distinctive role as the instructor of humanity in divine wisdom about life. He therefore designates himself as *Qohelet* in preference to his proper name.

This is exactly the role in which Solomon is presented in the book of Kings. Using the same root *qahal*, Solomon is said to "assemble" the people and then to address them as the embodiment of Israel's wisdom figure (1 Kings 8:1). The root *qahal* in noun or verb form occurs six times in this chapter of 1 Kings (8:1–2, 14, 22, 55, 65). Throughout the narrative, Solomon is prominent as the king who "assembles" the congregation and addresses them.

It may also be worth noting that traditionally the names "Agur" (Prov. 30:1) and "King Lemuel" (31:1) have been regarded as instances of the use of different names for Solomon in Israel's wisdom literature. Although current discussion has largely rejected this connection, no other satisfactory explanation of these words has been forthcoming.[23]

---

23. For a brief discussion of the use of these names for Solomon, see Crawford H. Toy, *A Critical and Exegetical Commentary on the Book of Proverbs* (Edinburgh: T. & T. Clark, 1904), 517–18. Toy notes that Agur is identified with Solomon "by many Jewish and Christian expositors" (518). See also Michael V. Fox, *Proverbs 10–31: A New Translation with Introduction and Commentary*, AB 18B (New Haven, CT: Yale University Press, 2009), 851–53, 884. Fox notes that the midrash "identifies Agur with Solomon" (852) and that traditional commentators "identified Lemuel with Solomon" (884).

(2) Though the dictum of Delitzsch has often been quoted, as indicated above,[24] its validity has been regularly questioned. As early as the 1920s, Princeton professor Robert Dick Wilson responded to Delitzsch's dictum by concluding that Delitzsch simply did not have enough materials to construct a proper "history" of the Hebrew language.[25] More recently, after four pages of detailed interaction with various theories regarding the language of Qohelet, one commentator observes: "We do not know the history of the Hebrew language or the foreign languages that influenced it well enough to use *Qohelet's* language as a barometer of the book's origin."[26] Another commentator reaches the same conclusion: "the language of Ecclesiastes does not at present provide an adequate resource for dating."[27] Still another study classifies among "outdated notions" the postexilic dating of Ecclesiastes on the basis of late language. This study regards the late dating of Ecclesiastes as one of the "great assured results" of modern scholarship that "need to be drastically revised."[28] He concludes that language is no longer a "criterion for date," and affirms a context for the language of Qohelet "in the pre-exilic period."[29] Though the linguistic argument has functioned in the past as a key consideration for the case against Solomonic authorship, more recent studies have brought that conclusion under closer scrutiny.[30]

24. See footnote 16 above.

25. Robert Dick Wilson, *A Scientific Investigation of the Old Testament* (London: Marshall Brothers, 1926), 105.

26. Longman, *Ecclesiastes*, 15.

27. Michael A. Eaton, *Ecclesiastes: An Introduction and Commentary* (Downers Grove, IL: InterVarsity Press, 1983), 19.

28. Ian Young, *Diversity in Pre-Exilic Hebrew* (Tübingen: J. C. B. Mohr, 1993), 140.

29. Ibid., 157. In comparing Ecclesiastes with Ben Sira (the Jewish author of the second-century B.C. wisdom document called *Ecclesiasticus*), Young concludes that Qohelet "is a work of pre-exilic Wisdom" (148).

30. The most thorough analysis of the language of Ecclesiastes and its relevance to the dating of the book is found in the three-hundred-page work of Daniel C. Fredericks entitled *Qoheleth's Language: Re-Evaluating Its Nature and Date*, Ancient Near Eastern Texts and Studies 3 (Lewiston, NY: Edwin Mellen Press, 1988). Fredericks closely analyzes the view that the number of Aramaisms in Ecclesiastes indicates that it was originally composed in Aramaic, as well as the more recent theory of Dahood regarding "heavy Canaanite-Phoenician literary influence" in Ecclesiastes. His preliminary conclusion is that "growing knowledge of ancient Near Eastern language shows that some often repeated claims can no longer be upheld" (24).

(3) The fact that Qohelet says that he "*was*" king in Israel does not by necessity imply that there was a time when the king was removed from his throne and then subsequently restored to his kingship. The author is simply saying that during the period when he tried all these various elements in life, he was king. It would not quite fit the situation for him to say, "I am king, and I am trying pleasure, riches, food and drink, work." Instead, he says, "I was king, and while reigning I tried these various things." When he tried pleasures, projects, wealth, and wisdom, he was a king on his throne. He could undergo all these experiences to the fullest degree just because he was king. As king, he had more access to all these experiences than anyone else. So the fact that he *was* king during this period, rather than disproving Solomonic authorship, adds a dimension of reality to his royal testimony.

Again, the author says that he increased in wisdom above all who had ruled before him in Jerusalem (Eccl. 1:16). This statement would appear to exclude Solomon, since only David his father had been king in Jerusalem before Solomon. Some have proposed in response that Qohelet could be including Melchizedek king of (Jeru)Salem (Gen. 14:18), Adonai-Zedek king of Jerusalem (Josh. 10:1), and the king of the Jebusites in Jerusalem during David's day (2 Sam. 5:6). While this explanation is possible, it seems more likely that Qohelet simply speaks in hyperbolic language. As the paragon of wisdom figures in Israelite history, Solomon was the indeed the greatest.

Fredericks thoroughly discusses grammatical patterns in Ecclesiastes in comparison with various stages of Hebrew, noting that the basic nature of language lies more in its grammatical structures than in its lexical stock (28–170). Then he investigates lexical considerations, including a detailed analysis of Mishnaisms, late Biblical Hebrew words, Aramaisms, Persianisms, and Greek words and phrases that may appear in Ecclesiastes (171–254). He notes that Ecclesiastes contains only two Persian words, which are "acceptable for even a pre-exilic book given the historical connections of Palestine with the East" (242, 244).

His conclusion as expressed in his more recent commentary (2010) is that the language of Ecclesiastes "is either vernacular in dialect or transitional in the history of the Hebrew language." If transitional, "it appears to be more transitional from early Biblical Hebrew to later Biblical Hebrew than between later Biblical Hebrew to the still later Mishnaic Hebrew" (Fredericks and Estes, *Ecclesiastes*, 61). He concludes that the probable date for the current text of Ecclesiastes is "no later" than an eighth- or seventh-century B.C. date. If it is an example of a more vernacular dialect, "then it could be earlier yet," and "does not necessarily preclude" Solomon, though it could be by a creative writer other than Solomon (31–32).

214

On another issue, it may seem incongruous that the authentic king of Jerusalem would speak with great concern over the suffering of his people under oppression, while he himself participates in the same sins. Indeed, Solomon is portrayed in Scripture as oppressing his own people (1 Kings 5:13–16; 9:15). Yet anyone who has lived in a bureaucracy knows full well that it is almost impossible for the "man on top" to control everything going on below him. Solomon may have perceived that things were going too far in the oppression of one level of society by another, but could have found it impossible to weed out all oppression. At the same time, this same objection would apply to the fictional person "impersonating" the king as author of the book. This fictional person would be just as guilty of serious hypocrisy, and his expressions of disappointment over oppression would have no more "ring of truth" than if they had been spoken by Solomon himself.

(4) Parallels with Akkadian forms of literature in which fictional autobiographies include the impersonation of kings long dead may provide distinctive insight into the format used by the author of Ecclesiastes.[31] But a more immediate source for understanding the literary form of Ecclesiastes may be found in a biblical model "closer to home" in terms of its relationship to Ecclesiastes. The ancient and regularly repeated form of *first-person personal testimony* as recorded in Scripture compares closely with the prevailing format adopted by the author of Ecclesiastes. This ancient form of *first-person confessional credo* was prominent across the centuries of Israelite history. From the days of the patriarchs, through the period of Moses and Joshua, and into the time of David, the psalmists, and the prophets, first-person personal testimony played its significant role in the life of God's people. This format will be explored in more detail in a subsequent section that deals with the literary form of Ecclesiastes. But at this point, it may

---

31. While comparison with Akkadian literary forms is significant, substance inherent in the form must also be considered when a comparison is being made. In this regard, Longman himself notes the obvious difference in the two works. The first-person narrative in Qohelet is "intellectual-religious," and the Cuthaean Legend is "political-religious" (Longman, *Fictional Akkadian Autobiography*, 121). One document wrestles with the frustrations of human life, while the other reports losses and victories on the battlefield. Still further, the first-person testimony of Ecclesiastes has a centuries-old precedent in the testimonies of aged believers, as discussed later in this material. In these biblical cases, the authenticity of the person's testimony is critical to the effectiveness of the personal witness.

be sufficient to note that first-person personal testimony is regularly found in the material of the patriarchs Jacob and Joseph, in the legislation of Moses, in the life of Joshua, in the last words of David, and regularly in the first-person witness of the psalmists and prophets. Here in this material may be found the most congenial literary framework that parallels the form and substance of Ecclesiastes. In this case, the search "near to home" may prove to be far more fruitful than a search abroad for insight into the genre of Ecclesiastes.

In this regard, it may be proper to suggest that if the basic form of Ecclesiastes is a first-person personal testimony, then the effectiveness of the book's message depends to a great extent on the authenticity of the experiences to which the author himself testifies. If the person depicted in Ecclesiastes did not experientially bask in the blessings of material affluence and personally experience the frustrations associated with a diligent search for the depths of human wisdom, then the authenticity of his first-person testimony must be brought into serious question. How could the invitation to get wisdom from this person be seriously entertained if the basis of his claims were fictional in what they affirm? Why should his personal affirmations be accepted as true regarding the vanity of pleasure and power if he had no authentic basis for these observations? When the book of Ecclesiastes is set in the context of ongoing personal testimonies among God's people regarding experiential reality, the necessity of personal integrity in the testimony must be maintained. From this perspective, a "fictional" representation of a dead man's speech would carry little weight.[32]

In conclusion, no final deathblow has been struck against the Solomonic authorship of Ecclesiastes. The person who wrote this book was king. He was king of Israel. He was king of Israel in Jerusalem. He was the most glorious king who ever ruled over God's people under the old covenant. In every way, this description suits Solomon and none other than Solomon. The biblical-theological circumstance in Solomon's day is right for the composition of a book such as Ecclesiastes. No other age quite matches it. In his day, the kingdom and the

---

32. Note the evaluation of Gordon J. Wenham, *Story as Torah: Reading the Old Testament Ethically* (Edinburgh: T. & T. Clark, 2000), 12: "Thus intrinsically history is a much more authoritative narrative than fiction." This principle would apply even more pointedly to first-person personal testimony.

kingship reached its highest hour of glory. Most fittingly, then, would the book of Ecclesiastes be written by the premier man of that era.

Date of Composition

In terms of the date of Ecclesiastes' composition, an old tradition proposes that in his youth, Solomon wrote the Song of Songs with its accent on love; in his maturity, he wrote Proverbs with its emphasis on how to deal with the practical problems of life; and then in his old age, he reflected on the frustrations of a lifetime and wrote Ecclesiastes.[33] Without affirming the tradition that Solomon was first deposed and later reinstated, the content of Ecclesiastes clearly favors the concept that he wrote these words in the latter years of his life. As he contemplated the course of his days, he wrote to provide much-needed wisdom for the generations to come. In this book he offered his mature reflections on how to cope with life's frustrations.

LITERARY FORM, STRUCTURE, AND SYNOPSIS

No written document can be fully understood or appreciated without some awareness of its literary form and structure. Otherwise, a segment of material may be greatly misunderstood or grossly exaggerated in terms of its true meaning and role in the total context of the document. Much frustration has arisen with respect to Ecclesiastes because of an inadequate awareness of the book's shape and structure. The following observations represent an effort to uncover something of the literary form and structure of Ecclesiastes. Both the larger framework and specific literary types will be considered.

Literary Form

First-Person Personal Testimony

As already mentioned, Ecclesiastes manifests an overall literary form that has deep roots and consistent usage throughout Scripture. The first-person personal testimony is not something invented by the

33. Gordis, *Koheleth*, 39.

author of Ecclesiastes. Instead, it goes back to the earliest traditions of Israel.

According to the record of Deuteronomy, a first-person personal testimony with a carefully structured format was legislated as a regular ritual for Israel. This confessional format "bears all the marks of great antiquity."[34] After entering the land of promise, the individual Israelite was to bring the firstfruits of the land to the divinely designated dwellingplace of God's name. He was then to present his firstfruits to the priest and declare his personal testimony:

> I testify this day to the COVENANT LORD your God that I have come into the land which the COVENANT LORD swore to our fathers to give to us. (Deut. 26:3)

The presiding priest then took the basket containing the firstfruits of the land and set it before the altar of the COVENANT LORD. The individual Israelite was then to continue his testimony:

> My father was a wandering [perishing] Aramean,[35] and he went down into Egypt . . . . So the LORD brought us out . . . . He gave us this land . . . . And now I bring the firstfruits of the ground. (Deut. 26:5, 8–10)

The individual Israelite offering this testimony was then to place the basket before the LORD and bow down before him. Then he himself, along with the priest and the aliens of the land, was to "rejoice" in all the good that the COVENANT LORD his God had given him and his house (Deut. 26:3–11).

The extent of parallels with the first-person testimony by the author of Ecclesiastes is quite extensive:

34. Gerhard von Rad, *Old Testament Theology*, vol. 1 (Edinburgh: Oliver & Boyd, 1962), 122. Von Rad's analysis of the Credo in Deuteronomy 26:5–9 has had great impact on subsequent studies in Old Testament biblical theology.

35. The word translated as "perishing" (Deut. 26:5) is rendered as "wandering" in most English translations, with the exception of the KJV and the NKJV. But the consistent usage elsewhere in the Old Testament indicates that the meaning "perishing" should be favored. This understanding suits well the original context of Jacob's descent into Egypt, for Jacob finally succumbs to the urgings of his sons because they are on the verge of "perishing" as a result of the relentless character of the drought in the land of Palestine.

- It is a public testimony.
- It is given in the first-person singular.
- It is given at the end of a long pilgrimage through life.
- It is given for future generations.
- The fruit of the land is prominent in this testimony.
- The testimony is given in the house of the LORD at the assembly of God's people.
- "Rejoicing" over the good things that the LORD has given to the individual and his household is a prominent factor in the testimony.

So the first-person personal testimony of the Israelite centers on the blessings of the firstfruits of the land. Quite striking when compared with Ecclesiastes is its expectation of rejoicing over personal enjoyment of the fruit of the land (cf. Eccl. 3:12–13; 5:18–19; 8:15; 9:7–9; 11:9).

Not only in this ancient credo, but repeatedly across the generations of redemptive history, God's people come forward to give their first-person personal testimony. Jacob before Pharaoh in Egypt declares, "The years of my pilgrimage are a hundred and thirty. My years have been few and difficult, and they do not equal the years of the pilgrimage of my fathers" (Gen. 47:9 NIV). Earlier Joseph had indicated his willingness to provide a testimony before Pharaoh on behalf of his family: "I will go up and speak to Pharaoh and will say to him, 'My brothers and my father's household, who were living in the land of Canaan, have come to me. The men are shepherds; they tend livestock, and they have brought along their flocks and herds and everything they own" (46:31–32 NIV). Joshua in his old age summoned all Israel and said, "I am old and well advanced in years. . . . I have allotted as an inheritance . . . all the land of the nations. [Remember] . . . the nations I conquered . . . . Now I am about to go the way of all the earth. You know with all your heart and soul that not one of all the good promises the LORD your God gave you has failed" (Josh. 23:1–4, 14 NIV). Again, he assembles all the tribes of Israel one final time to offer his own personal testimony even as he challenges the people: "Choose for yourselves this day whom you will serve . . . . But as for me and my household, we will serve the LORD" (24:15 NIV). King

David also offers his first-person personal testimony "when the LORD delivered him from the hand of all his enemies . . . : 'The LORD is my rock, my fortress and my deliverer; . . . I call to the LORD . . . , and I am saved from my enemies. . . . Therefore I will praise you, O LORD, among the nations . . . . He gives his king great victories . . . , to David and his descendants forever'" (2 Sam. 22:1, 4, 50–51 NIV). Once more: "These are the last words of David: '. . . The Spirit of the LORD spoke through me . . . . Will he not bring to fruition my salvation and grant me my every desire?'" (23:1–2, 5b NIV). In addition to all these first-person personal testimonies across the ages of redemptive history, a number of psalms are cast in the form of one man's witness to the truth (cf. Pss. 30, 34, 73, 77, 88, 101, 116, 138). Especially striking is the commitment of the psalmist to testify to the assembly of God's people about the LORD's faithfulness:

> I proclaim righteousness in the great assembly; I do not seal my lips, as you know, O LORD. I do not hide your righteousness in my heart; I speak of your faithfulness and salvation. I do not conceal your love and your truth from the great assembly. (Ps. 40:9–10 NIV)

These confessional psalms confirm the fact that first-person personal testimony before the assembled congregation served as an essential part of Israel's worship practices. Still further, among Israel's prophets, Jonah and Habakkuk stand out as making use of this particular mode of expression. While still in the belly of the great fish, Jonah offers his personal testimony: "In my distress I called to the LORD, and he answered me. . . . When my life was ebbing away, I remembered you, LORD . . . . I, with a song of thanksgiving, will sacrifice to you" (Jonah 2:1–2, 7, 9 NIV). Habakkuk offers personal testimony to his resolved acceptance of the LORD's purposes: "LORD, I have heard of your fame . . . . I heard and my heart pounded, my lips quivered at the sound . . . . Yet I will rejoice in the LORD, I will be joyful in God my Savior" (Hab. 3:2, 16, 18 NIV).

The first-person personal testimony of the book of Ecclesiastes fits precisely into this well-established pattern of literary form. Though speaking in reference to an international genre, von Rad indicates that the book of Ecclesiastes "is, according to its outward form, an off-shoot of a literary type which was cultivated particularly in ancient Egypt, namely the Royal Testament."[36] He notes that the book is "expressed predominantly in the first person" and purports to be "a wise man's personal experience of life."[37]

Some useful insights may be gained from extrabiblical materials. But this form of first-person personal testimony as found across the breadth of old covenant Scripture and experience, offered regularly in a person's old age and providing godly insight into the wise way of life, suits the broader context of the book of Ecclesiastes much better. Particularly in the area of basic integrity, the age-old tradition in Scripture speaks out strongly. To carry their own weight, the recorded testimonies must be genuine, or they have contradicted their own formal literary shape. If the first-person personal testimony cannot be believed, it has nullified its own profession. If Israel was not delivered out of slavery in Egypt and by God's grace granted the precious fruit of the land that had been promised, how minimalistic would be the testimony to God's faithfulness as declared by the Israelite? If the personal witness of Jacob, Joseph, Moses, David, the psalmists, and the prophets has no authenticity, what is its worth to a people facing equal challenges and needing encouragement? If the author of Ecclesiastes did not actually experience frustration to the extreme as he attests in his book, how can his words be given any credence?

The Hypothetical "Frame Narrator"

One alternative perspective speaks of the role of a hypothetical editor designated as the "frame narrator" of Ecclesiastes. This frame narrator's role is compared to the part played by the narrator in Joel Chandler Harris's Uncle Remus stories of the American South. These stories about Br'er Rabbit and the Tar Baby are introduced and concluded by the comments of a frame narrator. This literary format provides "a way of attesting to the reality of Uncle Remus, even though he did not actually exist." The genre conveys "not actual belief in Uncle Remus' reality" but belief in the "illusion of reality." Uncle

---

36. Gerhard von Rad, *Wisdom in Israel* (London: SCM Press, 1972), 226.
37. Ibid., 227.

Remus is a "bizarre character" that we can believe in only because of the peculiarity of the frame narrator's perspective.[38]

In a further comparison, it is also noted that Jonathan Swift in his *Gulliver's Travels* does not actually expect belief in his tall tales. Instead, he is only looking for a "suspension of disbelief" so that the reader can enjoy his fictional episodes.[39] In a similar way, the reader of Ecclesiastes must "look upon *Qohelet* as a real individual in order to feel the full force of the crisis he is undergoing."[40] Yet according to this view, actual belief in the "story" embedded in Ecclesiastes is never expected.

Contrast these fictional imaginatives with the very real first-person personal testimony of the Israelite whose ancestors have undergone the crushing burden of enslavement and their liberation at the Red Sea. This individual comes with the firstfruits of the land and testifies to God's faithfulness. Is his witness true? Or is it only a fictional story that calls for faith nonetheless? Similarly, when Qohelet describes his experiences with wisdom and wealth, is he offering only fictional images that are to be believed nonetheless? Or does not this literary framework of first-person testimony in Ecclesiastes call for a more substantial confidence in its objective truthfulness? In this regard, the larger literary form in Ecclesiastes will inevitably determine the way in which his witness is received.[41]

The Proverb

In addition to this larger literary framework, a number of other genres appear in Ecclesiastes. One author has listed several literary forms, including truth-statements, "better than" sayings, instructions, traditional sayings, malediction and benediction, autobiographical narrative, example story, anecdote, parable, and antithesis.[42]

The most significant genre among this listing is the proverb. Its presence throughout the book, though occurring more frequently in the second half, has bamboozled interpreters. How can a reasoned

38. Fox, "Frame-Narrative," 94–96.
39. Ibid., 100.
40. Ibid.
41. See the observation of Wenham, *Story as Torah*, in footnote 31 above, to the effect that history is a much more authoritative narrative than fiction.
42. James L. Crenshaw, *Ecclesiastes: A Commentary* (London: SCM Press, 1988), 29.

structural outline shape these independent, self-contained aphorisms? What are they doing in a book that begins and ends with unified topical treatments?

Yet is this not exactly the format of the book of Proverbs? Does it not begin with nine chapters of sensible admonitions promoting the virtues of wisdom over against folly? Does it not conclude with an acrostic poem unified about the topic of the virtuous woman? And does not the second half of the book abound with proverbial aphorisms that may extend in length from one verse to several verses? In all these regards, these two books of wisdom, both purporting to be authored by King Solomon, have these significant similarities of format.

The proverbs of Ecclesiastes may be viewed in this literary context rather than as foreign elements that disrupt any logical flow of thought. They are not enemies of order. Instead, they should be seen and treated for what they are: proverbs—pithy sayings that condense words of wisdom about the realities of life in short scope that can be easily remembered.

In terms of form, these proverbial sayings in Ecclesiastes appear in poetic parallelism, frequently following the standard patterns of a-b-b-a and a-b-a-b. In terms of substance, they express in a few well-chosen words a truth about reality that conforms to the concepts of the larger biblical perspective. Examples of proverbs may be found throughout Ecclesiastes, though a greater concentration appears in the later chapters of the book. A few illustrations from earlier chapters may confirm the role of the proverbial form throughout the book. In these cases, the specific proverb serves to underscore the point that has just been made in the immediately preceding narrative:

> I have seen all the projects done under the sun;
> Would you believe! Everything amounts to frustration and striving
>   after wind.
>   What is bent
>   cannot be straightened;
>   What is lacking
>   cannot be counted. (Eccl. 1:14–15)

Then I applied myself to the understanding of wisdom, and also of madness and folly, but I learned that this, too, is a chasing after the wind.

> For with much wisdom
>> comes much sorrow;
> The more knowledge,
>> the more grief. (Eccl. 1:17–18 NIV)

A proverb from Ecclesiastes that closely parallels a proverb from the book of Proverbs with the same structure and similar concepts reads as follows:

> Better is one full hand
>> with quietness
> Than two fistfuls of toil
>> and striving after wind. (Eccl. 4:6)

> Better is a dry morsel
>> with quietness
> Than a house full of feasting
>> with strife. (Prov. 17:1 KJV)

A few samples taken from one of the later chapters of Ecclesiastes may illustrate the more extensive use of the proverb as a literary form:

> Whoever digs a pit
>> may fall into it;
> whoever breaks through a wall
>> may be bitten by a snake.
> Whoever quarries stones
>> may be injured by them;
> whoever splits logs
>> may be endangered by them. (Eccl. 10:8–9 NIV)

> Words from the mouth of a wise man
>> are gracious;
> But the lips of a fool
>> swallow him up.
> At the beginning the words of his mouth
>> are folly;

And at the end his mouth
  is wicked madness,
    and the fool multiplies words. (Eccl. 10:12–14a)

No man knows
  what shall be,
  and what shall be after him
Who can know it? (Eccl. 10:14b)

Woe to you, O land,
  when your king
    is a child,
  and your princes
    feast in the morning.
Blessed are you, O land,
  when your king
    is a son of noblemen,
  and your princes
    feast at the proper time,
      for strength and not for drunkenness.
  (Eccl. 10:16–17)

The recognition of the presence of the proverbial saying may go a long way toward alleviating the sense of lack of structure in the book of Ecclesiastes. For typical of the proverb is the inherent unity of the single thought, so that expectations of longer narrative coherence cannot be presumed.

Quite remarkable is the way in which the proverbs in Ecclesiastes remain closely connected with the book's larger subject of coping with life's frustrations. Many topics of significance treated in the book of Proverbs make little or no appearance in Ecclesiastes. The adulterous woman, represented so extensively in Proverbs, finds only one verse in Ecclesiastes (Eccl. 7:26). The sluggard appears in two verses (4:5; 10:18), while the drunkard and the glutton are not once mentioned. Nothing is said of the son who willingly receives discipline in contrast with the son who resists his father's corrections. Even when the same topic is approached, the special perspective of Ecclesiastes is quite different from that of Proverbs. For instance, both books present the value of a good name. Says Ecclesiastes: "A good name is better than fine oil" (7:1a). In similar fashion, the book of Proverbs declares: "A good name is more desirable than great riches" (Prov. 22:1a NIV). But the two treatments of the same subject depart radically from each other in the second half of their respective proverbs. Proverbs reads: "to be esteemed is better than silver or gold" (Prov. 22:1b NIV). But the parallel phrase in Ecclesiastes declares: "and the day of death [is] better than the day of birth" (Eccl. 7:1b NIV). This observation does not establish two different authors for the two books. Instead, it underscores the firmness of intention on the part of Ecclesiastes' author to "stick to his subject."

"Better than" Contrast

An additional poetic device beyond the proverb in Ecclesiastes is the use of the "better than" contrast. In one chapter of Ecclesiastes, no fewer than eight of these contrasts appear:

> A good name is *better than* fine oil,
>> and the day of your death *better than* the day of your birth.
>>> (Eccl. 7:1)

> It is *better* to go to the house of mourning
>> *than* to go to the house of feasting, because there is an end to every man,
>> and the living will take it to heart. (Eccl. 7:2)

> *Better* is agitation
>> *than* frolicking, for a sad countenance is good for the heart. (Eccl. 7:3)

> *Better* to hear the rebuke of the wise
>> *than* to hear the song of fools. (Eccl. 7:5)

> *Better* is the end of a matter
>> *than* its beginning, and
> *Better* is a spirit that's longsuffering
>> *than* a spirit that's haughty. (Eccl. 7:8)

> Never say, Why were the former days *better than* these?
>> For it is not wise to ask this kind of question. (Eccl. 7:10)

226

In addition to these eight instances of the "better than" contrasts in this one chapter, an additional fifteen instances are found elsewhere throughout Ecclesiastes, making a total of twenty-three.[43] This fact in itself provides some significant insight into the outlook of the book. For despite the sometimes seemingly negative perspective of his realistic picture of life, the author can always point to something "better." Significant connection with the book of Proverbs may be seen in the fact that Proverbs contains no fewer than twenty-one of these "better than" contrasts.[44] With this kind of comparison, it becomes more difficult to mount the case for two contrasting outlooks on life to be found in Proverbs and Ecclesiastes.

Extended Topical Discourses

One final literary form that may be noted in Ecclesiastes is the extended topical discourse on various subjects, such as:

- The temporal character of everything in this life. (Eccl. 1:3–11)
- The frustrating character of wisdom, pleasure, and projects. (Eccl. 1:12–2:26)
- The divinely appointed time frames of life. (Eccl. 3:1–17)
- The agonies of oppression and labor. (Eccl. 4:1–12)
- The solemnity of worship. (Eccl. 5:1–7)
- The frustration of not enjoying the labor of your hands. (Eccl. 6:1–12)
- The shared destiny of the righteous and the wicked. (Eccl. 9:1–12)
- Advice to the young in view of their coming old age and death. (Eccl. 11:9–12:7)

Summary on Literary Form in the Book of Ecclesiastes

So it should be apparent that Ecclesiastes is quite diverse in its use of literary genre. The reader would do well to take the book for what it

---

43. In addition to the eight instances from chapter 7 mentioned above, cf. Eccl. 2:24; 3:12, 22; 4:2–3, 6, 9, 13; 5:5; 6:3, 9; 8:12, 15; 9:4, 16, 18.

44. These contrasts can be found in the following passages: Prov. 3:14; 8:11, 19; 12:9; 15:16–17; 16:8, 16, 19, 32; 17:1; 19:1, 22; 21:9, 19; 22:1; 25:7, 24; 27:5, 10; 28:6.

is. Nothing will be gained by attempting to force the material into a pre-conceived notion of what the form of the book ought to be. If it is treated with the respect given to a similar book such as Proverbs, it will prove to be a most valuable asset in learning how to cope with life's frustrations.

Structure

The basic structure of Ecclesiastes is apparent to all and agreed on by all. The book begins and ends with material in the third person, while the bulk of the book is in the first person. The resulting overall structure is as follows:

- Prologue (Eccl. 1:1–11)
- Body (Eccl. 1:12–12:7)
- Epilogue (Eccl. 12:8–14)

To this point, everyone basically agrees. But in terms of the structure and flow of thought throughout the body of the book, little agreement may be found. One commentator has collected four pages of materials representing differing viewpoints on the structure of Ecclesiastes.[45] Yet he comments that "the book of Qoheleth in its present form can be fully understood as a coherent text, if one takes into account its discursive character and considers the possibility of an ironic playing around with the traditional genres and themes."[46] Another commentator finds no linear development of thought or logical progression in Ecclesiastes. Instead, a unifying function is achieved "by a small number of leading concepts to which *Koheleth* returns again and again."[47] Still another commentator perceives an even looser connection of thought, noting that "at times *Qohelet's* words are almost stream of consciousness."[48]

In general, we may note that the more extended thematic sections appear in the earlier chapters (Eccl. 1–6), and the more proverbial sayings in the second section of the book (Eccl. 7–12). Even this

45. Kruger, *Qoheleth*, 5–8.
46. Ibid., 16.
47. Von Rad, *Wisdom in Israel*, 227.
48. Longman, *Ecclesiastes*, 200.

basic observation must be immediately qualified, in that a number of proverbial sayings may be found in the first section (4:5–6; 6:7–10), while one of the most extended thematic segments may be found in the second section of the book (11:9–12:7). Without attempting to develop a logical outline, a synopsis of Ecclesiastes follows, which may provide some sense of the flow of the book.[49]

Synopsis

This analysis of the materials in Ecclesiastes will not attempt to deal comprehensively with all the problems faced by the interpreter. The current author would not want to deny the reader the privilege

49. Various attempts have sought to uncover the inherent structure of Ecclesiastes, but none have succeeded in convincing many others of the correctness of their own analysis. Seow (*Ecclesiastes*, 43–46) notes that some see no structure, while others perceive multiple structures. Most convincing is the observation that identifies Ecclesiastes 6:10 as "the midpoint of the book," noted by the Masoretes in the margins and at the end of the book. Seow cites others who note 222 verses in the book, with 111 in Ecclesiastes 1:1–6:9 and 111 in 6:10–12:14 (45). He questions determining the book's structure on the basis of counting verses, since the ancients may not have had the same ideas about versification that prevailed in the medieval period when the verses were first marked (44). At the same time, he notes that D. N. Freedman had indicated to him that apart from the five Hebrew words in Ecclesiastes 6:9b translated as "this, too, is vanity and pursuit of wind" (says Seow, in reporting Freedman's statement), "we have precisely the same number of words in the first half of the book as in the second: 1,491 words in the first half (1:1–6:9a) and 1,491 words in the second (6:10–12:14)" (45). Seow regards this identical count as "a remarkable coincidence," but not "the author's or the editor's intention" (45). He nonetheless concludes that the book "is divided into two halves of roughly equal length" (46).

A. G. Wright, "The Riddle of the Sphinx: The Structure of the Book of Qoheleth," *CBQ* 30, 3 (1968): 313–34, had previously noted this twofold structure, and had provided a more detailed analysis of Ecclesiastes based on the distribution of certain key phrases or concepts. In the first half of the book (Eccl. 1:1–6:9), he noted eight recurrences of the phrase "chasing after the wind" that serve as concluding statements or markers ending various sections (1:14, 17; 2:11, 17, 26; 4:6, 16; 6:9; cf. also "toils for the wind" in 5:16c) (cf. Wright, "Riddle," 323). In most of these instances, this phrase does appear to mark the end of a section. Furthermore, as Wright observes, the phrase never occurs in the second half of Ecclesiastes, which adds further weight to its structural role in the first half. In the second half of the book (6:10–12:14), Wright focuses on the regular appearance of the phrase "Do not know . . ." or its equivalent in chapters 9, 10, and 11 (9:1, 5, 10, 12; 10:14–15; 11:2, 5–6), and the similar phrase "cannot find/who can find?" in chapters 7–8 (7:14, 24, 28; 8:17 [3 times]) (Wright, "Riddle," 323). His observations regarding the structural role of these latter phrases have some merit, but are not quite so convincing. The matter of structure within Ecclesiastes deserves further study, though it should be remembered that its extensive use of self-contained proverbs discourages too rigid a structural form.

of wrestling with some of these interpretive challenges for himself. Yet an overall grasp of the flow of thought in the book may be helpful.

Prologue (Eccl. 1:1–11)

The author is introduced as Qohelet, son of David, king in Jerusalem. He is the Convener of the assembly of God's people (Eccl. 1:1).[50] In this prologue, three key phrases emerge that recur repeatedly throughout the book. First, he summarizes the theme of his discourse with the phrase: *"Frustration of frustrations, all is frustration"* (1:2).[51] Second, he asks a penetrating question regarding the meaningfulness of human life: *"What's the profit?"* (1:3a). Third, he refers to the cycle of human life on this earth: *"under the sun"* (1:3b). As an initial elaboration of the significance of these three repetitive phrases, the author points to cosmic cycles that demonstrate the inevitable frustration associated with all human existence.[52] The sun rises, sets, and then eagerly pants after the place from where it rises (1:5). The wind

50. As previously discussed, "Convener," the person who calls for an assembly, may serve as a better English translation for *Qohelet* than "Preacher" or "Teacher."

51. A more extended discussion of this critical phrase in Ecclesiastes may be found in the section entitled "Frustration of Frustrations" below.

52. The strong emphasis on the cyclical pattern of life is clearly intended to underscore the frustration, the *hebel*, of all human existence. Yet at the same time, this cyclical aspect of life provides an essential insight into the role of wisdom literature in Old Testament biblical theology. As previously mentioned, the outworking of God's purposes in redemptive history does not move simply in a linear pattern. Always there has been the cyclical element. "Generation follows generation" is not exclusively a negative thought. Otherwise, the genealogies in Scripture would all have to be read in a purely negative manner. But—generation follows generation! Progress is being made across the generations. The divinely appointed goal will ultimately be realized. It may be objected that this positive perspective on the cyclical pattern does not accord with the wholly negative perspective that some ascribe to the book of Ecclesiastes. Yet this understanding of the total message of Ecclesiastes may rest rather strongly on the assumption that "meaningless, meaningless, all is meaningless" is the correct understanding of *hebel* in Ecclesiastes. If the phrase may be read more properly as "frustration of frustrations, all is frustration," then this "frustrating" character of human life may be mollified in Ecclesiastes by the word *hope*, even as the apostle Paul does when he employs the same word for "frustration" (ματαιότης) that translates *hebel* in the LXX (Rom. 8:20–21). In any case, it is clear that in the total picture of life as perceived by the writer of Ecclesiastes, this cyclical pattern is "going somewhere." His perspective on life begins with creation, makes its way through many divine directives in providence, and climaxes with God's finally bringing to judgment all deeds done by all people, whether good or bad.

blows to the south, turns to the north, going continually round and round (1:6). All streams flow into the sea, yet the sea is never full. To the place where the streams originate, there they inevitably return (1:7). The eye never has enough seeing, nor the ear enough hearing (1:8b). What has been will be again, what has been done will be done again, and there is nothing new under the sun (1:9).

Once firmly settled in the introduction, these three distinctive phrases occur repeatedly throughout the book. Taking into account their role in the preface joined to their permeating usage, we see that these three phrases serve to bind the book in a literary unit despite its diversity.

Body (Eccl. 1:12–12:7)

The author now offers a further identification of himself. He was king over Israel in Jerusalem. Then he begins his first-person personal testimony concerning wisdom (Eccl. 1:12–13). He records the frustrations that come with wisdom, pleasure, and projects. He notes that wisdom is better than folly, but that in the end the grave awaits the wise as well as the foolish. He concludes that the best thing to do in life is to eat, drink, and enjoy your work, while always recognizing that God alone is the one who gives wisdom, knowledge, and delight in life (1:14–2:26).

Next he stresses the sovereignty of God in the times and seasons of humanity (Eccl. 3:1–17). He presents fourteen different contrasting "times" that people can expect to undergo from birth to death. Some of these experiences are totally out of the control of people, while others call for the exercise of wisdom. But throughout this passage, God remains prominent. He is mentioned nine times in these seventeen verses, emphasizing that all of life is at his sovereign disposal. He has laid the burden of work on men, he has made everything beautiful in its time, he has set eternity in the hearts of men, he gives the gift of satisfaction in life, everything he does endures forever, nothing can be added to or removed from what he has done, and he will bring the righteous and the wicked to judgment (3:1–17).

Then the author notes how God humbles people by showing that in terms of what can be observed, humans are no better than the animals. All have the same breath; all die and go to the same grave. He alludes to the original curse on mankind, "Dust you are, and to dust you will return" (Gen. 3:19), by the similar words "all come from dust, and to dust all return" (Eccl. 3:20). Then for the third time he states that there is nothing better than for a person to enjoy his work, for that is his apportioned lot from God (3:18–22).

Next he discusses factors that intensify life's frustrations (Eccl. 4:1–16). First among these is oppression (4:1–3). Many peoples experience for decades the oppression that often comes through the powers that be. A Stalin, a Mao, or an Idi Amin brings perpetual tears to an oppressed people. Power belongs with the oppressor, and no comfort is available to the oppressed. Second among these factors that intensify a person's frustration is envy (4:4–6). Folded, idle hands can ruin a man. But the kind of envy that drives a person to get two handfuls increases frustration. Far better is a single handful with tranquility. Third, aloneness heightens frustration (4:7–12). Qohelet presents a vignette of a person all alone without son or brother. This lonely man labored endlessly with frustrating discontent. So it becomes clear that two are better than one. Fourth, successors can bring great frustration (4:13–16). A rootless youth may succeed the king. But a discontented people will not be long pleased with him. This, too, is frustrating, a chasing after wind.

In dealing with worship, Qohelet lays emphasis on the solemnity of taking a vow in God's house (Eccl. 5:1–7). The fool speaks far too much in God's presence, which is nothing but vanity. In contrast with this foolishness, Qohelet advises that you perform your worship in the fear of God.

Whether or not you have it, wealth will always bring frustration—unless God grants his gift of enjoyment (Eccl. 5:8–6:12). Higher officialdom that loves money will always bring oppression on those below. Man comes naked from his mother's womb, and as he comes so he departs. Wealth and the ability to enjoy it must come as a gift from God. But God does not grant this gift to everyone.

Wisdom enables a person to understand why some things are "better than" others (Eccl. 7:1–8:1). The day of death is better than the day of birth. The house of mourning is better than the house of feasting. A wise man's rebuke is better than the song of fools. Patience is better than pride. Wisdom is better than an inheritance. Wisdom makes a single wise person more powerful than ten rulers in a city. So commit yourself to the search for wisdom and the scheme of things, even though in its fullest dimension wisdom may forever remain beyond your complete comprehension. "Deep, deep," he says of wisdom. *Bathu Bathos* is the Greek translation. Who can find it out (7:24)? Elsewhere he speaks of the impossibility of understanding what God is doing in the world:

> Man cannot find out the whole of the work which God does, neither its beginning nor its end. (Eccl. 3:11)

> Man cannot comprehend the work that is done under the sun. (Eccl. 8:17)

> As you do not know the path of the wind, . . . even so you cannot know the work of God, who does all. (Eccl. 11:5)

Yet you can be assured that even a limited amount of wisdom invariably brightens a man's face and changes his harsh appearance (Eccl. 8:1).

Give proper respect to the king as a governing authority, even though someone may lord it over others to his own hurt (Eccl. 8:2–9). Because no one can comprehend why the wicked get what the righteous deserve and the righteous get what the wicked deserve, go ahead and enjoy your food, your drink, and your work during all the days that God gives you (8:10–17).

The righteous and the wicked, the wise and the foolish, share the same destiny. So enjoy life with the wife you love. Whatever your hands find to do, do it with all your might, for no one knows when his appointed hour will come (Eccl. 9:1–12). A poor but wise man may save a city, but he will soon be forgotten. A little folly can outweigh a great deal of wisdom (Eccl. 9:13–10:3).

Wisdom provides insight into all the different circumstances of life (Eccl. 10:4–20). Kings may err by entrusting fools with positions of responsibility. Calamity may come with lawful endeavors. The wise man speaks gracious words, but the fool speaks folly. Kings must not be reviled even though they bring curses on their people because of their self-indulgence.

Be always industrious rather than idly worrying about circumstances that you cannot control (Eccl. 11:1–6). As you cannot know the path of the wind or how a body is formed in the womb, so you must not expect to understand the workings of God your Maker. So keep busy morning and evening, not knowing which activity God will bless, or whether he will bless both.

As a young person just setting out in life, be happy and enjoy your life. But always remember two things: God will bring you into judgment for everything you do, and the challenges of old age and death are inevitable (Eccl. 11:7–12:7).

Epilogue (Eccl. 12:8–14)

The author rounds out the results of his search for wisdom. He reiterates his theme: Frustration of frustrations, all is frustration (Eccl. 12:8). He then locates this search by Qohelet the Convener in the larger context of a single "Shepherd" who is the ultimate source of all wisdom among multiple wisdom figures of God's people (12:9–11). He draws out the conclusion of this search with two admonitions: Fear God, and keep his commandments. These two final admonitions must be treated with great seriousness in view of God's coming judgment of all that every person has done, whether good or evil (12:12–14).

THE MESSAGE OF THE BOOK

Having reviewed the content of Ecclesiastes in summary fashion, we must now undertake a more careful analyzing of its message. This analysis will first consider the question of a unified message. Then the message itself will be considered as that message appears first in the repeated phrases of Ecclesiastes and then in the representation of God in the gospel of Ecclesiastes.

The Question of a Unified Message

The first and most basic question regarding the message of Ecclesiastes is whether the book has multiple messages or a unified message. Clearly, some statements of the book seem to stand in opposition to other statements.[53] But more significantly for current discussion, the critical question is this: do the book's final verses, written in the third person instead of the first person, present a perspective on life that is quite different from that of the body of the book? Prominent scholars have argued that the book's conclusion is written "in critique of" Qohelet, the author of the bulk of the book, rather than as a positive summation of the book's own message.

Two Authors?

Even without considering the matter of differing theologies, the question whether the prologue and epilogue are written by the same person who composed the body of the book requires thoughtful analysis. It can be reasonably proposed that a single author first introduces himself and his central topic in the third person, proceeds to record his first-person testimony, and then concludes with a final summation in the third person. Illustrations of writings in the first person with a conclusion in the third person may be seen in the personal testimonies given by David at the end of his life. He presents his rather lengthy song about the faithfulness of the LORD in delivering him from all his enemies in the first person:

> The LORD is my rock, my fortress and my deliverer . . . . I call to the LORD . . . , and I am saved from my enemies. (2 Sam. 22:2, 4 NIV)

In his conclusion he makes the transition from the first person to the third person:

> Therefore I will praise you, O LORD, among the nations . . . . He gives his king great victories; he shows unfailing kindness to his anointed, to David and his descendants forever. (2 Sam. 22:50–51 NIV)

This same transitional process occurs again with the "last words of David," this time at the beginning of David's psalm:

---

53. Regarding apparent contradictions of viewpoint in the book, Seow (*Ecclesiastes*, 41) observes that if the book as a whole is any reflection of the author's inner struggles, his "debates within himself," then the reader should not be surprised even with contradictory perspectives. For to Qohelet there are "all sorts of [apparent] inconsistencies in the world" (41).

> The oracle of David son of Jesse, the oracle of the man exalted by the Most High, the man anointed by the God of Jacob, Israel's singer of songs:
>
> "The Spirit of the LORD spoke through me; his word was on my tongue. The God of Israel spoke, the Rock of Israel said to me . . . ." (2 Sam. 23:1–3 NIV)

So nothing in terms of literary restrictions keeps an author from moving back and forth from first person to third person, and then again back to first person. These examples could quite naturally explain the transition in Ecclesiastes between third person in the prologue and epilogue, and first person in the body of the book.

At the same time, nothing excludes the possibility that a second author introduces and concludes the book of Ecclesiastes, speaking in the third person, while the body of the material originates with a different author. A similar situation may be seen in a document of the New Testament. The Gospel of John concludes:

> This is the disciple who testifies to these things and who wrote them down. We know that his testimony is true. (John 21:24 NIV)

It may be that the author of the Gospel refers to himself in the third person in these concluding words of testimony. This perspective would agree with the way in which he regularly speaks of himself throughout the Gospel as "the disciple whom Jesus loved" (John 13:23; 19:26; 20:2; 21:7, 20). At the same time, it may be that a different person added his comments as a witness to the veracity of the Gospel.

With regard to the book of Ecclesiastes, it is difficult to find compelling evidence that would resolve the question whether a second person has added the concluding remarks. The similarities of thought and language are so extensive that they could easily have been written by the same person. Yet it is also possible that a subsequent author composed the conclusion of the book.[54]

---

54. Fox, "Frame-Narrative," 84, offers a strong case for his insistence that a second "speaker" must be recognized in Ecclesiastes. He notes specifically the "says *Qohelet*" insertion that occurs in the middle of a first-person sentence in Ecclesiastes 7:27. According to Fox: "While one *can* speak of himself in the third-person it is unlikely

One Author in Conflict with Another?

A more serious matter arises with the proposition that the supposed two authors of Ecclesiastes are at significant variance with each other. One commentator sees the two sections of the book in serious conflict, promoting two drastically different messages. He quotes approvingly the observation of another critic of Qohelet, who notes that there are "good sages" as well as "evil ones."[55] Qohelet falls into the category of an "evil sage," while the author of the prologue and epilogue, designated as the "frame narrator," corrects the serious errors of Qohelet. This frame narrator warns his son about the "words of the wise ones," including the life perspective presented by Qohelet.

---

he would do so in the middle of a first-person sentence." The phrase "says Qohelet," however, could simply be understood as the speaker's self-identification, which is quite appropriate to the flow of the argument at this point. This self-identification appears within the initial first-person statement of the second half of the book (Eccl. 6:10–12:14). A statement just at this point reaffirming that none other than Qohelet the Convener speaks as the primary source of wisdom is quite appropriate. Coming essentially at the halfway point of the book, this self-identification connects the opening and closing identifications of the source of this material as coming from the wise person identified as Qohelet. In addition, it comes at a focal point in which great stress is now being placed on the role of "wisdom" in coping with life's frustrations. Five times over at this midpoint of the book, summary statements declare the role of "wisdom" as key to life, which makes the specific identification of Qohelet as the source of wisdom quite appropriate:

Summary Statement #1: "Wisdom, like an inheritance, is a good thing" (Eccl. 7:11–12 NIV).

Summary Statement #2: "All this I tested by wisdom and I said, 'I am determined to be wise'" (Eccl. 7:23–25 NIV).

Summary Statement #3: "Who is like the wise man? . . . Wisdom brightens a man's face" (Eccl. 8:1 NIV).

Summary Statement #4: "I applied my mind to know wisdom . . . . Even if a wise man claims he knows, he cannot really comprehend it" (Eccl. 8:16–17 NIV).

Summary Statement #5: "I also saw under the sun this example of wisdom . . . . Wisdom is better than strength" (Eccl. 9:13, 16 NIV).

For these reasons, the identity of Qohelet as the speaker in Ecclesiastes 7:27 is not as intrusive as might first appear. Fox concludes with a mind-straining proposal: "I suggest that all of 1:2–12:14 is by the same hand—not that the epilogue is by Qohelet, but that Qohelet is 'by' the epilogist" (91). That is, after all this effort to distinguish two voices, Fox concludes that the book is authored by one and the same person. The third-person voice has written the entire composition. This single author of Ecclesiastes has tried to represent faithfully the wise old man who speaks in the first person, even though in the end he has subtly inserted his own critiques in the third person. So: one author speaks in two voices in Ecclesiastes, with one of the voices subtly critiquing the other voice.

55. Longman, *Ecclesiastes*, 277, quoting Fox, "Frame-Narrative," 97.

In essence, the frame narrator says to his son, "*Qohelet's* thinking is dangerous material—be careful."[56]

In consistency with this viewpoint, this commentator regularly sets the message of Qohelet in a negative framework. Death renders every human achievement useless. Only God can make it possible for someone to enjoy life, and it is judged to be "clear throughout the book that *Qohelet* did not consider himself a person so blessed by God."[57] Qohelet's statements about God depict him as "distant, occasionally indifferent, and sometimes cruel."[58] There will be a final judgment, but Qohelet "does not expect to find justice there."[59] In addition, "*Qohelet* may well believe in divine providence, but it is no source of comfort to him as he faces the unpredictable chaos of life."[60] In Qohelet's understanding, "the universe is ruled by a God that just does not seem to care much about earthly concerns."[61] Qohelet is "a prime representative of skepticism in Israel" who agrees with Israel's skeptics that deny "God's goodness if not his very existence," and portray men and women as "powerless to acquire essential truth."[62] Even in the epilogue of the book, the goads and nails "are better taken as negative and harmful."[63] This commentator concludes by seeing Qohelet as giving expression to unbelief without hope. Only in the frame narrator who disagrees with the body of the book may be found a positive message.

This disagreement is said to be found in virtually everything the frame narrator says about Qohelet. Even his apparent commendations should be read in a negative light. The frame narrator may concede that Qohelet taught, heard, investigated, and put in good order many proverbs. Yet this description of Qohelet's task "lacks any honorifics or terms of respect."[64] In actuality, this frame narrator "subtly

56. Longman, *Ecclesiastes*, 281.
57. Ibid., 35.
58. Ibid.
59. Ibid.
60. Ibid.
61. Ibid., 36.
62. Ibid.
63. Ibid., 38.
64. Ibid., 277.

238

calls *Qohelet* a double failure."[65] Though Qohelet sought "words of delight," he did not find them. The book is better characterized as "difficult and problematic."[66] Though he attempted to write "words of truth," it must be concluded that the frame narrator was not ready to admit that Qohelet actually spoke the truth.[67]

The consequences of this perspective in terms of the canonical authority of the book of Ecclesiastes should be given full consideration. In this view, a maximum of 17 verses in Ecclesiastes give the right view of life, while 204 verses offer a view of life by an "evil sage" that is dangerous, without truth, full of skepticism and unbelief, and requiring that youth be warned of its contents.

Some years earlier, one commentator offered a penetrating comment and question regarding this dualistic perspective on Ecclesiastes:

> It is very odd to imagine an "editor" issuing a work with which he disagrees but adding extensive notes and an epilogue to compensate. Why should an orthodox writer reproduce a skeptical book at all, let alone add orthodox glosses to produce a noticeably mixed bag? . . . It is scarcely likely that anyone would [send out Ecclesiastes] if he were unhappy with the content of the work.[68]

A Unified Perspective

When the substance of the material found in the epilogue of Ecclesiastes is compared with the body of the book, far more agreement is found than disagreement. The proposed editor declares that the discourse is now finished. The "word" is completed. All has been heard. This proposed author of the conclusion (Eccl. 12:8–14) presents two pointed admonitions followed by two strong reasons that these admonitions should be heeded. Three of these four points are repeatedly anticipated in the body of the book.

First, the reader of the epilogue is told: "Fear God" (אֶת־הָאֱלֹהִים יְרָא—Eccl. 12:13). This precise phrasing also appears in

---

65. Ibid., 278.
66. Ibid.
67. Ibid.
68. Eaton, *Ecclesiastes*, 40.

the body of Qohelet's writings. As he discusses the seriousness of worship, Qohelet warns that in many dreams and a multitude of words there is much vanity. Therefore, he says: "Fear God" (5:6). In another passage, though not employing exactly the same phrase, Qohelet twice affirms the importance of "fearing God." It will go better with "the fearers of God who fear before him." To the contrary, it will not go well with the wicked, who will not prolong their days because they have no fear before the presence of God (8:12–13).

These references to the fear of God in the body of Ecclesiastes give no evidence that they communicate a different concept from the identical admonition to fear God found in the epilogue. To the contrary, they call for the same respect for God that is reinforced in the book's conclusion.

The second concluding admonition states: "Keep his commandments." This particular admonition has no specific precedent in the body of the book. The one earlier note regarding "keeping the commandment" by Qohelet refers to the responsibility of keeping the command of the king (Eccl. 8:5). This absence of parallel expressions regarding keeping the commandments slightly weakens the case for a unified message between the body of Ecclesiastes and its epilogue. Yet the repeated references in the book to doing what is right and just may be understood as essentially equivalent to the concluding exhortation to keep God's commandments.[69]

The epilogue concludes with two reasons that support the author's admonitions to fear God and keep his commandments. First, a rather sweeping observation responds to the large picture of frustration that permeates the entirety of the book: "For this is the whole of humanity" (Eccl. 12:13c). Translations generally insert the word *duty* in the phrase, so that it reads: "This is the whole *duty* of man." The insertion of the word *duty* captures one aspect of the "whole of humanity." But

69. A discussion of the relation between the "fear of God" and *torah* in Ecclesiastes may be found in Craig G. Bartholomew, *Ecclesiastes* (Grand Rapids: Baker Academic, 2009), 88–92, 370–71. Says Bartholomew: "There are clear indications that the reference to law may not be as alien to Ecclesiastes as some suggest" (88). Again, he says: "The indications that Ecclesiastes has a strong link with Genesis and several strong links with Deuteronomy make it more and more difficult to insist that the reference to law means that the epilogue must be a later addition" (92).

the original wording embraces more than simply the concept of duty. "The whole of humanity's reason for existence" communicates the idea better.[70] The entirety of Qohelet's discourse finally finds a proper resolution for all its inherent tensions. Humanity's existence makes sense only in relation to God the Creator, the Sustainer, the Lawgiver, the Judge. Therefore, fear God and keep his commandments. For apart from him, nothing makes sense. No greater reason for fearing him and keeping his commandments can be imagined.

The epilogue gives one final reason for obeying his admonitions. God will bring every work into judgment. This truth-statement of the epilogue finds its anticipation in the body of the book. The term for this "work" (מַעֲשֶׂה—Eccl. 12:14) that will be brought into judgment occurs seven times in the body of Ecclesiastes, and in several cases the context is one of judgment being exercised over a person's work. In his temporal judgments God may destroy the "work" of a person's hands (5:6). Qohelet himself exercises judgment over "every work" done in the present day (8:9). A "work" of evil must be judged quickly, or the hearts of the people will be filled with schemes to do wrong (8:11). These early references to the judgment of a person's work clearly anticipate the final judgment of every man's work as described in this last verse of the epilogue.

In one passage, Qohelet presents a very realistic picture of the defective judgments exercised in this present world order when he observes that he saw "wickedness" standing in the place of "justice" (Eccl. 3:16). But he immediately balances his perspective in direct anticipation of the final remarks found in the epilogue: "But then I said in my heart, 'Both the righteous and the wicked God will judge'" (3:17). As Qohelet states so plainly in rounding out his discourse: Be happy, young man. But be sure you understand: "For all these things God will bring you to judgment" (11:9 NIV).

According to the epilogue, this final judgment of God will include "every hidden thing" (Eccl. 12:14). The word for "hidden thing"

70. Says Derek Kidner, *Wisdom to Live By: An Introduction to the Old Testament's Wisdom Books of Proverbs, Job and Ecclesiastes* (Leicester, UK: Inter-Varsity Press, 1985), 104n3: "Strictly the phrase in 12:13b means 'for this is every man'—a concentrated way of saying, 'Every man is destined for, and should be wholly absorbed in, this.'"

(נֶעְלָם) is rare in the Old Testament. But quite strikingly, it is used to describe the depth of knowledge displayed by King Solomon. When the queen of Sheba visited him, nothing was "hidden" from the king that he could not explain to her (1 Kings 10:3; 2 Chron. 9:2). In a similar way, "our hidden sins" will be made apparent in the light of God's presence (Ps. 90:8). In the final day, the King of the kings will bring everything directly into the light for his judgment.

The activities to be judged are specifically identified as including both the "good" and the "evil" (Eccl. 12:14). Once more, the message of the epilogue finds repeated anticipation in the body of the book. According to Qohelet, there is nothing better than for a person to be joyful and *do good* while he lives (3:12). Yet there is not a righteous person who *does good* and does not sin (7:20). Although the "evil" described in the body of the book is not always morally wrong, in many cases it is indeed morally evil, and so subject to this final judgment of God. Fools go into the house of God, not knowing that they do evil (5:1). The hearts of the sons of Adam are full of evil (מָלֵא־רָע —9:3). Echoing these earlier statements, the final summation of the epilogue declares that every single good and evil deed arising from the hearts of men will be subjected to God's finalizing judgment.

In summary, it would be quite difficult to divorce the viewpoint of the author of the epilogue in Ecclesiastes from the perspective of the author of the body of the book. Virtually every point made in the epilogue finds its anticipatory counterpart in the book's body. It may be difficult to conclude whether the author of the epilogue is the same person as the composer of the body of the book. Yet despite many truths held internally in tension, the entire work clearly presents itself as a unified whole.

In addition to these large areas of agreement, the commendations of Qohelet and his work that find expression in the epilogue must be taken seriously. The author of the epilogue begins his comments by a repetition of the overarching theme introduced at the beginning of the book: "Frustration of frustrations, all is frustration" (Eccl. 12:8; cf. 1:2). This theme reappears in the epilogue without any suggestion of a negatively critical analysis.

Then the "epilogist" offers his personal evaluation of Qohelet and his work (Eccl. 12:9–10). This Convener of the assembly of God's people is characterized in a number of ways:

- He is "wise." All the commendations of wisdom found in the book may now be appropriately applied to Qohelet himself.
- He "taught the people knowledge." He has shown genuine interest not merely in the "elite." His concern has been for all of God's people, sensing their need for the truth of God's wisdom to deal with the frustrations of life.
- He "pondered, searched out, and set in order many proverbs." Qohelet has made his best effort to comprehend the truth of God about human life, and to make it easily understood and remembered.
- He searched diligently to find "words of delight," well-crafted words that would be efficient communicators in form as well as content. He was not interested merely in abstract truth. Instead, he diligently applied himself to the task of giving expression to truth in a most memorable and practical fashion.
- He was careful to write only statements that were upright and true.

In reviewing this concluding evaluation of the work of Qohelet the Convener, we find it difficult to imagine a more appreciative recommendation. Any author receiving an evaluation framed in these words would be compelled to respond with embarrassment and humble appreciation.

In light of this extensive commendation of the body of the book as found in the epilogue, it would indeed be difficult to support the idea of two conflicting messages in the one book of Ecclesiastes. If there are two authors, they are in total agreement. To cast these concluding commendations into a subtle critique that actually intends to discredit the body of the book requires a tour de force to the extreme. If this epilogue has

243

been written by a different person from the author of the book, he manifests little interest in correcting the analysis of life presented by Qohelet. Instead, he clearly manifests great appreciation for the book's author.

Various Frameworks for Interpreting the Message

The challenge of comprehending the overall message of Ecclesiastes has led to a variety of frameworks for interpretation. Among a number of possibilities, the following may be noted:

A False View of Life

S. R. Driver in his 1913 *Introduction to the Literature of the Old Testament* offers this evaluation of the message of Ecclesiastes:

> Of course, Qoheleth takes a false view of life .... His teaching, as a whole, if followed consistently, would tend directly to paralyze human effort, to stifle every impulse to self-denial or philanthropy, to kill all activity of an ennobling or unselfish kind.[71]

Needless to say, this viewpoint would have the effect of essentially expelling the book of Ecclesiastes from the canon of the Old Testament. An interpreter should think long and hard before dismissing the book from the collection of authoritative words from God simply because of difficulties in interpretation.

An Allegory of the Gospel

The history of the interpretation of Ecclesiastes has featured a long line of allegorical interpretations. Classic expression of this viewpoint may be found in the work of Peter Lombard of France (1096 B.C.). In discussing the reference to the flowering of the almond tree (Eccl. 12:5), generally taken to refer to the whitening of a person's hair in old age, Lombard offers this explanation:

> There are three things in the almond, viz., the rind, the shell, and the kernel; and Christ consists of three substances—the flesh corresponding with the rind, the mind with the shell, and the divinity with the kernel.

---

71. Driver, *Introduction*, 472.

The rind is bitter, the shell is strong, the kernel is sweet. But when shall the almond flower? In the resurrection, for it seemed dead and dry in his passion and death.[72]

This understanding of the message of Ecclesiastes in terms of an allegory of the gospel hardly needs refutation. Any curbs properly belonging to the process of exegesis have been effectively removed.

The Best of Human Wisdom

According to this perspective, the book of Ecclesiastes represents the best efforts of man's natural reason to understand the perplexities of human life. Yet as has been well said, "it does not seem to be worthy of God to occupy valuable space in the Bible with the arguments of the skeptic and of the natural man. We can buy those anywhere or have them for nothing. That is the difficulty with Scofield's theory."[73]

A Realistic Picture of Life

This perspective on Ecclesiastes views the book as providing a strong dose of realism. Far from being a sub-Christian theme, the unifying message of the book anticipates the words of the apostle Paul as found in Romans 8.[74] Paul employs the same Greek word found in the LXX translation of the opening verses of Ecclesiastes. God is the one who has "subjected the creation to *frustration*" (ματαιότητι—Rom. 8:20). Even those who are righteous in their union with the promised Christ will suffer many frustrations in this present world order. Yet they should always remember that God has subjected this world to frustration—*in hope* (Rom. 8:20). Though Ecclesiastes may not spell

---

72. Quoted in C. D. Ginsburg, *The Song of Songs and Coheleth (Commonly Called the Book of Ecclesiastes)*, Library of Biblical Studies (New York: KTAV, 1970), 108.

73. J. Stafford Wright, "The Interpretation of Ecclesiastes," in *Classical Evangelical Essays in Old Testament Interpretation*, ed. Walter C. Kaiser Jr. (Grand Rapids: Baker, 1972), 137, in response to the analysis of the message of Ecclesiastes as found in the original *Scofield Reference Bible*.

74. This is the viewpoint promoted by Wright, "Ecclesiastes": "Is it only by chance that Paul in Romans 8, after speaking of the vanity of the whole creation, goes on to speak of the sufferings that create a problem even for the Christian, and the confidence of the Christian in his daily life that all things work together for good for him?" (149).

out this hope in all its fullness, it is still present in the book. God ordains that the wicked will store up the product of his labors for the person who pleases him (Eccl. 2:26). God will subject to his just judgment the righteous and the wicked (3:17). The end of a matter is better than its beginning, and patience is better than pride (7:8). When the book concludes with the expectation that God will climax time and eternity with a judgment of the good and the evil, it may be legitimately expected that God will make all things right.

In this framework of a realistic perspective on life, the message of Ecclesiastes may be considered more closely. Both the message as contained in the repeated statements of the book and the God of the gospel in Ecclesiastes will be considered.

The Message Contained in the Repeated Statements of the Book

Ecclesiastes is distinctive in its use of particular phrases regularly repeated throughout the book. These phrases serve to emphasize overarching thought-patterns. As previously indicated, three specific phrases appear in the preface (Eccl. 1:1–11) and then permeate the book, which serves to strongly underscore the book's unity. These three phrases provide distinctive insight into the message of the book and deserve further consideration. The key phrases are "frustration of frustrations," "what's the profit," and "under the sun," all three of which occur in the first two verses of the book's text proper (1:2–3).

Frustration of Frustrations (הֲבֵל הֲבָלִים)

Serving as a dominant motto of the book, this key phrase has been described as "misunderstandable in the highest degree."[75] The noun appears seventy-one times in the Old Testament. More than half these occurrences (36) are found in Ecclesiastes, where the word appears at least once in each chapter except chapter 10. This thematic phrase that occurs at the beginning and ending of the book employs singular and plural forms of the same root: "*Hebel hebalim*, all is *hebel*" (Eccl.

---

75. Kruger, *Qoheleth*, 44.

1:2; 12:8). The root idea of the word is "wind" or "breath," as may be perceived in the parallelism of a verse from the prophet Isaiah:

> The wind
>> will carry them off,
> A breath [*hebel*]
>> will take them away. (Isa. 57:13)

Difficulty with determining a proper definition for this elusive term arises from the fact that the word derives from a figure of speech. For what can be more vague in communicating precise meaning than the image of "wind" or "breath"?[76]

The root *hebel* first occurs in Scripture with the naming of the second son of Adam and Eve as *Hebel* ("Abel") (Gen. 4:2).[77] The term also describes Israel's "worthless idols" that angered the LORD (Deut. 32:21; 1 Kings 16:13, 26). A striking phrase indicates that because the Israelites followed after "the *hebel* they became *hebel*" (הַהֶ֫בֶל וַיֶּהְבָּֽלוּ —2 Kings 17:15).

In Ecclesiastes, many things are declared to be *hebel*:

- Everything is *hebel*. (Eccl. 1:2)
- All that is done under the sun is *hebel*. (Eccl. 1:14)
- Pleasure is *hebel*. (Eccl. 2:1)
- Work is *hebel*. (Eccl. 2:11)
- Wisdom is *hebel*. (Eccl. 2:15)
- Laboring night and day is *hebel*. (Eccl. 2:23)
- Money is *hebel*. (Eccl. 5:10)
- Wealth, possessions, and honor are *hebel*. (Eccl. 6:2)
- A wandering appetite is *hebel*. (Eccl. 6:9)

---

76. Cf. K. Seybold, "*hebhel*," in *Theological Dictionary of the Old Testament*, ed. G. Johannes Botterweck and Helmer Ringgren (Grand Rapids: Eerdmans, 1978), 3:315. Seybold notes that because of its onomatopoeic origin, "the range of meaning of *hebhel* is open. It has a broad emotion-laden stratum with strong evocative possibilities, and it is especially suited therefore to be a keyword or catchword."

77. Seybold, in commenting on the name *Abel*, notes that "everything favors the view that the name is intended to signify the breath character of the fleeting life of the victim" (ibid., 3:316).

- The days of a man's life are *hebel*. (Eccl. 6:12)
- All that is coming is *hebel*. (Eccl. 11:8)
- Youth and vigor are *hebel*. (Eccl. 11:10)
- (Concluding as at the beginning): everything is *hebel* (Eccl. 12:8)

In reviewing this list of things declared as *hebel* in Ecclesiastes, we find that the critical nature of a proper understanding of the term becomes obvious. In this regard, the representation of the word as "meaningless" as found in the NIV is both unfortunate and seriously misleading.[78] Once everything mentioned in Ecclesiastes is understood to be "meaningless," a skeptical view of life cannot be escaped. With this perspective on the word, the whole of life must be viewed as having no meaning.

But precisely what is this *hebel* of which Qohelet speaks? What is the framework in which this idea may be properly understood? What is the source of this concept?

Already the pivotal role of the earlier chapters of Genesis in the book of Ecclesiastes has been noted. God made man upright at creation, but he has sought out many schemes (Eccl. 7:29; cf. Gen. 1:27, 31; 3:6). Labor is frustrating because a person is regularly denied the enjoyment that should come from his burdensome work (Eccl. 2:17–18, 23; 3:9–10; 5:15–17; cf. Gen. 1:28–29; 3:17b–19a). Humanity is destined to return to the dust, and incapable of carrying anything beyond this life (Eccl. 3:20; 12:7; cf. Gen. 3:19b). A terminating judgment sentence inevitably leads man into the declining years of old age as he moves toward death (Eccl. 7:2; 8:8; 12:1–7).

Yet despite the permeating character of this God-imposed *hebel*, fruitfulness and enjoyments can be found in life. God can bless a person's labor so that he rejoices in his food, his drink, his work, and the wife he loves (Eccl. 2:10, 24–26; 3:13, 22; 5:18–19; 8:15; 9:9). God has made everything beautiful in its time (3:11). Even aging and

---

78. Interestingly, Iain Provan, *Ecclesiastes, Song of Songs*, NIV Application Commentary (Grand Rapids: Zondervan, 2001), 51–53, strongly rejects the understanding of *hebel* as "meaningless," though this translation for *hebel* is retained even in the latest version of the NIV.

death can be viewed from a positive perspective, for ultimately the spirit returns to God who gave it (12:7b).

On the other hand, this *hebel* of Ecclesiastes can be a most unpleasant thing. Outside Ecclesiastes, the term frequently describes the "worthlessness" of idols (Deut. 32:21; 1 Kings 16:13, 26; 2 Kings 17:15; Jer. 2:5; 8:19; 10:8, 15; 14:22; 23:16; 51:18). These false gods are *hebel*; they are worse than useless in providing anything helpful to a fallen humanity under the curse of sin.

So not all that is *hebel* falls into the same category. Some passages communicate quite negative thoughts. *Hebel* refers to "vain," "worthless," "useless" things. But in other cases, hope is retained in situations described as *hebel*. The original divine judgment pronounced over man's labor and woman's conception communicated the expectation of blessing alongside curse. Despite God's judgment, the man will eat bread, and the woman will bear children.

One effort at understanding the term presents the most basic meaning of *hebel* in Ecclesiastes as "transitoriness." This concept properly represents the meaning of the term in certain Scripture passages outside Ecclesiastes as well as within the book itself.[79] Passages in Scripture outside Ecclesiastes supporting the idea of transitoriness include the following:

Man is like a breath [*hebel*],
His days a passing shadow. (Ps. 144:4)

Surely every man stands as a mere breath [*hebel*]!
Surely man goes about as a shadow.
Surely for breath [*hebel*] they are in turmoil. (Ps. 39:5–6)

---

79. See the extensive exploration of the term *hebel* in Daniel C. Fredericks, *Coping with Transcience: Ecclesiastes on Brevity in Life* (Sheffield, UK: JSOT Press, 1993), 11–32. Fredericks cites Fox, "Frame-Narrative," 83–106, as promoting a singular meaning for *hebel* on the basis of "the thematic declaration that everything is *hebel* and the formulaic character of the *hebel*-judgments" (17n1). Fredericks himself promotes the singular meaning "transience," though recognizing cases in which *hebel* may connote "futility" (24, 24n1). Seow, *Ecclesiastes*, 47, says that *hebel* refers to "anything that is superficial, ephemeral, insubstantial, incomprehensible, enigmatic, inconsistent, or contradictory." In summarizing his analysis of the term, he says: "[Qohelet] does not mean that everything is meaningless or insignificant, but that everything is beyond human apprehension and comprehension" (59). This concluding analysis is not the same as "superficial, ephemeral, insubstantial, . . . or contradictory."

I would not live forever.
For my days are breath [*hebel*]. (Job 7:16 ESV)

Passages within Ecclesiastes supporting the idea of transitoriness as the meaning of *hebel* include the following:

Man's fate is like that of the animals; the same fate awaits them both: As one dies, so dies the other. All have the same breath; man has no advantage over the animal. Everything is meaningless [transitory (*hebel*)]. (Eccl. 3:19 NIV)

Enjoy life with your wife, whom you love, all the days of this meaningless [transitory (*hebel*)] life. (Eccl. 9:9 NIV)

Qohelet's days are fleeting, as are the days of Job and the psalmist.

This transitory character of human existence has been captured by Shakespeare in the pungent lines placed in the mouth of Macbeth:

Life's but a walking shadow, a poor player,
that struts and frets his hour upon the stage,
And then is heard no more.[80]

This concept of *transitoriness* enlightens a number of passages in Ecclesiastes that use the term *hebel*. Yet a survey of the more than thirty passages in which *hebel* appears in Ecclesiastes uncovers many places where "transitory" simply does not function as the best option for communicating the meaning of the word.

In reviewing the use of the term throughout Ecclesiastes, the concept of *frustration* suits as many as twenty-five of the thirty-six contexts. As a sampling, the following passages may be noted:

- Everything done under the sun is "frustrating," a chasing after the wind. (Eccl. 1:14)
- Pleasure proves to be "frustrating." (Eccl. 2:1)
- All that Qohelet toiled to achieve proved to be "frustrating," a chasing after the wind. (Eccl. 2:11)

80. *Macbeth* act 5, scene 5, lines 26a–28.

- The fate of the fool will overtake the wise, which is "frustrating." (Eccl. 2:15)
- All his work was grievous, "frustrating," a chasing after the wind. (Eccl. 2:17)
- The person who takes over your job may be a fool, which would be "frustrating." (Eccl. 2:19, 21)
- A person may work day and night in great pain, which can be "frustrating." (Eccl. 2:23)
- Man ends his life like the animals, which is "frustrating." (Eccl. 3:19)
- A person living alone may toil endlessly and never enjoy his work, which is "frustrating." (Eccl. 4:7–8)
- Whoever loves money is never satisfied, which is "frustrating." (Eccl. 5:10)
- God gives a man wealth and honor, but he does not enable him to enjoy them, which is "frustrating." (Eccl. 6:2)
- A righteous man perishes in his righteousness, and a wicked man lives long in his wickedness, which is "frustrating." (Eccl. 7:15)
- The wicked receive praise in the holy place, which is "frustrating." (Eccl. 8:10)

If "transitoriness" or "vanity" may be viewed as representing the objective side of the word *hebel*, "frustration" best represents the effect of this transitoriness or vanity on the human psyche. A human being's normal reaction to the fleeting character of every experience in life is a sense of frustration. The companion phrase, "chasing after the wind," vivifies the significance of *hebel* in several passages (Eccl. 1:14; 2:11, 17, 26; 4:4, 6; 6:9).[81] Ever since the fall of man, all attempts to realize any goal possess this inherently frustrating character. Even

81. The phrase "chasing after the wind" is a difficult one. It could mean "vexation of spirit" or "toiling for the wind." Cf. Eaton, *Ecclesiastes*, 63. Eaton speaks of "frustration by the insoluble" or "ambition for the unattainable." Either meaning would suit this context. Cf. the discussion of Longman, *Ecclesiastes*, 81–82, who concludes that the idea communicated is that "life on earth is futile and frustrating." His additional assertion

251

though a specific goal may be achieved, each task undertaken will require more time and effort than the fruit produced should require. This universal experience of humanity may be properly characterized as "frustration of frustrations, all is frustration."

This understanding of the term connects appropriately with the word as it appears in a classic passage of the New Testament. When Paul writes to the Romans explaining that God has subjected the creation "to frustration" (τῇ γὰρ ματαιότητι—Rom. 8:20a), he deliberately alludes to the original curse that brought this world into its current experience of "frustration" or "futility." Yet according to Paul, this present order in creation survives despite the divine curse, continuing "in hope"—a hope that "the creation itself will be liberated from its bondage to decay" (8:20b-21). The judgmental sentence of inevitable deterioration rests on the whole of this fallen creation. Yet the prospect of restoration stands perpetually alongside the "frustration" arising from the curse.

What Is the Profit? (מַה־יִּתְרוֹן)

This phrase occurs ten times in Ecclesiastes, and nowhere else in the Old Testament. The phrase essentially means "What's the gain, the advantage, the profit?" The implied answer to this searching question that introduces the book of Ecclesiastes appears to be that there is no lasting profit, no enduring gain, no permanent advantage in return for all the hard work of a lifetime (Eccl. 1:3). Qohelet wrestles with the frustration that he has gained nothing from all his labor (2:11; 3:9). Man comes naked from his mother's womb, and returns naked with nothing to take with him as a fruit of all his toil (5:15–16).

In terms of what a person may carry out of this world, the statement of Qohelet is true. The probing question "What is the profit?" lingers as a challenge to every generation. There is "no profit" in terms of what a person may carry with him as he exits this present world. Even in the new covenant era, the statement remains true: "For we brought nothing into the world, and we can take nothing out of it" (1 Tim. 6:7 NIV).

---

that this concept reinforces the idea that life is "meaningless" does not exactly follow. "Frustrating" and "meaningless" are not the same thing.

Yet Qohelet qualifies his raw statement of fact, using the same word *profit* once more: "Yet I found that there is more profit in wisdom than in folly, just as there is more profit in light than in darkness" (Eccl. 2:13). The contrast could not be sharper. Wisdom brings profit that outshines the darkened shadows of folly. Subsequently he affirms that wisdom and knowledge provide some advantage, some profit, some gain. They give life to the one who possesses them (7:12). Wisdom is profitable in that it gives success (10:10).

So although this key phrase at first appears to communicate only negative thoughts in the mind of Qohelet, the end of the matter is quite different. Yes, it is true that there is "no profit" in the sense that things accomplished "under the sun" cannot be carried out of this world by the dead. But profit will come both in this life and in the life to come through God's gift of wisdom.

Under the Sun (תַּחַת הַשֶּׁמֶשׁ)

This phrase "under the sun" occurs twenty-nine times in Ecclesiastes and nowhere else in Scripture. But what does it mean?

"Under the sun" does not convey the idea of a view of life without God.[82] The phrase essentially describes the cycle of human life on this earth as it is defined by the regular rising and setting of the sun. "Under the sun" refers to a realistic perspective on life in this world in which humanity has fallen into sin. As a consequence, all the disorders, injustices, and calamities that come constitute an inescapable aspect of reality. "Under the sun," men's hearts are full of wickedness. In addition to this ever-present moral depravity under the sun, "evil" in the sense of calamitous circumstances manifests itself in this current life "under the sun" (Eccl. 9:3). "Under the sun," in the cycle of life measured by the rotation of the earth about the sun (to commit a deliberate anachronism), wickedness prevails in the place of righteousness (3:16). "Under the sun," power belongs to the oppressors, which bring tears

---

82. Longman, *Ecclesiastes*, 39, interprets "under the sun" to mean "apart from heavenly realities, apart from God." He understands the phrase to communicate "hopelessness . . . without recourse to God's redemption." With the all-permeating presence of God throughout the book, it is unlikely that this phrase speaks from this kind of atheistic or agnostic perspective. Instead, the phrase describes human life as it is actually perceived from the perspective of this present world order, while also presuming the reality of God the Creator.

to the oppressed (4:1). "Under the sun," no long-term gain may be realized from a lifetime of hard work, since the person who takes over your projects may have no appreciation for the things you have accomplished (2:11). Man is like a shadow "under the sun" that fades even as he passes through his life's course (6:12). After a person dies, he has no further interaction with things that transpire "under the sun" (9:6).

This description of the cycle of human life "under the sun" as it is currently being experienced appears in Ecclesiastes as an honest but healthy dose of reality. Yet despite all the apparent gloom associated with this perspective, the counsel of Qohelet is to enjoy your daily routine of life "under the sun." Enjoy your eating, drinking, and work "under the sun" (Eccl. 5:18). Rejoice with the wife whom you love as you live out the cycle of your life "under the sun" (9:9). For these enjoyments of life "under the sun" can come only from the hand of a beneficent God, the Giver of every good and perfect gift (8:15; cf. James 1:17).

In view of the life that God has given you "under the sun," what should you do? Rather than giving up because of life's frustrating character, live life to the fullest. Whatever your hand finds to do, do it with all your strength (Eccl. 9:10a). It's hard to imagine a more positive statement in view of the ever-present deterrents in this life "under the sun." In fact, the words sound very much like the new covenant admonition of the apostle Paul: "Whatever you do, do it heartily as to the Lord . . . , for you serve the Lord Christ" (Col. 3:23–24).

This vigorous admonition to throw yourself wholeheartedly into life finds itself balanced with a further challenge: "For there is no work or determination or knowledge or wisdom in the grave where you are going" (Eccl. 9:10b). What is the point if you only end up in the grave? But once more, the question may be asked: Is not Qohelet providing a strong dose of realism for his hearers? Is it not true? There is no work in the grave. No knowledge, no wisdom, no plan to be executed may be found in those narrow confines.

This statement of Qohelet may be compared to the remark of Jesus: "The night comes, when no man can work" (John 9:4).[83] It is a

---

83. Walter C. Kaiser Jr., *Ecclesiastes: Total Life*, Everyman's Bible Commentary (Chicago: Moody Press, 1979), 102.

true summation of the experience of human life, even presuming the reality of God the Creator. Once your time is over in this world, you are altogether finished in terms of contributions to this present life. Thus, consider carefully what you do "under the sun."

So these key phrases in Ecclesiastes convey basic truths that the author intends to communicate. This life will be filled with "frustration." Viewed from the perspective of the present world order of a fallen creation, life may seem to offer "no profit." Many discouraging factors appear in the cycle of human life as it is lived out "under the sun." Yet in the fear of the LORD (which is the beginning of wisdom), meaningfulness, enjoyment in this life, and profit now as well as beyond the grave can be the experience of reality.

God in the Gospel of Ecclesiastes

It may at first seem odd to speak of the "gospel" of Ecclesiastes in any sense. Indeed, nothing in the precise terms of justification by faith alone in Christ alone through grace alone is explicitly taught in Ecclesiastes. Yet as has been indicated, the book teaches lessons that are "essential, as preparatory to our enjoyment of the Gospel."[84] The New Testament, particularly in the book of Acts, as Christianity's gospel is first being formulated among all nations, speaks of the "good news" of the "gospel" in a broad framework. It speaks repeatedly of the "gospel" in terms of the *logos* (Acts 4:29; 6:4; 8:4, 21; 14:25; 15:7; 16:6); the *logos* of God (4:31; 6:2, 7; 8:14; 13:46; 17:13; 18:11); the *logos* of the Lord (8:25; 13:44, 48–49; 15:35–36; 16:32; 19:10, 20); and the *logos* of his grace (14:3; 20:32). In these contexts, the *logos* of the gospel includes more than simply explaining how a sinner is justified. Instead, it encompasses a comprehensive Christianity that embraces an entirely new concept regarding the meaning and experience of life. The good news, the *logos* of the kingdom of God (Matt. 13:19), has a vitalizing impact on all aspects of human life. So in this broader sense, Ecclesiastes is full of the gospel. More particularly, God emerges as the focal factor in the gospel of Ecclesiastes.

---

84. Charles Bridges, *An Exposition of the Book of Ecclesiastes* (London: Banner of Truth, 1960), vi.

This current treatment of Ecclesiastes appears as a chapter in this volume with the title *The Christ of Wisdom*. As a consequence, the reader may be eagerly looking to learn how Christ is focal to this rather challenging book of the old covenant Scriptures.

At this point it should be remembered that the concept of *Christ* has meaning only in the context of—*God*! Apart from the reality of God in all his self-contained glory, Jesus Christ the Son of God has only a truncated significance. As has been previously proposed, the target audience of the book of Ecclesiastes is humanity as a whole. Paul the apostle to the nations spoke in a similar way to the community of humanity in the marketplace of Lystra and the open forum of Athens. In both these addresses he focused on God as the Creator, the Giver of every good gift of human life, and the Judge of all (Acts 14:8–18; 17:22–31). In a similar way, Qohelet speaks to the whole of mankind. He also focuses on the reality of *God*—God the Creator, the Benevolent Sustainer, the Righteous Judge. In that well-formed context, he ultimately introduces the "one Shepherd" who serves as the ultimate source of all true understanding of reality in God's world (Eccl. 12:11).

So the fullness of Christ as revealed in the Scriptures of both the old and the new covenants may be perceived only in the context of the reality of God. Finding Christ in all the Scriptures must always be through comprehending the greatness of God.

Far from presenting a secularistic perspective on life, as some commentators would represent the message of Ecclesiastes, God stands front and center as the determining factor in every aspect of every human being's life. The word for *God* (אֱלֹהִים) appears forty times in the book. The major response to life's transitory nature, its vanity, and its frustrating character must be found in—*God*!! An analysis of the role fulfilled by God according to these numerous uses throughout Ecclesiastes underscores the permeating character of God in the total life of humanity:

God Is the Maker of All Things

God's workmanship is so profound that you can never fully understand his purposes. The circular path followed by the wind, the formation of a human body in the mother's womb remain beyond the grasp of human understanding (Eccl. 11:5). All of God's works are so perfect that they last forever. Nothing can be added to them and nothing taken from them (3:14). As the Creator, he is the one who ultimately gives all wisdom, knowledge, and happiness (2:26). He made mankind altogether upright. But sad to say, they have invented many sinful schemes (7:29).

A comparison with the substance of Paul the apostle's address to the Greek philosophers on Mars Hill in Athens (Acts 17:22–31) may help in rightly perceiving the "God of the Gospel" as he is presented in Ecclesiastes. In this Old Testament book, no mention is found of the covenant name *Yahweh*, as well as no reference to the saving activity of God with Israel. The God of Creation appears as the Giver to humanity of every daily gift. In a similar way, Paul's address to the Athenian philosophers makes no mention of Scripture, of the nation of Israel, of the ministry of John the Baptist, of the life of Jesus. Instead, the apostle to the nations speaks of God the Creator who gives life and breath and every blessing for humans to enjoy. Only in his last sentence does Paul mention that God has set a day in which he will judge the world in righteousness by the man he has appointed. But even at that crucial moment, he does not even mention the name of Jesus (17:31).[85]

The "God of the Gospel in Ecclesiastes" is quite similar to this perspective of Paul as he presents the gospel to the pagan philosophers on Mars Hill in Athens. Qohelet as king in Jerusalem addresses the whole of humanity. He speaks to all mankind about their Creator, their Sustainer, their Benefactor, their Sovereign, and their Judge. In these identities may be found the God of the gospel in Ecclesiastes. Since God is your Maker, you should always remember him as your Creator, particularly in the days of your youth (Eccl. 12:1). This remembrance must be done before the dust that constitutes human flesh returns to the ground from which it came and the spirit returns to God who gave it (12:6–7). In this assurance of God as Creator may be found a firm foundation for perceiving God as the basis for coping with the constant frustrations of life.

---

85. For a further development of these parallels between Paul's address in Athens and the message of Ecclesiastes, see Eaton, *Ecclesiastes*, 47.

God Has a Prevailing Purpose in Providence That Should Be Searched Out

Even though this searching will prove to be a challenging task, it must be done (Eccl. 1:13). God presents man with the burden of discovering what he has done in time and eternity. Everything he has made is beautiful in its time (3:10–11a). In shaping man like himself, God placed eternity in his heart, which drives him to seek an understanding of what God is doing in this world (3:11b). According to one commentator, "It is man's highest privilege to discern something eternal behind the transitory objects of the present world, and to be able to cling closely to this eternal substance."[86] Yet mankind can never quite grasp what God has done from the beginning to the end (3:11c). This wise man in Ecclesiastes has some comprehension of the broad picture of all that God has done. Yet its full meaning escapes him:

> No one can comprehend what goes on under the sun. Despite all his efforts to search it out, man cannot discover its meaning. Even if a wise man claims he knows, he cannot really comprehend it. (Eccl. 8:17 NIV)

This ordering of God that humanity cannot comprehend includes both good times and bad times. In experiencing these diverse seasons of a lifetime, you will not be able to straighten what he has made crooked. So in a good day, make the best of the good, and in a bad day, strive to be perceptive in your understanding of his purposes (Eccl. 7:13–14). For he assigns the days of a man's life, but no one can know whether good times or bad times are before him:

> So I reflected on all this and concluded that the righteous and the wise and what they do are in God's hands, but no man knows whether love or hate awaits him. (Eccl. 9:1 NIV)

The limitations of man's perception might seem to lead to despair. But the very fact that God has an overarching plan that embraces every

86. Hengstenberg, *Ecclesiastes*, 107.

human experience points in the opposite direction. You, your daily moment-by-moment circumstances, your final end are all "from the hand of God" (Eccl. 2:24). In this confidence you may deal with the vanity, the frustrations, the transitoriness of daily life.

God Is the Great Benefactor of Humanity

He provides pleasure, satisfaction, and sustenance in the daily routines of eating, drinking, and working. This ability to enjoy the routine matters of life comes directly from the hand of God (Eccl. 2:24). In fact, the enjoyment of the common things of life should be regarded as a distinctive gift from God: "that everyone may eat and drink, and find satisfaction in all his toil—this is the gift of God" (מַתַּת אֱלֹהִים הִיא—3:13 NIV).[87]

Yet these "simple" things of life are actually rather profound. God the Creator put man (*adam*, "humanity") in a garden and gave him access to all the trees that were beautiful to the eyes and good to eat (Gen. 2:9). In their desert wanderings, the people of God lived without the fruit of the trees. But upon their entering the land of promise, this basic blessing of life was restored. God directed them to annually celebrate this restoration to the enjoyment of the trees at the Festival of Tabernacles, which reminded them of their years of deprivation in the desert even as they feasted in the garden of their restored paradise:

> On the fifteenth day of the seventh month, when you have gathered in the produce of the land, you shall celebrate the feast of the LORD seven days. . . . And you shall take on the first day the fruit of splendid trees, branches of palm trees and boughs of leafy trees and willows of the brook, and you shall rejoice before the LORD your God seven days. (Lev. 23:39–40 ESV)

87. With an overemphasis on the transcendence of God in Ecclesiastes, Seow, *Ecclesiastes*, 56, asserts: "This deity does not relate personally with anyone." Yet God is indeed the "Great Benefactor" of humanity who gives enjoyment in all the things of life. He is the "one Shepherd" (Eccl. 12:11), a figure that communicates intimate, personal involvement in the day-by-day lives of his sheep. Elsewhere Seow, ibid., 122, says that the word for "chasing" in the phrase "chasing [*ra'ut*] after wind" "is related to the Hebrew *ro'eh*, 'shepherd'—that is, one who runs after and minds sheep." So must God be regarded as impersonal in his role as the (Good) Shepherd?

So when Qohelet speaks repeatedly of enjoying God's blessing of food and drink, of work and wife, he refers to no mundane matters. He echoes the enjoyment of the blessings of paradise. He takes his readers back to humanity's original condition at creation and to the creational ordinances of labor and marriage: "Subdue the earth" and "Be fruitful and multiply" (Gen. 1:28). Neither does he ignore the central element of worship (2:3; cf. Eccl. 5:1–7; 12:1).

Qohelet elaborates on this principle of God's common grace to humanity in several passages:

> Then I realized that it is good and proper for a man to eat and drink, and to find satisfaction in his toilsome labor under the sun during the few days of life God has given him—for this is his lot. Moreover, when God gives any man wealth and possessions, and enables him to enjoy them, to accept his lot and be happy in his work—this is a gift of God. He seldom reflects on the days of his life, because God keeps him occupied with gladness of heart. (Eccl. 5:18–20 NIV)

In fact, nothing can be better than for a man to eat, drink, and be glad in his work all the days of the life that God gives him (Eccl. 8:15; 9:7).

So from the perspective of Qohelet, the experience of all these blessings comes as a gift from God. God in the manifestation of his grace *gives* food, drink, work, and the ability to enjoy all these things. He *gives* wisdom, knowledge, and happiness. He places eternity in the heart of man as his *gift*. He *gives* the ability for someone to enjoy his inheritance from God. He *gives* wealth, possessions, honor, and everything the heart desires. He *gives* a wife and the ability to enjoy life with her. He *gives* the human being a spirit, which ultimately returns to God. He is indeed the *Giver* of every good and perfect gift (Eccl. 2:26; 3:11, 13; 5:18; 6:2; 8:15; 9:9; 12:7; cf. James 1:17).

The conclusion might be reached that these words encourage seeking personal pleasure as the primary and proper goal of life. Many commentators have categorized Qohelet as a blatant Epicurean.

But a vivid passage from Isaiah describes what a true Epicurean looks like. Even as siege is being laid against Jerusalem, "Behold! Joy and gladness, killing oxen and slaughtering sheep, eating flesh and drinking wine. 'Let us eat and drink, for tomorrow we die,'" they are saying (Isa. 22:13 ESV). They have made defensive preparations against an imminent assault, but have failed to look to "him who made it" or show any respect "to him who planned it long ago" (22:11 NASB). That's real Epicureanism—feasting in face of calamity and disregarding altogether the divine purpose and plan.

Only by a determined distortion could Ecclesiastes be read in this way. Yes, enjoy your eating and drinking; but recognize that your enjoyment is possible only as a gift from God. Yes, face up to the realities of coming hardships, including aging and death. But do it with faith that God assigns the lot to every person and that he makes everything beautiful in its time.

This message of encouraging the enjoyment of God's gifts may be compared to a portion of one of the earliest recorded sermons of the apostle Paul to a community of pagan idol-worshipers in Lystra as they are in the process of deifying the apostle and Barnabas his companion:

> Men, why are you doing these things? We also are men, of like nature with you, and we bring you good news, that you should turn from these vain things to a living God, who made the heaven and the earth and the sea and all that is in them. In past generations he allowed all the nations to walk in their own ways. Yet he did not leave himself without witness, *for he did good by giving you rains from heaven and fruitful seasons, satisfying your hearts with food and gladness.* (Acts 14:15–17 ESV)

Paul subsequently emphasizes this same point in his first letter to Timothy when he instructs him to charge the rich

> to put their hope in God, who richly provides us with everything for our enjoyment. (1 Tim. 6:17 NIV)

The repeated observation of Qohelet is quite similar to the message of Paul regarding the enjoyment of the good gifts of the Creator. This perspective on life serves as a vital portion of "The God of the Gospel" in Ecclesiastes. In addition, the clear indicator in Ecclesiastes of God's role as final Judge of all enjoyments should make it quite clear that Qohelet is no Epicurean: "Know that for all these things God will bring you to judgment" (Eccl. 11:9 NIV). So recognizing God as the Giver of everything good should help immensely in comprehending the God of the gospel.

God Expects Men to Revere Him in Worship, and as a Consequence to Take All of Life Seriously

Far from being purely secularistic in his perspective, the writer of Ecclesiastes insists on a proper reverence before God, which inevitably leads to seriousness and sobriety in life. Engaging God in worship is assumed to be an essential part of human existence. In one significant passage, Ecclesiastes underscores the proper approach to God in worship:

> Guard your steps when you go to the house of God. Go near to listen rather than to offer the sacrifice of fools, who do not know that they do wrong. Do not be quick with your mouth, do not be hasty in your heart to utter anything before God. God is in heaven and you are on earth, so let your words be few. As a dream comes when there are many cares, so the speech of a fool when there are many words.
>
> When you make a vow to God, do not delay in fulfilling it. He has no pleasure in fools; fulfill your vow. It is better not to vow than to make a vow and not fulfill it. Do not let your mouth lead you into sin. And do not protest to the temple messenger, "My vow was a mistake." Why should God be angry at what you say and destroy the work of your hands? Much dreaming and many words are meaningless. Therefore stand in awe of God. (Eccl. 5:1–7 NIV)

A number of matters related to the worship of God stand out in this passage.

(1) Formal worship with the people of God in his designated place of assembly is expected. You are to "go into the house of God." Secularistic postmodern humanity views worship purely as a matter of personal taste. But the writer of Ecclesiastes sees formal worship in the house of God as a regular aspect of human life.

(2) Proper worship involves personal intimacy with God. The worshiper is expected to "draw near" to him.

(3) The worshiper must draw near to listen to what God's messenger will say. He must not offer the "sacrifice of fools," which is to be hasty in speaking rather than in listening.

(4) Approaching the deity in worship requires great reverence and self-restraint. Neither with the mouth nor with the heart should the worshiper be rash in his commitments to God. God is in heaven and you are on earth; therefore, let your words be few.

(5) Yet vows and oaths uttered before God are a vital part of worship. The solemn oath that binds the individual as well as the community in fidelity to their God is an inevitable part of worship.

(6) Once an oath is taken, be sure to fulfill it. Otherwise, you will be sinning even in the process of your worship. Better not to vow than to fail to fulfill your commitments to God.

(7) Do not try to get out of a vow once taken, or God will destroy the work of your hands. Do not attempt to persuade God's minister that your oath was a mistake.

(8) In all your worship, remember to fear God. Always stand in awe of him.

When these various elements of proper worship are considered, it becomes clear that the book of Ecclesiastes presumes an aspect of human life that has been totally negated in the secularism of the modern age. God is very real, and a vital focus of human life is the worship of God.

One area of practical outworking of this worshipful relation to God is the fulfillment of obligations to civil authorities. "Obey the king's command, I say, because you took an oath before God" (Eccl. 8:2). The oath of allegiance to civil authorities actually involves a pledge in the presence of the Omnipotent God. He is the ultimate authority. Anyone rebelling against the lawful rules of civil governments is at the same time rebelling against him. As a consequence, worship eventually has a significant effect on the whole of human life.

God Is Judge and Distinguishes between the Righteous and the Wicked

According to Qohelet, God makes a clear distinction between the righteous and the wicked, the good and the evil, the wise and the foolish. Despite all his stated frustrations over life, Qohelet nonetheless recognizes this basic distinction that God makes within humanity.

Mankind as a whole is perceived from the viewpoint of its original and permeating depravity:

- God made man upright, but he has gone on a search for innumerable wicked schemes. (Eccl. 7:29)
- There is not a righteous man on the earth who does what is right and does not sin. (Eccl. 7:20)
- The hearts of people are filled to the brim with schemes to do wrong once it becomes clear that no just punishment will come quickly on the wicked. (Eccl. 8:11)
- The sinner is not content to commit one crime; he will do the same thing a hundred times. (Eccl. 8:12)
- The hearts of men are full of evil, and madness resides in their hearts. (Eccl. 9:3b)
- Madness and folly are the prevailing characteristics of humanity. (Eccl. 1:17)

Yet Qohelet also affirms that there are good and righteous people who fear God. To those who are good in his sight, God gives wisdom, knowledge, and happiness (Eccl. 2:26). Life will go better for God-fearing people (8:12). At the same time, the frustrating enigma of experience also demonstrates cases in which "the righteous perishes in his righteousness and the wicked lives long in his evil" (7:15). Situations commonly occur in which righteous people get what the wicked deserve, and wicked people get what the righteous deserve (8:14). The writer summarizes this puzzling circumstance in memorable fashion: "as it happens to the good, so it happens to the sinner" (כַּטּוֹב כַּחֹטֶא—9:2).

Quite significant is the fact that Ecclesiastes recognizes the presence of righteous, good, God-fearing people in the midst of this fallen, sin-filled world. Even the "wise" are viewed by God not merely as being savvy; they are "righteous" (Eccl. 9:1). Similarly, foolishness is not simply silliness; it is "wickedness" (7:25).

But in view of his prior description of the permeating depravity of humanity, how can the writer characterize anyone as "good," "righteous," and "wise"? After declaring so specifically that the hearts of men are "full of evil" (Eccl. 9:3b) and that not a person on this earth does good and does not sin (7:20), how could he also affirm the existence of "good," "righteous," and "God-fearing" people?

From his unique perspective as the Convener of all humanity, Solomon could speak with clear understanding of the depravity of the sinful heart while at the same time assuring the world of good and righteous people who experienced the blessedness of God's benedictions. Whether this document is viewed as written by Solomon himself or by a personification of Solomon, it is still Solomon's perspective that defines the book's point of view. Qohelet is son of David, king in Jerusalem (Eccl. 1:1). This man Solomon must have grown up with a keen awareness of the peculiar circumstances that brought him eventually to the throne. He was son to the king only because David his father had illegitimately taken to himself another man's wife and murdered her husband. His father's grievous sins of adultery and murder were the deeds that eventually brought Solomon into this world. Yet Solomon must also have been fully aware that his father had confessed his sin before God and received the LORD's forgiveness. For in Israel's worship services, the nation regularly celebrated the blessedness of the man whose transgressions were forgiven, whose sin was covered, according to psalms composed by David his father (Pss. 32, 51). Despite the heinousness of the sin, Solomon's father David was reckoned by God as a "righteous man."

God in his grace continually makes this critical distinction among humanity. In the eyes of God, there are the good and the evil, the righteous and the wicked, the wise and the foolish. From this perspective, the frustrations of life are more understandable. This understanding also makes it possible to live with these frustrations. This is the God in the gospel of Ecclesiastes.

God Tests Humanity in a Variety of Ways

A partial explanation for the seeming inconsistency in God's dealings with the righteous and the wicked may be found in the fact that God is constantly testing people as a way of either exposing their failed perspectives on life or perfecting their virtues. As Qohelet observes:

I also thought, "As for men, God tests them so that they may see that they are like the animals. Man's fate is like that of the animals; the same fate awaits them both: As one dies, so dies the other. All have the same breath; man has no advantage over the animal. Everything is meaningless [frustration]. All go to the same place; all come from dust, and to dust all return. Who knows if [or, better, recognizes that] the spirit of man rises upward and if [or, that] the spirit of the animal goes down into the earth?[88] So I saw that there is nothing better for a man than to enjoy his work, because that is his lot. For who can bring him to see [cause him to see] what will happen after him? (Eccl. 3:18–22 NIV)

Just before these verses that compare the fate of humanity to the fate of an animal, Ecclesiastes had emphasized that God will call everything in the past to account and will bring to judgment both the righteous and the wicked (Eccl. 3:15, 17). This assertion clearly anticipates ongoing existence beyond the grave for the sake of accountability before God. But now the author states that man has no advantage over the animals. All have the same destiny. Both turn to dust. Simply on the basis of normal observation, that fact is indisputable. So does the human spirit rise upward while the spirit of the animal goes downward?

This passage provides two perspectives on human existence. On the one hand, Qohelet views mankind in terms of his accountability before God. Both in this life and in the life to come, God exercises just judgments based on a person's deeds, whether good or bad. At the same time, Qohelet views life from the realistic perspective of what can actually be perceived. The human body decays in the grave just as does the body of an animal. So far as basic human perception is concerned, that is it. No one can deny these realities.

88. The sentence contains no "if", and has no sign of the interrogative. For a full discussion supporting the affirmative character of the statement, see Hengstenberg, *Ecclesiastes*, 118-121. Cf. also Eaton, *Ecclesiastes*, 87-89; Kaiser, *Coping With Change*, 108-110. The text may be rendered, "The spirit of the sons of man, it is the one going up into the upper realm, and the spirit of the beast, it is the one going down to the lower realm into the earth." The introductory "Who knows that [recognizes that]" could refer to the scarcity of people who acknowledge this fact. Hengstenberg, op. cit., 118, says that the words "Who knows..." "direct attention to the difficulty of discerning this superiority [of mankind over beast]." Longman, *Ecclesiastes*, 130-131, affirms that the Masoretic pointing treats the words as a statement rather than a question, but suggests that "perhaps the Masoretes wanted to turn Qohelet into a more traditional theologian who believed in the distinction between humans and animals,..." (131).

266

God tests man by the inherent limitation of these perceptions. By restricting man's ability to see beyond the grave, God tests man's loyalty to him. Will he serve the unseen God by living in righteousness? Or will he abandon the reality of God? He cannot totally escape reality as he perceives it. Man, like the animal, returns to the dust. At the same time, he must respond to his limitations of perception by faith in the unseen. Both these perspectives are real, and both are presented side by side in the book of Ecclesiastes. By this limitation of human perception, God tests humanity.

God also tests people by giving them possessions but not allowing them to enjoy them (Eccl. 6:2). Sometimes he orders good days and at other times bad days (7:14). God has made the one as well as the other. So a human being can never determine what the future will bring.

So what should be the result of this testing through uncertainty regarding the future? The final verses of the book answer this question. Rather than despairing over the uncertain state of the future, man should "fear God and keep his commandments, . . . for God will bring every deed into judgment, including every hidden thing, whether it is good or evil" (Eccl. 12:13–14 NIV). At that time, God will perform his final test of mankind.

God Will Finally Call All People to Account

This seventh and final point about God's role in the life of humanity clearly sets the writer of Ecclesiastes apart from the secularist. A realistic observation of human life cannot help but note that man returns to dust just as does the animal. But from the beginning God the Creator has set people apart from animals. They must all give account to their Maker. He will call all deeds of the past to account (Eccl. 3:15). He will bring to judgment both the righteous and the wicked (3:17). A young man may be encouraged to enjoy life in his youth. But he must know that "for all these things God will bring [him] to judgment" (11:9).[89] The dust may return to the ground it came from, but the spirit will return to God who made it (12:7). The proper conclusion to the whole matter is found in the final words of this book:

---

89. Seow interprets Ecclesiastes 11:9c to mean that God "calls people into account for not enjoying themselves" (ibid., 56). To the contrary, the text affirms that God will bring people into judgment for the precise manner in which they did enjoy themselves.

Now all has been heard; here is the conclusion of the matter: Fear God and keep his commandments, for this is the whole *duty* of man [the whole of human life]. For God will bring every deed into judgment, including every hidden thing, whether it is good or evil. (Eccl. 12:13–14 NIV)

With this understanding, a person should be enabled to cope with the vanities, the transitoriness, the frustrations of life. God and God alone can make everything beautiful in its time, even the final judgment yet to come.

The Final Message and the Final Messenger

The writer of the epilogue to Ecclesiastes marks his final summarizing statement as "the conclusion of the matter" (סוֹף דָּבָר—Eccl. 12:13). This conclusion states the book's response to the frustrating, perplexing problems of human life:

Fear God and keep his commandments,
   for this is the whole *duty* of man [whole of human life].
For God shall bring every work into judgment
   with every hidden thing,
      whether good or bad. (Eccl. 12:13–14 NIV)

Living in the fear of God is the "beginning [and the end] of wisdom." This pious fear of God will manifest itself concretely in the keeping of all of God's commandments. These few words capture the "whole of human life." God will ultimately judge every work of each human being on the basis of his commandments. The hidden will be fully known, and the good will be distinguished from the evil. This is the final message of Ecclesiastes.

And the final messenger? Ecclesiastes describes Qohelet in his final words as a "wise" person who imparted knowledge to the people. He pondered, searched out, and set in order many proverbs. He strained to find just the right words. What he wrote was upright and true (Eccl. 12:9–10).

This very special Convener of humanity finds support from other "wise ones" who also serve as messengers of divine wisdom:

The words of the wise ones
   are as goads;

and as nails firmly embedded
>   by the masters of assemblies.
They are given
>   by one shepherd. (Eccl. 12:11)

A plural noun designates these companions of Qohelet as "wise ones." The book of Proverbs also refers to these "wise ones" (Prov. 22:17; 24:23). They may be identified as other laborers in the school of divine wisdom. A multiple of persons serve as sources of wisdom for God's people. Their function is twofold. As "goads," they spur the people to a vitality of life that should mark every servant of God. As "nails firmly embedded," they provide stability to the life of the people.

These "wise ones" are also called the "masters of assemblies" (בַּעֲלֵי אֲסֻפּוֹת).[90] As such, they have the responsibility of convening the people and instructing them in the ways of wisdom.

While recognizing the great value of these "wise ones," Qohelet insists on indicating that their sayings are "given by one shepherd" (Eccl. 12:11). That is, their words of wisdom do not originate with themselves. Instead, they all have a single source. One good shepherd who cares for his sheep provides these insights into life. This singular chief shepherd supplies these words of wisdom to the undershepherds.

So who is this "one shepherd" that serves as the ultimate source of truth for God's flock? Many commentators have directly identified this "one shepherd" as God, the source of all wisdom.[91] But in the context of Ecclesiastes, this single shepherd should be more immediately identified with Solomon, the king of Israel in Jerusalem, the primary

---

90. Various English versions translate this phrase differently: "collected sayings" (NIV, ESV); "masters of these collections" (NASB); "masters of assemblies" (KJV); "words of scholars" (NKJV). Robert Alter, *The Wisdom Books: Job, Proverbs, and Ecclesiastes: A Translation with Commentary* (New York: W. W. Norton, 2010), 390, says: "The meaning of the Hebrew is uncertain, but a reference to anthologists or collectors of sayings is plausible in context." The phrase literally refers to "masters of assemblies," which could refer to gatherers of people (assemblies) or gatherers of sayings (collections). Most likely, they are the "wise ones" following in the tradition of Solomon.

91. Both the NIV (1984) and the ESV capitalize "Shepherd," thereby directly identifying God as the "one Shepherd." Interestingly, the NIV (2011) removes the capitalization. In contrast, the two "King James" versions reverse the hermeneutical process. The original KJV reads "shepherd," while the more modern NKJV renders the word as "Shepherd."

269

source of wisdom as indicated in the opening statement of the book of Ecclesiastes (Eccl. 1:1). As the embodiment of wisdom par excellence, King Solomon naturally fills the role of the "shepherd" who cares for all humanity. In a distinctive way, he functions as the major source of wisdom for all people. His international fame as a wisdom source pinpoints him as the one shepherd who rules his people in greatest wisdom.

Yet even in the context of Solomon's original establishment as a wisdom figure, his insightful comprehension of reality originated with a higher source. In answer to his prayer, the God of heaven and earth gave him all the wisdom he possessed. Even before he asked, God had given him the wisdom to ask for wisdom! So from this perspective, God is the Shepherd-source of all of Solomon's wisdom. God himself is the Divine Shepherd of Israel's royal undershepherd. This imagery of God as the Shepherd of his people is as old as the patriarchs (Gen. 48:15; 49:24) and as familiar as Psalm 23. It even survived the devastations of the nation's exile (Ps. 80:1; Ezek. 34:11–12).

So God himself is the one Shepherd, the ultimate source of all wisdom, including all the wisdom embedded in the book of Ecclesiastes. The words of this book are not ultimately to be attributed to Solomon, but to God himself, the source of all wisdom. By this concluding reference to God as the one Shepherd-source of wisdom, the book of Ecclesiastes claims for itself divine inspiration. This book is God's word of wisdom to a humanity perplexed and frustrated over the fallen condition of the world in which they must live out their lives.

Eventually in the processes of redemptive history, a wisdom figure superior to Solomon arose. The promised messianic King whom Solomon foreshadows by his wisdom ultimately proves to be that one Shepherd of God's people. In this wisdom figure are hidden all the treasures of wisdom and knowledge (1 Cor. 1:30; Col. 2:2c–3). He is the Good Shepherd who gives his life for the sheep (John 10:11). Only in him may be found the wisdom and grace necessary for salvation and survival in the midst of this fallen, corrupted world.

He, like Solomon/Qohelet, also spoke of himself in the third person as the wisdom figure par excellence: "A greater than Solomon is here," said Jesus (Matt. 12:42; Luke 11:31). Not in empty boastfulness, but in the spirit of one who was himself truly "meek and lowly of heart" (Matt. 11:29), Jesus claimed his rightful role as the "good shepherd" (John 10:11, 14). Every true undershepherd will hear his voice as the only ultimate source of wisdom and knowledge.

CONCLUSION

So the writer of Ecclesiastes is anything but a secularist. God is everywhere providing his perception of human life. He lays the foundation for understanding human life in the context of the reality of God as Creator. The writer affirms and reaffirms that God is the providential Sustainer of the life of all humanity. He identifies God as the source of food, drink, and labor as the basic elements of meaningful human existence. He explains good and bad days as having their origin in the mysterious plans and purposes of God. He finds the consummation of all things in the final judgment to be presided over by this same God, the Creator and Sustainer of all life.

So the gospel in its broadest terms may be found in the book of Ecclesiastes. Not so much in the perfected doctrine of justification by faith alone in Christ alone. But in this realistic view of God as Creator, Sustainer, the Giver of every good and perfect gift, the righteous Judge who will bring every deed to account—in this perspective on God may be found the proper foundation of a true gospel that truly saves. As has been well said:

> Thus *Qoheleth* holds up the mirror to man, showing him the transience of his work and the fact that God's work alone endures. This is the corrective which man needs to his perennial conviction that he can make unlimited progress; for until the end of the age and the break-in of God's full reign, Paul's words in Romans 8:20ff. still apply to us. But whereas *Qoheleth* can only say that God's work alone will last, Paul proclaims that God has acted in Christ, and that the groaning and travail of the present age will not be in vain.[92]

Some centuries earlier, Martin Luther summarized the message of Ecclesiastes in these words:

92. Derek Kidner, *The Wisdom of Proverbs, Job & Ecclesiastes* (Downers Grove, IL: InterVarsity Press, 1985), 115.

271

The main point in this book is, that there is no higher wisdom on earth under the sun than that every man should fill his post industriously and in the fear of God, not troubling himself whether or no his work turn out as he would fain have it, but contenting himself, and leaving the ordering of all things great and small entirely to God. In fine, that he be contented, and abide by that which God gives him at the present moment, taking for motto the words, "The Lord's behest will turn out best." And thus a man should not worry and question and trouble himself how things will or should turn out in the future, but think within himself—God has entrusted me with this office, with this work, and I am resolved to discharge it diligently: if my counsels and plans do not succeed as I expected, let God dispose, ordain, and rule as He will.[93]

In the regular daily struggles with life's frustrations, it may be helpful to remember the wideness of God's mercy toward humanity. Even this constant living with frustration may prove beneficial if it is understood to have the divine intention of leading us back to God. A poem of George Herbert's may sharpen the focus on the positive dimension of God's intention in man's frustration:

> When God at first made man,
> Having a glass of blessing standing by;
> Let us (said He) pour on him all we can:
> Let the world's riches, which dispersed lie,
>   Contract into a span.
>
> So strength first made a way;
> Then beauty flowed, then wisdom, honour, pleasure,
> When almost all was out, God made a stay,
> Perceiving that alone of all His treasure,
>   Rest, in the bottom lay.
>
> For if I should (said He)
> Bestow this jewel also on My creature,
> He would adore My gifts instead of Me,
> And rest in nature, not the God of nature:
>   So both should losers be.

93. Quoted in Hengstenberg, *Ecclesiastes*, 32.

> Yet let him keep the rest,
> But keep them with repining restlessness:
> Let him be rich and weary, that at least,
> If goodness lead him not, yet weariness
> May toss him to My breast.[94]

SELECTED BIBLIOGRAPHY FOR ECCLESIASTES

Bartholomew, Craig G. *Ecclesiastes*. Grand Rapids: Baker Academic, 2009.

Bridges, Charles. *An Exposition of the Book of Ecclesiastes*. London: Banner of Truth, 1960.

Crenshaw, James L. *Ecclesiastes: A Commentary*. London: SCM Press, 1988.

Delitzsch, Franz. *Commentary on the Song of Songs and Ecclesiastes*. Edinburgh: T. & T. Clark, 1891.

Driver, S. R. *An Introduction to the Literature of the Old Testament*. 9th ed. Edinburgh: T. & T. Clark, 1913.

Eaton, Michael A. *Ecclesiastes: An Introduction and Commentary*. Downers Grove, IL: InterVarsity Press, 1983.

Forman, Charles C. "Koheleth's Use of Genesis." *JSS* 5, 3 (1960): 256–63.

Fox, Michael V. "Frame-Narrative and Composition in the Book of Ecclesiastes." *Hebrew Union College Annual* 48 (1977): 83–106.

Fredericks, Daniel C. *Coping with Transcience: Ecclesiastes on Brevity in Life*. Sheffield, UK: JSOT Press, 1993.

———. *Qoheleth's Language: Re-Evaluating Its Nature and Date*. Ancient Near Eastern Texts and Studies 3. Lewiston, NY: Edwin Mellen Press, 1988.

Fredericks, Daniel C., and Daniel J. Estes. *Ecclesiastes & The Song of Songs*. Downers Grove, IL: InterVarsity Press, 2010.

Ginsburg, C. D. *The Song of Songs and Coheleth (Commonly Called the Book of Ecclesiastes)*. Library of Biblical Studies. New York: KTAV, 1970.

Gordis, Robert. *Koheleth—The Man and His World*. New York: Bloch, 1955.

———. "Was Koheleth a Phoenician?" *JBL* 71, 2 (1952): 103–14.

Hengstenberg, E. W. *Commentary on Ecclesiastes*. Edinburgh: T. & T. Clark, 1869.

Kaiser, Walter C. Jr. *Coping with Change: Ecclesiastes*. Ross-shire, Scotland: Christian Focus Publications, 2013.

———. *Ecclesiastes: Total Life*. Everyman's Bible Commentary. Chicago: Moody Press, 1979.

---

94. Quoted in Derek Kidner, *The Message of Ecclesiastes: A Time to Mourn and a Time to Dance* (Leicester, UK: Inter-Varsity Press, 1976), 109–10.

Kidner, Derek. *The Message of Ecclesiastes: A Time to Mourn and a Time to Dance*. Leicester, UK: Inter-Varsity Press, 1976.

———. *The Wisdom of Proverbs, Job & Ecclesiastes*. Downers Grove, IL: InterVarsity Press, 1985.

Kruger, Thomas. *Qoheleth: A Commentary*. Minneapolis: Fortress Press, 2004.

Longman, Tremper, III. *The Book of Ecclesiastes*. Grand Rapids: Eerdmans, 1998.

———. *Fictional Akkadian Autobiography: A Generic and Comparative Study*. Winona Lake, IN: Eisenbrauns, 1991.

Miller, Douglas B. *Ecclesiastes*. Scottdale, PA: Herald Press, 2010.

Murray, John. *Principles of Conduct: Aspects of Biblical Ethics*. Grand Rapids: Eerdmans, 1957.

Provan, Iain. *Ecclesiastes, Song of Songs*. NIV Application Commentary. Grand Rapids: Zondervan, 2001.

Rad, Gerhard von. *Old Testament Theology*. Vol. 1. Edinburgh: Oliver & Boyd, 1962.

———. *Wisdom in Israel*. London: SCM Press, 1972.

Reimer, David J. "Introduction to the Poetic and Wisdom Literature." In *ESV Study Bible*, 866–68. Wheaton, IL: Crossway, 2008.

Robertson, O. Palmer. *The Christ of the Covenants*. Phillipsburg, NJ: Presbyterian and Reformed, 1980.

Scott, R. B. Y. *Proverbs, Ecclesiastes: Introduction, Translation, and Notes*. AB 18. Garden City, NY: Doubleday, 1965.

Seow, C. L. *Ecclesiastes: A New Translation with Introduction and Commentary*. AB 18C. New York: Doubleday, 1997.

Seybold, K. "hebhel." In *Theological Dictionary of the Old Testament*, edited by G. Johannes Botterweck and Helmer Ringgren, 3:313–20. Grand Rapids: Eerdmans, 1978.

Wenham, Gordon J. *Story as Torah: Reading the Old Testament Ethically*. Edinburgh: T. & T. Clark, 2000.

Williams, A. Lukyn. *Ecclesiastes*. Cambridge Bible for Schools and Colleges. Cambridge: University Press, 1922.

Wilson, Robert Dick. *A Scientific Investigation of the Old Testament*. London: Marshall Brothers, 1926.

Wright, A. G. "The Riddle of the Sphinx: The Structure of the Book of Qoheleth." *CBQ* 30, 3 (1968): 313–34.

Wright, J. Stafford, "The Interpretation of Ecclesiastes." In *Classical Evangelical Essays in Old Testament Interpretation*, edited by Walter C. Kaiser Jr., 133–50. Grand Rapids: Baker, 1972.

4

Lamentations
How to Weep

Chapter Outline

Introduction
  I. Introductory Questions
     A. Historical Setting
     B. Authorship, Date, and Place of Writing
     C. Literary Type
     D. Poetic Elements
        1. The Alphabetic Acrostic
        2. Figures of Speech
        3. A Specific Lament Meter?
     E. The Biblical-Theological Significance of Lamentations
 II. Major Themes of Lamentations
     A. Calamity Has Come
     B. Sin Has Caused It
        1. Confession of Sin in Lamentations 1
        2. Confession of Sin in Lamentations 2
        3. Confession of Sin in Lamentations 3
        4. Confession of Sin in Lamentations 4
        5. Confession of Sin in Lamentations 5
     C. God Has Ordered It
     D. Hope Nonetheless

INTRODUCTION

Many people are brought into crisis situations respecting their faith because they fail to grasp a proper biblical view regarding calamities that can come into their lives. Failing to recognize that life's circumstances may bring times of weeping as well as times of rejoicing can foster serious disillusionments. Sincere believers may mistakenly assume that their faith will free them from all earthly troubles.

The book of Lamentations teaches God's people how to weep. Inevitably, weeping over tragedies will come into the lives of all people. Yet there is a proper way and an improper way to weep. In the gracious purposes of God, the book of Lamentations has provided directions regarding how the LORD's people should weep in response to the tragedies that come into their lives. Its central message explains how to weep.

But before looking more closely at the message of the book, we must consider a number of introductory questions. These include the historical setting, the authorship, the date and place of composition, the literary type, the poetic elements, and the biblical-theological significance of the book. After treating these basic introductory questions, we will address the message of the book.

INTRODUCTORY QUESTIONS

Historical Setting

The laments of the book of Lamentations arose in response to the final destruction of the city of Jerusalem by the Babylonian invaders under King Nebuchadnezzar in 587 B.C. This fall of the sacred city occurred in stages: in 605 B.C., in 597 B.C., and in 587 B.C. Although the earlier conquests of the city by the Babylonians were a most serious matter, it was the city's total destruction in 587 B.C. that brought about the responses found in the book of Lamentations.

Just a few short years before these tragic events, good King Josiah had been slain by Pharaoh Necho of Egypt in 609 B.C. Josiah had led the nation through its last great reform. On the occasion of his death, Jeremiah the prophet led the nation in a period of mourning by composing laments to give the people a proper framework for expressing their grief:

> Jeremiah composed laments for Josiah, and to this day all the men and women singers commemorate Josiah in the laments. These became a tradition in Israel and are written in the Laments. (2 Chron. 35:25 NIV)

Several conclusions may be reached on the basis of this succinct statement from the book of Chronicles:

(1) A specialized form of literature, called the *Laments*, existed in Israel at least a full generation before the fall of Jerusalem in 587 B.C. This type of literature was distinctive enough to have its own collection maintained across the years.

(2) Though it may have been originally composed orally, this type of literature in its written poetic form was introduced to the community at this early stage.

(3) These lamentations were presented for use in public worship, involving specifically male and female singers. This fact strongly supports the idea that these materials were provided to choirs in the form of written compositions. The acrostic form of Lamentations may well represent a preservation of this publicized form of the text.

(4) Multiple laments might be composed by one author as commemorations for a single event. These various laments, it could be imagined, might have been celebrated individually or as a group.

(5) The prophet Jeremiah was personally involved in the composition of multiple laments that were preserved in the collection of Israel's Laments at around 609 B.C., the year of the untimely death of Josiah. So the prophet would be recognized in the community as one

gifted in the composition of laments as much as twenty years before the fall of Jerusalem in 587 B.C.

Once an untimely death snatched good King Josiah from his ruling role in Israel's monarchy, the nation quickly slipped back into its corrupting, idolatrous ways. Very soon the Israelites reached the "point of no return," for none of Josiah's sons or his grandson who ruled in Jerusalem after him had the passion for reform as did Josiah. As a consequence, the regular celebration of the laments over Josiah prepared the way for the larger laments associated with the fall of Jerusalem.

Shortly after the fall of Jerusalem, the survivors of Judah's devastation by the Babylonians instituted regular fasts to lament the destruction of their sacred city. References in the prophecy of Zechariah dating to 520 B.C. recall the regular fasts lamenting Jerusalem's fall. These references indicate that public laments continued over a period of at least fifty years.[1] These fasts were held annually during the fourth, fifth, seventh, and tenth months (Zech. 7:4–5; 8:18–19). They possibly commemorated the various phases by which the destruction of Jerusalem occurred:

- Tenth month: Nebuchadnezzar began his siege of Jerusalem. (2 Kings 25:1; Jer. 39:1)
- Fourth month: Nebuchadnezzar conquered Jerusalem. (Jer. 39:2; 52:6–7)
- Fifth month: Nebuchadnezzar burned the temple and the city. (Jer. 52:12–13)
- Seventh month: Gedaliah the governor of Judah appointed by Nebuchadnezzar was assassinated. (2 Kings 25:25; Jer. 41:1–2; dated according to Jewish tradition)[2]

The book of Lamentations should be read in this context of national lament over the fall of Jerusalem and all the attendant tragedies. The

---

1. Zechariah 7:5 refers to seventy years of fasting, which would have begun with the first assault of Jerusalem by Nebuchadnezzar in 605 B.C.

2. Cf. C. F. Keil, *Biblical Commentary on the Old Testament: The Twelve Minor Prophets* (Edinburgh: T. & T. Clark, 1871), 2:305–6. These tragic moments related to the destruction of Jerusalem are still recognized in contemporary Judaism.

fact that an inspired portion of Scripture is given over to lamentation over disaster has great significance. The tragedies that Israel experienced in connection with the destruction of Jerusalem by the Babylonians in 587 B.C. have been and will be reflected in one way or another in the life of every new generation. God's people will undergo devastation, for "man is born to trouble as surely as sparks fly upward" (Job 5:7). As Jesus predicted, there will be "wars and rumors of wars, . . . famines and earthquakes" (Matt. 24:6–7). Men's hearts will fail them for fear (Luke 21:26). Parallels in the modern circumstance may be seen in the plagues, murders, thefts, rapes, suicide bombings, tsunamis, invasions, and wars that continue unabated. These tragedies come to both individuals and communities. It does no good—in fact, it does great harm—for believers in Christ to "hide their heads in the sand." To pretend that great calamities will not come to the Christian individual and the Christian community can lead to serious disillusionment, bringing tragedy on top of disaster.

The book of Lamentations has its vital place in the canon of Holy Scripture for this very reason. An entire book of inspired Scripture is given over to this topic. Through the experience of Israel, God's people must learn how to weep. For there is a wrong way and a right way to weep. There is a God-honoring way to respond to the deepest tragedies of life, and there is a seriously harmful way for the people of God to react to their calamities, both as individuals and as a body. In every previous generation, the message of the book of Lamentations has been greatly needed. Its message continues to be needed, so that the people of God may maintain a proper balance in their lives as they pass through this alien, wilderness world as strangers and pilgrims.

Authorship, Date, and Place of Writing

The book of Lamentations does not begin by specifically identifying its author, the date of composition, and the place of writing. But the whole context presumes the destruction of a great city, namely, Jerusalem. "How deserted lies the city, once so full of people," announces the first verse of the book (Lam. 1:1 NIV). This dramatic declaration is immediately followed with direct reference to Judah's exile, to the mournful state of the roads leading to Zion, to the fading of her splendor, and to Jerusalem's fond remembrance of all the treasures she once possessed (1:3–4, 6–7). The tenor of the book presumes the perspective of an eyewitness to the tragic fall of Jerusalem. Nothing suggests that the writer was distanced by time and circumstance from the tragedy he describes. So it may be concluded with some confidence that Lamentations was composed by an eyewitness to the fall of Jerusalem in 587 B.C., writing in the vicinity of Jerusalem shortly after the disaster had occurred.[3]

But who was this individual? No specific identification may be found in the wording of the book itself. Perhaps the oldest identification of the prophet Jeremiah as the author of Lamentations may be found in the opening verse of the majority of LXX texts, though not found in Hebrew manuscripts:

> So after the captivity of Israel, and after Jerusalem had been left deserted, Jeremiah sat weeping as he lamented his lament over Jerusalem, saying . . . .

Basically every question regarding authorship, date, and place of composition finds an answer in this old pre-Christian tradition dating into the third century B.C. Jeremiah is the author, the 587 B.C. fall of Jerusalem fixes the date, and the setting is near the ruins of the city.[4] While some have disputed this tradition, little or no evidence points in a different direction.[5] Until more recent days, the overwhelming majority opinion has supported these conclusions.

---

3. Some critics affirm that chapters 1, 2, and 4 of Lamentations were written by the same author at the time of the fall of Jerusalem, but that chapters 3 and 5 were added later by a different author. Cf. Claus Westermann, *Lamentations: Issues and Interpretation* (Minneapolis: Augsburg Fortress, 1994), 105. Norman K. Gottwald, *Studies in the Book of Lamentations*, Studies in Biblical Theology 14 (London: SCM Press, 1954), 21, does not believe that Jeremiah wrote Lamentations, but affirms a single author for the first four chapters. Other writers suggest that Jeremiah composed chapters 1, 2, and 4, but that chapters 3 and/or 5 may have been written by someone else. But the unity of perspective and similarity of structure in the five chapters argue strongly for a single author of the book.

4. Westermann, *Lamentations*, 105, states that the "greatest likelihood" is that Lamentations was written "on the soil of Judah/Jerusalem." He indicates that nothing argues for an origin outside Judah somewhere else among the exiles.

5. Iain W. Provan, *Lamentations*, NCBC (Grand Rapids: Eerdmans, 1991), 9–11, 17–19, is skeptical concerning any specific conclusions about the author, date, or site

Literary Type

Since the beginnings of the twentieth century, particularly with the ascendancy of the technical approach to the materials of Scripture called *form criticism*, much discussion has focused on the lament as a distinctive literary type. Quite interesting is the existence of laments outside the bounds of biblical literature. Particularly striking is the collection of extant laments over the fall of Sumerian cities dating to the early second millennium B.C.[6] But the temporal distance of some

---

of composition. Adele Berlin, *Lamentations: A Commentary*, Old Testament Library (Louisville: Westminster John Knox, 2002), 32, says that the author should be viewed as an "affective persona, not a historical individual." In terms of the date of composition, she concludes that the book was written "not during or immediately after the destruction of Jerusalem, but during the exilic period, possibly near or at its end" (35). F. W. Dobbs-Allsopp, *Lamentations*, Interpretation: A Bible Commentary for Teaching and Preaching (Louisville: John Knox, 2002), 4, judges that Lamentations has survived "in a mostly decontextualized state." He regards the internal evidence as "certainly compatible" with a locale and dating near the 586 B.C. destruction of Jerusalem. He also affirms a single author (5), contrary to what he denotes as the "nihilistic position" of Iain Provan.

Despite current skepticism, hardly a writing of Scripture so closely relates to a specific event of redemptive history as Lamentations. In addition, the ancient testimony of the LXX should not be cast aside so easily. Though it cannot be absolutely affirmed, circumstantial evidence points strongly to Jeremiah as the author, who wrote in Palestine shortly after the city's destruction before he was dragged down to Egypt.

6. Cf. the discussion of Robert Gordis, *The Song of Songs and Lamentations: A Study, Modern Translation and Commentary* (New York: KTAV, 1974), 127–28. Gordis rejects the view of S. N. Kramer that the biblical book was directly influenced by Sumerian models. He notes that while the parallels cited by Kramer are interesting, "none are verbally exact or even sufficiently close to demonstrate dependence by the Biblical poet" (127). Hillers, *Lamentations*, 35n47, notes that in the first edition of his commentary (1972), he "expressed skepticism about any direct connection" with the Mesopotamian laments. In this later edition (1992), he concludes that "some kind of connection" exists (35). Westermann, *Lamentations*, 11–23, offers a "conjecture" in which he attempts to explain the similarities by a common reference to the "primordial history." This conjecture assumes the unhistorical character of this primordial history, and seeks to find the meaning of real history in myth. Such a search could provide little comfort for those individuals and communities that have experienced the harsh realities of true tragedy. Dobbs-Allsopp, *Lamentations*, 7–12, discusses at length the comparison of Lamentations with the "city-lament genre." His conclusion stresses the uniqueness of the Israelite lament. Lamentations is "no simple Mesopotamian city lament." There is "very little of the Mesopotamian genre that has been taken up (however mediated) wholly into Lamentations." This distinction is made apparent in that in Lamentations the sin of the people is the cause of their city's destruction, while in the Mesopotamian lament the capricious decision of the divine assembly is the cause of the destruction. Furthermore, there is no mention of the restoration of the city in Lamentations, while that theme serves as the basis for the extrabiblical laments. For

fifteen hundred years between the Sumerian materials and the book of Lamentations, alongside the geographical distance between the Sumerian kingdom and Judah, excludes any likelihood of explicit dependence. Yet as has been appropriately noted, "similar circumstances will lead to similar descriptions of conditions and similar expressions of mood."[7] If one ancient Near Eastern community laments the destruction of its cities, it should not be surprising that other communities follow similar modes of expression.

More specific analysis of the "type" in which the book of Lamentations presents itself leads to a consideration of whether its literature may be characterized as a funeral dirge, a communal lament, an individual lament, or a combination of elements from these different literary forms of lamenting. Though the term *literary form* may be applied to these distinctions, it is largely a question of the writings' material substance that is more directly under consideration.[8] Some specific literary characteristics of a funeral dirge and a community lament may be identified.[9] But the question more precisely boils down to whether the various poems in the book of Lamentations speak figuratively as a funeral dirge over a city's "death" or more gener-

---

the text of the poems regarding the Mesopotamian city-lament, see James B. Pritchard, ed., *Ancient Near Eastern Texts Relating to the Old Testament*, 3rd ed. (Princeton, NJ: Princeton University Press, 1969), 455–63, 611–19, 646–51.

7. Gordis, *Song of Songs and Lamentations*, 127.

8. Note the caution offered by Gottwald, *Lamentations*, 33–34. Delbert R. Hillers, *Lamentations: A New Translation with Introduction and Commentary*, 2nd ed., AB 7A (New York: Doubleday, 1992), 32, concludes that "we derive relatively little help" from the older genre analysis of Herman Gunkel, who treats chapter 5 as a communal lament, chapter 3 as an individual lament in the main, and chapters 1, 2, and 4 as funeral dirges for a nation, but then concludes that all but chapter 5 have an admixture of alien elements. As Hillers summarizes, in Gunkel's view Lamentations comes so late that "even the dominant motif of a particular type may be lost."

9. See Westermann, *Lamentations*, 96, who notes that in the dirge may be found "an announcement of the death, a summons to wail and to engage in mourning rites, a description of the state of distress that has befallen the survivors, and eulogies for the deceased set in contrast to the distress of the survivors." Similar elements may be found in the modern funeral service, which suggests the universal character of the dirge. Strikingly absent in Westermann's description of the ancient dirge are the acknowledgment of guilt and expression of hope, which clearly mark the distinctiveness of the book of Lamentations as well as the Christian funeral. The assignment of these elements exclusively to the "communal lament" is an arbitrary distinction imposed by Westermann.

ally as a community's lament over their city's destruction. From a cultic perspective, the question is whether the materials of the book of Lamentations have been shaped more directly by a funeral service or a worship service.

In answer to this question, both these cultic and cultural elements appear to make their contribution to the five poems of the book of Lamentations. "Death of a City" is definitely a theme in the first poem, as seen in the extended personification of the city as a weeping widow who lies deserted (Lam. 1:1–7). Yet elements common to certain psalms composed for Israel's worship are also present, including confession of sin and petition to the Almighty for mercy. It is generally agreed that the second, fourth, and fifth poems (chaps. 2, 4, and 5) primarily reflect the characteristics of a community lament similar to expressions found in the psalms. The third poem (chap. 3) is distinctive in that the first major portion of the poem occurs in the first-person singular (3:1–24, with the exception of verse 22, which is in the first-person plural). Extensive discussion has centered on the identity of this "I." Does it refer exclusively to a single person? Or does the "I" represent a personification of the entire community from the perspective of "corporate personality"? Or could this "I" combine both these elements by referring to a single individual through whom the experience of the whole community is embodied?

In considering this question, some mistakenly assume that the entirety of chapter 3 appears in the first person. But to the contrary, the poem fluctuates from a singular "I" (Lam. 3:1–24) to an impersonal "he" (3:25–39) to a plural "we" (3:40–47), and then returns to the singular "I" (3:48–66). In addition, this third poem is by no means unique in its fluctuation among persons. The first poem begins with the impersonal "she" in reference to the city of Jerusalem (1:1–11a). Then the singular "I" represents the city itself as speaking (1:11b–16). Next, Zion and Jerusalem reappear briefly in the third-person personified (1:17), followed by a return to the first-person "I" (1:18–22). Similar exchanges of persons are found in chapters 2 and 4. The most consistent of the five poems in terms of the pronominal persons is chapter 5. In this last poem, the first-person plural is used throughout, except for

283

the final verses, which make use of the second-person singular "you" as the LORD is called upon by the people (5:19–22).

What may be deduced from these observations regarding the interchange of persons among the various poems? Certainly no firm conclusions should be asserted regarding the distinctiveness of chapter 3 simply because it begins with a first-person section. Contrariwise, the fluctuation among persons throughout the first three chapters suggests a unity of literary type throughout the book. This fluctuation among speakers contributes to the vitality of the book. It takes on the character of a "living organism" that communicates a distinctive message regarding tragedies among God's people both individually and corporately.

Who, then, is the "I" of these various poems? Clearly, at some points it is a personification of the city of Jerusalem that is speaking in the first person (cf. Lam. 1:9c, 11c–22). At other points, this "I" is an individual who looks on the sufferings of Jerusalem with great sympathy (2:11–17). This person could be anyone who was an eyewitness to the destruction of Jerusalem. But Jeremiah the prophet remains as the most likely candidate. At other times, this "I" could be a single person functioning as representative of the whole of God's people. In this manner, the suffering of the individual as well as the community would be underscored. As a further consideration, this distinction of the "I" from the whole of the community provides a dramatic demonstration of the principle of *aloneness* that accompanies every tragedy. As the opening verse of Lamentations exclaims: "How deserted is the city that once was filled with people" (1:1). Whether it be the tragedies associated with war and all its horrors or the loss of a precious loved one in death, aloneness haunts the person experiencing disaster.

In sum, with respect to the literary type of Lamentations, the book clearly fits into the cultural mode of its day. Elements of both the funeral dirge and the communal lament blend into a single piece of literature that provides a framework for the expression of grief felt by community and by individual. For this reason, the book continues to speak significantly to every community, every culture, and every individual today.

Poetic Elements

Three elements of a poetic nature deserve special attention when considering the book of Lamentations. Most significant is the alphabetic acrostic that shapes the form of the book. Matters of secondary importance are the employment of figures of speech and the question of a specific meter designed for the expression of laments.

The Alphabetic Acrostic

The book of Lamentations presents the most extensive use of the alphabetic acrostic in the biblical materials.[10] *Alphabetic acrostic* refers to a poetic form in which every subsequent stanza opens with a word that begins with the next letter of the Hebrew alphabet. Since twenty-two letters constitute the Hebrew alphabet, each of these poems contains twenty-two stanzas, with each subsequent stanza being introduced by the next letter of the Hebrew alphabet. Three exceptions to this basic arrangement as it relates to Lamentations should be noted. The third poem (chap. 3) consists of three verses beginning with each subsequent letter of the Hebrew alphabet rather than a single verse, making a total of sixty-six verses. The fifth poem contains twenty-two stanzas, but without any representation of the various letters of the Hebrew alphabet.[11] In addition, the second, third, and fourth poems contain a "curious and unexpected disturbance" of the alphabetic order.[12] Instead of the customary arrangement in which the letter *ayin* precedes the letter *pe*, the sequence is reversed so that *pe* precedes *ayin*. This reversal of order has been interpreted as indicating that a normative sequence of letters had not yet been determined for the Hebrew alphabet at the time of the composition of the book of Lamentations in the

10. Generally fourteen acrostic poems have been identified in the Old Testament Scriptures. Beyond the first four chapters of Lamentations, additional acrostics include Psalms 9–10, 25, 34, 37, 111, 112, 119, 145, and Proverbs 31:10–31. Nahum 1:2–8 is generally recognized as a partial acrostic.

11. Other biblical poems with twenty-two lines but without the alphabetic acrostic include Psalms 33, 38, and 103. Hillers, *Lamentations*, 25, comments that "it is reasonable to suppose that in all of these cases the number of lines is chosen intentionally, though none is an acrostic." These poems may be designated as *quasi-acrostics*.

12. Gottwald, *Lamentations*, 24.

sixth century B.C.[13] It is more likely that this different order of letters may have provided an additional "peg" for the memorization of the entire poem.

As a further factor in the poetic shape of the book, some difference exists in the total number of stanzas and lines found in the various chapters. Chapters 1 and 2 consist of twenty-two stanzas with three lines to each stanza, making a total of sixty-six lines in each of the first two chapters. But only the introductory line of each stanza reflects the alphabetic sequence of letters. Chapter 3 also consists of sixty-six lines as in the case of the first two chapters. Three lines form each stanza in chapter 3 as in chapters 1 and 2, making a total of 22 stanzas in each of the first three chapters. But in chapter 3, each of the three lines in each stanza begins with the same sequential letter (A, A, A; B, B, B; C, C, C; etc.). Because those who introduced versification into the Bible chose to assign a verse number to each of these lines, chapter 3 counts 66 verses even though it has the same number of lines and stanzas as chapters 1 and 2. As a consequence, chapter 3 is no longer than the first two chapters in terms of total lines. Chapter 4 contains two lines to each stanza for a total of forty-four lines, with only the first line of each stanza reflecting the alphabetic sequence. Chapter 5 contains no indicator of alphabetic sequence, and consists of only one line to each stanza. As a consequence, it is the shortest of the poems, with only 22 lines total. If the book was designed for public reading, it might be imagined that three readers would present the first three chapters, with each reader reciting a single line in sequence. Then one of the readers would drop out at the end of the third chapter, so that only two readers remained to present the fourth chapter. Finally, only one reader would remain to conclude with the reading of the final poem, which contains only one unalphabetized line to each stanza. If this arrangement were followed, a sense of the declining state of the city and its

---

13. Westermann, *Lamentations*, 98. Hillers, *Lamentations*, 29, says that the proposal that the order of these letters was not yet fixed "has seemed rather improbable in view of the consistent sequence *ayin-pe* in Ugaritic abecedaries almost a millennium older than Lamentations." But he then cites the Qumran manuscript of Lamentations and other documents as evidence of "an authentic early Hebrew tradition of alphabetic order divergent from the Ugaritic and Phoenician order that became dominant" (29–30). Westermann, *Lamentations*, 99, indicates that acrostic poems are also found in Akkadian, Ugaritic, and Paleo-Canaanite documents, but does not discuss the consistency of their alphabetic order.

people would be vividly demonstrated through the decline of readers as the poems progressed. The absence of any alphabetic order in the final poem might also underscore the chaotic state of the besieged city.

But why did the author of Lamentations employ this particular poetic form? Several answers to this question have been proposed:

(1) It has been proposed that the acrostic form gave witness to a belief in the magical power of letters. This view finds no support in the old covenant Scriptures and contradicts the biblical abhorrence of anything "magical" or superstitious. One need only sense the revulsion of the God of Israel toward resorting to any means of seeking to know his will apart from the word of his prophets to appreciate just how alien would be a magical access to any aspect of divine truth.[14]

(2) It has been proposed that the acrostic form served as a device designed for teaching the alphabet. This reason for the acrostic form is unlikely, considering the substantial character of the content of Lamentations. This material clearly was not designed for infantiles or juveniles.

(3) It has been proposed that the acrostic form served as a means of making possible the easier memorization of the entire book of Lamentations. Because a time of tragic loss places individuals and communities in a state of mental anguish that often excludes clarity of perception and propriety of expression, the acrostic form would enforce "the most judicious economy" of expression on the individual as well as on the community. In addition, this form would demand an expression of emotions that would be "disciplined and restrained" despite the depth of the tragedy.[15] Anyone who has undergone traumatic suffering can appreciate the need for restraint in mode and substance of expression.

(4) It has been proposed that the acrostic form would encourage "completeness in the expression of grief."[16] Following the order of the entire alphabet means that

> one comes as close as man may to a total development of any theme or the complete expression of any emotion or belief. If the subject

---

14. See the treatment of the teaching of Deuteronomy 13 and 18 in O. Palmer Robertson, *The Christ of the Prophets* (Phillipsburg, NJ: P&R Publishing, 2004), 48–51.

15. Gottwald, *Lamentations*, 31.

16. Ibid., 28. This same principle was expressed a century earlier by C. F. Keil, *Biblical Commentary on the Old Testament: Jeremiah and the Lamentations of Jeremiah* (Grand Rapids: Eerdmans, 1980), 2:337.

is to be exhausted, the alphabet alone can suffice to suggest and symbolize the totality striven after.[17]

The Judean tradition that Adam transgressed the whole law "from aleph to taw" (*A* to *Z*) and that Abraham kept the whole law "from aleph to taw" supports this understanding of the use of the acrostic form. Especially in response to human tragedy, a balanced mode of expression before God is necessary. Indeed, a person or a community may rightly sense a need to give full expression to the depths of distress. But alongside a manifestation of grief must be found both the confession of sin and the declaration of hope.

These deeper reasons for the use of the acrostic support the view that the original shape of the book of Lamentations possessed this acrostic form. For from the beginning, the nation's grief could be properly expressed only within the restraints of appropriate repentance and faith. An irrational or excessive expression of despair would never be appropriate for God's covenant people. When the Israelite psalmist declared his deepest despair, he did not say, "O God, why have you forsaken me?" Instead, trust in God bridled his most painful exclamations: "*My* God, *my* God, why have you forsaken me?" (Ps. 22:1 NIV).

It has been suggested that the rigidity of the acrostic form does not suit the deeply moving quality of human lamentation, and that this form has the effect of introducing additions, transpositions, insertions, and even "genre-alien elements" that exclude a steady flow of thought.[18] But such a negative analysis of the acrostic form minimizes the positive effects of proper restraint in the expression of laments. The acrostic form properly requires a judicious use of words that will not allow for the free run of unchecked emotions. At the same time, this very form encourages the needed balance among expressions of grief, confession of sin, and certainty of hope.

Figures of Speech

As in the case of the book of Job and other biblical wisdom literature, figures of speech play a prominent role in vivifying wisdom's

17. Gottwald, *Lamentations*, 29.
18. Westermann, *Lamentations*, 100.

message in Lamentations.[19] If more than three hundred figures may be found in the forty-two chapters of the book of Job, Lamentations features even more, proportionately speaking, with its total of seventy-five to eighty figures in only five chapters.[20] This concentrated use of figures of speech should be seen as a vital part of the concept of wisdom in biblical revelation. King Solomon's three thousand proverbs anticipate King Jesus' constant instruction through parable. Without a parable he did not teach, vivifying his determination to teach only and exclusively "as they were able to understand" (Mark 4:33–34). In a similar way, figures of speech skillfully employed can illuminate truth and drive it home in a most effective manner.

Approximately twenty figures of speech occur in each of the first four chapters of Lamentations, which constitutes an average of almost one figure per stanza in chapters 1, 2, 3, and 4. In significant contrast, chapter 5 contains only three comparisons in its twenty-two stanzas/verses/lines. It might be proposed that this difference indicates that this last chapter was composed by a different author. As previously indicated, however, the book contains an inherent progression by shrinking the number of lines in each stanza of its successive chapters. The three-line stanzas of chapters 1, 2, and 3 are followed by the two-line stanzas of chapter 4. Chapter 5 concludes the book with only one line to a stanza. This gradual reduction of lines, along with an abandonment of the alphabetic acrostic and the drastic reduction of figures of speech, reinforces the unadorned statement of tragic truth that characterizes chapter 5. Although all these factors could be used to support the argument for a different author for chapter 5, they may be more appropriately understood as supporting the wholeness, the united structure of the book of Lamentations.

In reviewing the extensiveness of figures of speech in Lamentations, one commentator concludes that this mode of expression indicates that these songs of lament "arose among simple folk."[21] This

19. Berlin, *Lamentations*, 3–4, indicates her intent to unpack the significance of metaphors in Lamentations, which she regards as being generally neglected.

20. Westermann, *Lamentations*, 106, counts seventy-five comparisons in the 264 lines of Lamentations. The count may go slightly higher into the eighties, depending on whether a use of the same figure more than once may be counted twice or even three times. Cf. the comparison of God's "swallowing up" the dwellings of Jacob (Lam. 2:2), his "swallowing up" Israel and all its palaces (2:5), and Israel's enemies' "swallowing up" Jerusalem (2:16).

21. Ibid.

conclusion ignores the genius necessary for a skillful use of figures of speech in poetry. These vibrant, carefully crafted images hardly come from the hands of "simple folk." To the contrary, they clearly display the poetic genius of the person responsible for the composition of this magnificent piece of literature.[22]

The truth-substance communicated by the figures of speech in Lamentations lends strong support to four major topics of the book. As a consequence, these topics will be introduced by noting a selection of the figures of speech that vivify each of these points. Rather than providing a simple list of the various figures of speech, they will be introduced in connection with the development of these four major themes of Lamentations. These themes are as follows: Calamity has come; sin has caused it; God has ordered it; hope nonetheless. The role of each of these themes in Lamentations will be discussed subsequently.

A Specific Lament Meter?

Significant efforts have been made to uncover a specific meter that characterizes the poetic rhythm of the lament.[23] In some cases, it may appear that a stress pattern following a 3:2 sequence of accents among words or syllables may be detected. This meter has been characterized as a "limping" meter, suggesting that "something was wrong."[24] Yet a proper caution may be found in the following analysis:

All that is now known of Ancient Near Eastern poetry suggests that there was a degree of accentual freedom available to Semitic composers which was unknown to the Greeks and Romans. It cannot be urged too strongly, therefore, that analogies from Classical poetry can be misleading, since in Hebrew the number of unstressed syllables which can occur between stresses is variable. Hebrew poetry is concerned primarily with intellectual rather than phonic or rhythmic

22. Berlin, *Lamentations*, 3–4, notes that "most studies of biblical poetry have slighted metaphors in favor of formal poetic devices."

23. R. B. Salters, *A Critical and Exegetical Commentary on Lamentations* (London: T. & T. Clark, 2010), 17, notes that C. Budde in 1882 and 1898 drew attention to the predominance of a 3:2 meter in Lamentations 1–4.

24. Salters, *Lamentations*, 17. Cf. Walter C. Kaiser, Jr., *Grief and Pain in the Plan of God: Christian Assurance and the Message of Lamentations* (Ross-shire, Scotland: Christian Focus Publications, 2004), 37–38.

considerations, and has as its predominant aim the balancing of one thought against another by using syllabic accentual values which most probably never corresponded to strictly measurable units.[25]

The net result of extensive academic research into the specific meter of the Hebrew lament is that little in terms of agreed conclusions has been realized.[26] One commentator urges caution in this matter of a lamentation meter when he observes the presence of the so-called "lament meter in poetic passages that do not have lamentation as their theme (cf. Song 1:9–11), while passages that clearly have lamentation as their theme give no evidence of the supposed lamentation meter" (cf. 2 Sam. 1:17–27).[27] Since possible considerations of meter would have only minor impact on the communication of the book's message, the tendentious nature of this research should not create great difficulty in understanding and appreciating the message of Lamentations.

The Biblical-Theological Significance of Lamentations

Comparisons with extrabiblical parallels may prove helpful in understanding the biblical laments. At the same time, these parallels may tend to blur the unique role of the lament in Israel's relationship to her God. For the biblical lament cannot be properly comprehended

---

25. R. K. Harrison, *Jeremiah and Lamentations: An Introduction and Commentary*, TOTC (Nottingham, UK: Inter-Varsity Press, 1973), 202–3.

26. A thorough effort to provide an analysis of specific meter from Lamentations may be found in Gordis, *Song of Songs and Lamentations*, 118–21. Gordis begins with the affirmation that one beat per thought unit is "basic to Biblical poetry." But then he modifies this basic principle with various qualifications. One word may receive two stresses instead of one; two words may receive one stress; or two words may receive two beats. The choice among these options is to be decided case by case according to the demands of the meter, which should primarily have the result of "thus preserving the 3:2 pattern." In this instance, it appears that the presumption of a 3:2 pattern plays a large role in discovering the 3:2 pattern. Gordis further notes that *the poetic caesura will diverge from the logical caesura*, that is to say, the thought will continue beyond the pause imposed by the meter pattern" (italics his). He further notes that in Lamentations "this divergence is so common that it may fairly be regarded as a special characteristic of the poet." So his original affirmation that "thought unit" is the prevailing principle in the meter of Hebrew poetry must receive serious modification in the case of Lamentations, where divergence from this principle has become a "special characteristic of the poet."

27. Salters, *Lamentations*, 17.

apart from the divine covenant initiated by the LORD with Israel. It is not before a god in the abstract that Israel expresses its sorrows over the tragic fall of Jerusalem. Only in the context of the divinely initiated covenants with Israel across the generations may the people's laments be properly understood. A conviction of violation of divine law that has brought about the national calamities, a prospect of hope despite desperate circumstances, and a focus on a single innocent sufferer may be comprehended only in the context of divinely initiated covenants with Abraham and the patriarchs, with Moses and the nation, with David and his successors.

More specifically, the rehearsal of these awesome calamities may be properly understood only in terms of the nation's response to the curses of God's covenant. The nation understood all too well that curses would come in the event of disobedience to the covenant's demands.

These words of covenantal judgment were deeply engraved in the minds of the nation by the form of a "song," a poem that Israel must rehearse in the day of its calamity, antedating Israel's exile in the nation's memory by almost a thousand years. In the covenantal document of Deuteronomy, God informs Moses:

> "These people will soon prostitute themselves to the foreign gods of the land they are entering. They will forsake me and break the covenant I made with them. On that day I will become angry with them and forsake them; I will hide my face from them, and they will be destroyed. Many disasters and difficulties will come upon them . . . .
>
> "Now write down for yourselves this song and teach it to the Israelites and have them sing it, so that it may be a witness for me against them." . . .
>
> And Moses recited the words of this song from beginning to end in the hearing of the whole assembly of Israel . . . .
>
> Moses came with Joshua son of Nun and spoke all the words of this song in the hearing of the people. (Deut. 31:16–17, 19, 30; 32:44 NIV)

This "Song of Moses" as recorded in Deuteronomy 32 (NIV) anticipates the same basic elements subsequently found in the book of Lamentations. Despite the constant favors of the LORD to the Israelites, "they have acted corruptly toward him" (Deut. 32:5). As a consequence, the COVENANT LORD was angered by his sons and daughters, and determined to "heap calamities upon them and spend [his] arrows against them" (32:19b, 23). Famine, pestilence, and wild beasts will consume them (32:24). Young men and young women, infants and gray-haired men will all be destroyed (32:25). Yet in the midst of their calamities, the LORD will "have compassion on his servants when he sees their strength is gone" (32:36). The nation may rejoice, "for he will . . . make atonement for his land and people" (32:43).

The similarity of substance between these curses of the covenant and the book of Lamentations makes it appear that this book was written specifically to confirm the faithfulness of God to his covenantal Word. As the prophet, the author of Lamentations, himself declares:

> The COVENANT LORD has done
>   what he determined;
> He has carried out his Word
>   which he decreed ages ago. (Lam. 2:17)

So the response to the most calamitous dealings of the LORD with his people must involve the affirmation of his faithfulness to his covenanting Word. Just as the Israelites sang the song of deliverance at the Red Sea, so they must sing the song of devastation at their destruction.

This kind of response to calamity can come only as a consequence of the work of God's Spirit. As the restoration prophet Zechariah declares after the remnant of Israel has been restored from its exile:

> And I will pour out on the house of David and the inhabitants of Jerusalem a spirit of grace and supplication. They will look on me, the one they have pierced, and they will mourn for him as one mourns for an only child, and grieve bitterly for him as one grieves for a firstborn son. On that day the weeping [lamentation] in Jerusalem will be great, like the weeping [lamentation] of Hadad Rimmon in the plain of Megiddo. (Zech. 12:10–11 NIV)

The prophet Zechariah first looks back in time to the laments of Jeremiah composed on the occasion of the death of Josiah at the pass of Megiddo (cf. 2 Chron. 35:22–25). But then he looks forward to an even greater lament when the nation will look on "me," the COVENANT

LORD himself, the One they have pierced (Zech. 12:10). The concept is unimaginable, but proves to be prophetically true. Israel's greatest lamentation occurred when the people looked on the One they had pierced. Their lamentation was as one who mourns for an only child and grieves bitterly for a firstborn son (Zech. 12:10; cf. John 19:34, 37).

In that consummate context, the message of Lamentations reaches its greatest fulfillment in terms of new covenant realization. The curses of the covenant, a part of redemptive history across the ages, reached their old covenant climax with the prophetic projection of Zechariah, based on the lamentations of Israel over the death of good King Josiah, which ultimately anticipated the fall of the nation and its temple in Jerusalem. The new covenant realization of these same covenantal curses came to pass with God's heaping the guilt of all his people through all the ages on his only beloved Son. That crux of moments in the history of redemption found the Son on the cross crying out of the all-embracing darkness, "My God, my God, why have you forsaken me?" (Matt. 27:46). In that moment he embodied all the accumulated agonies of the "I" of the book of Lamentations.

MAJOR THEMES OF LAMENTATIONS

Having dealt with the principal introductory questions regarding the book of Lamentations, we now find it appropriate to review the book's major themes. As indicated earlier, these themes are essentially four: Calamity has come; sin has caused it; God has ordered it; hope nonetheless. In each of these themes, the figures of speech so characteristic of the book play a significant role in making vivid each aspect of the book's message.

Calamity Has Come

Numerous descriptions and images of calamity permeate the book of Lamentations. Each chapter has its own specialized collection of vivid figures of speech, descriptions, and literary images. The city weeps, she is betrayed by friends, she mourns, her priests groan, her maidens grieve, her enemies laugh at her destruction, she is bound in a yoke that saps her strength. After affliction and harsh labor, the people of God have gone into exile, they are captive before the foe, outside the sword bereaves, inside there is only death (Lam. 1:2, 4, 7, 9, 14, 3, 5, 20). She is set under a cloud, her splendor is hurled down to earth from heaven, her people are destroyed, her infants faint like wounded men in the streets, her wound is as deep as the sea, her walls shed streaming tears, her young men and maidens have fallen by the sword, there are terrors on every side (2:1, 11–13, 18, 21–22). The sufferer is walled in, weighed down, mocked, hunted like a bird, cast into a pit (3:7, 14, 52–53). The inhabitants of Jerusalem are destitute and lie in ash heaps, they are blacker than soot, their skin is shriveled on their bones, they are racked with hunger and waste away for lack of food, they grope as blind men, they cry "Unclean" as lepers, they are stalked, pursued, and chased (4:5, 8–9, 14–15, 18–19). They have become orphans and widows, their skin is hot as an oven, they experience the fever of famine, their women have been raped (5:3, 10–11).[28]

Most striking is the fact that it is God's city, the city of Jerusalem, the royal habitation of Zion, the focal place for the life of the chosen people of Israel, that suffers these massive calamities. The very first word of the book gives expression to the grief of the city of Jerusalem with a heart-rending exclamation: "Ahhh!" (אֵיכָה): How could it be! How is it possible! What a stunning reality!

Not only is this calamity astounding; it is unbelievable. How could God's own sacred city, temple, and people suffer such calamity? This devastation at the decree of the Almighty

> marks the most horrendous national catastrophe in the history of Judah, the most colossal break in the entire relationship between God and Israel since its beginning. The very foundations of Judah have crumbled: the country has been conquered, the Davidic monarchy brought to an end, the temple destroyed, and the people exiled from their land. No matter that Deuteronomy had envisioned it and the

---

28. Berlin, *Lamentations*, 7, provides a summation of the distinctive perspective of each successive chapter on the devastation that has come. In her analysis, chapter 1 focuses on the city itself; chapter 2 centers on God the perpetrator of the destruction; chapter 3 portrays the process of exile from the perspective of a lone male; chapter 4 depicts the utter degradation of the people; chapter 5 presents the prayer of the Judean remnant.

prophets had foretold it; nothing could prepare one for the cruel reality and the apparent finality of the situation.[29]

The radicalness of this calamitous event may be fully appreciated only with the backdrop of Israel's "Zion theology" in full view. For hundreds of years, the nation had regularly celebrated the "psalms of Zion" in its worship. In these psalms, the chosen place of God's dwelling was hailed as altogether invincible. Any enemy would be utterly decimated if it dared to assault Zion. Concerning the "city of God," the psalmist says:

> God is within her,
>   she will not fall;
> God will help her
>   at break of day.
> Nations are in uproar,
>   kingdoms fall;
> He lifts his voice,
>   the earth melts. (Ps. 46:5–6 NIV)

Again the psalmist celebrates the theme of the unconquerable nature of God's city:

> How awesome!
> The kings assembled themselves,
> They invaded as one man.
> They saw with their own eyes,
>   they were astounded.
> They panicked,
>   they were put to flight.
> Trembling seized them
>   right where they stood,
> Anguish
>   like a woman going into labor.
> With a strong wind from the desert
>   you smashed the ships of Tarshish.

---

29. Ibid., 18.

As we heard the report, so we witnessed for ourselves,
  in the city of the COVENANT LORD of Hosts,
  in the city of our God.
God firmly establishes her forever. (Ps. 48:4–8)

With God's dwelling in the midst of Zion as the foundation of its impregnable character, how can the destruction of city and temple be comprehended? The only answer to this perplexing question is found in the visionary experience of a prophet who lived contemporaneously with the fall of Jerusalem. Though residing as an exile in distant Babylon, Ezekiel witnessed in his vision the step-by-step departure of the Glory from its residence in the temple of Jerusalem: first from the Holy Place to the threshold of the temple (Ezek. 8:9–10; 9:3); next from the threshold to the east gate (10:18–19); finally from above the city to the Mount of Olives (11:22–23). Once that removal of the LORD's presence had taken place, the once-sacred city and its temple were as vulnerable as any other fortified locale.[30] A comparison of the words of the psalmist with the sad echo of identical phraseology in the Laments vivifies the tragic defamation of the city:

Beautiful for elevation,
  the joy of the whole earth
Is Mount Zion, in the far North,
  the city of the Great King. (Ps. 48:2)

Is this the city that was called
  "The perfection of beauty,
  the joy of the whole earth"? (Lam. 2:15c NIV)

A principal consequence of this tragedy is the aloneness of the city. Once Jerusalem teemed with multitudes, particularly during the three solemn festivals of the old covenant calendar. Pilgrims from every town and village flooded the city. But after this disaster has struck, Jerusalem experiences the isolation of aloneness.

---

30. For a fuller treatment of the place of Zion theology in the context of the book of Lamentations, see Bertil Albrektson, *Studies in the Text and Theology of the Book of Lamentations*, Studia Theologica Lundensia 21 (Lund: CWK Gleerup, 1963), 219–30.

Every tragedy brings this sense of aloneness. At a death in the family, friends and relatives gather to express their sympathy. But eventually they must return to their own life schedules, leaving the bereaved alone with that awesome sense of emptiness. When sickness strikes, friends speak words of comfort and encouragement. But the afflicted must spend bedridden hours alone. If sin brings tragedy into life, the guilty must bear his accusing conscience alone. Just as the plague of darkness that struck Egypt caused every person to sit alone, so every calamity inevitably brings aloneness (cf. Ex. 10:22–23).

None have experienced aloneness with the intensity felt by the promised Suffering Savior. He is prophetically described as "a man of sorrows, and acquainted with grief" (Isa. 53:3 KJV). "Behold and see," says the author of Lamentations, "if there be any sorrow like unto my sorrow" (Lam. 1:12 KJV). These words emerge appropriately as the pathos-filled cry of the Suffering Savior in Handel's *Messiah*. "My God, my God, why have you forsaken me?" he groaned from the abyss of his abandonment (Ps. 22:1). While the old covenant psalmist may have felt abandonment, the new covenant chanter of this same psalm actually experienced the awful desolation of absolute aloneness (Matt. 27:45–46).

Not only the city of Jerusalem suffers these calamities. All the particular peoples of the city undergo these birth pangs of lamentation. Look at the infants of Jerusalem and it will break your heart. They "faint in the streets of the city" (Lam. 2:11c). They say to their mothers, "'Where is bread and wine?' as they faint like wounded men in the streets of the city, as their lives ebb away in their mothers' arms" (2:12 NIV).

No citizen of the assaulted city can claim exemption from these extreme calamities. Her princes are "like deer that find no pasture; in weakness they have fled before the pursuer" (Lam. 1:6 NIV). Young men and maidens have gone into exile (1:18c). Priests and elders perish in the city as they search for enough sustenance to support life (1:19). Prophets no longer experience visions from the LORD (2:9c). Young women have bowed their heads to the ground (2:10c). Children faint from hunger at the head of every street (2:19). Priests and prophets are murdered within the sanctuary of the LORD (2:20c). Young and old lie together in the dust of the streets; young men and maidens have fallen by the sword (2:21). Even the LORD's anointed, their noble king, has been caught in their trap (4:20).

A concentrated vision of the sufferings of every category of person is rehearsed in the final chapter of the book:

Women
    have been ravished in Zion,
And virgins
    in the towns of Judah.
Princes
    have been hung up by their hands;
Elders
    are shown no respect.
Young men
    toil at the millstones;
Boys
    stagger under loads of wood.
The elders
    are gone from the city gate;
The young men
    have stopped their music.
Joy
    is gone from our hearts;
Our dancing
    has turned to mourning. (Lam. 5:11–15 NIV)

So this first message of Lamentations cannot be missed. Calamity has come. It has come to God's own covenant people. It has come in the past and at various times will come to all of God's people. By the grace of God, your personal or communal calamity may not be as severe as the devastations experienced by the people of Jerusalem. But it may be. God's people living in peaceful and prosperous communities must not forget their suffering and persecuted brothers and sisters in other lands. Genocide, church bombings, public executions of Christians before the watching world, an Ebola epidemic, a tsunami—all these calamities envelop Christian as well as non-Christian populations.

But this modern heresy of "health and wealth" as the assured possession of all of God's people all the time must be firmly repudiated on the basis of the truth of God's Word and the repeated experience of God's people. Otherwise, even greater tragedies could eventually come. As the apostle Peter has wisely advised God's people across the ages:

> Do not be surprised at the painful trial you are suffering, as though something strange were happening to you. But rejoice that you participate in the sufferings of Christ . . . .
>
> So then, those who suffer according to God's will should commit themselves to their faithful Creator and continue to do good. (1 Peter 4:12–13, 19 NIV)

Sin Has Caused It

But all this suffering. Why? Is it the work of blind fate? Is it simply the inevitable consequence of being human? Is it a manifestation of the principle of "tooth and claw," the "law of the jungle"? Not according to the book of Lamentations.

Vivid imagery underscores the sinfulness, the corruption of God's people that has brought about these calamities. Jerusalem has filth on her skirts; she is altogether an unclean thing (Lam. 1:8–9). God's people have become heartless, behaving like ostriches in the wilderness (4:3).

To avoid misunderstanding, it must be emphasized that Lamentations does not teach that calamity comes in this life precisely in proportion to a person's sinfulness. Clearly, the Babylonians, whom God used as his instrument of judgment on his own people, were an extremely sinful people, a people full of idolatry and brutality. Eventually they would also suffer God's judgment for their sin. But at this moment in time, they served as God's instrument of chastening judgment on a people that may well have been "more righteous than they" (Hab. 1:13). No one should torment himself each time tragedy strikes with the assumption that every suffering comes in proportion to sin. Jesus clarified this matter once and for all when he pointedly asked:

> Do you think that these Galileans were worse sinners than all the other Galileans because they suffered this way? I tell you, no! . . . Or those eighteen who died when the tower in Siloam fell on them—do you think they were more guilty than all the others living in Jerusalem? I tell you, no! (Luke 13:2–5a NIV)

Neither pagan Galileans nor pious Jews undergo tragedy because they are more sinful than everyone else around them. Yet Jesus immediately repeats his balancing statement, "But unless you repent, you too will all perish" (Luke 13:3b, 5b NIV; cf. John 9:1–3).

The book of Lamentations does not assume that suffering comes in proportion to sin, or that every calamity in life comes because of a particular sin. At the same time, a person has earned no congratulations if he is relatively free from suffering compared to the experience of other people. God in his own wisdom may "pamper" some people because he knows they are not mature enough to benefit from his chastening hand.

The book of Lamentations never asserts that some people suffer more than others because they are more sinful. Yet every chapter in Lamentations includes confession of the sin of God's people, affirming that their guilt has brought divine judgment. Chapter by chapter, poem by poem, this reality is acknowledged:

Confession of Sin in Lamentations 1
The LORD has brought her grief
     because of her many *sins*. (Lam. 1:5 NIV)

Jerusalem has *sinned greatly*
     and so has become unclean. (Lam. 1:8 NIV)

My sins have been bound into a yoke;
     by his hands they were woven together. (Lam. 1:14 NIV)

In all three of these passages, the multitude of sins is the reason for the people's calamity. Not once, but many times across the fourteen hundred years since the days of their father Abraham, the people of Israel have sinned.

See, O LORD, how distressed I am!
    I am in torment within.
    In my heart I am disturbed,
for I have been most rebellious. (Lam. 1:20 NIV)

The poet manifests a sorrow for sin that serves as an essential part of proper repentance. He represents the people as being distressed, disturbed, in torment. Why are they in this situation? The rebellious-ness of their souls against the LORD OF THE COVENANT has brought about this distress of soul.

Confession of Sin in Lamentations 2
The visions of your prophets
    were false and worthless;
They did not *expose your sin*
    to ward off your captivity.
The oracles they gave you
    were false and misleading. (Lam. 2:14 NIV)

Their ministers, their prophets, set apart by God to declare his word to the people—they have delivered false and worthless messages by failing to expose the people's sin. If only these spokesmen for God had fulfilled their responsibility of warning the people of the conse-quences of their wrongdoing, the nation's calamity might have been avoided. But because the people continued unchecked in their wicked ways, divine judgment became inevitable.

What a word of warning this message of Lamentations holds for preachers and teachers of God's Word today. Not without good reason, the apostle James severely warns people who presume to take to themselves the office of prophet/pastor/teacher:

Not many of you should presume to be teachers, my brothers, because you know that we who teach will be judged more strictly. (James 3:1)

Confession of Sin in Lamentations 3
Why should any living man complain
    when punished *for his sins*?
Let us examine our ways and test them,
    and let us return to the LORD.
Let us lift up our hearts and our hands
    to God in heaven, and say:
"*We have sinned and rebelled*
    and you have not forgiven." (Lam. 3:39–42 NIV)

Sin removes any basis for complaint against the LORD. Never has the LORD mistreated a single one of his creatures, much less his own children. Whatever chastening a person undergoes in this life, it is far less than what his sin deserves. So why should any sinner complain about the chastenings of the LORD, however severe those chastenings might be? With Job, every sinner must declare, "I am unworthy—how can I reply to you? I put my hand over my mouth" (Job 40:4 NIV). When a person rails against God for the calamities that come to his life, he demonstrates that he has not comprehended the depth of his own sin, or the depth of God's wisdom in all his purposes and plans.

In all the history of humanity, only one person could legitimately complain against his calamity, and that was Jesus the Christ, the altogether innocent Lamb of God. Yet knowing that his sufferings provided the only way of redemption for his beloved people, Jesus gave expression to not a single complaint. Like a lamb led to the slaughter, he opened not his mouth in complaint. As he anticipated the coming events of the fateful next day while in the garden of Gethsemane, his final word was: "Shall I not drink the cup the Father has given me?" (John 18:11). His "My God, my God, why . . . ," cried out from the cross, was not in complaint but in response to the sudden, stunning realization of what it meant to actually experience separation from the Father, equivalent to hell itself (Matt. 27:46). How awesome is the response to suffering by this single Innocent One who bore the just punishment for our sins in his body on the tree without uttering even a whisper of complaint.

Confession of Sin in Lamentations 4
The iniquity of my people
   is greater than the sin of Sodom
which was overthrown in a moment,
   and no one wrung their hands for her. (Lam. 4:6)

How could it be that God regards Israel's sin as greater than the depravity of Sodom and Gomorrah? The difficulty in answering this question is displayed in numerous English translations that render the Hebrew words that normally mean "iniquity" and "sin" (חַטָּאת ,עָוֹן)

as "chastisement" or "punishment" (NIV, ESV, RSV).[31] As a consequence, the passage is interpreted to mean "Our punishment is greater than Sodom's" rather than "Our iniquity is greater than Sodom's."

But the parallelism of these two words that mean "iniquity" and "sin" in an overwhelming number of cases strongly favors understanding these terms in their most basic meaning. The phrase declares that Israel's sin, not Israel's suffering, has been greater than Sodom's.

But how could it be? The patriarchal city of Sodom fully displayed its depravity when the entire male community, both young and old, stormed Lot's threshold and demanded that he release his visitors so that they could homosexually gang-rape them (Gen. 19:4–5, 9).

The reason that Israel's sin may be judged as greater than Sodom's is twofold. On the one hand, Israel's degeneration into sin was indeed extreme. Along with the increase of idolatry came the introduction of Baal-worship with its temple prostitution as well as child sacrifice (cf. 2 Chron. 33:3–6, 9). Though the sin of Sodom was great, it never reached this low point realized by the people bearing God's name. As a second consideration, God's just judgments always take into account the illumination of truth that has been made available to a particular people. For centuries, the LORD had sent to Israel and Judah his servants the prophets. They had proclaimed the truth to these people in ways never before experienced by any other nation of the world. For that reason if for no other, it could be rightly said that Israel's sin and guilt were greater than Sodom's. So it should not have surprised anyone that Judah experienced the devastations of its exile.

31. The Hebrew words are *avon* (עָוֹן) and *chatat* (חַטָּאת). While *avon* on occasion may convey the idea of "punishment," the concept of "iniquity" prevails in the great majority of cases. The second term, *chatat*, almost exclusively means "sin" or "wrongdoing." Taken together, the concept of "iniquity" or "sin" is strengthened, since the consistent use of *chatat* would impact the meaning assigned to *avon*. The LXX recognizes these prevailing significances by translating both words as ἀνομία, "lawlessness." The NIV translates the first word as "punishment," and leaves a blank for the second, more definitive word. The ESV translates the two words as "chastisement" and "punishment." The KJV as well as the NKJV combines the two concepts by rendering the first word as "punishment of the iniquity," and the second word as "punishment of the sin." Only the NASU offers the more justifiable rendering of the two words as "iniquity" and "sin."

This principle of God's exercising his just judgments on the basis of available light of truth must be factored into every evaluation of the sinfulness embedded in various cultures and generations. As Jesus said of the cities of his own day, "It will be more tolerable on the day of judgment for the land of Sodom than for you" (Matt. 11:24 ESV; cf. Matt. 10:15; Luke 10:12). The greater light of truth provided by God's grace to favored cities and nations of the world today magnifies the guiltiness that falls on them as a consequence of their sin.

Additional confession of sin is found in this fourth poem:

> The kings of the earth did not believe, nor did any of the world's
>   people,
>   that enemies and foes could enter the gates of Jerusalem.
> But it happened *because of the sins of her prophets and the iniqui-*
>   *ties of her priests,*
>   who shed within her the blood of the righteous. (Lam. 4:12–13 NIV)

The unbelievable has happened—unbelievable even to the pagan nations surrounding Israel. How is it possible that the city chosen by the mighty God of the exodus, the conquest, and the glorious kingdom of his Messiah could fall prey to its enemies? Only one explanation is adequate. It must have happened because of the sins of its people— sins committed particularly by its religious leaders, its prophets and priests. They are the ones who shed the blood of the righteous. As a consequence, the nation could not escape God's just judgments.

Confession of Sin in Lamentations 5

> *Our fathers sinned* and are no more,
>   and we bear their punishment. (Lam. 5:7 NIV)[32]

> Joy is gone from our hearts;
>   our dancing has turned to mourning.
> The crown has fallen from our head.
>   Woe to us, *for we have sinned*! (Lam. 5:15–16 NIV)

---

32. In this case, the translation of *avon* as "punishment" is justified, since this *avon* is described as a burden to be borne that has been brought about by *chatat*, which in this case must be translated "sin."

This last chapter of Lamentations continues to drive home the same theme. Sin has caused the people's calamities. Both the sins of the fathers and the sins of the sons, who inevitably reflect the sins of the fathers, are cited as the reason for their miserable, unhappy state. How could they manifest joy and celebrate with dancing when they are so conscious that their sin has caused these calamities?

What does a person do when he recognizes that his sin has caused his calamity? If you cannot justify yourself, how can you endure your tragedies? What can you do with the burdensome sense of guilt in your soul in the day of disaster? You cannot forget it. You cannot suppress it. You cannot do adequate penance for it. Obviously, you cannot rejoice and dance over it.

What, then, do you do?

You confess it. You acknowledge your guilt. In true repentance as you repudiate the sinful act, you cry out to God for his mercy. That's all you can do. That's what the suffering people of God must do in the process of their lamentations.

In a time of grief and calamity, it is essential to bare the sins of your soul before God. A critical part of godly sorrow must be confession of sin. It has been observed that no such thing as a "clear conscience" exists at a graveside. All the mourners know that they could have done more for the deceased than they have done. Part of godly sorrow is the work of repentance, of confession before God of all wrongdoing, acknowledging sins of omission as well as commission. Apart from an ordered acknowledgment of sin, the perplexities arising from calamity will never be properly resolved.

So Lamentations repeatedly acknowledges the sin of God's people. Their root sin was the idolatrous turning away from the worship of the one true and living God. This false worship resulted in the most heinous of sins: they have sacrificed their own infant children and have consumed their own infants' flesh (2 Chron. 33:6; cf. Lam. 2:20; 4:10).

God Has Ordered It

As many as eighteen images occur in the first sixteen verses of Lamentations 3, all of them driving home the truth that the COVENANT LORD himself, the God of Israel, is the source of all his people's calamities. The constant reference throughout these verses to a singular person as the recipient of these chastening judgments from the LORD has the effect of personalizing the awareness of God's involvement in your tragedies. God's wrath directs his rod of chastening specifically toward each individual as well as toward the community as a whole. Even the prophet himself is identified by this all-inclusive "I."

God has driven this person like cattle. God has made him dwell in darkness like those who have been long dead. He has walled him in and weighed him down in chains. Like a bear lying in wait, like a lion in hiding, God has mangled him. The LORD OF THE COVENANT has drawn his bow and shot arrows into his liver. He has filled him with gall and bitter herbs. He has broken his teeth with gravel and made him grovel in the dust (Lam. 3:1–16).

These startling images of God's direct involvement in the calamities that come into the lives of his people can create serious difficulties. Is it actually God that drives you along, pushing, shoving, relentlessly pressuring? Is he the one that brings unexpected calamities into your life, as a bear might attack with suddenness and strength? Has not our Lord said, If a son asks for bread, will his father give a stone instead? Or a serpent instead of a fish, a scorpion for an egg (Luke 11:11–12)? Yet life invariably takes on this puzzling perspective. Many people attribute these kinds of trials to Satan rather than God.

The question why a singular individual is represented as receiving these chastening blows may be answered in different ways. Just as the singular "she" of chapter 1 refers to the city of Jerusalem and its multiple inhabitants, so this singular "he" of chapter 3 may embody a reference to multiple sufferers among God's people. At the same time, the singular form underscores the involvement of individuals as individuals in these tragedies. The individualization of the suffering image enables every sufferer to identify with the agonies, the pains, the prayers of this lamenter. Each and every person living through all the attendant tragedies of Jerusalem's fall, together with every sufferer among the people of God across all ages, may identify himself with the "I" of Lamentations. If the poet had not spoken in this individualistic way, this universal identity of the sufferer in Lamentations with "Everyman" would not have been so easy.

Even beyond the representation of Everyman, there also resides that unique figure of someone who suffers for others. Jeremiah the prophet also suffers. In a very essential sense, he may be seen as an innocent sufferer. The weeping prophet bears in himself the pain of others. So the prophet embodies a prophecy within himself.

In addition to the vivid imagery of chapter 3, several other sections in Lamentations attribute this tragedy to the plans and purposes of Israel's God:

> The COVENANT LORD has caused her grief. (Lam. 1:5)

> Is any suffering like my suffering that was inflicted on me,
>   that the LORD brought on me in the day of his fierce anger?
>   (Lam. 1:12 NIV)

The poet vividly depicts the role of the LORD in all his people's sufferings in a section extending across three consecutive stanzas in the first chapter. God has sent fire into his bones, has spread a net for his feet, has made him faint all day long, has woven a yoke about his neck, has summoned an army to crush his young men, and has trampled the virgin daughter of Judah in his winepress (Lam. 1:13–15).

Even more extensively, twenty-four lines in eight consecutive stanzas of the second song describe the LORD's role in their devastations.[33] The LORD has covered the daughter of Zion with the cloud of his anger, he has swallowed up all the dwellings of Jacob, he has cut off every horn of Israel, he has burned like a flaming fire, he has slain all who were pleasing to the eye, he has multiplied mourning and lamentation for the daughter of Judah, he has spurned both king and priest, he has rejected his altar and abandoned his sanctuary, he has torn down her wall and made ramparts lament (Lam. 2:1–8). In a raw statement of God's involvement in these calamities, the poet gives recognition to the fulfillment of the LORD's specific purpose in Israel's devastation:

---

33. A single exception in these verses that identify the LORD as the source of their trials (Lam. 2:1–8) may be found in the last line of Lamentations 2:7, which states that "they," the Babylonians, have raised a shout in the house of the LORD. But in all the remaining twenty-four lines of the eight stanzas (counting one extra line in verse 6), it is "He," God, who has initiated all of Judah's calamities.

308

The COVENANT LORD has done
    what he determined;
He has carried out his Word
    which he decreed ages ago. (Lam. 2:17)

The fulfillment of precisely what the LORD had planned and decreed in these tragic events may be seen as consummately anticipating the divine ordering of all events related to the climactic sufferings of God's holy servant:

Indeed Herod and Pontius Pilate met together with the Gentiles and the people of Israel in this city to conspire against your holy servant Jesus, whom you anointed. They did *what your power and will had decided beforehand should happen.* (Acts 4:27–28 NIV)

The wicked forces of men and nations may do their worst in the devastations worked on the people of God. But in the end they will accomplish only what the LORD himself has determined.

The fourth poem in Lamentations continues this theme of the sovereignty of the LORD in the sufferings of his people:

The LORD has given full vent to his wrath;
    he has poured out his fierce anger.
He kindled a fire in Zion
    that consumed her foundations. (Lam. 4:11 NIV)

The LORD himself has scattered them;
    he no longer watches over them.
The priests are shown no honor,
    the elders no favor. (Lam. 4:16 NIV)

The LORD's destruction of the city's foundations as well as the withdrawal of his watchcare suggests some finality in his actions against the city and its people. Yet in this very affirmation that the LORD has done these things may be found a seed of hope. Because of God's purpose in their devastation, a hope for the future may be expressed. As the final chapter of Lamentations declares:

You, O LORD, reign forever;
    Your throne endures from generation to generation. (Lam. 5:19 NIV)

On this basis, and on this basis alone, the people of God may have hope even in the deepest darkness of their distress. This fact leads to the final truth of the book of Lamentations: Calamity has come. This calamity has come because of the people's sin. Whatever the calamity might be, God has ordered it. In view of God's direct involvement in their sufferings, his people may hope nonetheless.

Hope Nonetheless

The message of hope in the book of Lamentations is not nearly so extensive as the depiction of God's involvement in Israel's judgments. In fact, one commentator describes the message of Lamentations as "a theology ending in a question mark."[34] So it should not be surprising that images vivifying that hope are also limited. But a word of hope is clearly present, and serves as a necessary balancing factor in the godly expression of grief.

Hope in Lamentations 1

The opening image of the book provides some small ray of hope. For Israel is not portrayed as a woman divorced but as a widow in despair (Lam. 1:1).[35] In contrast with Hosea's earlier picture of unfaithful Israel (Hos. 2:4–5), this image speaks more of pity than of blame.

In the first chapter, encouragements of hope come only in the form of a modest prayer, a plea for the LORD to look, to see, to observe, to consider the devastated condition of his people:

> Look, O LORD, on my affliction,
>   for the enemy has triumphed. (Lam. 1:9c NIV)

> Look, O LORD, and consider,
>   for I am despised. (Lam. 1:11c NIV)

> See, O LORD, how distressed I am!
>   I am in torment within, and in my heart I am disturbed. (Lam. 1:20)

---

34. Provan, *Lamentations*, 24, quoting J. Renkema. In his own evaluation, Provan says: "After many struggles, it is doubt, not hope, with which the book leaves us; and to characterize Lamentations as a hopeful book is therefore to mislead" (22–23).
35. Berlin, *Lamentations*, 8.

If only the LORD OF THE COVENANT would take notice, that would be enough. How could he fail to intervene on their behalf if he sees his own covenant people in their suffering?

Hope in Lamentations 2

The second chapter of Lamentations continues to arouse some faint movements of hope by the direct involvement of the prophet himself. First, he positions himself as someone who might intervene so that they could receive some comfort from him:

> What witness shall I give about you?
>> To what shall I compare you,
>>> O daughter of Jerusalem?
> What can I liken you to,
>> that I may comfort you,
>>> O virgin daughter of Zion?
>>> For as vast as the sea is your wound.
>>> Who can heal you? (Lam. 2:13)

The prophet looks for a way to provide comfort to his suffering people. He seeks some comparison that might stir the Almighty to action and relieve them of their trials. For none but the LORD can help them. This depth of care by the prophet provides some small ray of hope for Israel.

Second, the prophet urges the people to never stop pleading with the LORD:

> The hearts of the people cry out to the Lord.
> O wall of the Daughter of Zion,
>> let your tears flow like a river day and night;
>> give yourself no relief, your eyes no rest.
> Arise, cry out in the night, as the watches of the night begin;
>> pour out your heart like water in the presence of the Lord.
> Lift up your hands to him for the lives of your children,
>> who faint from hunger at the head of every street. (Lam. 2:18–19 NIV)

By urging this constant pleading, the poet seeks to move the heart of the LORD, which is the only hope for this devastated people. The intensity of their prayer is vividly depicted in the image of tears flowing from their wall, in the persistence of prayers that continue day and night, in the pouring out of the heart as they present before the LORD their children, fainting from hunger in the streets.

Third, the poet offers his own dramatic pleadings in behalf of his people:

> Look, O LORD, and consider;
>> whom have you ever treated like this?
> Should women eat their offspring,
>> the children they have cared for?
> Should priest and prophet be killed
>> in the sanctuary of the Lord? (Lam. 2:20 NIV)

How could the LORD OF THE COVENANT close his eyes forever to the calamities of his own people? Must their suffering go to these extremes? Must these agonies continue forever? The prophet pleads his case on their behalf even as he simultaneously affirms that they have received no more than they have deserved for their sins.

In these pleas may be found a faint glimmer of hope. For if there were no hope, what would be the point of crying out to the COVENANT LORD in the midst of all these distresses?

Hope in Lamentations 3

The message of hope climaxes in the central section of the third poem. To this point, expressions of hope have appeared only in the form of prayers—prayers offered by prophet and people. Yet steps of progress have been steadily advancing toward a full manifestation of the prophet's hopefulness. For only after the pleadings in hope may be found the assurances of hope. Let no one presume that God will intervene even in the most tragic of circumstances apart from the heartfelt cries of his people.

The most significant image of hope for God's lamenting people is embedded in the description of God himself as their personal possession: "The LORD is my portion; therefore I will wait for him" (Lam. 3:24 NIV). This phrase echoes the words of the psalmist:

You are my portion, O LORD; I have promised to obey your words. (Ps. 119:57 NIV)

I cry to you, O LORD; I say, "You are my refuge, my portion in the land of the living." (Ps. 142:5 NIV)

Jeremiah himself had expressed his hope in terms of God as Jacob's portion:

He who is the Portion of Jacob is not like idols. For he is the Maker of all things. (Jer. 10:16; cf. 51:19)

More anciently, this concept of the LORD himself as the portion of his people finds its roots in the declaration that the Levites would have no portion of the land assigned to them. Instead, the LORD himself would be their inheritance (Josh. 18:7; cf. Num. 18:20; Deut. 10:8–9; 18:1–2; Josh. 13:33). This dramatic figure of God himself as the portion of his people instills hope, just as the phrase in Lamentations indicates: "The LORD is my portion; therefore I will wait for him" (Lam. 3:24 NIV). The devastated people of the LORD may put their hope in the fact that they are a nation of priests who possess the LORD himself as their portion. Even if the sacred city and temple are destroyed, even if the whole of the land is taken from them, nothing can take away the LORD. As a holy priesthood of the Maker of heaven and earth, they have all creation as belonging to the Creator that forever remains their portion. On this firm basis they can found their hope in the future.

A further ray of hope finds expression in the turn of the image of a "yoke" from a negative to a positive perspective. In Lamentations the "yoke" first appears as a sign of the burdensome chastenings imposed on Israel from the LORD (Lam. 1:14). But subsequently this same image appears in a positive light: "It is good [!] for a man to bear the yoke in his youth" (3:27). Suddenly all their tragedy is viewed from a different perspective. It can actually serve to mature a person and a nation so that they can give greater glory to their Creator and Redeemer. Even in the harshest of experiences that Israel has undergone through the destruction of Jerusalem, God does not intend "to crush underfoot all prisoners in the land" (3:34).

In this climactic section of the book, the essential characteristics of Israel's COVENANT LORD provide the foundation for hope despite devastation. Several aspects of the nature of her God are underscored. First among these characteristics are the covenant love of the LORD (חַסְדֵי יְהוָה) and the tenderness of his compassion (רָחַם). As the prophet says:

> I keep returning to this one reality in my heart;
> > therefore I have hope.
> Because of the multiple manifestations of his covenant love
> > we are not consumed. (Lam. 3:21–22)

> For though he brings grief,
> > yet he shows compassion by the breadth of his covenant love.
> > > (Lam. 3:32)

Nothing in these affirmations of the LORD's covenant faithfulness denies the fact that the sufferings of the people occur by the LORD's purposes. He is the one who brings the grief. Yet because he forever remains faithful to his own covenantal initiatives, they can live in hope despite their disasters. The tenderness of his heart toward his people restrains him from totally consuming them.

Other sources of hope find their roots in God's faithfulness and goodness. As the poet says:

> His tender mercies never fail;
> > they are new morning by morning.
> Great is your faithfulness. [רַבָּה אֱמוּנָתֶךָ] (Lam. 3:22–23)

> How good is the COVENANT LORD [טוֹב יְהוָה]
> > to those who wait for him,
> > to the one who seeks him with all his being. (Lam. 3:25)

God has always been faithful to fulfill his Word. Once he speaks a promise, he never fails to bring it to complete realization. For this reason, his people can continue in hope even in the midst of the most devastating circumstance. In addition, this God is simply and profoundly *good*! No malice can be found in him. This goodness embraces each and every one of his thoughts and actions. Therefore, his people can anticipate a positive final outcome from his every action, no matter how drastic the circumstances may appear at the time.

It is not always recognized that the familiar hymn "Great Is Thy Faithfulness" arises directly out of these hope-filled words in Lamentations 3:

> Great is thy faithfulness,
>   O God my Father;
> there is no shadow
>   of turning with thee.
> Thou changest not,
>   thy compassions, they fail not;
> as thou hast been
>   thou forever wilt be.
>   Great is thy faithfulness!
>   Great is thy faithfulness!
>   Morning by morning
>   new mercies I see.
>   All I have needed
>   thy hand has provided—
>   Great is thy faithfulness,
>   Lord, unto me![36]

Hope is also encouraged by firm affirmations of what the LORD will not do, and what will never be found in his heart:

> The Lord will not cast off forever. (Lam. 3:31 KJV, ESV)

> He does not afflict from his heart
>   or grieve the children of men. (Lam. 3:33 ESV [2016])

Sometimes in the midst of tragic circumstances, a person may be tempted to attribute wrong goals or evil motives to the LORD. But the LORD OF THE COVENANT must never be accused of even contemplating anything wrong.

36. Thomas O. Chisholm, "Great Is Thy Faithfulness" (1923).

In view of the LORD's covenant love, his compassion, his faithfulness, and his goodness, the prophet encourages his people to respond positively to their disasters. They are to "have hope," to "wait for the LORD," to "seek him," to "wait with quiet expectation," to "bear the yoke," to "examine and test their ways," to "return to the LORD," to "lift up heart with hands to God in the heavens" (Lam. 3:21, 24, 25, 26, 27, 29, 40, 41).

A most important element of godly lamentation is found in this challenge to hope. Each and every admonition intends to stir up the people's trust in the LORD despite their disasters. Apart from a manifestation of ongoing hope in the LORD, the expression of grief will be distorted. Whether the tragedy is one of individual loss or of corporate calamity, hope must be given its proper place. Otherwise, the very nature of God as good, merciful, faithful, and compassionate will be tragically denied.

The contrasting conclusion of the life of Peter and of Judas vivifies the difference between weeping in hope and entertaining remorse in despair. Peter wept over his denials of the Lord (Matt. 26:75), but later leaped into the water to swim to Jesus and be restored to him (John 21:7–15). But Judas in his remorse flung the thirty pieces of blood money into the temple and then went out and hanged himself (Matt. 27:3–5). "Godly sorrow brings repentance that leads to salvation and leaves no regret, but worldly sorrow brings death" (2 Cor. 7:10 NIV).

The final section of this middle chapter of the book speaks once more in the first-person singular (Lam. 3:48–66). First, this pious individual intercedes for his suffering people (3:48–51). His eyes fill with tears when he sees them in their pain. He vows to continue his mourning "until the LORD looks down from heaven and sees" (3:50 NIV). Then he remembers how he had called on the LORD, who took up his case and redeemed his life from all his enemies (3:52–58). Finally, he asks the LORD to vindicate his cause and pay back his enemies exactly what they deserve (3:59–66).

This portion of the third poem presumes the reality of an innocent sufferer, the rightness of his cause, and the proper character of a prayer for judgment on his enemies. This innocent sufferer speaks of the wrong that has been done to him (Lam. 3:59a). He pleads with the LORD: "Uphold my cause" (3:59b). Twice he refers to "all their plots against me" (3:60–61). So it is altogether appropriate that he anticipates by prayer the utter destruction of these enemies of the LORD and his chosen people.

In the full context of redemptive history, these truths may be fully appreciated only when the perfect and innocent Christ in union with his people is brought into full view. Apart from him, there can be no sufferers who may be regarded as genuinely innocent. But in union with the Righteous One, all his people appear in the perfections of his righteousness and holiness. In sharpest contrast, their tormentors show themselves to be malicious by all their maltreatments. As a consequence, they deserve the destructive judgment that the LORD will eventually bring on them. In the end, the final comfort of God's suffering people can be anticipated only in connection with the destruction of all his and their enemies.

Hope in Lamentations 4–5

The final two chapters of Lamentations return to a more modest expression of hope for the people. Though placed in a negative framework, the mention of their Messiah, the Anointed King of Israel, provides a slight ray of hope when read in its fullest context. The poet declares:

> The Lord's Anointed, our very life breath,
>> was caught in their traps.
> We thought that under his shadow
>> we would live among the nations. (Lam. 4:20 NIV)

A dark shade of disappointed expectation hovers over the image of their King/Messiah/Savior. Yet two verses later, the message of hope revives:

> O Daughter of Zion, your punishment will end;
>> he will not prolong your exile. (Lam. 4:22 NIV)

If their exile comes to an end, then their Anointed King must return to his throne. So despite the disappointment that their King had failed to establish them firmly in an honorable status among the nations of the world, they must not surrender their hope in him as they look to the future. This hope finds full expression in the later prophecies of Jeremiah as well as in the exilic and postexilic prophets.[37] But even as the holy city of Jerusalem smolders in the ashes of the Babylonian invasion, hope of return from exile is clearly evident.

The final chapter of the book begins and ends with a prayer for the LORD to remember the Israelites in their calamity and to bring them back from their exile:

> Remember, O COVENANT LORD, what has happened to us;
>> look, and see our shame. (Lam. 5:1)

> Cause us to return to yourself, O COVENANT LORD, so that we will
>> be able to return;
>> make our days brand-new, just as they were in ancient times.
>> (Lam. 5:21)

In multiple ways, these concluding prayers manifest a total dependence on the COVENANT LORD for every hope of restoration. The LORD must remember the people's disaster and their shame. He must take the initiative in causing them to return. To him and to no other they must return. The only way that they will be able to return is for him to enable them. Only he can renew their days. Just as all the blessings of ancient times depended wholly on him, so he alone can reinstitute those days of blessing.

As a preface to his final petition, the prophet lifts the people's vision beyond the immediate time and circumstance of their current calamity:

> You, O COVENANT LORD, sit enthroned forever;
>> your throne endures from generation to generation. (Lam. 5:19)

Far beyond the reaches of rising and falling nations, including even the kingdom of Israel, the LORD sits undisturbed on his throne. His sovereign reign extends across the generations. This very fact provides a basis of hope for the future. For as sovereign LORD, he can restore the people beyond all their experience of calamity.

---

37. Cf. some references to this hope as it develops through the prophets anticipating exile, experiencing exile, and restored after exile in Robertson, *The Christ of the Prophets*, 204–6 (Hosea); 209–10 (Amos); 220–27 (Isaiah); 276–78 (Jeremiah); 300–317 (Ezekiel); 373–89 (Haggai and Zechariah).

Yet in one final expression of the people's humbling themselves before the LORD, the prophet acknowledges the LORD's sovereignty in determining whether or not this restoration will occur:

Make our days brand-new, just as they were in ancient times,
   unless you have utterly rejected us
   and are provoked in your anger against us to the ultimate.
    (Lam. 5:21b–22)

This level of humility opens the way for great hope among God's devastated people. They recognize with all honesty that they do not deserve restoration. Yet they know of the mercy of the LORD, and lay a strong grip on the promises of his covenant.

CONCLUSION

The amazing testimony of the book of Lamentations centers on the reality of the COVENANT LORD's unswerving commitment to redeem a people to himself. Despite the seriousness of the calamity that has come on his own people, they can still count on him to accomplish his ultimate goal of their salvation. How striking it is that this conquering nation of Babylon, the instrument in God's hand for the chastisement of his people, in a few short years disappears altogether from the pages of human history. But this weakened, defeated, devastated people rise again in the second temple of Israel's restoration, and climactically in the third temple in the body of their Messiah. It is the work of God's grace that no man can destroy. This grace is seen in the resilience of the defeated nation's faith. Though the "gods" of the Babylonians had apparently triumphed over the people, they refused to transfer their faith from the LORD OF THE COVENANT to the god of the idols. As one commentator has noted, they "refused to concede victory to the deities of their conquerors and instead continued steadfastly to engage Yahweh, prayerfully, liturgically, even if not always in unabashed adulation."[38]

From the five poems of this book, God's people across the generations may learn how to weep in a godly fashion. They must recognize that calamity both corporately and individually has come even to God's people, and will continue to come. They must confess with humble,

---

38. Dobbs-Allsopp, *Lamentations*, 41.

self-searching, penetrating thoroughness that their own sin has caused it. Indeed, not in every case of calamity is sin directly the cause. Yet always searching of soul and confession of sin must provide its healing balm. They must affirm that God in the wisdom of his justice and his grace has ordered it. They must triumphantly affirm by their faith that they hope nonetheless. In this way of godly weeping, they will learn that godly sorrow works salvation.

Selected Bibliography for Lamentations

Albrektson, Bertil. *Studies in the Text and Theology of the Book of Lamentations*. Studia Theologica Lundensia 21. Lund: CWK Gleerup, 1963.

Berlin, Adele. *Lamentations: A Commentary*. Old Testament Library. Louisville: Westminster John Knox, 2002.

Dobbs-Allsopp, F. W. *Lamentations*. Interpretation: A Bible Commentary for Teaching and Preaching. Louisville: John Knox, 2002.

Gordis, Robert. *The Song of Songs and Lamentations: A Study, Modern Translation and Commentary*. New York: KTAV, 1974.

Gottwald, Norman K. *Studies in the Book of Lamentations*. Studies in Biblical Theology 14. London: SCM Press, 1954.

Harrison, R. K. *Jeremiah and Lamentations: An Introduction and Commentary*. TOTC. Nottingham, UK: Inter-Varsity Press, 1973.

Hillers, Delbert R. *Lamentations: A New Translation with Introduction and Commentary*. 2nd ed. AB 7A. New York: Doubleday, 1992.

Kaiser, Walter C. Jr. *Grief and Pain in the Plan of God: Christian Assurance and the Message of Lamentations*. Ross-shire, Scotland: Christian Focus Publications, 2004.

Keil, C. F. *Biblical Commentary on the Old Testament: The Twelve Minor Prophets*. Edinburgh: T. & T. Clark, 1871.

———. *The Prophecies of Jeremiah and the Lamentations of Jeremiah*. Biblical Commentary on the Old Testament. Grand Rapids: Eerdmans, 1980.

Pritchard, James B., ed. *Ancient Near Eastern Texts Relating to the Old Testament*. 3rd ed. Princeton, NJ: Princeton University Press, 1969.

Provan, Iain W. *Lamentations*. NCBC. Grand Rapids: Eerdmans, 1991.

Robertson, O. Palmer. *The Christ of the Prophets*. Phillipsburg, NJ: P&R Publishing, 2004.

Salters, R. B. *A Critical and Exegetical Commentary on Lamentations*. London: T. &. T. Clark, 2010.

Westermann, Claus. *Lamentations: Issues and Interpretation*. Minneapolis: Augsburg Fortress, 1994.

THE SONG OF SONGS
HOW TO LOVE

CHAPTER OUTLINE

INTRODUCTION

Now comes the king with his bride. All the pomp and circumstance that would be expected for a royal wedding permeate this poem. Yet the quiet intimacies of relationship between a man and a woman are also present.[1] It's all in holy Scripture, teaching God's people "how to love."

As in other wisdom literature of the old covenant Scriptures, the king serves as the abiding model for God's work of restoring his people to the fullness of life. This unique piece of literature vividly depicts the intimacies of love in the marriage relationship as experienced by king and queen, anticipating the life of "Everyman" redeemed by God's work of restoring his fallen creation. As a poem about human love, this best of all songs "looks at what it is like to be in love from both a woman's and a man's point of view, and it relies exclusively on dialogue, so that we learn about love through what lovers say about it."[2]

---

1. The assertion that there is no wedding and therefore no proper marriage in the Song of Songs overlooks the larger context of the message of the Song in terms of a restoration of the original relation of man to woman as it existed in the garden of Eden. Adam and Eve had no wedding ceremony to seal the original relationship. Yet they were clearly "married" in the eyes of their Creator. The Song of Songs should be read in this context—as a picture of the restoration of fallen humanity to their original state in the garden.

2. J. Cheryl Exum, *Song of Songs: A Commentary* (Louisville: Westminster John Knox, 2005), 1. Says Exum: "By presenting the lovers in the act of addressing each other, the poem gives us the impression that we are overhearing them and observing their love unfold" (4). She continues: "The key to this unfolding is the dialogue. The dialogue format, though not unique, is certainly unusual. . . . It represents itself as offering both points of view, a woman's and a man's. . . . As is the case with any good writer, their voices seem authentic" (4). Exum's commentary is distinctive in that its prose comments on the text

INTRODUCTORY MATTERS

Title of the Book

The books of Proverbs, Ecclesiastes, and Song of Songs among the wisdom books of the old covenant each possess a title that communicates relevant information concerning the specific literary piece.[3] This particular wisdom book contains the title "The Song of Songs, which is Solomon's" (Song 1:1). By the phrase "song of songs," this work presents the "best of songs," celebrating the greatest theme among earthly experiences that humans ever sing about.[4]

The additional phrase "which is Solomon's" could indicate that the material is "about" Solomon, "dedicated to" Solomon, "written by" Solomon, or even "in critique of" Solomon. A similar breadth of possible meanings may be found in the common notation titling a number of psalms. The recurrent phrase *ledavid* is frequently translated "of David," which may mean that the specific psalm is "about" David, "dedicated to" David, or "written by" David. The additional relative pronoun found only in this title of the Song of Songs, "which is" Solomon's (אֲשֶׁר לִשְׁלֹמֹה), might provide further testimony supporting the Solomonic authorship of the Song, though the phrase could be interpreted otherwise.[5]

---

of the Song take on a poetic character, which is quite fitting for the subject matter, but seldom even approximated in biblical commentaries.

3. In the traditions of Judaism, the Song of Songs is the first of the five Megilloth or "Rolls" (i.e., "Scrolls") read in connection with certain annual festivals. The Song was read at Passover, Ruth at Pentecost, Lamentations at the Ninth of Ab (generally early August), Qohelet at the Feast of Booths, and Esther at the Feast of Purim. Cf. S. R. Driver, *An Introduction to the Literature of the Old Testament*, 9th ed. (Edinburgh: T. & T. Clark, 1913), 435n.

4. Comparable phrases indicating the superlative include "holy of holies," "heaven of heavens," and "servant of servants" (Ex. 29:37; Deut. 10:14; Gen. 9:25).

5. Christian D. Ginsburg, *The Song of Songs* (London: Longman, 1857), 2, observes that the additional "which is" Solomon's is "owing to the article" in "The Song of Songs," "which generally, though not always, is followed by this pronoun." Ginsburg concludes that the meaning "respecting Solomon" is contrary to usage. He affirms subsequently that the title "designates Solomon as the author," although he proceeds to assert: "but internal evidence is against it" (124).

The Question of Solomonic Authorship

Extensive discussion has concentrated on the question of Solomon's role as author of the Song of Songs. Three considerations stand out as the principal arguments against authorship by Solomon: (1) the language of the Song suits a date later than Solomon; (2) the Song consists of a collection of love songs composed across several centuries, which would naturally exclude Solomonic authorship; (3) Solomon cannot be considered as a suitable model for a proper marriage relationship.

In response to these concerns, several observations may be noted. First, recent studies have seriously questioned the decisive character of linguistic considerations in dating the Song well beyond the tenth-century B.C. era of Solomon.[6] Second, despite differences among the various songs that constitute the book, an inherent unity of perspective binds the songs together. Says one commentator:

> The individual poems themselves attest a world of imagery, a literary style and form, and a pathos that point in the direction of a unified composition rather than a mere anthology.[7]

Third, with respect to the propriety of Solomon's serving as a role model for the ideal marriage, Solomonic authorship would underscore one important truth that permeates Scripture. God's grace toward

---

6. Regarding the appropriateness of the book's language for Solomonic times, cf. the thorough investigation into the distinctive features of the language of the Song in Ian Young, *Diversity in Pre-Exilic Hebrew* (Tübingen: J. C. B. Mohr, 1993), 157–65. Young notes that only the Song among all the biblical books consistently uses *se* to the exclusion of *aser* for the relative pronoun (163). He observes that in proportion to the size of the book, the Song has more *hapax legomena* than any other book in the Old Testament, even exceeding the number found in the 150 chapters of Psalms, supporting the book's poetic authenticity and antiquity. Among other observations about the inconclusive character of dating the Song as late on the basis of linguistic considerations, including supposed Persian or Greek words, Young refers to the "first criterion" for using loanwords to date biblical books: "that the word must have a firmly established origin and etymology. Neither of the two loanwords which have been used to date the Song of Songs late, or to split it up into a disunity, passes even the first test" (162). G. Lloyd Carr, *The Song of Solomon: An Introduction and Commentary* (Leicester, UK: Inter-Varsity Press, 1984), analyzes the linguistic distinctives of the book, and concludes that the poem, "essentially complete, probably originated in the time of Solomon or shortly thereafter" (18).

7. Roland E. Murphy, *The Song of Songs: A Commentary on the Book of Canticles or The Song of Songs*, Hermeneia (Minneapolis: Fortress Press, 1990), 3.

a fallen humanity extends to all aspects of human life. The divine bestowal of blessing in the marriage relationship may occur despite extreme corruption in moral behavior. Solomon with his seven hundred wives and three hundred concubines can hardly be regarded as a paragon of virtue in the marriage relationship. Yet he can experience the blessings of the creational ordinance of marriage, which clearly displays the extent of God's grace. But let no one ever appeal to this grace as a basis for corrupting the sacred order of marriage. As the apostle Paul says, "Shall we continue in sin that grace may abound? God forbid!" (Rom. 6:1–2 KJV). Yet the manifestation of God's grace to Solomon could well provide a framework for understanding God's blessing in marriage relationships despite prevalent distortions of the ordinance.

Nothing inherent in the Song excludes the possibility of Solomon's authorship. To the contrary, several considerations favor him as the author: (1) The title is most likely read as an affirmation of authorship.[8] (2) The broad knowledge of nature suits well the description of Solomon as a person who had a thorough understanding of plant life "from the cedar of Lebanon to the hyssop that grows out of walls." In addition, he "taught about animals and birds, reptiles and fish" (1 Kings 4:33). This description of Solomon corresponds well with the fact that twenty-one varieties of plant life and fifteen different animals are mentioned in the short compass of the Song.[9] (3) The book gives evidence of an "insider's" knowledge of royal luxury. (4) Geographical references are balanced between the northern and southern regions of Palestine, suggesting a composition before the kingdom rivalry between north and south that developed after Solomon's death.[10] Even the northern city of Tirzah is favorably mentioned, which would not

---

8. Tremper Longman III, *Song of Songs*, NICOT (Grand Rapids: Eerdmans, 2001), 4, concludes that the superscription "is making the claim that Solomon wrote the Song in its entirety." He then proceeds to cite several reasons that Solomon may have written portions of the Song, but not the Song in its entirety.

9. C. F. Keil, *Introduction to the Old Testament* (Edinburgh: T. & T. Clark, 1869), 1:502, characterizes Solomon as "an eminent naturalist."

10. Mention is made without discrimination of locales in the north as well as the south of Palestine, including sites such as Jerusalem, Carmel, Sharon, Lebanon, Engedi, and Hermon.

have been done so easily after it had served as the rival capital of the northern kingdom once the division occurred at the beginning of the reign of Solomon's son Rehoboam (Song 6:4; cf. 1 Kings 15:33).[11] (5) Perhaps most significantly, Scripture specifically indicates that Solomon's "songs" "numbered a thousand and five" (1 Kings 4:32). All these various considerations provide strong internal evidence for the Solomonic authorship of the Song of Songs.

Two or Three Principal Players

Directly relevant to the matter of authorship is whether two or three persons constitute the principal individuals represented in the Song. In other words: Is the Song "in praise of God for his gift of marriage as demonstrated in the life of King Solomon"? Or is it "in praise of God for the fidelity of a young woman manifesting integrity in marriage despite the lurings of King Solomon"? Does the Song depict the beauties of marriage in the relation between Solomon and his bride? Or is the woman in the Song remaining faithful to her country lover while lecherous old Solomon attempts to add one more maiden to his collection of bedroom trophies? May the message of the Song be summarized as being "in praise of Solomon," or "in critique of Solomon"?

The idea that the Song includes three principal persons (Solomon, the Shulamite maiden, and her country lover) eliminates any problem associated with Solomon's being the ideal model for marriage.[12] For in this reading, Solomon is firmly rebuked by the young maiden's refusal

---

11. Marvin H. Pope, *The Song of Songs: A New Translation with Introduction and Commentary* (Garden City, NY: Doubleday, 1977), 22–23, has assembled various strands of internal evidence supporting the origin of the book in the days of Solomon. For fuller discussion regarding authorship, see the treatment of Longman, *Song*, 2–9. A response to each of Longman's points denying Solomonic authorship may be found in Duane Garrett, *Song of Songs*, WBC 23B (Nashville: Thomas Nelson, 2004), 24–25.

12. The identity of the woman as a "Shulamite" maiden has provided a challenge to interpreters through the ages. It has been objected that this name "Shulamite" should never be applied to a historical person from a specific place because "the main players are poetic types and not historical personages" (Longman, *Song*, 192). Yet this conclusion appears to operate on the basis of presuppositional consistency rather than on linguistic analysis of the term. Among other options, it is linguistically possible that the term represents a feminine form of the masculine *Solomon*. But as Pope, *Song*, 600, has noted, "the final word has not been written on the term *sulammit*."

to yield to his enticements. The three-player view also promotes virtue to its highest level in the realm of relations between men and women. For the young maiden remains true to her commitments to her country lover despite all the wooings of a wealthy king.[13]

The largest problem with this view is that it requires a subtle redirection of speeches, particularly when the dialogue suddenly addresses someone who is not even present. For instance, in their earliest recorded interchange, Solomon addresses the Shulamite maiden:

> You are so lovely, my dearest!
>   So strikingly beautiful!
> Your eyes have the calm beauty of doves. (Song 1:15)

The Shulamite maiden responds by addressing Solomon:

> You are so handsome, my lover!
>   So pleasant to be with.
> Our bed is luxuriant. (Song 1:16)

But in the three-player view, the maiden does not address Solomon with these expressions of affection. Instead, she directs her speech toward her country lover, who is altogether absent from the scene of this interchange between herself and Solomon. In order to accomplish this abrupt diversion of her speech, one commentator renders the biblical text so that instead of reading "*You [Solomon]* are so handsome, my lover," the passage is read "*My lover* is well-formed!," even though the text says "you" as she stands in the presence of Solomon. In this representation of the text, it is assumed that the woman addresses her absent country lover. Only through this redirection of the maiden's speech by a modification of the biblical text can this three-player rivalry among lovers be sustained.[14]

---

13. The three-player interpretation is at least as old as the twelfth century A.D., as seen in the treatment of Ibn Ezra. The tradition is maintained quite impressively by Calvin Seerveld, *The Greatest Song* (Chicago: Trinity Pennyasheet Press, 1967). Cf. also Iain W. Provan, *Ecclesiastes and Song of Songs* (Grand Rapids: Zondervan, 2001), 246.

14. Seerveld, *Song*, 25. Apparently Seerveld has substituted the Hebrew "Behold" (הִנֵּה) for "Behold you" (הִנְּךָ), which would enable him to have the woman address her country lover rather than Solomon. But manuscript evidence is lacking for this departure from the

One commentator favoring the three-player view supposes that the maiden addresses her beloved "as if he were present," asking him to tell her where he tends his flock (Song 1:7). At this point, the "watchful king . . . immediately comes forward" and tries to win her affections, "but without effect" (cf. 1:9–11). Then "as soon as the king retires" (which is nowhere noted in the text), the maiden "shows her unabated attachment to her shepherd" (1:12).[15] In order to accomplish a crisscross conversation that includes an altogether absent country lover, this commentator identifies the maiden's "nard" as a reference to her beloved but absent shepherd. Says this commentator: "Two distinct persons are here spoken of; *the king* at the table, and *a beloved shepherd*, called 'nard'."[16]

This hypothetical three-way interchange among speakers that includes an admittedly absent country lover is not convincing. The more natural reading of the text envisions two people, Solomon and the Shulamite maiden, interchanging speeches weighted with loving admiration. For this reason, the two-player perspective is to be preferred. In this view, Solomon and the Shulamite maiden exchange their words of awe and affection for each other.

FRAMEWORK FOR INTERPRETATION

A decision about the literary form or genre of the Song of Songs, as much as any other book of the Bible, will determine how a person interprets and applies the book. Once the book's literary nature has been determined, details can be explained with greater consistency.[17] Four different frameworks for interpretation of the Song of Songs may be considered: the allegorical, the typological, the natural, and the redemptive-historical.

But before considering these various frameworks for interpretation that have been proposed, we must recognize the genius of the Song

---

Masoretic text. The LXX text reads "behold you" (ἰδοὺ εἶ), which supports an address to Solomon on her part, not to her country lover.

15. Ginsburg, *Song*, 8.

16. Ibid., 138.

17. For an extended history of the interpretation of the Song, see Pope, *Song*, 89–229. According to Pope, 89, a thorough survey of the history of the interpretation of the Song "would require the lifelong labors of teams of scholars."

of Songs as a piece of literature. It has been hailed as "a masterpiece of pure poetry."[18] Goethe, the famous German poet, described the Song as "the most tender and inimitable expression of passionate yet graceful love that has come down to us."[19]

Allegorical

First among possible frameworks for interpretation is the allegorical method. From this perspective, the words of the Bible represent only an outer shell that conceals the inner, true meaning of the text. Rabbi Aqiba, dating around 100 A.D., gave early support to the allegorical interpretation while inadvertently revealing the existence of a difference of opinion. While Aqiba does not explicitly designate the Song as an allegory, his exalted estimate of the book points to the conclusion that he viewed the Song as giving expression to the love of God for the Israelite people rather than depicting the intimacies of the human marriage relationship.[20] Says Aqiba:

> Whoever sings the Song of Songs with a tremulous voice in a banquet hall and [so] treats it as a sort of ditty [thereby inadvertently revealing the existence of an alternative opinion] has no share in the world to come.[21]

He further indicates his high respect for the book by noting that

> all the writings [of Scripture] are holy, but the Song of Songs is the Holy of Holies.[22]

This allegorical perspective manifests itself regularly in the traditions of Jewish interpretation.[23] Rashi, an influential Jewish scholar

---

18. Denis Buzy as quoted in Exum, *Song*, 30.

19. Quoted in Exum, *Song*, 30.

20. Pope, *Song*, 19, concludes: "It is clear that Aqiba must have understood the Song allegorically." He indicates that he will later provide samples of his interpretation of selected verses that confirm this conclusion.

21. Quoted in Murphy, *Song*, 13.

22. Ibid., 6.

23. Interestingly, the LXX translation of the Song gives no evidence of an allegorical interpretation. Says Pope, *Song*, 20: "There is no clear evidence that the translator was influenced by the allegorical interpretation which the Synagogue and Church later applied to the text."

of the eleventh century A.D., expresses his view that Solomon saw by the Holy Spirit that the Israelites would be carried into exile, and then would remember God's former love to them. So "Solomon produced this book by divine inspiration in the language of a woman saddened by a living widowhood, longing for her love."[24] According to a popular Jewish interpretation, the book opens with a scene in which Israel (the woman) begs the man (God) to kiss her. Palestine is their bedroom, the kissing is the giving of the law, the maiden's confession of blackness represents their idolatry in the wilderness, and the comparison of the woman to Pharaoh's chariot intentionally reminds of the exodus from Egypt.[25]

This allegorical interpretation has been supported across the centuries by Christian as well as Jewish interpreters. It took Origen (third century A.D) twelve volumes to explain the Song's allegorical significance in terms of the love of Christ for his church.[26] Bernard of Clairvaux died in 1153 after composing eighty-six sermons on the Song, having reached only the end of the second chapter.[27] The King James Version of the English Bible, printed in 1611, popularized the allegorical interpretation by placing headings at the top of each page to indicate how the Song related to Christ's love for his church.[28] This Christian allegorical reading of the Song has fostered several applications. The allegory could represent the intimacy of love between Christ and the church, Christ and the individual believer's soul, or even Christ and the virgin Mary, as proposed by Ambrose in the fourth century.[29]

The insuperable problem with the allegorical framework for interpretation is the impossibility of expounding the intimacies of the Song in terms of the relation of God or Christ to his people. The bizarre character of efforts in this direction may be illustrated by the analysis of Cyril of Alexandria (ninth century), who proposed that the two

24. Quoted in Pope, *Song*, 102.
25. Longman, *Song*, 25.
26. Franz Delitzsch, *Commentary on the Song of Songs and Ecclesiastes* (Edinburgh: T. & T. Clark, 1891), 2.
27. Ibid.
28. Seerveld, *Song*, 11.
29. Robert Gordis, *The Song of Songs and Lamentations: A Study, Modern Translation, and Commentary*, rev. and augmented ed. (New York: KTAV, 1974), 3.

330

breasts of the woman in Song 1:13 represent the Old and New Testaments, and that Christ is the little pouch of myrrh that hangs between these breasts.[30] A more modest explanation suggests that the pouch of myrrh between the breasts stood for "the pleasantness of the society of Christ to the saint."[31] Typically this view among Christian interpreters will not elaborate on the physical parts of the human body. Instead, the interpretation will go directly to what might be considered the "spiritual equivalent" of bodily references. Desiring to be kissed with Christ's mouth (1:2) expresses the "desire of the pious heart, that the Lord Jesus would give us manifestations of the love which none but his dearest friends can receive."[32] Milk and honey under the tongue (4:11) refer to "the words of repentance, faith, prayer, and praise, offered at the mercy-seat by the contrite heart."[33]

Illustrations of this type of allegorical interpretation could be multiplied, particularly because "there are no well-defined hermeneutical canons to guide the interpreter in determining the precise meaning and application if the allegorical view is adopted."[34] Yet nothing present in the text itself even remotely suggests that the various parts of the human anatomy in the Song mean something other than what is explicitly indicated. The heart of the Song inescapably resides in these intimacies of description. The message of the book will inevitably be lost once these intimacies are subjected to fanciful suppositions.

Typological

A second major framework for interpreting the Song of Songs is the typological method. The typological analysis of the book represents a modification of the allegorical tradition. In one version of this method, it is proposed that the substance of the Song refers to an actual event in Solomon's life. Yet all along, the book intends to

30. Cyril on Song 1:13, as indicated in Seerveld, *Song*, 12.
31. George Burrowes, *A Commentary on the Song of Solomon* (London: Banner of Truth, 1958), 156.
32. Ibid., 73.
33. Ibid., 303.
34. John Murray, as quoted in Carr, *Song*, 23. Carr cites Murray as indicating that he "cannot now endorse the allegorical interpretation of the Song of Solomon." The context of Murray's change of mind is not made clear.

display the intimacies of the relation of Christ to his church. As one commentator notes, this relation of Christ to his church in the Song is to be found "not in all the subordinate details . . . but only in the main outlines."[35] This commentator continues:

> It requires a really mature soul to appreciate the spiritual beauties which are latent in the book. Not without justification is the old rabbinical requirement that no Jew should read the Song of Songs until he had attained the age of 30.[36]

This line of argument actually provides a stronger case against the typological view than in favor of it. For as a consequence of this view, the most distinctive aspect of the Song of Songs, which is its intimacy of detail, must be relegated to the level of "subordinate details." Yet at the same time, this view denies a desperately needed biblical book to the youth of the church.

One analysis of this allegorical/typological perspective on the Song begins with a definition of *allegory* as a piece of literature in which the events of a narrative "obviously and continuously refer to another simultaneous structure of events or ideas."[37] On the basis of this definition, the conclusion is reached that "it is clear . . . that the Song of Songs is not an allegory," and that no one can "dispute this fact."[38] Still further, in critique of the typological interpretation, it is affirmed that there is "absolutely nothing in the Song of Songs itself that hints of a meaning different from the sexual meaning."[39] On the basis of this conclusion, it is affirmed that the assignment of any "spiritual meaning" to the text takes on an "incredibly arbitrary character."[40] As this author further indicates: "The book itself has no signals that it is to be read in any other way than as a love song."[41]

---

35. Gleason L. Archer, *A Survey of Old Testament Introduction* (Chicago: Moody Press, 1964), 475f.

36. Ibid., 478. Cf. the opening sentence of Richard S. Hess, *Song of Songs*, BCOT (Grand Rapids: Baker Academic, 2005), 11: "The Song of Songs is an adult book."

37. Longman, *Song*, 23, quoting *The Princeton Encyclopedia of Poetry and Poetics*.

38. Ibid., 23.

39. Ibid., 36.

40. Ibid.

41. Ibid., 23.

Yet despite these clear denials of any basis for viewing the Song as an allegory, this particular author affirms that this conclusion "does not end the discussion."[42] He then proceeds to make a distinction between an "allegorical piece of literature" and an "allegorical interpretive strategy."[43] He subsequently notes his intention to "come full circle in order to affirm the legitimacy of a theological reading" of the book.[44] He explains that the Song "has a clear and obvious relevance to the divine-human relationship."[45] He concludes by noting that the allegorical approach "was not wrong" in reading the Song as relevant to our relationship to God. For from the Song "we learn about the emotional intensity, intimacy, and exclusivity of our relationship with the God of the universe."[46]

Several observations may be made regarding this particular proposal for interpreting the Song:

First of all, the distinction between an allegorical "piece of literature" and an allegorical "interpretive strategy" raises serious questions regarding the basic method of interpretation being used. This distinction promotes one meaning for the actual wording of the text (the natural or literal), while simultaneously offering a different meaning for the interpretation of the text (the allegorical or typological). Once a distinction is made between the intended message as found in the words of the text and a different message to be developed by the interpreter, controls in the process of interpretation have been altogether compromised.

Second, if the Song effectively communicates the truth of God about the tenderness, the mutual respect, the exclusiveness, the grandeur that is manifest in the intimacies of human love between a man and a woman in the broader context of God's redemptive work, then this piece of inspired literature need do no more. If the Song communicates these truths in the canonical context of the redemption found ultimately in the Christ, that is surely an adequate basis for underscoring the book's Christ-centered nature. No further "message" needs to

42. Ibid.
43. Ibid.
44. Ibid., 67.
45. Ibid.
46. Ibid., 70.

be found. If it is affirmed that the Song focuses on the glories of human love in the creational ordinance of marriage as restored in redemption, that is a sufficient reason for its existence. The relation of love between Christ and his church, not found in the wording of the Song itself, need not be introduced to expand the Christological center of the book. His work of redeeming the human marriage relationship is enough and more than enough for this one book of the canon.

Third, the author cannot so easily undo his own categorical exclusion of the allegorical interpretation. Obviously, there is a place for developing insights into a person's relation to God through marriage imagery. This development is found explicitly in other portions of inspired Scripture.[47] But as the author himself indicates, the relation of God to his people in connection with marriage imagery is nowhere to be found in the explicit love language of the Song of Songs. Without question, the book contains a message that has potential for great good for the church that will not be discovered in any other inspired book of the Bible. But that good will not be found by imposing an interpretation on the book that is admittedly absent from the words themselves.

Natural

A third major framework for interpretation of the Song is the literal or natural method. This view of the Song has not been without serious opposition. Already the ancient Jewish tradition has been cited: "He who trills his voice in the chanting of the Song of Songs, and treats it as a secular song, has no share in the world to come."[48] Theodore of Mopsuestia was posthumously condemned by the Council of Constantinople in 533 A.D. for holding to the literal view of the Song.[49] The Protestant Westminster Assembly meeting in England in the seventeenth century rejected the literal interpretation of the Song, noting that some Jews and Christians have received it "as an hot carnall pamphlet, formed by some loose Apollo or Cupid."[50]

---

47. See in particular Ps. 45:1–17; Isa. 54:5; 62:4–5; Hos. 2:2, 19–20; Eph. 5:25–33.
48. Gordis, *Song*, 9, quoting a statement of Jewish tradition regarding the Song.
49. E. J. Young, *An Introduction to the Old Testament* (London: Tyndale, 1964), 336.
50. Cf. H. H. Rowley, "The Interpretation of the Song of Songs," in *The Servant of the Lord and Other Essays on the Old Testament* (London: Lutterworth Press, 1952), 233n3,

Despite these stringent objections, the "literal" or "natural" interpretation has continued to be promoted by many interpreters, even though sometimes combined with an allegorical or typological application.[51] The largest consideration supporting this view is that it takes the text of Scripture seriously for what the words actually describe in terms of the intimacy of a physical relationship between a man and a woman. "Kisses of the mouth" means "kisses of the mouth." The reference to the woman's "two breasts" describes the sexual attractiveness of the female's breasts. Indeed, figures of speech must be treated as images of substantial realities depicted by the author. "Milk and honey under the tongue" do not describe the enjoyment of special treats that might be found on the king's banquet table. Instead, they depict the personal intimacies naturally developing from the passionate relationship between a male and a female. The concreteness of the situation is emphasized by the fact that the amorous relationship depicted is "a love that is being celebrated in the present."[52] The lovers are constantly enjoying their ecstatic moments, or just about to do so. This realistic experience of love is depicted through the book's continuing dialogue:

> Desire in the Song is always on the brink of fulfillment, and has an urgency about it (come! tell me! make haste!). Fulfillment is simultaneously assured, deferred, and, on a figurative level, enjoyed.[53]

At the same time, this naturalistic view cannot help but raise serious questions. Is this vividness of description an appropriate vehicle for communicating God's truth to his redeemed people? If that is the case, what precisely is the truth being communicated? One interpreter, accepting the "literal" or "natural" interpretation, concludes that the Song is "entirely secular, indeed, sensuous, in character," as "the only book in the canon lacking a religious or national theme."[54] If this were

---

quoting the Westminster Assembly's *Annotations upon All the Books of the Old and New Testament*, 2nd ed. (1651), i.

51. Cf., among others, Delitzsch, Rowley, Young, and Longman.

52. Exum, *Song*, 5.

53. Ibid., 11.

54. Gordis, *Song*, 1.

the case, it would indeed be a biblical book with no precedent. For the Bible from Genesis to Malachi, from Matthew to Revelation, sees everything in life as "religious." Secularism is just as much a "religion" as is Buddhism, Hinduism, Islam, or Judaism. As a consequence, secularism inevitably functions as a rival to the religion of the Bible. So if the Song of Songs is "entirely secular," it represents the imposition of another religion into the sacred Scriptures, thus destroying its unified perspective on the truth about the one true, living God.

Redemptive-Historical

A fourth framework for interpreting the Song of Songs may be designated as the redemptive-historical perspective. This analysis, though approaching the text essentially from a "natural" method of interpretation, does so in terms of the redemptive work of God in restoring humanity to the situation prevailing at the time of their creation.

Considering the Song of Songs in this larger canonical context, the book may be seen as a vital part of the restoration promised in this uniquely revealed religion of the Scriptures. The human being who shares in God's redemption from sin's curse passed down by his original parents may experience a restoration of the initial blessing of man and woman in their relation to each other, just as when they first stood in each other's presence "both naked" but feeling "no shame" (Gen. 2:25). This Song rejoices in the fullness of God's redemption of the marriage relationship.

Strenuous objection has been raised to this perspective by some interpreters. Instead of reading the Song as a restoration of the beauties of the original marriage relationship established at creation, this alternative viewpoint imagines a couple sinking into the sin of premarital sex. Says one commentator:

> There is no way around it. These two people are simply in love with one another, and are planning to sleep together without anyone else's permission, without benefit of marriage license or church ceremony. And *that* is in the Bible![55]

---

55. H. Gollwitzer, *Song of Love: A Biblical Understanding of Sex* (Minneapolis: Fortress Press, 1979), 29, as quoted in Carr, *Song*, 46.

The crass statement that these two people are "planning to sleep together without anyone else's permission" totally overlooks the repeated allusion to the role of the mothers of both the man and the woman throughout the text of the Song (3:4, 11; 6:9; 8:2, 5). In addition, the observation that they have neither marriage license nor church ceremony ignores the cultural differences between today's Western civilization and the ancient Near East of three thousand years ago. Still further, this viewpoint fails to take into account the extensive imagery of a restoration to Paradise, with the presence of all its delicate flora and fauna. While a marriage ceremony as such will not be found in the text of the Song, specific reference is made to King Solomon's wedding day (Song 3:11). It might also be worth remembering that neither did Adam and Eve, the original "bride" and "groom," possess marriage license or church ceremony that might justify their intimate relationship. Yet God himself brought them together in their intimate union (Gen. 1:28; 2:22, 24).

At the same time, the underlying presumption throughout the Song is the long-term commitment in body and soul of one woman to one man and one man to one woman. This commitment to a monogamous relationship has always been a vital part of the essence of divinely instituted marriage.

Perhaps the finest, most poetic expression of this renewed relationship may be found in one particular author's description of the "kerygmatic outreach today" of the Song of Songs. A quite lengthy quotation is necessary to communicate the impact of this statement that summarizes the message of the Song of Songs when viewed from a "natural" perspective in a redemptive-historical context:

> It would not be popular today to press the *kerygma* of The Greatest Song: unless your love be enflamed by the fear of Jahve, it profits you nothing. But that is what the Word of God says. An evil ascetic idea of love has long passed for being Christian. Men have prided themselves on being virtuous because they were sexually inhibited, had never "fallen" for a woman, because they lead a monotone married existence. Renowned theologians have posited a sexless *agape* opposite a demonic *eros* and hinged the dilemma with a doubledfaced *caritas*, in the name of Augustine, as the best possible deal in a most ambiguous matter. Believers, as well as unbelievers, still read the

famous alphabet poem concluding Proverbs [31:10–31] as the Bible's picture of the perfect woman, and envision an industrious, middle-class, somewhat homely, churchgoing housewife.

But the "spirituality" framing such conceptions of bodily human love are conditioned more by pagan Greek philosophical anthropologies than the holy Scriptures. The apostle Paul [still often misread as a Stoic] explicitly condemned a strait-laced, kill-joy approach to life [1 Timothy 4:1–5]. To be repressive or dull is not at all biblical, and certainly not Old Testament, where men are called to one holy passion in life, from worship of God to war to sleeping with a woman. The Greatest Song is overpowering scriptural evidence of how earthy minded Jahve is [and remember the incarnation—*sarx! egeneto*], and how happy He is for us creatures to glory thankfully in what He has made, because it is good.

It is so that Proverbs [31:30] says, "Charm is deceptive; prettiness is a passing thing; a woman who fears Jahve—she is worth boasting about." But the thought context is another proverb [11:22]: "A beautiful woman without discretion is a fine gold earring in a hog's nose"—to which the Shulammite adds positively: "My bronze and ruddy lover is one in a thousand!" [5:10]. "My lover! . . . Let us go spend the nights among the henna blossoms. . . . There I will give you my caresses . . . saved up for you, my lover!" [7:12–14]. That is, glory in the body, glory in a woman and in her beauty, revel in the embraces of your lover, get carried away! When and because it is glorying in the Lord. But if maidenhood, bodily splendor, the thrill of touch, have lost its relation to Jahwe and erected itself into idolatry without bounds, then indeed, shun it like the devil.

It is this two-edged truth—exuberance in Jahve-bonded passion! Or lost in numberless vanities—that well-meaning pseudo-Christian saints have read with a veil over the eyes, and lamentably often stunted God's handiwork and given perceptive unbelievers an excuse to experiment licentiously.[56]

The redemptive-historical reading provides the best framework for understanding the Song of Songs. When this perspective is fully comprehended, no need exists to "find Christ" in the Song in any way other than as the Redeemer and Restorer of the original marriage

---

56. Seerveld, *Song*, 80–81.

relationship first celebrated by Adam and Eve. This inner connectivity of two persons, male and female, must be viewed as one of the most amazing manifestations of God's creative powers. How wondrous it is that this very physical relationship could be such a way of uniting two souls into one, such a means for communicating love, such a source of giving and receiving pleasure, and at the same time such a program for extending and expanding the human race as well as the people of God across countless generations! The intimate relationship of man and woman shines forth as one of God's greatest creative acts. Christ's restoration of this relationship by his death and resurrection shines forth as one of his greatest gifts to a renewed humanity.

From this perspective, Christ is preached in the Song, not by finding him allegorically or typologically. Instead, by considering the Song in the broader context of redemptive history, the work of Christ in reconstituting the marriage relationship confirms him as the cosmic Christ. Indeed, this relationship may be comprehended more fully by recognizing that the reconstitution of marriage is possible only through the expression of the same kind of self-sacrificing love that Christ showed for his church. But the message of the Song does not center on the love of Christ for his church. Instead, the purpose of the Song is to focus on the love between redeemed man and woman in the context of the cosmic Christ's re-creative work.

It could be urged that this "natural" interpretation of the Song, even from a redemptive-historical perspective, is far too explicit for our young people. But the manner in which the Song provides intimate descriptions of the beauty of the human body brings out the uniqueness of this amazing piece of inspired literature. The various parts of the woman's body are described with a full appreciation for their attractiveness. Three times the man presents detailed descriptions of the woman's body, going once from her head down (Song 4:1–5); once concentrating on the various parts of her head (6:4–7); and once going from her feet to her head (7:1–5). These descriptions are "intimate, suggestive, and even explicit"; yet the use of metaphors functions "as much to hide the body as to display it."[57] A "heap of

---

57. Exum, *Song*, 20.

wheat encircled by lilies" describes the woman's belly, and a scarlet ribbon depicts her lips. The alluring aspects of the feminine physique are clearly depicted. But what have we actually learned about the specific characteristics of her body? The woman's description of the man's body is quite different from his description of hers. Now the images depict firmness and solidity: arms compared to rods of gold, a torso of polished ivory, marble pillars for legs, an overall appearance resembling a cedar of Lebanon (5:14–15). Indeed, the elements of tenderness are also present when she compares his cheeks to beds of spice, his lips to lilies dripping with myrrh, and his mouth to sweetness itself (5:13, 15).

Interestingly, a difference in the circumstance that evokes these differing descriptions may also be clearly detected. The woman responds in answer to a question put to her by her comrades (Song 5:9). But three times, the man in "spontaneous outbursts inspired by the sight of her" is moved to speak eloquently of her beauty.[58]

In any case, the extensive use of metaphors dampens any inclination to read the Song erotically. It enables the author to control to a significant degree what the reader sees. Instead of looking with lust, he is inspired to look with wonder. As has been noted:

> The Song also keeps us out of the garden of eroticism. It renders our looking less voyeuristic, and our pleasure more aesthetic than erotic, by clothing the lovers' bodies in metaphors, which never quite gives access to the body being described. The images may be strongly visual, but they are literary, part of a text not a picture. Metaphor . . . is a sophisticated literary technique for managing the reader's gaze.[59]

Of course, no one can be totally prevented from turning something that is beautiful into something that is crude or obscene. Satan has had continual success across the generations in corrupting God's good gift of sexuality so that it becomes a sordid and selfish thing. But in a unique way, this piece of inspired literature paints a picture that inspires wondering awe rather than wandering lust.

58. Ibid., 21.
59. Ibid., 24.

The possible consequences of not reading the Song from this naturalistic, redemptive-historical perspective are that young people of today may be deprived of a message that they desperately need from God's Word. All through history, men and women have struggled with temptation to sexual sin. But in the twenty-first century, the proliferation of electronic devices that are ever-present in the hand, the pocket, and the purse makes the possibility of sexual temptation massively more immediate. It is therefore critical that the church of Christ reclaim a thoroughly biblical understanding of the purity, propriety, and legitimate enjoyment of sex within its God-given bounds, as expressed in his Word.

This Word of the Lord could save many people from a tragic relationship, and at the same time enrich their life in a marriage that will happen "at the proper time." One way or another, young people will learn the "facts of life." The modern schooling textbooks for very young children are far more explicit and far more sexually provocative than the Song of Songs. How much better if young people learn about male and female relations in the context of a godly community that listens to God's Word as it speaks of human sexuality.

Other Frameworks for Interpretation

A number of other frameworks for interpreting the Song of Songs have been proposed. Among the several, a few alternatives may be briefly considered:

A Prophetic History

According to Cocceius, a Reformed theologian known for his contribution to the development of covenantal theology, the Song of Songs should be read as a prophetic history of the Christian church, culminating in the Protestant Reformation.[60] Cocceius has done for Protestant Christianity what Jewish scholars attempted to do millennia earlier by interpreting various elements of the Song in terms of Jewish national history. But these treatments of the Song have no solid foundation in the actual wording of the book.

---

60. Cf. the discussion of R. K. Harrison, *Introduction to the Old Testament* (Grand Rapids: Eerdmans, 1969), 1053.

An Adaptation of a Pagan Liturgy

According to this theory, the Song is based on a Babylonian myth in which a god dies and a goddess descends to him into the underworld, signifying the dying and rising of nature. However, as has been pointed out, the Song makes no reference to someone's dying, or to a descent into the underworld, or to the decay of nature.[61] As has been well said:

> One is, of course, at liberty to assume that our book represents a secular reworking of a no longer extant litany of an assumed Israelite cult which has left no record of its existence behind it. Such a complex of unsubstantiated hypotheses recalls the argument that the ancient Hebrews must have known of wireless telegraphy, because archaeologists in Palestine have found no wires in their excavations.[62]

A Cultic Celebration of Love in a Funeral Ritual

In a massive work of over seven hundred pages, one author indicates his view that "the cultic interpretation, which has been vehemently resisted from its beginnings, is best able to account for the erotic imagery" of the Song.[63] He continues:

> Sex is so significant that it has been mythologized as a divine prerogative, too good to be permitted mankind (cf. Gen. 3:5). But our blessed Mother Eve filched the forbidden fruit of the Tree of Knowledge of Good and Evil and shared it with her less venturesome mate, thus bestowing the bittersweet blessing and curse of sexuality on humanity and with it the final dread Death.[64]

This author concludes his extended introduction by connecting the Song with the pagan funeral feasts of the ancient Near East that were "love feasts celebrated with wine, women, and song."[65] These

---

61. Gordis, *Song*, 7–8. Cf., for further references and critique, E. J. Young, *Introduction to the Old Testament*, 335. Additional analysis of cultic options may be found in Longman, *Song*, 44–46.

62. Gordis, *Song*, 8.

63. Pope, *Song*, 17.

64. Ibid.

65. Ibid., 228.

love feasts frequently featured "orgiastic revelry, drunkenness, gluttony, cannibalism, incest, and sundry other excesses."[66] He then connects the Song with these funeral feasts "as expressive of the deepest and most constant human concern for Life and Love in the ever present face of Death."[67]

Such an interpretation runs aground on the divine direction given the first humans to "multiply and replenish the earth" (Gen. 1:28 KJV). God's blessing on sex was clearly pronounced before Adam and Eve had ever eaten the forbidden fruit. At creation their Maker declared that "a man will . . . be united to his wife, and they will become one flesh" (2:24). This foundational evidence in Scripture is sufficient to counter the idea that the Song embodies a "cultic" idea of sex. The rooting of this Song in the grossest of pagan rituals is revulsive to the extreme, and has the effect of raping the virgin daughter of Scripture. This proposal has no foundation in the wording of the Song, and contradicts the model of monogamous purity that permeates its pages.

A Collection of Love Songs

Comparisons with descriptive poems associated with wedding celebrations in the Middle East have led to the proposal that the Song of Songs represents a collection of ancient love songs.[68] These wedding songs traditionally describe the beauty of the bride and groom in a way similar to the descriptions found in the Song. This perspective is used to explain the lack of orderly progression in the narrative throughout the Song. From this perspective, the Song has been described as "an anthology of love poems, a kind of erotic psalter."[69]

While this perspective offers some rationale for understanding what is otherwise presumed to be a disjointed piece of literature, it also introduces serious problems in its treatment of the book. First

---

66. Ibid., 227.
67. Ibid., 229.
68. Prominent in the development of this hypothesis is J. G. Wetzstein, who was Consul in Damascus, Syria, for a number of years during the latter part of the nineteenth century. An extensive sample of his work may be found in Delitzsch, *Song*, 162–76. A more recent presentation of this view may be found in Longman, *Song*, 43–44, 55–56.
69. Longman, *Song*, 43.

among these difficulties is the splintering of a unified literary piece into an indefinite number of fragments. In one instance, the impression is given that virtually every verse is a separate poem. In another case, an effort is made to identify precisely twenty-three songs.[70] In addition to the difficulty of determining the exact number of poems, it is acknowledged that "while there are clear poems in the text, the individual poems are of uncertain and often even of doubtful connection with one another."[71] As a consequence, the overall message of the book becomes disconnected and muddled. As one commentator has noted, this approach "has broken The Greatest Song up into many disconnected songs of aphoristic length," with the result that it "cannot exposit the work as an Israelite-oriented, Old Testament directed and concentrated, Holy Spirit-breathed revelation."[72]

In this regard, the burden of proof must rest on the person promoting the disunity of the treatise. If twenty or thirty different poems are contained within this singular piece of literature, the person urging this disunity must clearly display the inherent substance in each piece that makes it different from the others.

It is quite true that the Song does not progress in narrative form from beginning to end, from chapter 1 through chapter 8. A cyclical element in the poem is clearly present. But a comparable cyclical pattern may be seen in other wisdom books of the Old Testament, including the three rounds of speakers in the book of Job and the five rounds of lament in the book of Lamentations. The cycles of painful/pleasant searching and finding of lovers, climaxing in intimacy of relationship, provide the key to understanding the unity of the Song. The repetition of an identical refrain at a climax of intimacy in three of the five major portions of the book speaks strongly for a designed structure rather than twenty or more disconnected segments loosely strung together (cf. Song 2:7; 3:5; 8:4). A narrated story from start to finish obviously is not the format of the Song. But a description leading repeatedly to the height of marital union finds a natural climax in the central scene of the book (4:16–5:1). The poem concludes with its

70. Ibid., 43–44.
71. Ibid., 43.
72. Seerveld, *Song*, 15.

most exalted expression of the glories of marital love (8:5–14). Only as the book is read as a whole does its message come through clearly. These and other factors in the Song point to something other than a random collection of love songs.

Conclusion regarding Framework for Interpretation of the Song of Songs

Of all the options that have been explored across the centuries, the "natural" interpretation of the Song in a redemptive-historical context best suits the substance of the Song itself. The intimacy of detail describing the love relationship between a man and a woman may be regarded as the unique feature of this book of wisdom when compared to other books of the Bible. Very little biblical material even comes close to reaching the same intimacy of descriptiveness as found in the Song. The fondling of a virgin's breasts in the book of Ezekiel may be the closest thing to this level of intimacy (Ezek. 23:8). But in the case of Ezekiel, the descriptions are specifically placed in the context of an allegory depicting the love relationship between harlotrous Israel and her idolatrous "lovers." In sharpest contrast, nothing in the Song even suggests that the intimacies are to be understood in any way other than the physical relationship between a man and a woman.

This uniqueness in the Song clearly identifies the focal message of the book. God in the grace of the covenant has redeemed man and woman from their fallen condition. He has made it possible for them to taste the wonders of the sexual relationship as intended by God at their creation. In Christ the Redeemer, this precious gift of intimacy in relationship can be experienced once more.

Explicit underscorings of the purity of God's design regarding marriage should be fully appreciated for their straightforward affirmations. Jesus answers the query regarding divorce by plainly stating that "at the beginning the Creator made them male and female," and declaring that "for this reason a man will leave his father and mother and be united to his wife, and the two will become one flesh" (Matt. 19:4–5). Jesus clearly affirms by these words that sexual union between husband and wife is altogether pure, rooted in the explicit purpose of the Creator. He seals this understanding of sex as coming directly from God by his interpretive comment: "Therefore what *God* has joined together, let man not separate" (Matt. 19:6b NIV). Further confirmation of the total propriety of sexual union comes to expression in the letter to the Hebrews: "Marriage should be honored by all, and the marriage bed kept pure, for God will judge the adulterer and all the sexually immoral" (Heb. 13:4 NIV).

TYPE OF LITERATURE

The literary type of the Song of Songs is closely related to the question of its framework for interpretation. Yet the two questions are quite different. "Framework for interpretation" refers to the hermeneutical principle that must govern the overall interpretation of the book. "Type of literature" points to the literary genre of the piece. In this regard, several alternatives may be considered with respect to the type of literature found in the Song of Songs.

A Song?

The title of this piece of literature presents itself as a "Song," as the "Song of Songs." Does the title mean that this Song was meant to be "sung"? No musical notations regarding tunes or instruments accompany the Song, as in the case of many psalms. Possibly this "song" was chanted, in accord with the traditions of Judaism. At the same time, the phrase "song of songs" could refer to the exalted substance of the Song rather than a notation regarding the manner in which its message was to be presented.

A Drama?

Is it to be supposed that the Song of Songs should be treated as a drama to be enacted before the community of God's people? This supposition is not very likely, since no precedent in the literature of the Old Testament can be found. As one commentator indicates, the idea that the Song has the literary form of a drama to be enacted has an "insuperable difficulty" in that "among the Semites generally, and the Hebrews in particular, drama as such was unknown."[73] As another scholar has analyzed the situation, the Song of Songs "was never intended to be acted, but recited, and that while it is certainly dramatic, it is not scenic."[74]

A Dramatic Reading?

The substance of the Song itself provides a significant clue to its literary type. As the book progresses, more than one voice speaks. First a woman addresses a man; then a man responds to the woman. Quite remarkable is the extent to which the woman speaks, and the boldness with which she expresses her desire for her lover.[75] Clearly, the image of this woman is not that of a "wilted flower" under the domination of a male chauvinist. Instead, she appears with the strength of a "helper corresponding to" the man, as was God's intent for womanhood from the beginning (Gen. 2:18).

A chorus of ladies also offers its contribution to the interchange. At certain points, a narrator is helpful if not required. This alternation among speakers continues throughout the book. Yet in clear contrast with the book of Job, the various speakers in the Song are never identified as they speak. In Job, each subsequent speaker is specifically presented as he steps forward. First Eliphaz is introduced and offers his comments; then Job is identified as responding. Next Bildad speaks, and Job responds. Then Zophar; then Job; then Elihu; then God; then Job again; then finally God. At each point, the person of the speaker is specifically noted. But speakers in the Song of Songs can be identified only by noting the change between male and female, between singular and plural pronouns.

These multiple voices may be read quietly to oneself. Or they could all be spoken aloud by a single reader, with or without distinctive articulations that might help the hearer follow the progress of the book.

But it is equally possible that the various persona in the Song could be represented by various presenters, by male and female voices, by

73. Harrison, *Introduction to the Old Testament*, 1054.
74. Rowley, "Interpretation," 211n1, quoting W. W. Cannon, "The Song of Songs Edited as a Dramatic Poem" (1913).
75. Hess, *Song*, 19, cites Brenner, who notes that the female voice accounts for 53 percent of the text, and the male voice 34 percent.

single and multiple participants.[76] Clear and obvious precedent for this type of presentation in the biblical tradition may be found in a number of psalms. Psalm 2 presents four different scenes with multiple persons represented as speaking in their turn. Psalm 118 alternates between a single speaker and multiple persons who respond to his speeches. Many other psalms follow this pattern of interchanging speakers.

Assuming that very few individuals of the community possessed their own copy of the book, they could intuitively understand the message much more readily if different speakers, both male and female, read the various portions of the Song in accordance with the book's original design.

With this perspective in mind, the translation of the Song included in this study is presented in the form of a dramatic reading. The translation includes a limited number of interpretive comments interspersed throughout the text. Principal speakers are a commentator, the bride, the groom, and a chorus of ladies. The presence of this group of ladies in the context of the intimacies of the dialogue underscores the author's intention to instruct regarding the wonders of the marriage relationship by this unique device of the dialogue. As has been indicated, "The lovers do not view the presence of these women as either intrusive or embarrassing."[77] Instead, their presence and participation in the dialogue invites every subsequent reader and listener to view these words as though they were addressed to them as well.

The book naturally divides into five scenes, structured according to the repetitive pattern of seeking and finding on the part of the lovers. Three of these five sections conclude with an identical chorus.[78] The final section climaxes the whole work with a lofty poem exalting the beauties of human love, all to be viewed in the context of the

---

76. The treatment of the text of the Song as a dramatic reading appears in two Greek translations. Pope, *Song*, 34, indicates: "Codex Sinaiticus of the fourth century, and Codex Alexandrinus of the fifth century, supplied marginal notes to the text indicating the speakers and the persons addressed."

77. Exum, *Song*, 7.

78. This structure of the Song into five sections is found in Carr, *Song*, 45. Carr notes that three of these sections conclude with the theme statement, and that the other two "conclude with a common theme of consummation." Additionally, he notes that each of the sections begins with the idea of arousal (Song 2:10; 5:2; 8:5) or the arrival of one of the lovers and the invitation of the other (1:2, 4; 2:8, 10; 3:6; 5:2; 8:5f.).

redemptive, restorative work of the promised Christ. The translation is designed to be read before a community of God's people, with the intent of communicating as effectively as possible the message of the Song to current believers.

Major Themes

Several major themes emerge as the narrative of the Song of Songs moves through its cyclical pattern. These themes unite to underscore the didactic dimension of the Song, which teaches the beauties of the marriage relationship in the context of God's redemptive work of restoration. The following emphases may be noted:

(1) The regal setting of the Song elevates the love relationship of every husband and wife beyond the realm of the commonplace. The ecstatic experience of human love in its most intense form may be claimed as the possession of every "Adam" and every "Eve" who have been renewed by God's work of restoration and redemption.

(2) The blessings of union in marriage may be best experienced and comprehended in the context of the beauties of a creation preserved and renewed in the grace of God. Aromatic flowers, flowing streams, grazing sheep, graceful gazelles, cooing doves, and blossoming vines all combine to enrich the romantic setting of the marriage relationship.

(3) The extensive use of figures of speech serves as a literary device that lifts the subject matter of "The Greatest Song" beyond the level of prosaic narrative. This heightening of the experience of marital love through the instrumentality of poetic device leads to a fuller appreciation of this great gift of God's redemptive, restorative grace.

(4) Through the presence of "learners" who continually appear and reappear throughout the narrative, the Song stresses that this message of marital love renewed by redemption obligates individuals to be either teachers or learners. Marital union in the blessings of redemption is a vital truth that must be transmitted from generation to generation. As Paul the apostle instructs Pastor Titus, the older women must "train the younger women to love their husbands" (Titus 2:4). It may be assumed that this instruction in how a younger woman should love her husband would include all aspects of the marital relationship.

349

(5) Though not specifically indicated in the words of the Song, the message of monogamy is powerfully communicated throughout the narrative. Only one man and one woman committed unequivocally and exclusively to each other can experience the wonders of the marriage relationship in all its richness.

(6) The person and work of Christ may be seen in the Song, but not by means of allegorical or typological extension of the language into a realm not inherent in the meaning of the words themselves. Instead, Christ's glory is seen in the restoration of this marvelous union of one man and one woman as first established at creation and now experienced in redemption.

The Best Song

Arranged as a Dramatic Reading Featuring Multiple Voices with Interpretive Comments

COMMENTATOR (reads the following introduction)

Today, great confusion characterizes the public perspective on the intimacies of male and female relationships. Only an understanding of the Creator's intention in the restoration of a fallen humanity can clarify people's thinking on this critical issue.

The biblical book entitled "The Song of Songs" has been written to instruct God's people on the subject of "how to love." The didactic Song communicates God's perspective on human love in the larger context of his redemptive purposes. It vividly describes the beauties of the intimacies of the marriage relationship, and emphasizes that the bed is undefiled and marriage is to be held in honor by all (Heb. 13:4).

Contrary to this understanding of the Song of Songs, efforts have been made across the ages to read the book as an allegorical picture of God's love for his people rather than depicting the intimacies of the human marriage relationship. For the church has found it difficult to accept the public declaration of human love at the level of explicitness found in the Song of Songs.

Yet these very intimacies of description make it most difficult to "spiritualize" the Song and interpret it in terms of the relation of God to Israel or of Christ to his church. It simply does not seem appropriate to describe Christ as a bundle of myrrh dangling between the two breasts of the old and new covenant Scriptures (Song 1:13), or for the church to long for Christ to kiss her with the kisses of his mouth (1:2).

With all its difficulties, the "natural" interpretation of the Song from a redemptive-historical perspective represents the apparent intent of the text with greater integrity.

The present treatment favors this "natural" interpretation of the Song in a redemptive-historical context. From this perspective, this book is titled "The Song of Songs" because its subject matter is the most wonderful of all human themes about which people may sing. It is the best of all songs. According to the book of Proverbs, one of the "things . . . too amazing" to comprehend is "the way of a man with a maiden" (Prov. 30:18–19).

The straightforwardness of the language of the Song may at points appear rather shocking to the reader. But it must be remembered that this book presents itself as the inspired Word of God. As such, its message should be trusted as God's Word that speaks directly to man's need.

In this context, the strong undertone of a monogamous relationship in marriage throughout the Song of Songs must be appreciated. It is only in the commitment of one man to one woman that the beauties of the marriage relationship may be fully appreciated and experienced.

Some of the figures of speech in the Song may sound rather bizarre in a modern context. Today's woman would not be especially impressed if her teeth were compared to a "flock of sheep freshly shorn" (Song 4:2), or her hair to a "flock of goats reclining on a mountainside" (4:1). But every generation's love language will invariably sound strange and stilted to subsequent generations.

Questions have arisen around the phrase "The Song of Songs, *which is Solomon's*." How could a proper song about pure love in the marriage relationship be composed by a man who had seven hundred wives and three hundred concubines (1 Kings 11:3)?

One solution to this problem has been to suppose that the Song of Songs depicts a love triangle. While lecherous old Solomon tries to add one more girl to his bedroom trophies, this Shulamite maiden maintains her fidelity to her country lover.

This analysis of the Song has been called the *three-player view*. It has many built-in attractions. But a primary problem with this view relates to the subtle redirection of speeches among various parties required to make sense out of the text. At certain points, Solomon and the Shulamite maiden are alone. The king speaks to her in praise of her beauty: "You are so lovely, . . . so strikingly beautiful" (Song 1:15). The woman accordingly responds: "You are so strikingly handsome, my lover . . . . Our couch is luxuriant" (1:16). Yet according to the three-player interpretation, the woman directs her speech not to Solomon, the only person currently with her, but to her absent lover. It is as though the woman, having heard the love language of Solomon, responds by looking over his shoulder as she envisions her absent lover, and speaks to him instead. It is rather difficult to make a convincing case for this kind of redirection of speeches between two people alone with each other.

A better solution to this problem of Solomon's role as author of this book on marital love is to recognize the immensity of God's grace in his redemptive working among fallen humanity. Despite all his deficiencies, King Solomon still represents the apex of wisdom figures under the old covenant. His departures from the perfections of God's laws regarding marriage were indeed great. Yet the moral failures of other "heroes" of the old covenant were equally great. Abraham brought curses rather than blessings on Egypt because of his deceit regarding his wife (Gen. 12:11–13, 17), Moses was denied entry into the land of promise for his outbreak of anger (Deut. 32:48–52), and David brought the curses of internecine war on his people because of his lust for a woman (2 Sam. 12:9–10). From this perspective, God in his grace may use Solomon as a source of wisdom for the life of God's people despite Solomon's sin.

The present version of the Song supposes that only Solomon, his Shulamite bride, and a chorus of ladies are present. The various verses have been divided among these speakers. At some points, the original language of Scripture clearly indicates the change of speakers. At other points, it is not so clear which person speaks. But the message nonetheless comes across most strongly: God is the author of human love, and people who have been re-created in Christ may rejoice in this good gift of the Father.

The current translation has divided the Song into five scenes, reflecting the cyclical pattern of seeking and finding that prevails throughout the book. The "meandering" nature of the narrative "reflects the repetitive pattern of seeking and finding in which the lovers engage."[79] Immediately following an announcement of the title of the work, Scene One opens with a speech of the bride, which begins *in medias res*, that is, "in the middle of the story," in appropriate literary fashion.

Scene One (Song 1:1–2:7)

COMMENTATOR (announces: "Scene One")

1:1   The best of all songs, which is Solomon's song.

BRIDE

1:2   Oh, let him kiss me
            with the kisses of his mouth.
         For your caresses
            are better than the best of wines.

1:3   The fragrance of your ointments
            is so enticing.
         Just mentioning your name
            is like pouring out perfume.
         It's no wonder so many maidens
            adore you.

COMMENTATOR

From these opening lines, it becomes clear that this Best of Songs will not avoid explicit love language. "Kisses of the mouth," "caresses

79. Exum, *Song*, 11.

better than wine," "enticing" fragrances vividly depict the physical aspect of human love. All things ordained by God are pure in themselves, and to be received with thankfulness.

BRIDE

1:4a   Take me away with you!
       Let us run together.
       The king has brought me into his bedchamber.

CHORUS

1:4b   We will find delight in rejoicing with you.
       We will celebrate your loves more than wine.

BRIDE

1:4c   It is fitting that they adore you.

COMMENTATOR

Very early the reader is introduced to the didactic nature of the Song. The "we" in these phrases refers to a chorus of young ladies.

It's not that this troop of girls belong to the harem of Solomon in the sense that they expect to eventually share in his love. Neither will they observe the intimacies of relationship between the Shulamite maiden and her royal lover. Nor are they rivals to the Shulamite, biding their time, competing for Solomon's attentions. Instead, they are learners, maidens being instructed in the mysteries and wonders of marital love.

As king among God's people, Solomon receives the admiration of these maidens. He represents the perfect picture of the man who has been reestablished to his rightful place in creation by the grace of God's redemptive work. Holding this exalted position, he is celebrated by all and becomes the instructor of all. Along with these maidens, let us listen and learn all we can about the greatness of this aspect of God's creation.

BRIDE

1:5   Darkened am I,
        yet beautiful, O daughters of Jerusalem;
    Dark as the tents of the northern nomads,
        beautiful as the tapestries of Solomon.

1:6   Do not stare at me
        because I am blackened,
        burned by the sun.
    My brothers
        were incensed at me.
    They made me
        keeper of the vineyards.
    My own vineyard, which is mine alone,
        I have neglected.

COMMENTATOR

The bride speaks of her body as her own "vineyard." This figure of speech will play a prominent role throughout the remainder of the book. The woman compares her body to a vineyard rich in delightful fruits.

BRIDE

1:7   Please, let me know where you will be.
        For I am the one who loves you with my whole being.
          Where will you shepherd your flock?
          Where will you let them lie down
            during the noontime heat?
        Why must I walk about as a veiled woman
          among the flocks of your friends?

COMMENTATOR

"Where will you shepherd your flock?" asks the bride. Nothing in Scripture suggests that Solomon ever served as a shepherd of sheep, as did his father, David. But the king of Israel was often compared to the shepherd of a flock because of his responsibility to care for the well-being of his people. Now the Shulamite maiden addresses her lover as a shepherd, and expresses her desire to meet with him among the beauties of God's creation.

GROOM

1:8   If you, the most beautiful of women,
      do not know where to find me,
      then follow the footprints of the flock,
        and let your young goats graze
        by the tents of the shepherds.

1:9   My dearest, you are like one of the trotting horses
      among Pharaoh's chariots.

1:10   Your cheeks are resplendent with their ringlets,
      the curve of your neck with its string of beads.

COMMENTATOR

Lovers lauding features of beauty in one another is a universal phenomenon. As in so many other ways, this hymn to married love is the "best of all songs." The descriptions of physical beauty are most appealing. Yet the cultural conditioning of these descriptions is quite obvious. Comparing a beautiful woman to a trotting horse would not be taken as the nicest of compliments in the modern world.

CHORUS

1:11   We will fashion for you
      strands of gold sparkling with silver.

COMMENTATOR

The learning maidens cannot resist presenting their own glamorous gift to the bride. They are totally taken up in their admiration of this beautiful woman.

BRIDE

1:12   While the king reclined on his couch,
        my fragrance dispelled its inviting aroma.

COMMENTATOR

This imagery of a perfumed fragrance coming from the woman expresses her longing for the man. She extends herself to him by her aroma, both figuratively and literally.

BRIDE

1:13   A bundle of myrrh
        is my lover to me.
        He nestles between my breasts.

1:14   A cluster of blossoms
        is my lover to me,
        selected from the gardens of Engedi.

GROOM

1:15   You are so lovely, my dearest,
        so strikingly beautiful!
        Your eyes have the calm beauty of doves.

BRIDE

1:16   You are so handsome, my lover!
        So pleasant to be with.
        Our bed is luxuriant.

GROOM

1:17   The beams of our house
            are cedars;
        our rafters
            are cypress.

BRIDE

2:1   I am a mere meadow flower
            from the plains of Sharon,
        a common lily
            from the valleys.

GROOM

2:2   Indeed, as a lily
            among the thorns,
        so is my companion
            among other maidens.

COMMENTATOR

The rapid interchange of compliments between bride and groom indicates the intensity of their affection for each other. Never does their relationship appear as a one-sided affair.

BRIDE

2:3   As an apple tree
            in the midst of other trees of the forest,
        so is my lover
            among the young men.

        I take great delight
            sitting in his shadow,
        and his fruit
            is so sweet to my taste.

359

2:4   He led me
      into his house of delights,
    and his covering over me
      was love.

2:5   Nourish me
      with raisin cakes,
    refresh me
      with apples,
      for I am enraptured with love.

2:6   His left hand
      is under my head,
    and his right hand
      embraces me.

2:7   I make you pledge, O daughters of Jerusalem,
      by the deer and the antelope of the field,
    never to awaken or arouse love
      until love's desires come properly.

COMMENTATOR

The first scene is over. The pattern of seeking and finding has been resolved, but it will recur with increasing intensity. Anyone who has tasted love knows the meaning of this pleasantly painful seeking, longing, searching, and finding.

The admonition of the bride to the learning maidens literally says that they are not to awaken or arouse love "until it pleases." The meaning most likely is that intimate relations should not be entered into "until love's desires come properly." This refrain recurs in two other places (Song 3:5 and 8:4). In each of these three cases, the bride has sunk into the arms of her lover. In the didactic context of the Song, she turns to the young women learning from her, and as it were draws a curtain of solitude and privacy behind her. At the same time, she admonishes the young maidens not to arouse or excite love indiscriminately.

SCENE TWO (SONG 2:8–3:5)

COMMENTATOR (announces: "Scene Two")

Now the bride and groom begin their process of searching and finding once more. This scene concludes with the repetition of the refrain that ended the first scene.

BRIDE

2:8   The voice of my lover!
        Ahh. He's coming!
    Bounding over the mountains,
        leaping over the hills.

2:9   My lover is like an antelope
        or a young stag.
    There he is!
        Standing outside our wall,
        gazing through the windows,
        peering through the lattices.

2:10a My lover responds to my longing.
      He invites me, saying:

GROOM

2:10b Arise, my companion, my beautiful one,
      come away with me.

2:11   Look! The winter is past,
      the rains are over and gone.

2:12   The flowers blossom
      across the land,
    the time for song
      has come,
    and the cooing of the turtledove
      is heard in our land.

2:13   The fig tree
        sweetens its early fruit,
    and the blossoming vines
        dispel their fragrance.
    Arise, my companion, my beautiful one,
        come away with me.

2:14   My dove, in the clefts of the rock,
    in the secret places of the mountainside,
        let me see your form,
        let me hear your voice.
            For your voice is sweet
            and your form is lovely.

BRIDE

2:15   Restrain the foxes, those little foxes
        that spoil the vineyards.
    For our vineyards are in bloom.

2:16   My lover is for me,
        and I am for him.
    He browses among the lilies.

2:17   When the evening breezes blow
    and the shadows flee,
        turn, my lover,
        like an antelope or a young stag
        on the divided mountains.

COMMENTATOR

The bride prepares to meet her lover in their secret place as he has proposed. But she is conscious of all the little glitches that can spoil the intimacies of a relationship. So she asks both his friends and hers to help in restraining all such interferences. Since their time is right, she offers herself willingly to her lover.

BRIDE

3:1 While lying on my bed night after night
    I sought the one I love with my whole being.
    I sought him, but did not find him.

3:2 So now I will arise
    and traverse the city.
  In the streets and roadways
    I will search for the one I love with my whole being.
  I searched for him,
    but I could not find him.

3:3 The watchmen who patrol the city
    found me.
  "Have you seen the one I love with my whole being?"
    I asked.

3:4 As I hurried past them,
    I finally found the one I love with my whole being.
    I embraced him and would not let him go
      until I brought him into the house of my mother,
      into the very room where she conceived me.

COMMENTATOR

The bride refers to the house of her mother, to the very room where she had been conceived. More than once the Song uses this type of reference to suggest that society's approval rested on the bride and groom's marital union. They were not sneaking behind the backs of their parents and relatives. To the contrary, they sought and attained the approval of the generations that had journeyed on the path of love before them.

Young people would greatly benefit from this principle of divine wisdom. The interest and concern expressed by parents and friends regarding their love life should never be resented. God has ordained the involvement of others for the good of his covenant people. The bonds of marriage include not merely two people, but two families—indeed, a whole community of believers.

BRIDE

3:5   I make you pledge, O daughters of Jerusalem,
        by the deer and the antelope of the field,
    never to awaken or arouse love
        until love's desires come properly.

COMMENTATOR

The refrain appears for the second time. The cycle of seeking and finding has been completed once more. With these words, the bride admonishes her learners to remain true to their single lover.

The cyclical nature of the Song means that the narrative should not be interpreted in a purely temporal sequence, moving from courtship through engagement into marriage. Instead, these earlier scenes of seeking and finding must be understood as occurring within the marriage bond.

Once more, the bride draws the curtain of privacy about her as she admonishes her attending maidens. They are not to arouse love indiscriminately.

The third cycle begins at this point, and contains the most descriptive hymn to marital love. The chorus ends the cycle by expressing its approval of the love displayed between bride and groom.

SCENE THREE (SONG 3:6–5:1)

COMMENTATOR (announces: "Scene Three")

CHORUS

3:6   Who is this coming up from the wilderness
        among billows of smoke,
        perfumed with purest incense and myrrh,
        engulfed in all the enchanting aromas of the merchant?

3:7 Look! Solomon's carriage
with sixty mighty men surrounding it
from the mightiest of Israel.

3:8 Each of them wields a sword,
possessing expertise in combat.
Every man wears his sword at his thigh,
armed against nightly terror.

3:9 King Solomon made for himself
a sedan chair of Lebanon wood.

3:10 Its columns he made from silver,
its base of gold,
its cushion of purple velvet,
its interior lovingly decorated
by the daughters of Jerusalem.

3:11 Daughters of Zion,
hurry out and gaze on King Solomon,
wearing the crown with which his mother crowned him
on his wedding day,
the day his heart pulsed with joy.

COMMENTATOR

Solomon makes a glorious impression in this wedding procession. Upon his arrival, he addresses his chosen bride, declaring his appreciation for her beauty:

GROOM

4:1 You are truly beautiful, my friend,
truly beautiful.
Your eyes behind your veil
have the calm beauty of doves.
Your hair is like a herd of goats
descending the slopes of Mount Gilead.

4:2   Your teeth are as a flock of sheep freshly shorn,
        coming up from the washing.
    Each one has a twin,
        and not a single one is bereaved.

4:3   Your lips are as a scarlet thread,
        and your mouth is captivating;
    your temples are like a slice of pomegranate
        behind your veil.

4:4   Your neck is as the tower of David,
        a model for builders,
            with a thousand shields hung on it,
            all the armor of mighty men.

4:5   Your breasts are like young fawns,
        twins of a doe,
        browsing among the lilies.

4:6   When the evening breezes blow,
    and the shadows flee,
        I will come to the mountain of myrrh
        and the hill of perfume.

4:7   You are altogether beautiful, my friend,
    and there is not a blemish in you.

4:8   Come with me from Lebanon, my bride.
    You must come with me from Lebanon!
    Come down
        from the peak of Amana,
        from the crest of Shinar and Hermon,
        from the dens of the lions,
        from the mountain haunts of the leopards.

4:9   You have captivated my heart, my sister, my bride.
    You have captivated my heart
        with a single glance of your eyes,
        with a single ornament of your neck.

4:10   How lovely are your caresses, my sister, my bride.
How much better
    are your caresses than wine,
    and the fragrance of your oils than all spices.

4:11   Your lips drip sweetness as the honeycomb, my bride.
Honey and milk
    lie under your tongue,
and the aroma of your clothing
    is as the fragrance of Lebanon.

4:12   An enclosed garden
    is my sister, my bride;
an enclosed spring, a sealed fountain.

4:13   An enclosed paradise of pomegranate trees
    is your budding,
    with delicious fruits, clusters of blossoms, and nard.

4:14   Nard with crocus, calamus, and cinnamon,
    with every variety of flowering trees, myrrh, and aloes,
    with all the finest spices.

4:15   A garden fountain,
    a well of living water,
    and rushing streams from Lebanon.

BRIDE

4:16   Stir, stir, north wind.
Come, wind of the south.
Blow over my garden, disperse its fragrance.
    Let my beloved come into his garden,
    and let him eat its delicious fruits.

COMMENTATOR

The bride responds most willingly to the call of the groom. She expresses her deep desire to belong to him, body and soul.

Between this verse and the next, a marriage union occurs. The chorus of ladies responds with their wholehearted approval.

Subsequent seeking and finding may be understood as a rehearsal of their earlier days of courtship, or as the searchings arising from separations that inevitably interrupt the marriage bond.

GROOM

5:1a   I have come into my garden, my sister, my bride.
        I have gathered my myrrh with my spices.
        I have eaten my honeycomb with my honey.
        I have drunk my wine and my milk.

CHORUS

5:1b   Eat, friends!
        Drink deeply, lovers!

SCENE FOUR (SONG 5:2–8:4)

COMMENTATOR (announces: "Scene Four")

Now the fourth cycle of the Song begins. It continues until the next repetition of the refrain. Once more, the bride and groom exchange flattering descriptions of each other throughout this section.

BRIDE

5:2a   I was sleeping,
      but my heart remained awake.
        The call of my lover—he's knocking!

GROOM

5:2b   Open to me, my sister, my companion,
        my dove, my perfect one.
    For my head is drenched with the dew,
        my locks with the damp of the night.

BRIDE

5:3   [But] I have taken off my dress!
        Oh, shall I put it on again?
    I have washed my feet.
        Shall I soil them again?

5:4   My lover
        withdrew his hand from the lock,
    and my deep desire
        was agitated with the thought of him.

5:5   I leaped to open for my lover.
        My hands dripped with myrrh,
        and my fingers with liquid myrrh
           on the handles of the bolt.

5:6   I opened to my lover,
        but my lover had left—he was gone!
    My soul had yearned when he spoke.
        I sought him, but could not find him.
        I called out to him, but he did not answer me.

5:7   The patrolling guards of the city found me.
        They beat me;
        they bruised me;
        they snatched my shawl from me,
           those guards of the wall!

5:8   I make you pledge, O daughters of Jerusalem,
        if you should find my lover,
        what will you say to him?
          Tell him I languish with love.

CHORUS

5:9   You are indeed the loveliest of women.
        But tell us how your lover excels another lover.
        If you make us pledge,
          then tell us how your lover excels another lover.

COMMENTATOR

If they are to be brought under oath, the chorus must ask the bride for proof of her lover's worthiness. She most gladly responds:

BRIDE

5:10   My lover is bronze and ruddy,
        conspicuous among ten thousand.

5:11   His head
        is of the finest gold,
    his locks wave on wave,
        black as a raven.

5:12   His eyes are as doves by streams of water,
        bathed in milk, and richly set.

5:13   His cheeks are like a bed of sweet herbs,
        banks of luscious plantings.
    His lips are like lilies,
        dripping with liquid myrrh.

5:14   His arms are like golden cylinders,
        set with jewels.
    His waist is carved ivory,
        inlaid with sapphires.

5:15   His legs are marble pillars
        built on gold foundations;
    his form as Lebanon,
        distinguished as the cedars.

5:16   His palate is most sweet,
        and all of him appears desirable.
    This is my lover; this is my friend,
        O daughters of Jerusalem.

COMMENTATOR

The bride's description of her lover has convinced the chorus that they should support the bride in her search for him. So now they are prepared to lend their help. But they need some direction.

CHORUS

6:1   Where has your lover gone,
        O most beautiful of women?
    In which direction has your lover turned?
        We will search for him with you.

BRIDE

6:2   My lover has gone down to his garden,
        to the beds of sweet spices,
    to browse in the gardens
        and to gather lilies.

6:3   I am for my lover and my lover is for me.
    He feeds among the lilies.

GROOM

6:4   You are so beautiful, my companion—
        beautiful as Tirzah,
    as lovely as Jerusalem,
        awesome as bannered hosts.

6:5   Turn aside your eyes from me,
        for they overwhelm me.
    Your hair is like a herd of goats
        descending the slopes of Mount Gilead.

6:6   Your teeth are as a flock of ewes
        coming up from the washing.
    Each one has a twin,
        and not a single one is bereaved.

6:7   Your temples are like a slice of pomegranate
        behind your veil.

6:8   There are sixty queens,
    and eighty concubines,
    and virgins without number.

6:9   My dove is one by herself—my perfection!
        She stands alone before her mother.
        She is choice to the one bearing her.
            Daughters see her
                and bless her.
            Queens and concubines
                praise her, saying:

6:10   "Who is she that looks down like the dawn,
        beautiful as the moon,
        bright as the sun,
        awesome as bannered hosts?"

BRIDE

6:11   I went down to the grove of nut trees
        to see the budding flowers by the brook,
        to see the blossoming vine,
        and the blooming pomegranates.

6:12   Unknowingly my longing soul had brought me
        right to the chariots of the prince's companions.

CHORUS

6:13a Turn, turn, O Shulamite.
      Turn all around,
         that we may wonder at you.

BRIDE

6:13b Why would you wonder at the Shulamite,
         as at the dance of a double company?

GROOM

7:1   How beautiful are your sandaled feet,
        O princely daughter.
     The curves of your thighs
        are as an ornament made by the hands of an artisan.

7:2   Your navel is like a rounded goblet,
        never emptied of spiced wine.
     Your belly is like a mound of wheat,
        compressed with lilies.

7:3   Your two breasts
        are like two fawns,
        twins of a doe.

7:4   Your neck
        is like an ivory tower;
     your eyes
        are as the pools in Heshbon by the populous gate.
     Your nose
        is as the tower of Lebanon which looks toward Damascus.

7:5   Your head
        crowns you as Carmel,
     and the locks of your hair
        are like a dark purple.
           Even a king is captivated in those strands.

7:6   How beautiful, how captivating, my love,
      with all your charms.

7:7   Your stature
      is like a palm tree,
    and your breasts
      like its clusters.

7:8   I said, "I will climb
      the palm tree;
    I will grasp
      its date clusters.
    Your breasts will be
      as clusters of the vine,
    and the faint fragrance of your nostrils
      as fresh apples,

7:9a   and your palate
      as the best wine . . ."

BRIDE

7:9b   . . . going down smoothly for my lover,
      gliding over the lips of one who sleeps.

7:10   I am for my lover,
      and he yearns for me.

7:11   Come, my lover,
      let us go to the field,
      let us take up lodging
        among clusters of blossoms.

7:12   Let's start out early in the morning
      among the vineyards.
    Let's see if the vine flowers, the buds open, the pomegranates bloom.
      Out there I will give you my loves.

374

7:13 The love-apples
  give forth a fragrance,
and at our doors
  may be found everything sweet.
Things new and old, my lover,
  I have treasured up for you alone.

COMMENTATOR

The bride declares that she has kept herself as a treasure for him alone. Note this great principle of the Song of Songs. The intimacies of love must be reserved for one and only one. The treasures of affection must not be lavished on just anyone. They must be kept for only a single other person.

BRIDE

8:1 Oh! If you were like a brother to me
  that nursed at my mother's breasts!
I would find you in public, I would kiss you,
  and they would not scorn me.

8:2 I would lead you, draw you
  to the home of my mother who taught me.
I would make you drink
  spiced wine, the juice of my pomegranate.

COMMENTATOR

Again the Song celebrates the instruction in love that the bride has received from her mother. The blessings of marriage are secured by the bonds of the covenant established between God and the generations of believers yet to be born.

BRIDE

8:3 His left hand
  is under my head,

and his right hand
    embraces me.

8:4   I make you solemnly pledge, O daughters of Jerusalem,
    never to awaken or arouse love
        until love's desires come properly.

COMMENTATOR

Now for the third and last time the refrain is repeated. The lesson has been communicated well. Love must not be aroused indiscriminately. It must be for one, only for one, only for the one to whom you are wholly committed, and who is wholly committed to you.

Scene Five (Song 8:5–14)

COMMENTATOR (announces: "Scene Five")

CHORUS

8:5a   Who is this coming up from the wilderness,
        leaning on her beloved?

BRIDE

8:5b   Under the apple tree
        I awakened you.
    Here your mother
        was in labor with you.
    Here she was in labor;
        she gave birth to you.

8:6   Set me
        as a seal on your heart,
        as a seal on your arm.

For love
  is as strong as death,
passionate love
  as intense as Sheol.
    Its flames are blazing flames,
    a fire of the LORD himself.

8:7   Many waters
        cannot quench love,
      and rivers
        cannot overflow it.
      If a man should give all the wealth of his house for love,
        he would be utterly despised.

COMMENTATOR

No more beautiful description of love may be found anywhere in human literature. If you are looking for language by which you may give renewed expression to your wedding vows, you may find it here: "Love is as strong as death . . . . Its flames are blazing flames, a fire of the LORD himself. Many waters cannot quench love, and rivers cannot overflow it. If a man should give all the wealth of his house for love, he would be utterly despised." Love cannot be bought at any price. It is a gift freely and willingly bestowed.

CHORUS

8:8   We have a little sister,
        and her breasts have not yet formed.
      What shall we do with our sister
        on the day in which she is spoken for?

8:9   If she puts up a wall of discretion,
        we will fashion on her a crown of silver.
      If she is a door,
        we will confine her with cedar planks.

COMMENTATOR

Now the chorus responds for the last time. They are considering how they will transmit the principles of the best of all songs to future generations.

When their young sister approaches the age of maturity, they will observe her closely. If she shows herself to be a wall, if she exercises discretion in responding to her suitors, they will honor her with a crown.

But if she behaves as a door, swinging open to every flattery, they will enclose her with a sturdy, long-lasting cedar fence.

BRIDE

8:10   I was a wall,
        and my breasts like towers.
    Then at the proper time
        I was in his eyes as one who found peace.

COMMENTATOR

The bride testifies to her exercise of discretion. She did not cast herself on everyone that came along, but preserved herself in modesty and purity for her husband alone.

BRIDE

8:11   Solomon had a vineyard
        in Baal-Hamon.
    He turned over the vineyard
        to keepers.
    Each man was to bring in a thousand shekels of silver
        for its fruit.

8:12   My vineyard, which is mine alone,
        is at my disposal.
    The thousand shekels still come to you, O Solomon,
        and those who have preserved its fruit even get their
        two hundred.

COMMENTATOR

The bride returns to the earlier figure of the vineyard. Solomon possessed a vineyard, and could demand revenues of a thousand shekels from those who reaped its harvest.

The Shulamite is the sole owner of her own vineyard, which is her body. Yet Solomon receives freely from her hand all its precious fruits.

GROOM

8:13   O you who are always at home in the gardens,
        your companions have paid close attention to your voice.
    Now let me hear it!

COMMENTATOR

The groom assures the bride that she has done well in teaching her companions. She has communicated many truths about love.

But now the groom's patience is ended. He wishes to have the opportunity to listen to her alone.

BRIDE

8:14   Hurry, my lover,
        be like an antelope or a young deer
        on the mountains of spices.

COMMENTATOR

Love is beautiful. The biblical pattern for human love is the most beautiful. As the redeemed in Christ, men and women have the privilege of entering into this most beautiful of relationships with the wisdom that only God can provide.

Selected Bibliography for the Song of Songs

Archer, Gleason L. *A Survey of Old Testament Introduction*. Chicago: Moody Press, 1964.

Burrowes, George. *A Commentary on the Song of Solomon*. London: Banner of Truth, 1958.

Carr, G. Lloyd. *The Song of Solomon: An Introduction and Commentary*. Leicester, UK: Inter-Varsity Press, 1984.

Delitzsch, Franz. *Commentary on the Song of Songs and Ecclesiastes*. Edinburgh: T. & T. Clark, 1891.

Driver, S. R. *An Introduction to the Literature of the Old Testament*. 9th ed. Edinburgh: T. & T. Clark, 1913.

Exum, J. Cheryl. *Song of Songs: A Commentary*. Louisville: Westminster John Knox, 2005.

Garrett, Duane. *Song of Songs*. WBC 23B. Nashville: Thomas Nelson, 2004.

Ginsburg, Christian D. *The Song of Songs*. London: Longman, 1857.

Gordis, Robert. *The Song of Songs and Lamentations: A Study, Modern Translation, and Commentary*. Rev. and augmented ed. New York: KTAV, 1974.

Harrison, R. K. *Introduction to the Old Testament*. Grand Rapids: Eerdmans, 1969.

Hess, Richard S. *Song of Songs*. BCOT. Grand Rapids: Baker Academic, 2005.

Keil, C. F. *Introduction to the Old Testament*. Edinburgh: T. & T. Clark, 1869.

Longman, Tremper, III. *Song of Songs*. NICOT. Grand Rapids: Eerdmans, 2001.

Murphy, Roland E. *The Song of Songs: A Commentary on the Book of Canticles or The Song of Songs*. Hermeneia. Minneapolis: Fortress Press, 1990.

Pope, Marvin H. *The Song of Songs: A New Translation with Introduction and Commentary*. Garden City, NY: Doubleday, 1977.

Provan, Iain W. *Ecclesiastes and Song of Songs*. Grand Rapids: Zondervan, 2001.

Rowley, H. H. "The Interpretation of the Song of Songs." In *The Servant of the Lord and Other Essays on the Old Testament*, 187–34. London: Lutterworth Press, 1952.

Seerveld, Calvin. *The Greatest Song*. Chicago: Trinity Pennyasheet Press, 1967.

Vawter, Bruce. "Prov 8:22: Wisdom and Creation." *JBL* 99, 2 (1980): 205–16.

Young, E. J. *An Introduction to the Old Testament*. London: Tyndale, 1964.

Index of Scripture

Genesis
1:27—248
1:28—113, 203, 260, 337, 343
1:29—203
1:31—248
2:1–3—203
2:3—260
2:9—259
2:16—203
2:18—94, 347
2:19—5
2:22—337
2:24—337, 343
2:25—336
3:6—130, 248
3:19—232, 248
4:2—247
9:25—323n4
10:9—32
12:8—36
12:11–13—353
14:18—214
14:19—55n28, 56
14:19–20—56
14:21–23—56
14:22—55n28, 56
18:19—45

19:4–5—304
19:9—304
26:22—36
29:1—14n10
41:8—5, 13
41:33—5
41:39—6
46:31–32—219
47:9—219
48:15—270
49:24—270

Exodus
3—xiii
7:11—6, 13
7:22—6
8:7—6
8:18—6
10:22–23—298
14:31—106
15:16—55n28
20:3–17—87
23:4—34n1
28:3—9
29:37—323n4
31:3—9
35:31—9

Leviticus
23:39–40—259
25:1–12—25
25:25—152
25:48—152

Numbers
18:20—313

Deuteronomy
3:23–25—194
4:2—104
6:3—41
6:5—12
6:6–9—109
8:5—34n1
10:8–9—313
10:14—323n4
12:32—104
13—287n15
17:4—188n37
18—287n15
18:1–2—313
26:3—218
26:3–11—218
26:5—218, 218n35
26:5–9—218n34

381

389

4:3—366
4:4—366
4:5—366
4:6—366
4:7—366
4:8—366
4:9—366
4:10—367
4:11—331, 367
4:12—367
4:13—367
4:14—367
4:15—367
4:16—367
4:16–5:1—344
5:1—368
5:2—348n78, 368–69
5:3—369
5:4—369
5:5—369
5:6—369
5:7—369
5:8—370
5:9—370
5:10—370
5:11—370
5:12—370
5:13—370
5:14—370
5:15—371
5:16—371
6:1—371
6:2—371
6:3—371
6:4—326, 371
6:5—372
6:6—372
6:7—372
6:8—372
6:9—337, 372
6:10—372
6:11—372

6:12—372
6:13—373
7:1—373
7:2—373
7:3—373
7:4—373
7:5—373
7:6—373
7:7—373
7:8—373
7:9—373
7:10—373
7:11—373
7:12—373
7:13—374
8:1—374
8:2—337, 374
8:3—375
8:4—344, 360, 376
8:5—337, 348n78, 376
8:5–14—345
8:6—xi, 376
8:7—377
8:8—377
8:9—377
8:10—378
8:11—378
8:12—378
8:13—379
8:14—379

Isaiah

10:15—32
11:1–3—8
11:14—14n9
13:1—103
19:11–12—14
22:11—261
22:13—261
41:2—14n10
43:5—14n10
50:10–11—33

53:3—298
54:5—334n47
57:13—247
57:15—34n1
59:19—33
62:4–5—334n47

Jeremiah

2:5—249
8:19—249
10:8—249
10:15—249
10:16—313
14:22—249
23:16—249
23:33–38—103
24:9—33
31:29—32
39:1—278
39:2—278
41:1–2—278
49:28—14:10
51:18—249
51:19—313
52:6–7—278
52:12–13—278

Lamentations

1—280n3, 286, 289,
    295n28
1–4—290n23
1:1—279, 284, 310
1:1–7—283
1:1–11—283
1:2—295
1:3—295
1:3–4—280
1:4—295
1:5—295, 301, 308
1:6—298
1:6–7—280

391

1:7—295
1:8—301
1:8–9—300
1:9—295, 310
1:11—310
1:11–16—283
1:12—298, 308
1:13–15—308
1:14—295, 301, 313
1:17—283
1:18—298
1:18–22—283
1:19—298
1:20—295, 301, 311
2—280n3, 283, 286, 289, 295n28
2:1—295
2:1–8—308
2:2—288n21
2:5—288n21
2:9—298
2:10—298
2:11—298
2:11–13—295
2:11–17—284
2:12—298
2:13—311
2:14—302
2:15—297
2:16—288n21
2:17—293, 309
2:18—295
2:18–19—311
2:19—298
2:20—298, 306, 312
2:21—298
2:21–22—295
3—280n3, 285, 286, 289, 295n28, 306, 308, 315
3:1–16—307
3:1–24—283

3:7—295
3:14—295
3:21—316
3:21–22—314
3:22—283
3:22–23—314
3:24—313, 316
3:25—xi, 314, 316
3:25–39—283
3:26—316
3:27—313, 316
3:29—316
3:31—315
3:32—314
3:33—315
3:34—313
3:39–42—302
3:40—316
3:40–47—283
3:41—316
3:48–51—316
3:48–66—283, 316
3:52–53—295
3:52–58—316
3:59—316–17
3:59–66—316
3:60–61—317
4—283, 286, 289, 295n28, 303
4:3—300
4:5—295
4:6—303
4:8–9—295
4:10—306
4:11—309
4:12–13—305
4:14–15—295
4:16—309
4:18–19—295
4:20—299, 317
4:22—317

5—283, 286, 289, 295n28
5:1—318
5:3—295
5:7—305
5:10–11—295
5:11–15—299
5:15–16—305
5:19—218, 309
5:19–22—283
5:21—318

Ezekiel

8:9–10—297
9:3—297
10:18–19—297
11:22–23—297
14:14—122
14:20—122
16:1–63—69
16:44—32
17:1–24—69
18:2—32
23:1–49—69
23:8—345
25:4—14n10
25:10—14n10
34:11–12—270

Daniel

1:17—9
9:25—25

Hosea

2:2—334n47
2:4–5—310
2:19–20—334n47

Jonah
2:1–2—220
2:7—220
2:9—220

Micah
1:11—211n20

Nahum
1:1—103

Habakkuk
1:1—103
1:13—300
3:2—220
3:16—220
3:18—220

Zechariah
7:4–5—278
7:5—278n1
8:7—14n10
8:18–19—278
9:1—103
12:10—294
12:10–11—293

Malachi
1:1—103
3:16–17—33

Matthew
2:1—14n10
2:2—27
5:32—112
5:44—34n1
10:15—305
11:19—68
11:24—305

11:29—270
12:42—27, 114, 270
13:1–23—70
13:19—255
13:31–32—11
13:34–35—6n3, 11, 129
19:4–5—345
19:6—346
19:9—112
21:33–45—11
22:36–38—12
23:12—34n1
24:6–7—279
26:75—316
27:3–5—316
27:36—294
27:45–46—298
27:46—303
28:19–20—175

Mark
4:33–34—288

Luke
1:31—114
1:50—34
2:52—27
10:12—305
10:25–28—12
10:25–37—11, 70
11:11–12—307
11:31—270
11:49—212
13:2–5—300
13:3—301
13:5—301
14:15–24—67, 70
16:8—137
18:9–14—70
20:9–19—67, 70
21:26—279

John
1:1—58
1:1–3—54, 69
1:3—58
4:23—187
9:1–3—301
9:4—254
10:11—270-71
10:14—271
13:23—236
14:6—46
18:11—303
19:26—236
19:34—294
19:37—294
20:2—236
20:19—160
20:30–31—35
21:7–15—316
21:7—236
21:20—236
21:24—236

Acts
2:36—60
4:27–28—309
4:29—255
4:31—255
6:4—255
6:2—255
6:7—255
7:22—13
8:4—25
8:14—255
8:21—255
8:25—255
9:2—45
9:31—105
10:35—34
13—58n34
13:33–34—58n34
13:36—25

INDEX OF SUBJECTS AND NAMES

three-player interpretation, of Song of
  Songs, 326–28, 352–53
timeless truths, 33
Titus, 349
tongue, 79
torah, 12
tragedy, 279, 284
transgender, 112
transgenerational wisdom, 111
"transitoriness," 249–51
trials, 133, 172, 193, 307
Trinity, 63
trouble, 51
trust, 105–7, 187
truth, 82, 239
tsunamis, 279, 299
typology, 331–34

Ucal, 89
Ugaritic texts, 286n13
unbelief, 238, 239
Uncle Remus, 221–22
"under the sun," 253–55
undershepherds, 269
ungodly, 137
union with Christ, 8, 46, 317
uniqueness, 42, 345
unity, 111, 124–25
universe, 140
uprightness, 9
useless, 249

vagueness, 138
Valentinian, 65n46
value, 53
vanity, 251
Vawter, Bruce, 56n31, 57n33
vengeance, 71, 87
vindictive, 148
vineyard, 356, 379
virgin Mary, 330
virtue, 327
vows, 263, 377

walking in wisdom, 43–46
Waltke, Bruce K., 20n26, 24n37,
  40n19, 62n45, 110n89
warning, 71–72
wars, 279
watchfulness, 97–98
Way, the, 45–46
way of the wicked, 49–50
wealth, 48, 206n12, 232, 247
wedding, 322, 337, 365
weeping, xi, 21, 26, 276, 320
Wenham, Gordon J., 216n32
Wertzstein, J. G., 343n68
Westermann, Claus, 164n21, 169n23,
  170n23, 280n4, 281n7, 282n10,
  286n13, 289n20
Western culture, ix
Western secularism, 94
Westminster Assembly, 334
Whybray, R. N., 17n20, 36n5, 37n11,
  41n20, 87n63, 90n67, 91n68,
  124n7, 164n21, 170n23, 186n35
wicked, 49–50, 53, 76, 78, 146, 154–
  55, 161, 191–92, 233, 241, 264
wicked vinedressers, 70
wilderness, 18, 24, 202, 279, 300, 330
Williams, A. Lukyn, 208n16
Wilson, Robert Dick, 213
wisdom
  in ancient Near East, 13–16
  at creation, 52
  biblical terminology for, 8–13
  existence before creation, 54
  in Old Testament theology, 24–26
  personification of, 35, 44, 51–69
  regal role of, 5–8
  ultimate source of, 164–65
  in the ungodly, 136–37
  walking in, 43–46
wisdom books, identification of, 16–21
wisdom literature, 14–15, 17n22,
  21–24, 74n52
Wisdom of Solomon, 17n22, 20n27
wisdom theology, 108–9
wise, 79

wise men, 35, 42
wise ones, 39, 84–87
woman, 79, 339–40
womanhood, 347
words, 53
work, 112–13, 204, 247, 254, 260
worldviews, 41
worship, 26, 201, 203, 232, 260, 262–63, 277, 283, 296
worthless, 249
Wright, A. G., 229n49
Writings, 17

Yahweh, 42, 45, 101, 104, 133–34, 202, 204, 257
yirat Yahweh, 11–12
yoke, 313–14
Young, Ian, 213n29, 324n6
youthful passions, 52

Zechariah, 278, 293–94
Zion theology, 296–97
Zophar, 124, 142, 154–55, 157–59, 184, 347